Future Public Health

Future Public Health

Burdens, Challenges and Opportunities

Edited by

Sandra Dawson
KPMG Professor of Management, Judge Business School, University of Cambridge, UK

and

Zoë Slote Morris
Senior Research Associate, Engineering Department, University of Cambridge, UK

First published 2009 by
PALGRAVE MACMILLAN

Palgrave Macmillan in the UK is an imprint of Macmillan Publishers Limited,
registered in England, company number 785998, of Houndmills, Basingstoke,
Hampshire RG21 6XS.

Palgrave Macmillan in the US is a division of St Martin's Press LLC,
175 Fifth Avenue, New York, NY 10010.

Palgrave Macmillan is the global academic imprint of the above companies
and has companies and representatives throughout the world.

Palgrave® and Macmillan® are registered trademarks in the United States,
the United Kingdom, Europe and other countries.

ISBN-13: 978 -0-230-01359-9   hardback

A catalogue record for this book is available from the British Library.

A catalogue record for this book is available from the Library of Congress.

10   9   8   7   6   5   4   3   2   1
18   17   16   15   14   13   12   11   10   09

Transferred to Digital Printing in 2014

Contents

Notes on Contributors

Jenny Amery, MB ChB, MSc, FFPHM, public health doctor, is Senior Health Adviser with the UK Department for International Development (DFID), currently based in New Delhi, India. The views expressed here are not necessarily those of DFID.

Sue Atkinson, CBE, BSc, MB.BChir, MA, FFPH, is an independent Public Health Consultant, previously Director of Public Health for London and Health Advisor to the Mayor and Greater London Authority. She holds a number of Non-Executive and Honorary posts, including Visiting Professor at the Department of Epidemiology and Public Health, University College London.

Sarita Bhalotra, MBBS, MHA, PhD, Assistant Professor at the Heller School for Social Policy and Management, Brandeis University, is Director of Undergraduate Programs and the Leadership Program in Health Policy and Management at the Heller School, and Associate Chair for Health: Science, Society and Policy, at Brandeis University.

Kalipso Chalkidou, MD, PhD, is the acting director for Policy Consulting at the National Institute for Health and Clinical Excellence (NICE).

Joanna Coast, BA (Econ) (Hons), MSc, PhD, is Professor of Health Economics at the University of Birmingham.

Laura Corbett is a doctoral candidate in the faculty of Social and Political Sciences at the University of Cambridge.

Anthony Culyer, CBE, DEcon (Hon), FRCP (Hon), FRSA, FMedSci, is Professor of Economics at the University of York, England; Ontario Chair in Health Policy and System Design, University of Toronto; Chair of the Office of Health Economics, London; Chair of the Research and Development Advisory Committee of the National Institute for Health and Clinical Excellence (NICE); Co-Editor of the Journal of Health Economics.

Sandra Dawson, DBE, D.Sc (Hon), MFPHM, BA, is KPMG Professor of Management and former Director of Judge Business School, University of Cambridge and Master, Sidney Sussex College.

Yvonne Doyle is Regional Director of Public Health and Medical Director of the Government Office for the Southeast/Southeast Coast Strategic Health Authority and an honorary lecturer at the London School of Hygiene & Tropical Medicine.

Terry Flynn, MACantab, MSc, PhD, is a research fellow in health economics at the Medical Research Council Health Services Research Collaboration, University of Bristol.

Richard J. Fordham, PhD, MA, BA (Hons), FFPH, is Senior Lecturer in Health Economics and Director of the Health Economics Support Programme, University of East Anglia, and Visiting Lecturer, University of Cambridge.

Jeff French, PhD, MBA, MSc, Dip HE, BA, CertEd, is Director of the National Social Marketing Centre (www.nsmcentre.org.uk).

Stephen Gillam, MD, FRCP, FFPH, FRCGP, is a general practitioner and public health specialist. He works in the NHS and directs public health teaching at the Clinical School of Cambridge University. He is a Visiting Professor at the University of Bedfordshire.

Scott L. Greer, PhD, is Assistant Professor of Health Management and Policy at the University of Michigan School of Public Health and Honorary Senior Research Fellow of the Constitution Unit, University College London.

Ini Grewal, MA, BA (Hons), was Senior Researcher in the Qualitative Research Unit at the National Centre for Social Research.

Martin Karlsson, PhD, is Research Fellow (economics) at the Oxford Institute of Ageing.

Jane Lewis, BA (Hons), is Director of the Qualitative Research Unit at the National Centre for Social Research.

Graham Lister, PhD, MSc, is a Senior Associate of Judge Business School, University of Cambridge and Visiting Professor in Health and Social Care at London South Bank University.

Peter Littlejohns, MD, FRCP, is Clinical and Public Health Director of the National Institute for Health and Clinical Excellence (NICE).

Dominic McVey, BSc (Hons), MSc, is the Research Director at the National Social Marketing Centre at the National Consumer Council and Associate Research Fellow at the London School of Hygiene and Tropical Medicine.

Leslie Mayhew, PhD, is Professor of Statistics in the Faculty of Actuarial Sciences and Insurance at Cass Business School, City University, London and Director of The Risk Institute at Cass Business School. He is an Honorary Fellow of the Faculty of Public Health and of the Institute of Actuaries and director of Mayhew Associates Ltd.

David McDaid, is a research fellow in the Personal Social Services Research Unit (PSSRU) at the London School of Economics and Political Science and editor of Eurohealth.

Martin McKee CBE, MD, DSc, MSc, FRCP, FRCPI, FFPH, FmedSci, is Professor of European Health Policy at the London School of Hygiene and Tropical Medicine.

Zoë Slote Morris, PhD, is Senior Research Associate in the Department of Engineering, University of Cambridge.

Miranda Mugford, DPhil, BA, is Professor of Health Economics at the University of East Anglia. She works on methodological issues with colleagues at the Centre for Reviews and Dissemination at the University of York, and chairs the advisory group of the NHS Economic Evaluation Database.

Bhash Naidoo, BEng, MSc, PhD, is a Technical Advisor within the Centre for Public Health Excellence at the National Institute for Health and Clinical Excellence (NICE).

Lucy Natarajan, BA (Hons), MAOxon, MScLSE, was Senior Researcher in the Health Research department at the National Centre for Social Research.

Justin Needle, is Lecturer in Health Services Research and Policy at the Centre for Allied Health Professionals Research at City University, London.

Abiodun Olukoga, BSc, MBCHB, MBA, MPH, MCom (Econ), FMCPH, is a specialist public health physician and economist at the School of Medicine, Health Policy & Practice, University of East Anglia.

Tim Peters, BSc (Hons), MSc, PhD, is Professor of Primary Care Health Services Research at the University of Bristol.

Ben Rickayzen, BSc, PhD, FIA, is Senior Lecturer in Actuarial Science in the Faculty of Actuarial Science and Insurance, Cass Business School, City University.

Donald S. Shepard, PhD, is Professor at the Schneider Institute for Health Policy at the Heller School, Brandeis University.

Martyn Sherriff, PhD, ANCRT, BSc, MIMMM, FSS, MRSC, is Reader in Biomaterials at King's College London Dental Institute at Guy's, King's College and St Thomas' Hospitals.

Kerry Sproston, BA (Hons), MACantab, is a Research Director at the National Centre for Social Research in London.

Edward Wilson, BSc (Hons), MSc, is a researcher in Health Economics at the University of East Anglia.

List of Figures

List of Tables

List of Boxes

Appendices

List of Abbreviations

ADLs	Activities of Daily Living
AIDS	Acquired Immunodeficiency Syndrome
ASHA	Accredited Social and Health Activist
BCR	Benefit Cost Ratio
CBA	Cost Benefit Analysis
CCA	Cost Consequences Analysis
CEA	Cost Effectiveness Analysis
CMA	Cost Minimisation Analysis
CMO	Chief Medical Officer
CMS	US Centers for Medicare and Medicaid Services
COBRA	Cabinet Office Briefing Room A
COPC	Community-Oriented Primary Care
CPHE	Centre for Public Health Excellence
CUA	Cost Utility Analysis
CVD	Coronary Vascular Disease
DALY	Disability Adjusted Life Years
DCLG	Department for Communities and Local Government
Defra	Department of Environmental, Food and Rural Affairs
DH	Department of Health
DPH	Director of Public Health
ECDC	European Centre for Disease Prevention and Control
EPP	Expert Patient Programme
EQ-5D	EuroQol – 5 Dimensions
ESRD	End Stage Renal Disease
EU	European Union
EYLL	Years of economically active life lost
GHQ	General Health Questionaire
GOF	Goodness of Fit
GP	General Practitioner
HAF	Health Attribution Fractions
HALE	Health Adjusted Life Expectancy
HALS	Health and Lifestyle Surveys
HDA	Health Development Agency
HIV	Human Immunodeficiency Virus
HPA	Health Protection Agency
HSE	Health Survey for England
ICER	Incremental Cost Effectiveness Ratio
IMCI	Integrated Management of Childhood Illnesses
LAA	Local Area Agreement

LMPD	Medicare Lifestyle Modification Program Demonstration
LTC	Long-Term Care
MDGs	Millennium Development Goals
MoD	Ministry of Defence
MPP	Midwestern Prevention Project
NCC	National Consumer Council
NGO	Non-Governmental Organisation
NHS	National Health Service
NICE	National Institute for Health and Clinical Excellence
OMEP	Orthogonal Main Effects Plan
ONS	Office for National Statistics
PCT	Primary Care Trust
PSS	Personal and Social Services
QALY	Quality Adjusted Life Year
QOF	Quality Outcomes Framework
RCT	Randomised Controlled Trial
RDPH	Regional Director of Public Health
SARS	Severe Acute Respiratory Syndrome
SEM	Structural Equation Modelling
SHA	Strategic Health Authority
SM	Social Marketing
SNP	Scottish National Party
SPSS	Statistical Package for the Social Sciences
STI	Sexually Transmitted Infection
TB	Tuberculosis
TEHIP	Tanzania Essential Health Interventions Project
TROP	Tobacco Policy Options for Prevention
UNAIDS	Joint United Nations Programme on HIV and AIDS
UNFPA	United Nations Population Fund
UNICEF	United Nations Children's Fund
WHO	World Health Organisation
WHP	Workplace Health Programme
YLL	Years of Life Lost
YLD	Years lived with disability

Acknowledgements

The origins of the book lie within the Policy Futures for UK Health programme of work generously supported by the Nuffield Trust between 1998 and 2007. The work has taken many turns as we proceeded down paths of building scenarios, challenging governments, reviewing literature, commissioning work and consulting stakeholders. Throughout the programme we had steadfast support from the trustees of the Nuffield Trust, in particular from its chairs, Sir Maurice Shock, Professor Sir Denis Pereira Gray and Professor Dame Carol Black, and its senior officers John Wyn Owen, Max Lehman and Kim Beazor. We join with all our colleagues, who over the years have worked on the Cambridge team on this programme of work, in extending our gratitude to the trustees and officers of the Nuffield Trust for their support and inspiration.

More specifically this book is a development from a conference we organised in Cambridge in 2006 under the title of The Future of Health: Burdens, Challenges and Opportunities. From the 50 or so papers presented, we made the selection which appears here. We are grateful to all the conference delegates & especially the track chairs and rapporteurs who helped to derive and synthesise the presented material in ways which enabled the structure of this book to be created.

The papers which appear in the book are the result of further endeavours by their authors. We are extremely grateful to them all for listening to editorial comment and being patient and attentive in redrafting.

Over the course of our policy futures work in Cambridge we have benefited enormously from dedicated support from colleagues, notably Charlotte Sausman (nee Dargie), Marie-Anne Kyne-Lilley, Linda Chang, Beth Altringer, Kay Fieldhouse, Agnés Aubert, Jenny Ridgeon and Yasmine Kobeh. Our work was based in Judge Business School where many colleagues in academic, administrative and operational roles have made significant contributions to the understandings and structures which nurtured our programme of work, and we are very grateful to them all.

Two people however stand out for very special mention. Pam Garside has been co-director with Sandra Dawson of the overall programme of Policy Futures work in Cambridge since its inception. Although not directly involved with the production of this collection, Pam has been a friend and inspiration in every aspect of the wider programme, and we are extremely grateful to her. Lastly, Will Erickson has been the ultimate research assistant. He has generously given his intellect, political understanding, analytical and empathetic skills and good humour to the completion of this book and its index. No reference was too obscure or contributors too elusive to put him off completing the tasks necessary for the dispatch of the manuscript to the publishers. He has worked to wonderful effect without complaint and in the process has contributed a huge amount of energy, inspiration, intellect and good humour to the production of this particular volume.

Thank you to everyone: colleagues, friends and family who in many different ways have made a contribution to the completion of this collection.

Sandra Dawson & Zöe Slote Morris, Cambridge, August 2008

Foreword

Perhaps next to health care it is inevitable that public health is a 'poor relation' in the eyes of government. To an extent the same may be true as individuals – we pay most attention to immediate problems rather than longer
term maintenance of our health and well being. Yet the most important
issue is not whether somehow attention and resources for population public health issues should trump demands and expenditure on health care, but
how to achieve an appropriate balance of effort and expenditure on both.

Against a background of rising threats to population health in particular
from obesity, suboptimal exercise and diet, interest in public health waxes
and wanes. In recent years there has been sustained focus, evidenced by government policy for example to reduce avoidable mortality from significant
killer diseases, reduce childhood obesity, and reduce inequalities in health
between socioeconomic groups. While there have been some notable successes, they have been partial. And while Derek Wanless has argued successfully for more 'upstream' investment in prevention to reduce 'downstream'
costs of ill health, he equally lucidly pointed to the lack of hard evidence of
impact of benefits for the costs of investment in activities to improve public
health. Given the likelihood of greater parsimony in public financing of the
public sector in the short to medium term, there is a risk that the agenda to
improve population public health is largely shelved, as it has been in the
past. There is more hope in the immediate term of investment in secondary
prevention of ill health in the NHS, via better support of older people with
chronic conditions and better predictive modelling to identify who might be
most at risk of ill health in future. While welcome this activity is far from a
more holistic effort to tackle the wider determinants of health which is critical if current threats to health are to be minimised.

It is therefore very timely to take a hard and unbiased look at what can be
done to boost these efforts, and to identify the complex and dynamic factors which hinder them. This book is an admirable attempt in that direction,
thoughtfully analysing the evidence, unsolved issues, and suggesting where
next for the future. The next challenge will be in how these ideas will be
acted on by the public health community.

Dr Jennifer Dixon
Director
The Nuffield Trust
October 2008

Introduction

Sandra Dawson and Zöe Slote Morris

Public health is the foundation of a healthy society. To understand and improve public health requires that one do more than aggregate what one understands about individual health. We know some of the components that influence individual health: genetic predisposition or determination, social background, disposable income, climate, advances in health technologies and caring protocols, organisational capacity for multisectoral and multidisciplinary working, peer influence, personality, motivation and capacity and willingness to look after oneself and one's family, friends and neighbours. For public health, however, one needs to do more than quantify the sum, or the mean, of the health of all the individuals within a society or population and consider the context in which individuals and societies live, for example, the role of the state as regulator, provider of social and physical infrastructure, and educator. One needs to develop optimum routes to secure public goods without creating the moral hazard of undercutting individual responsibility. One needs to consider attributions of legitimacy and accountability between members of diverse professions and lay public members; and in the 21st century one needs to consider the impact of globalisation on human lifestyles and microbial life patterns. Thus to understand and act upon the burdens, challenges and opportunities encountered in promoting individual health, itself a herculean task, only gets one part way on the journey to understanding and acting upon the burdens, challenges and opportunities encountered in promoting public health. Yet that is what this book sets out to do.

An historical and comparative perspective can provide evidence of specific celebrated successes in advancing public health in England. They are often prompted by notorious incidents sparking widespread fear and/or remarkable leadership. Three weeks of the infamous London smog of 1952, killing more people than did bombs dropped on London for the entirety of 1939–1945 war, was crucial in the formation and enactment of the Clean Air Act in 1956 (Holland and Reid, 1965). The results of poor sanitation, another environmental hazard, were evident for all to smell in the 'Big

1

Stink' of 1858 on the Thames (Holland and Stewart, 1998) and so followed public investment in a sewer building programme of unprecedented proportions. Similar stories can be told about advances in the control of infectious diseases, like the removal by local authorities during the 1854 cholera epidemic in London of the handle to the Broad Street pump made famous by John Snow (Johnson, 2006), or more recently the distribution of insecticide-treated mosquito nets as part of a combination of preventative measures in malarial zones (Nyarango *et al.*, 2007); the introduction of oral rehydration therapy, which has brought the number of children dying from diarrhoea worldwide from 4.6 million in 1980 to 1.5 million in 2000 (Victora *et al.*, 2000); and public programmes of vaccination, like the compulsory vaccination against smallpox in England and Wales in 1853 (Durbach, 2005), and the coordinated worldwide battle against smallpox which led to the last case of naturally-occurring smallpox being recorded in Somalia in 1977 (Breman and Henderson, 2002). Given their complexity, it is difficult to apportion costs and benefits of public health interventions even though, for example, it is undisputed that some of the changes in life expectancy in England and Wales from 49 for men and 53 for women in 1910 (itself a dramatic rise from just over 40 for men in the 35 years since the 1875 Public Health Act) to 75 for men and 80 for women in 1998, can be attributed to public health interventions (Holland and Stewart, 1998).

Yet if such benefits can be suggested, why is public health so often the 'poor relation' when it comes to share of expenditure and attention in the 21st century? Five reasons come immediately to mind as the scene is set for this book: the effect of strong competitors fighting for resources and attention in the same health tent; lack of rigorous measurement and clarity on outcomes and value for money from public health investments; expansion of the ambit of public health from seeking to 'control others' who are creating health hazards for members of a population, to seeking to influence whole populations to control, minimise or eradicate aspects of their own behaviours which are damaging to individual and public health; the dilemma of comprehensive coverage versus tackling inequalities; and finally the sheer complex indeterminacy of the issues and the task.

One might be forgiven for thinking that as the UK has a health system which is predominantly funded through public taxation, and as investments in public health would arguably reduce the call on expensive services for acute and chronic care, it should be easy to advocate and sustain public health investment. But that is to ignore the first reason for its partial eclipse: the extremely powerful political, professional, industrial and advocacy groups that argue, with confident justification, within a highly politicised arena, for more expenditure from the health pot on their celebrated causes. Sausman and Dawson (2005) describe the complex stakeholder web of interests and drivers for supply and demand in the UK health care system which create remarkable complexity and almost by default leave health promotion in the shadows of health care. Thus the very fact that in England expenditure on public health comes from the same health pot as does expenditure on health care for individuals with acute and chronic illness is itself a hazard limiting investment in public health. The 2008 UK Budget lists £91.7b in spending on the NHS in England[1] whereas *Choosing Health* (Department of Health, 2004), the government's public health strategy, identifies £1b for supporting the public health agenda. Approximately half of the £1b was to be passed through Primary Care Trusts[2] and half through national programmes. As the allocation was not formally ring-fenced and budget crises were evident in the system, it cannot be certain that even this allocated amount of money has been spent on public health. The NHS, with its remit to provide health care, its focus on hospitals and its workforce concentrated on dealing with people with illness, receives considerably more public, media and political attention than the institutions and professions that are employed to promote the less emotionally-charged and less immediate public health agenda. Instant, sudden attention can be focused on public health issues in a time of crisis or fear, as we saw internationally in respect of SARS (BBC, 2004) or locally when an outbreak of meningitis appears (BBC, 1999); but as the crisis and fear subsides, so too does the policy priority.

The second reason is lack of clear and focused evaluation. Wanless and colleagues (2007), when invited to look back at the five years since Wanless' 2002 report, noted that 'it is impossible to track trends in public health or health promotion spending since 2002 as no official figures are kept' (p. xxiii). In an age of targets and performance measurement, any lack of measurement of input or outcome is a serious invitation to ignore the activity, or to assume that none has taken place. Wanless *et al.* observed that 'it is also indicative of the relatively low priority given to public health that, while non-public health medical staff numbers have increased by nearly 60 per cent since 1997, and real spending on the NHS is up 50 per cent since 2002, the number of public health consultants and registrars has gone down overall' (Wanless *et al.*, 2007, p. xxiii). They chided the government for never having implemented the public health portion of the 2004 review (Wanless, 2004) and placed progress on population health as somewhere 'between slow uptake and solid progress' (Wanless *et al.*, 2007, p. 38). Wanless had not expected public health to generate its own momentum; he knew it would require focused public investment, and at the time he had been modest and, he thought, realistic. The 2007 assessment observed that 'the 2002 review estimated health promotion expenditure in England of around £250m – less than the NHS spends in a day and a half' (p. xxiii).

The third reason why the challenges in public health promotion are particularly profound is that we have seen a shift in the emphasis of public health programmes; the target has moved from specific offenders to the citizenry at large. This has excited some ambivalence about the extent to which we 'the public' wish to encourage external intervention focused on our own or others' lifestyles. At base there is a generic argument about what constitutes individual freedom. Is it not up to all of us to live our lives as we choose? What is the justification for seeking to change behaviour or lifestyle by cajoling, embarrassing or incentivising through an institution-alised system of punishments and rewards,[3] or outright forcing with the rule of law? Few of a *laissez-faire* persuasion want to be surveilled, molly-coddled and restricted by what some would call a 'nanny state'.[4] Coote argues that fear of this label increases politicians' wariness of placing too much attention on prevention rather than cure (Coote, 2004).

There are degrees to which there is acknowledgement that help is needed for those who are particularly disadvantaged, by background or disability, but for the ordinary citizen the argument is easily accepted that each citizen has a 'right' to choose how much investment they make in their own health; it is in essence their choice. The debate becomes more complicated if and when it is demonstrated that one individual's free choice endangers another's without their consent, e.g. through passive smoking. At this juncture the issues become more like those associated with infectious diseases, where there is greater acceptance of the need to prevent contagion, provided it is not thought to damage those whose freedom the intervention some-how effects. Even those at the interventionist end of the spectrum may dis-tinguish between the sanctity of their own freedoms and the desirability of intervention with others. It may be easy to agree that 'others' need to be held to account, observed, cajoled, educated into adopting healthy life-styles which will avoid obesity, addiction, unsafe sexual behaviour and dys-functional family life: but surely, the argument goes, this does not apply to 'us' and our particular behaviour?

The opportunity for such debates to dampen enthusiasm for public health interventions reflects a change in their emphasis. Although public health victories in the 19th and 20th century were won by focusing attention on the burdens or 'externalities' that third parties imposed on the health of populations by their actions or inactions which polluted air or water, and remediation was therefore to require these third parties to reduce and/or pay for the burdens they imposed upon others, in the 21st century public health victories need much more attention to the burdens of poor health we inflict on ourselves. Thus improvements in public health require 'us' to behave differently, often on the basis of arguments and investments made through PCTs which often are themselves disadvantaged by a lack of 'crit-ical mass' to change attitudes and make the case for prevention (Bacon, Orchard, Milne, 2007).

The fourth reason why public health investment rarely triumphs in a spending round, or its impact is limited, is that policy development bal-ances on a tightrope strung between comprehensive coverage and targeting inequities. Patterns of eating, drinking, sexual behaviour, community rela-tions, and substance addiction are not randomly distributed amongst a national population. Tackling inequity needs to be at the heart of public health policy (*Choosing Health*, 2004). Yet an ideology of comprehensive coverage may result in 'successful programmes' dealing with, for example, nutrition or exercise being disproportionately taken up by those who are already relatively advantaged. Thus whilst the indices of coverage champion success, their very success may in fact exaggerate differences, leaving the disadvantaged in what relatively is poorer health (Commission on the Social Determinants of Health, 2008).

The fifth and last reason for public health's 'poor relation' status in terms of expenditure, the overwhelming complexity and indeterminacy of the issues and the task, will be made evident throughout the book.

This book seeks to provide evidence on the nature of the issues that must be addressed if public heath policy is to be successfully developed in the 21st century, to summarise what we know about successful interventions and to emphasise the need for appropriate means of evaluation and measurement if change is going to be sustained. Thus it is structured in three parts. The first, Policy Frameworks, covers the political, social and institutional context in which policy is formed. The second, Influencing Outcomes, shows ways in which success can be created, and the third, Evaluation and Measurement for Public Health, examines how a more robust framework of measurement needs to underpin developments so that progress may be evaluated and learning for the future secured.

Policy frameworks

The opening paper by Greer illustrates the impact of political institutions in shaping the policy context. With devolution to the home countries of the UK, policies for health and health care have substantially diverged and created very different conversations about the state's role in public health. In Scotland, the focus is much more on the conditions which influence people's lifestyles and decisions about health than on personal responsibility, which catches the focus in England. Greer describes how in Wales and Scotland, the most significant opposition to the ruling Labour party comes from the left, whereas in England it comes from the right. Thus it is easy to see that it is really only in England that the debate about individual, personal responsibility lies at the centre of public health thinking and policy. In Chapter 2 Amery and Gillam use the sharp lens of public health policy in developing countries to remind the reader that robust primary care services are the foundation for any public health programme. Robust health systems are vital to population health in both resource poor and well-resourced settings. Strong primary care enables a more effective response to current and future health needs and contributes to greater equity of health outcomes.

Atkinson, in Chapter 3, takes the perspective of an ideal policymaker and describes the imperatives they face in terms of the need to balance on several tightropes. They need to sustain balance between competing claims: to focus on individual behaviour and lifestyle and on the broader social determinants of individual behaviour; to be able to demonstrate action within the limits of politically- dictated timetables and to pursue an evidence-based approach; to develop cross-sectoral collaboration and working partnerships between government departments and to secure specialist input to the policy process; to utilise the resources of health professionals and institutions to achieve an integrated approach to health initiatives in institutions with a primary focus which is not health but work, education and urban planning.

In Chapter 4 French advocates the application of social marketing in public health policy. He argues that public health has tended to adopt overly paternalistic views that do not sufficiently emphasise joint, shared responsibility for health. Rather than viewing consumerism and a market-based society as part of the problem, social marketing integrates public health advocacy into the existing market-oriented society such that it can compete more effectively with other market messages in an attempt to guide people's behaviour. It encourages choice and responsibility on the part of providers and consumers.

Influencing outcomes

Part II of the book contains six papers that deal with how to influence outcomes and secure change in individual behaviour, social norms and social structures, and thereby in indicators of health and sickness, morbidity and mortality. In Chapter 5 Corbett opens with a sustained argument for public health policy to embrace the findings of health psychology on how social and psychological factors influence health attitudes, beliefs, values and behaviours. She reviews various initiatives based on different theoretical models, concluding that there is no one-size-fits-all theory to public health; selection must be contingent on context and target audience. She advocates a mix of mass communications, empowerment schemes, skills development and community improvement programmes appropriate to defined community needs and available resources.

Morris and Dawson follow in Chapter 6 by advocating the need to embed public health policy in the social as well as the psychological context. Taking the example of sexual health policy programmes that aim to change behaviour, they discuss how lay people interpret and respond to perceived risks to their health, and how policy can be adjusted to achieve change in light of this. They show that lay perceptions of risk may not be those which are guiding policy and that until deeper insight into how people conceive risk is developed, the impact of policy will continue to be limited. For example, people may do nothing to avert risk because they see risk factors as outside their control; or because risk taking is viewed with positive excitement, rather than negative avoidance, or because in a choice between two perceived risks, one is seen as more acceptable, or less undesirable, than the other. There are some basic policy guidelines that have been shown to help people manage risk more effectively, but there is less evidence about how to deal with risk aversion, reactance, and compensation. Because some things work for some people some of the time, interventions that are not only embedded in context, but also employ a number of strategies and channels, are also likely to be the most successful.

In Chapter 7 Karlsson, Mayhew and Rickayzen open the first of three papers that, whilst dealing with different aspects, focus attention on one of the critical public health issues of the 21st Century: ageing. They develop an econometric model to analyse the effects of cohabitation on disability over time whilst taking account of socioeconomic differences as captured by educational qualifications. Changing family structure for the elderly (higher divorce rates, longer life expectancy and an increase in lone-person households), a predicted shortage in informal carers (as spouses or children are no longer willing or available for a dominant caring role) and increased demand for care by the elderly in the future highlight the importance of securing estimations of costs. The analysis provides further evidence of the positive influence on health of cohabitation, a factor that is not directly amenable to health policy. Once more we are reminded of the need to locate our understanding of population health in wider social context, since household formation stands firmly outside the health policy domain but clearly impacts upon it. Given these results, it could be a wise public health policy that invested in programmes to promote cohabitation, as well as to support partners through bereavement, not out of sympathy but for the sake of their health. The chapter also provides the potential for calculating long-term care insurance premiums.

In the second paper on ageing, (Chapter 8) Doyle, Sherriff and McKee set out to refine the concept of 'successful ageing' beyond the oft-employed objective measures, to include subjective evaluations of levels of engagement and feelings of confidence and self esteem. 'Successful ageing' is shown to be linked to social engagement, physical activities and recent health experience more than with experience of disease and disability. The theme of social inequality is raised yet again, in that certain groups, such as women, the obese, and the less affluent are less likely to be active in old age. The messages for policy are clear: there needs to be support to create and sustain opportunities for older people to engage in social, cultural and physical activities and to enhance their social esteem by enabling them to more easily and visibly contribute to society and the economy. Housing is also important, and more and stronger alternatives need to be found to living either an isolated, vulnerable life alone at home, or in a care home with little sense of confidence or esteem.

In the last of the trio on ageing (Chapter 9) Coast, Flynn, Grewal, Lewis, Natarajan, Sproston and Peters develop an index of capability for older people as providing a new form for measuring public health interventions. The authors seek to move beyond the measurement of QALYs (quality of adjusted life years), arguing that they are overly focused on health outcomes and insufficiently focused on older peoples' quality of life and well-being. The paper's empirical contribution is to identify five components of quality of life in older people: 'love and friendship' (attachment); 'doing things that make you feel valued' (role); 'enjoyment and pleasure' (enjoyment); 'thinking about the future without concern' (security); and 'being independent' (control). Of these, attachment was found to be the most important to the subjects of their study, and security the least. The authors indicate that education, social care and crime would also influence quality of life as measured in their framework. Once again, the focus of intervention is shown to be much wider than what would normally be circumscribed as health.

In Chapter 10, the concluding paper in Part II on influencing outcomes, Bhalotra and Shepard review recruitment into lifestyle modification programmes intended to encourage and facilitate patient-centred care and evidence-based medicine in the management of increasingly prevalent chronic diseases, from which English policymakers might draw lessons. They report on their study of one such US-based programme that ran from 2000 to 2006, and that was designed to control health costs and reduce cardiac problems amongst the elderly through a focus on healthy diet, regular exercise and stress reduction. Low enrolment was a problem tackled by a variety of initiatives, with mixed results. Financial incentives alone were found to be largely ineffective, whereas a combination of the tools of social marketing, organisational restructuring and patient empowerment were found to have some effect. During the study, which ran from 2000 to 2006, success factors for increased enrolment included establishing programme champions within the service provider organisations, interest by referring physicians, data systems for keeping track of patients as they moved, and patient support systems for encouragement, anxiety relief and, when needed, transportation.

Evaluation and measurement

Echoing Wanless' lament that we need harder evidence of policy impact – on the benefits, and costs, where they are borne, and over what timescale – the third and last part of the book takes the complexity described earlier in its stride and determines to set out what can usefully be done in evaluation and measurement for public health. In Chapter 11 Lister, Fordham, Mugford, Olukoga, Wilson and McVey seek to develop a common approach to evaluating the societal costs of potentially preventable illnesses and high risk behaviour. Taking alcohol misuse, smoking, obesity, preventable cardiovascular disease and preventable mental illness, the paper shows that despite many studies on their prevention, there is no common methodology or set of shared assumptions, and few where illness or high-risk behaviour is evaluated in terms of its wider costs to society. The authors consider costs to individuals and households, NHS treatment and care services, the rest of the public sector, employers and wider social impacts and costs. They provide a much more holistic analysis than is currently the norm, and demonstrate that costs (especially those incurred outside the NHS) are generally much higher than are officially counted in health and care statistics. They conclude that while costs to the health service of these diseases and behaviours might not present a clear cut case for increased investment in their prevention, the costs to society certainly do.

In Chapter 12, McDaid and Needle provide a review of existing economic evaluations of public health interventions. This is a growing area of work, notwithstanding that evidence is hard to retrieve and often buried in studies geared toward reporting some other kind of result. Half of the studies included came from the USA, and many of these took place in the workplace. In the US employers have a very clear incentive to keep their employees healthy. Most evaluations were of interventions that were medically oriented, such as prevention of communicable diseases and early detection of cancer. Underresearched areas were mental health and socioeconomic determinants of health. Commenting on the centrality to public health of cooperation and coordination between agencies in public health interventions, the authors emphasise that economic evaluations must reach across agencies and budgets, as well as outside the health sector altogether into such venues as schools and workplaces. For example, if an intervention is shown to be highly cost-effective, but takes place in a school, and is only evaluated from within the school's perspective and budget, it might seem very expensive to local school systems if they did not realise (or care about) the benefits of such an investment, from a wider social perspective. Incentives, or transfers of funding, might be necessary to make such an intervention happen, for which economic evaluation would be a very important foundation. A corollary example is a situation where a health intervention is not shown to deliver large health gains, but demonstrates large non-health ones, like economic performance or community cohesion. In conclusion they warn that unless the funding of public health interventions and evaluations is dramatically increased, what we know about what works in public health will continue to lag behind richly funded (and, they argue, much less cost-effective) health care interventions.

Fordham, in Chapter 13, continues on the theme of economic evaluation in public health, arguing that it has been less effective in responding to cries to demonstrate the burden of economic proof than have advocates of acute care, and that this may partially explain the comparative higher rates of growth of investments in acute care. Like McDaid and Needle he unearths more studies than have been popularly assumed to exist, and like Lister *et al.*, he argues for more consistent methodologies and standardised practice. He critically evaluates the applicability of different approaches to economic evaluation in health, and emphasises the importance of values in defining and evaluating outcomes. As an example of what he means by the inevitability of value judgements, he illustrates the choice between equity and efficiency in screening programmes; to focus on the former would lead to measuring take-up as an outcome, and on the latter to measuring disease outcomes. He finds that comparing programmes by cost per QALY (quality adjusted life year) has proven more effective than other methods, and that further use of this unit may help provide the momentum to shift policy toward prevention and behaviour/lifestyle change programmes and away from expensive treatments of illnesses which have not been prevented. The chapter, like so many others, stresses the importance of appreciating the wider social context in public health and the dangers of reading across from the majority of cost-effectiveness studies which originate in the USA directly to the UK where different incentives and values prevail.

Moving through the book we discover then that the field is not as 'data-free' as we might have supposed. There is data which can guide choices, and many of these studies favour a broad cross-sectoral, yet context-specific, public health policy domain. However, in order to maximise the effectiveness of economic evaluation on future public health, economists need to develop and agree standard methodological practices in order to assist policymakers in their decisions. The National Institute for Health and Clinical Excellence (NICE) has begun this process and we turn to their activities in the last chapter (Chapter 14) in this part, in which Chalkidou, Culyer, Naidoo and Littlejohns give an insiders' perspective on the challenges of developing cost-effective public health guidance. They acknowledge the often conflicting aims of consistency and cross-evaluation comparability on the one hand and the need for methods that are most appropriate for public health guidance on the other. Their chapter chronicles NICE, from the framework set out in the Wanless reports to its current state, including its additional remit to evaluate 'health' as well as clinical interventions.[5] It identifies the five principal issues posed by attempts to use economic evaluation for the purposes of valuing public health initiatives: (1) appropriate outcome measures, which may supplement or replace the QALY and are better at including externalities (positive and negative) in the evaluation; (2) processes to synthesise different literatures that use different techniques; (3) systems to weigh costs and benefits appropriately in a way that is fair and equitable, without assuming a homogeneous public; (4) conceptualising the role of equity in public health priorities; and (5) securing the inclusion of public health interventions and motivating relevant behaviour changes in environments that are not the explicit domain of health (e.g., schools and workplaces) and which operate according to different aims and incentives.

The development of public health policy is thus hugely challenging. Serious investment in public health is on occasion relatively unattractive to citizens who resist control, unattractive to members of strong professionally qualified workforces in health care who would rather the investment went into their 'patch', and unattractive to politicians because it is unattractive to key interest groups and if effective, which it may not be, is likely only to be so revealed in longer time spans than electoral cycles. Yet even though it is sometimes difficult to find loud champions for public health, the burdens of poor public health are felt at state level as financial, social, and political consequences, as well as at the individual and community level in terms of suffering, despair and fear.

The situation is complex and dynamic and as we finish the book there are signs of a real change in public and political attitudes, so public health may yet emerge as an arena full of mainstream public champions. For example, it is barely a year since smoking was banned from all public places in the UK; and yet public acceptance is high.[6] Furthermore in the last few months we have seen a change in public and political attitudes and behaviour towards policies to tackle what is now described as the looming epidemic of obesity.[7] Perhaps after all the burdens on the public's health can be reduced and the opportunities for improving health status be seriously seized.

Notes

1 Available at http://www.hm-treasury.gov.uk/media/7/3/bud08_chapterc.pdf

2 Primary Care Trusts (PCTs) are the NHS bodies that serve chiefly to compensate GPs and commission services like hospital and mental health care, though they still provide some services directly. Most share boundaries with local authorities.

3 NHS Trusts have discussed the possibility of refusing operations to smokers until they quit, and smokers are now urged to give up smoking in the time leading up to their operation. See, for example, http://www.timesonline.co.uk/tol/news/uk/health/article1875561.ece

4 Nanny state is a derogatory term referring to what critics see as excessive state intervention to control economic or social policy and practices. It was probably coined by the Conservative British MP Iain Macleod who wrote 'what I like to call the nanny state ....' in his column 'Quoodle' in the December 3, 1965 edition of The Spectator.

5 NICE produces guidance on public health interventions and programmes with the aim of helping public health professionals and practitioners in local government and NHS organisations achieve the targets set out in the 2004 white paper *Choosing Health: Making Healthy Choices Easier.*

6 Weeks after the smoking ban in public places came into effect on 1 July 2007, 75 per cent of the population supported the law, and more smokers supported it (47 per cent) than opposed it (37 per cent) (Smokefree England, 2007). It was reported in January 2008 that the number of people successfully using the NHS' Stop Smoking Service was up 28 per cent from April to September 2007 over the same period in 2006 (BBC, 2008). There is now support for the policy idea of removing cigarettes from view in pubs and shops (BBC, 2008).

7 In January 2008 the government made cooking classes compulsory for children aged 11–14 (BBC, 2008). The City Council in Liverpool is discussing banning fast food restaurants from giving away free toys, though this is still in discussion stages (BBC, 2008). The debate is much more geared toward combating child obesity than that of adults, possibly because it sidesteps, to some extent, the nanny state argument.

References

S. Bacon, C. Orchard and R. Milne, 'Specialist Capacity in Public Health: Are we Hitting the Target?', *Public Health*, 121:2 (2007), 148–56.

BBC, 'Meningitis: the 1999 Panic', http://news.bbc.co.uk/1/hi/health/293501.stm, 9 March 1999, accessed 12 June 2008.

BBC, 'Timeline: SARS Virus', http://news.bbc.co.uk/1/hi/world/asia-pacific/2973415.stm, 7 July 2004, accessed 12 June 2008.

BBC, 'Cookery classes to be compulsory', http://news.bbc.co.uk/1/hi/education/7200949.stm, 22 January 2008, accessed 12 June 2008.

BBC, 'Smokers Kicking Habit After Ban', http://news.bbc.co.uk/1/hi/health/7214849.stm, 29 January 2008, accessed 12 June 2008.

BBC, 'New plan to cut childhood obesity', http://news.bbc.co.uk/1/hi/england/mersey-side/7263106.stm, 25 February 2008, accessed 12 June 2008.

BBC, 'Cigarette Display Ban Considered', http://news.bbc.co.uk/1/hi/uk_politics/7310884.stm, 24 March 2008, accessed 12 June 2008.

J. G. Breman and D. A. Henderson, 'Diagnosis and Management of Smallpox', *New England Journal of Medicine*, 346 (2002), 1300–8.

Commission on the Social Determinants of Health, Closing the Gap in a generation: health equity through action on the social determinants of health: Final report (Geneva: World Health Organization, 2008).

A. Coote, *Prevention Rather Than Cure: Making the Case for Choosing Health* (London: King's Fund, 2004).

Department of Health, *Choosing Health: Making Healthy Choices Easier* (London: HM Treasury, 2004).

Nadia Durbach, *Bodily Matters: The Anti-Vaccination Movement in England, 1853–1907* (Durham: Duke University Press, 2005).

HM Treasury, *Budget 2008* (London: HM Treasury, 2008).

W. W. Holland and D. D. Reid, 'The urban factor in chronic bronchitis', *The Lancet*, 1 (1965) 445–8, as quoted in W. W. Holland and S. Stewart, *Public Health: The Vision and the Challenge* (London: The Nuffield Trust, 1998).

Steven Johnson, *The Ghost Map: The Story of London's Most Terrifying Epidemic – and How it Changed Science, Cities and the Modern World* (New York: Riverhead Books, 2006).

P. M. Nyarango, T. Gebremeskel, G. Mebrahtu, J. Mufunda, U. Abdulmumini, A. Ogbamariam, A. Kosia, A. Gebremichael, D. Gunawardena, Y. Ghebrat and Y. Okbaldet, 'A steep decline of malaria morbidity and mortality trends in Eritrea between 2000 and 2004: the effect of combination of control methods', *Malaria Journal*, 5:33 (2006).

Smokefree England, 'Awareness, Attitudes and Compliance Three Months After the Commencement of Smokefree Legislation: A Summary Report', http://www.smoke-freeengland.co.uk/files/three-month-report-factsheet.pdf, 2 November 2007, accessed 12 June 2008.

C. G. Victora, J. Bryce, O. Fontaine and R. Monasch, 'Reducing deaths from diarrhoea through oral rehydration therapy', *Bulletin of the World Health Organization*, 78 (2000), 1246–55.

D. Wanless, Securing Good Health for the Whole Population (London: HM Treasury, 2004).

D. Wanless, J. Appleby, A. Harrison, D. Patel, *Our Future Health Secured? A Review of NHS Funding and Performance* (London: King's Fund, 2007).

Part I
Policy Frameworks

1
Devolution and Public Health Politics in the United Kingdom

Scott L. Greer

Intergovernmental relations may be intricate and dull, but understanding the law and politics of devolution is necessary for understanding the politics of public health in the UK. On the most basic level, power and responsibility in public health – and the chances for meaningful policy change – are shaped by the constitutional politics of the devolution settlement; everything from distinctive communicable disease notification rules to the possibility of a ban on smoking in public places is conditioned by devolution. The different politics of England, Northern Ireland, Scotland and Wales change the policy landscape; politicians and political agendas differ systematically in each jurisdiction, and consequently there is variation in the construction of the public health agenda.

The case of devolution in the UK also makes a broader point about the political nature of public health policymaking. Public health has long-term payoffs and short-term political costs, so it is a wonder that any politicians care to engage with it (Hunter, 2003). The answer is partly – fortunately – that politics can change the costs and benefits of policy. Public health policy, like any other policy, is ineradicably political. Basic public health ideas, such as evidence-based policy, are of little consequence if the political system does not share the values and approach of public health advocates. Public health practice – such as basic communicable disease tracking – depends on allocations of powers, resources and responsibility, and coordination mechanisms that are shaped by political decisions.

That means that a good evidence base and passionate, professional advocacy is not enough to produce public health policy. Understanding of politics is also necessary. The need to understand what policies have a chance, and the patterns in decisions of governments, means paying attention to the concrete politics of public health policymaking. That means avoiding the temptation to add in politics as an afterthought – as in an otherwise

*I would like to thank the Nuffield Trust for its support for this research.
+This chapter was received for publication in Winter 2006.

well-informed chapter that remarks on its last page, after long reviews of Scottish population health statistics that are not particularly distinctive, that 'a final influence on health policy in the new Scotland is, of course, the influence of politics, specifically party politics' (Tannahill, 2005). Such naiveté, if it is anything other than a rhetorical strategy, ill suits public health advocates who would influence policies made by none other than party politicians.

This chapter focuses on ways that the political process produces different understandings of, and policies toward, public health. It first discusses structures: the often poorly understood institutions that allocate responsibility for public health and create multiple challenges. Secondly it describes the political forces – the policy communities and party systems – that drive and sustain divergence. It also highlights the main contours of public health policy divergence, complementing reviews published elsewhere (Griffiths and Hunter, 2007; Rowland, 2006). It concludes that public health in the UK needs to take greater account not only of the institutions and politics of devolution, but also their structural fragility, which could endanger both policy advance and the coordination necessary to pursue basic public health goals such as control of communicable disease.

Devolution and public health: institutions and responsibilities

Because of the asymmetry in the UK devolution settlement, it is only possible to understand the distribution of power and responsibility by examining England (the UK government), Northern Ireland, Scotland and Wales on a case by case basis. They all have substantial public health powers – in fact, what is striking about the UK in comparative perspective is the scope for policy divergence that it permits (Greer, 2007).[1]

Scotland

The Scotland Act lists the powers of the UK government and allocates all other powers to the Scottish Parliament; the 'retained' powers of the UK government in health are relatively weak. Much public health legislation is directly under the control of the devolved Government (formerly known under Labour as the Executive), and indeed has long diverged from England; consider, for example, different lists of notifiable communicable diseases (Rowland, 2006). Major resource allocation to health in health care and public health as well as in education and local government are under the control of the Scottish Government. Public health policy that overlaps with social inclusion policy presents thornier problems for Scotland and the other devolved systems because it is 'interstitial', requiring the resources and participation of both the Scottish Government (with its health, education, and other powers) and the UK government (with its powers over social security and tax).

This is not to understate the potential difficulties that devolution law can present; Scotland could ban smoking in public places because its law was framed as being health legislation (devolved). If it had been viewed as health and safety regulation, it would have been a UK power and the Scottish Parliament would not have been able to pass the legislation. In other words, it was imperative that Westminster agreed with the Scottish Government's legal argument if the ban was to avoid potentially fatal challenge. There is a nice illustration of the potential for unexpected outcomes to be found in the intergovernmental relations of a ban on smoking in public places. It took some time for the interested parties to realise that it had thereby banned smoking in military barracks – soldiers posted in Scotland might think of their barracks as home, but for the relevant power, the Scottish Government, they are public places and smoking in them is therefore illegal (interview, MoD official, October 2006).

The Scottish Parliament was designed to differ from Westminster. Above all, the Scottish Parliament is elected under a system of proportional representation that provides representation for more parties while trimming the number of seats gained by the biggest parties. This means that Scotland is more likely to be governed by a coalition. Since devolution this has meant a Labour-Liberal Democrat coalition, but the other large Scottish party – the Scottish National Party (SNP) – could also plausibly lead a coalition government; a development that could have exciting constitutional consequences.[2] Other institutional features – a strong role for committee work and a petitions process – are also intended to make politics more participative and approachable to an involved public.

Wales

Wales is altogether more complicated. Understanding its devolution settlement involves interpreting two complicated – and flawed – pieces of legislation: The Government of Wales Act 1998 and the Government of Wales Act 2006; and the Transfer of Functions orders which are the decisions in which UK politicians actually pass certain functions to the National Assembly for Wales (Trench, 2006). Unlike Scotland, which shows some clear constitutional thinking, those who framed the Welsh system handed the powers of the Secretary of State for Wales over to the new body. The National Assembly for Wales was born with the powers of a UK cabinet minister rather than a parliament. This has created two fundamental problems in the Welsh devolution settlement that make it difficult to formulate simple statements about the powers of the Welsh Assembly Government, and more difficult to practise Welsh politics. First, the legislation does not use the Scotland Act's technique of listing UK powers and leaving the rest to the devolved politicians; rather, it denies primary legislative powers (like Scotland's) to the National Assembly and instead lists the secondary legislative powers of the National Assembly for Wales. The result is that the distribution of powers and resources in Wales is very complicated; understanding what Wales legally can and cannot do requires specific analysis of the legislation in a given area, while the power to implement policies does not always cleave to the power to make the policies in Wales.

Second, the lack of primary legislative powers means that the Welsh Assembly cannot make major policy changes without the agreement of Westminster. Until the Government of Wales Act 2006 the National Assembly had to ask Westminster for primary legislation. Past 2006 there is a specified process that still allows Westminster MPs to veto the Welsh National Assembly's requests for primary legislation. A compromise between the National Assembly and largely sceptical Welsh Labour MPs, the Government of Wales Act 2006 combines lack of clarity with a great deal of hierarchy and is likely to create very serious problems to the extent that governments in Cardiff Bay and Westminster are different political colours (Trench, 2006).

Insofar as it is possible to capture the Welsh settlement in any given area without pages of legal analysis, it is safe to say that health is one of the areas where the Welsh Assembly Government is highly autonomous – secondary legislation is the characteristic tool of UK health policymaking, particularly health services policymaking, and secondary legislation is the place to look for Welsh power. For example, Wales still operates under the 1984 Public Health (Control of Disease) Act, which applied to both England and Wales, but with most of the secondary legislative and other powers to organise and command that the Act gives to the Secretary of State for Health in England.

The Welsh electoral system is like the Scottish in that it does not produce consistent one-party majorities. But while Scotland settled at least for the first few years into a stable Labour-Liberal Democrat coalition, Wales saw mostly Labour government, but with a tiny majority (one vote) or as a minority government dependent on shifting alliances with the different parties in the National Assembly. It also saw the painful dismantling of an odd experiment in collective government – a mixture of utopian thought and local government practice – that originally blended government and opposition in a committee-based system. Even the concept of a responsible government (the Welsh Assembly Government) distinct from the legislature (the National Assembly for Wales) emerged only after years of contortions (Osmond, 2003; Rawlings, 2003b).

Northern Ireland

Northern Ireland has in most matters a well-deserved reputation for complexity, but its role in public health is relatively straightforward. On paper, when devolved, Northern Ireland has many of the same powers as Scotland. It also has its own civil service, the Northern Ireland Civil Service, which is responsible for most forms of public health policy. It has traditionally relied on the UK for its communicable disease control, with an outpost first of the Public Health Laboratory Service and now a branch of the Health Protection Agency.

But its government is also complex. The first complexity is that devolution in Northern Ireland is not a generally agreed end in itself, as it is in Scotland and Wales. Rather, it is a highly contested part of the larger 'peace process'. Politicians of all parties are willing to make decisions that undermine devolution if it suits their ideological and electoral interests (Wilson, 2003). The result is that the UK government has suspended Northern Irish devolution for most of its 1998–2007 history for the simple reason that the various parties that would need to form a joint executive have been unwilling to work together. When Northern Irish devolution was suspended, government meant 'direct rule', a system in which the UK government deputised junior ministers to run systems under the authority of the Secretary of State for Northern Ireland. This means UK politicians, from Great Britain, were in charge. They had no possible electoral connection to Northern Ireland (which has its own parties), and a strong incentive to both stay in Westminster and to take their policy direction from Whitehall. It is in Westminster and Whitehall, after all, that their futures will be made. That has been the *status quo* for Northern Ireland for almost every year since the late 1960s through to 2007.

The second complexity comes from this joint executive; in order to entice parties into office, the Belfast Agreement distributes seats in the Executive (not the Assembly) by proportional representation (Wilford, 2001; Wilford and Wilson, 2003; Wilson and Wilford, 2004). A party that has enough Assembly members gets one or more ministers. The result essentially eliminates both government and opposition, and with it collective responsibility. Parties are free to run their ministries as fiefdoms while more or less overtly undermining the Assembly. The result is a persistent set of problems in interdepartmental coordination under devolution, and a series of efforts to rewrite the Belfast Agreement to increase collective responsibility. The third Northern Irish complexity is the 'north-south' agenda. This refers to a 'strand' of the Belfast Agreement, inserted largely to satisfy nationalist and republican advocates of Irish unification that creates cross-border agencies in areas such as health. These agencies, born of sectarian and constitutional politics, are not necessarily useful, but they are political cover for, and sometimes political vehicles for, the cross-border coordination that is imperative for health policy (such as communicable disease control and hospital planning) on the UK's only (and heavily trafficked) land border (Jamison, Legido-Quigley and McKee, 2006).

England

The fourth jurisdiction of the UK is, of course, England – what has been called the 'gaping hole' in the devolution settlement (Hazell, 2006). The UK's devolution settlement was a pragmatic response to specific problems:

calls for strong devolution to Scotland, weaker calls for Welsh devolution, and the willingness to put almost any aspect of Northern Irish government on the negotiating table in the search for an end to violence. There was no such call from England. A referendum in the north-east made that rather clear, with an overwhelming majority opposed to establishing an assembly.

England is also remarkable for being the largest single public health system in the western world. Every other country uses some combination of territorial and functional decentralisation to split its health service into something far smaller than the English 49 millions (Greer, 2006b). The result is that English policymaking is often accused of being too large-scale. Governments of both parties have, since the early 1990s, responded by regionalising field services in 'Government Offices' of the regions, with territorial authority distributed across the eight 'standard regions' plus London[3] with public health in the shape of Regional Directors of Public Health (RDPHs) from 2001. Subsequently Strategic Health Authorities were also fitted to the standard regions from 2006[4] (Sandford, 2005). This sense that English policymaking is overly large-scale and a cause of central overload means that decentralisation, if not elected regional governments, will continue to be an issue.

The UK

The UK government in Whitehall is not just the government of England, however. It is the elected government of the UK, and while its responsibilities are overwhelmingly English, it has two other roles.[5] The first is as the international face of the UK, in the EU, World Health Organisation, World Trade Organisation, and other international organisations that influence health. The second is that the UK government, as a practical matter, holds itself responsible for coordination, especially in times of disaster, and has the military resources that are often used. An outbreak of pandemic influenza, for example, would not be handled by ordinary public health channels; it would be headed by the UK Cabinet crisis committee COBRA (short for 'Cabinet Office Briefing Room A', the Whitehall room where it meets) (interviews, Department of Health and public health specialists, London, October 2005). The question is whether devolved interests, devolved information, and the interests of devolved autonomy would be well represented.[6] If they are not, the consequences could be negative in both practical and constitutional terms.

The same problem holds for the EU and other international organisations. Specialists in a few areas of public health will have noticed a much stronger EU role. For example, the Blood Directive (2002/98 EC), passed to fulfil an EU power over blood and tissue created in the aftermath of the BSE crisis, has reshaped blood services across the EU (Faber, 2004). Communicable disease specialists will know of the European Centre for Disease Prevention and Control (ECDC) in Stockholm, which networks existing public health surveillance services and expertise across the EU (www.ecdc.eu.int). But the EU role in public health is far greater than that (McKee and Mossialos, 2006; Rowland, 2006). The EU is predominant in areas close to public health such as agriculture, consumer protection, and food safety. Furthermore, the EU is expanding its role as a regulator of health services, with its legal decisions grounded more in internal market law than in any consideration of health or public health policymaking. This means that the connection between devolved systems, the UK government and the EU is crucial. What we find is not particularly encouraging; Whitehall is perfectly capable of ignoring Scotland even when they are attempting to work together harmoniously (Fraser, 2007; Greer, 2006a). On the international level, the same problem exists. The UK government participated in the negotiations leading up to the new International Health Regulations (Calain, 2006) that it signed, but the devolved public health systems will have to implement them. Potential for irritation exists on all sides.

This means that the informality of UK intergovernmental relations presents a problem. On the official level, the systems have distanced themselves insensibly but inexorably. The Department of Health's 'Change Programme', which cut staff numbers by 1400 in 2004–2005 (Department of Health, 2005: 1, 26–27; Greer and Jarman, 2006), had the unintended effect of disrupting UK-wide networks – 'when we call the telephone just rings' complained a senior devolved public health official in a 2004 interview. This comes with rapidly declining interest on the part of Whitehall in the devolved countries. One devolved special advisor noted that while he used to be regularly contacted by Whitehall special advisors, in recent years he has had almost no contact (as of December, 2006). On the unofficial level, there has been a myopic reliance on the Labour Party and its unity; there is essentially no plan to cope with deliberately created intergovernmental conflict. When it works badly, we can expect something like the miserable experience of foot and mouth disease in Wales in 2001, when the National Assembly for Wales and UK government repeatedly suffered from failures to coordinate, exchange information, agree decisions and deploy resources (House of Lords Select Committee on the Constitution, 2002). Given that this looseness is between basically friendly Labour-led governments, it is easy to imagine how much trouble intergovernmental relations could cause for devolved government if it were a Conservative government eager to embarrass devolved Labour (for example), or the SNP chose to highlight the powerlessness of the Scottish Parliament in many areas (such as nuclear weapons).

Finally, devolution finance is basically common across the UK. The UK funds devolution through a mechanism known as the 'Barnett formula' (Bell and Christie, 2002; Heald and McLeod, 2002; McLean, 2005). This is a formula that allocates new money to Northern Ireland (excluding security), Scotland, and Wales on a rigid per capita basis; if a devolved population is

X per cent of England's, then it will receive X per cent of whatever new money is spent in England. The formula should operate to reduce the greater per-capita expenditure in Northern Ireland, Scotland, and Wales. It takes no account of health need or of internal divergence (most analyses find stunningly high levels of per-capita government spending not in Scotland or Northern Ireland, but in London) (McLean, 2005). It is also, like all aspects of the devolution settlement, Westminster's policy; the Barnett formula might occupy an important constitutional role, but it is basically a spreadsheet in the Treasury in London.

The Barnett formula has two consequences for public health policy. One is that because it is a bloc formula, the devolved politicians can transfer money from one budget head to another. This was particularly well illustrated in late 2001 when UK Chancellor Gordon Brown announced major increases in funds for the English NHS. This translated to large 'Barnett consequentials', that is, new money, for Northern Ireland, Scotland, and Wales. Scottish and Welsh politicians both made haste to say that they would match English increases in health expenditure (despite their already higher per-capita spending on health). Both later backtracked, emphasising their commitment to health rather than health services, in order to justify spending money on public health, infrastructure and social inclusion rather than putting it all into the NHS, as happened in England. It was political, rather than legal, pressure that made the Scottish politicians promise to spend the money on health, and public health arguments allowed them to divert it where they thought it would be more useful.

The other consequence of the Barnett formula is that the finances of Northern Ireland, Scotland, and Wales are determined in London by spending decisions for England.[7] This is both constraining and liberating. It is constraining because it means that the budgets of English spending departments, not anything in Northern Ireland, Scotland, or Wales, explains the devolved budgets. It is also constraining because it means that the devolved leaders lack a range of tools (taxes) that can be used to shape their societies. It is certainly therefore a constraint on democratic responsibility. But it is liberating because it insulates them from the economic consequences of their actions. This matters because public health policies can be damaging to short-term economic growth. Reducing binge drinking – an obvious public health policy goal – would certainly hurt the alcohol and hospitality trade. Lost jobs and reduced city-centre activity would be the immediate effects, while the advantages to the population or budget of decreased cirrhosis and violence would be easy to miss. It also matters because Northern Ireland and Wales (and, depending on assumptions about oil, Scotland) would not be able to fund their large public sectors on their economies and potential tax bases. The result is that devolved politics can be about running the welfare state and regulating society within a limited scope, with many crucial economic trade-offs made elsewhere. It should hardly be surprising that devolved politicians, equipped primarily with regulatory powers and the labour-intensive bit of the welfare state, should be interested in making a mark through regulation and changes to the welfare state's priorities.

The politics of devolution and public health

Public health, then, is an open field for devolved politics and the politics of devolution – for devolved political systems to make different decisions, and for intergovernmental politics to produce unexpected policy and constitutional outcomes. The structure of intergovernmental relations in the UK is permissive. The distinctiveness of policy debates means that the four systems of the UK take advantage of that permissiveness to develop distinctive policies. The basic reason is that there are systematic differences in the party politics and policy communities of the UK.[8]

A party system is the term for a set of parties that are significant in a given system (usually meaning they have elected representatives or threaten to elect them), and their interactions – the voters they attract, the voters they repel, and the voters they dispute with other parties (Sartori, 1999[1986]). They shape the incentives politicians have, and direct their worries towards some voters and issues rather than others. Crudely, politicians will focus their attention on the voters that they might lose to another party. Voters who do not have the option of defecting to another significant party are unlikely to be given much attention; voters to the left of Labour in England have little alternative, while voters to the left of Labour in Scotland can choose between the SNP, the Greens, and the various descendants of the Scottish Socialist Party. Party systems can differ even when the populations do not. The populations of Scotland and England are quite similar in their preferences towards most policy issues (and are very similar indeed when regressions explaining left-right preferences incorporate class identification or income as well as nationality (Paterson *et al.*, 2001). That does not matter, though, if the main electoral threats to Labour come from different directions (the right in England and the left in Scotland). Even if Labour loses office, the opposition party that replaces it will work to retain the voters that gave it the margin of victory – meaning that Labour and the Conservatives in England will try to address the preferences of the voters who swing between them, to the possible detriment of voters elsewhere in the electorate. Scottish leftists, who hold the votes needed by both Labour and the SNP, will be much better positioned than their English counterparts. Furthermore, there is often a case for devolved Labour to distinguish itself from London Labour, in order to burnish its nationalist credentials against its more nationalist opponents. The resulting party positioning can be seen in policy, but also in something as easy to deride as party rhetoric. Party position statements are, if not necessarily a guide to policy, a guide to positioning, and the differences between them highlight how the parties wish to be seen. What stands out in them, when discussed below, is the different expectations each party system imposes on Labour and its main competitor.

A policy community is the complement to a party system. It is the group of people who are professionally engaged with policy issues in a given jurisdiction – the policymakers, academics, consultants, journalists, and others who try to engage in debates and put forth their arguments. They vet each other and ideas, and it is usually among members of a policy community that we find the advocates who put forth ideas such as banning smoking in public places, improving school diets, or adopting new vaccination policies. Most adopted ideas come from people with credible positions in the policy community. Ideas with evidence around the world are unlikely to be noticed by politicians if they are not put forth to the politicians by policy advocates in the local policy community.

Party systems structure the incentives of politicians – set the political problems that they must solve if they are to avoid bad headlines or cope with a problem. Policy communities, in turn, offer ideas and filter out others. When a politician and a problem coincide with a policy idea, the result is the policy (Greer, 2005; Kingdon, 1995; Zahariadis, 1995). If party systems differ, politicians will day in and day out have to solve different political problems – respond to attacks from different quarters and contest the loyalty of different voters. And if there are differences in policy communities, the politicians will hear different advice, different policy ideas, and different readings of evidence. And, indeed, the party systems and policy communities of the UK vary substantially – so the public health policies do as well. For health policy overall the results are coherent because the policy communities and party systems are reasonably well aligned – the supply of policies of certain kinds fits with the demand for such policies: Scotland's trajectory is professionalist, with a strong role for professional organisations and values in policy; Welsh policies are localist, with a focus on local orientation and local government; English policies are pro-market, with competition and choice brought in to improve health service responsiveness and efficiency; and Northern Ireland's trajectory is one of permissive managerialism, in which managers have great latitude so long as they keep direct rule or otherwise-engaged devolved ministers out of trouble (Greer, 2004).

Scotland

Scottish politics tug leftward. It has two major parties: the Labour Party and the Scottish National Party (SNP), which is generally to the left of Scottish Labour and well to the left of the UK Labour party on most questions. Both the SNP and Labour face threats from small parties and independent candidates on their left; while the Scottish Socialist Party is in trouble, the Greens are thriving and their presence means leftist voters can punish Labour or the SNP for moving right. As a consequence Scottish public debate is structurally more favourable to public health arguments; consider the language of a typical SNP position statement:

The SNP believes that health policy should be as much about preventing ill-health as treating it. It makes sense, for the individual as well as the NHS, to focus on preventing serious illnesses such as heart disease rather than having to deal with them years down the line.[9]

And, in its 2007 manifesto:

Health policy should be as much about preventing ill-health as treating it. The SNP will focus on improving public health, as well as ensuring good and timely medical treatment. We will pay particular attention to reducing health inequalities within Scotland – as well as between Scotland and the rest of Western Europe.

Compare this to Labour's 2003 Scottish Parliamentary elections manifesto, just a bit to the right with its discussion of personal responsibility, but more explicit about inequality:

Too many of us have to acknowledge that we have failed to take responsibility for our own health. Despite medical advance and our National Health Service, we still have the worst health record in Europe... Labour is committed to improving Scotland's national health and we have backed that commitment with significant resources...We know that inequalities of wealth lead to inequalities of health. This social injustice must be tackled.[10]

And its 2007 manifesto:

Scottish Labour will take the bold decisions needed to improve the health of everyone in Scotland. Our drive to end child poverty, achieve full employment, improve housing and regenerate deprived communities is also vital to improving Scotland's health. Health cannot be tackled in isolation. Scottish Labour will continue to champion public health across devolved government and will tackle Scotland's big challenge: obesity, poor diet, inactive lifestyles, alcohol and substance misuse, and smoking.

Both parties operate in the same political environment and have large sections of their publications dedicated to public health as a result.

Scottish public health has also had a longstanding, serious, policy connection that we do not see elsewhere. Every publication on Scottish health policy notes this strong professional role (Dingwall, 2003; Nottingham,

2000; Spry, 2002; Woods and Carter, 2003). Professionals are comparatively powerful and well integrated in policymaking in Scotland, and the profile and engagement of academic public health and medical officers has made them credible and, as public health advocates go, close to power. This feeds on itself; Scotland has made major investments in capacity-building and research in public health, with considerable academic input into both public health priorities and interventions in general, as well as institutional developments such as first a Glasgow Centre for Population Health and perhaps now a Scottish equivalent centre.

So Scottish policy in public health has been traditional in form and structure but determined and coherent in scope and objectives. Scotland rebalanced its funding formula to match health services needs to health services expenditure, principally by spending more money in and around Glasgow. Public health has benefited from the improved integration and planning within the health services that came from the abolition of the internal market and unification of the Scottish NHS into fourteen health boards with public health responsibilities (Donnelly, 2007; Scottish Executive Health Department, 2003b). At the same time, Scotland left the micro-level position of public health – largely in the NHS – intact. The ability to network between the far smaller numbers of people in fourteen health boards also means that other questions, such as the exact relationship between the public health function and the NHS, are more academic. Very small groups enjoy more of the luxury of informality.

This means that while Scotland's priorities look much the same as the rest of the UK (reflecting similar societies and shared epidemiological debates), the implementation can be different. The priorities are healthy eating, smoking, alcohol, mental health, homelessness and sexual health (Scottish Executive Health Department, 2003a). Any distinctiveness is in the approach. On the level of government rhetoric, there is much less about lifestyle choice than in England. That rhetoric reflects and enables Scottish managers, medical professionals and public health specialists to pursue relatively left-wing policies that focus on wider determinants of health. This is difficult to measure because it is in the realm of the autonomy of the front lines – but we do know that both the WHO and television chef Jamie Oliver endorsed the Scottish Executive's health food programmes (Donnelly, 2007)!

Scotland also used its regulatory powers, most prominently to ban smoking in public places (Cairney, 2005). The smoking ban illustrated the virtues of devolution: the idea came to prominence in the UK when it was adopted in New York City and then the Republic of Ireland. Politically, adopting a ban gave Scotland a leading position in a prominent public health field, distinguished it from England (by its wiliness and speed), and allowed the Scottish Executive to set part of the health agenda while making a mark that voters would notice. The Scottish policy community, meanwhile, had strong public health and professional representation, and interest groups and others who represent affected industries were less prominent – the key tobacco, food and drinks lobbies are largely based in London where association headquarters can be found. The result is that Scottish Labour had few reasons not to embrace the cause.

Wales

Welsh politics are like Scottish politics: the opposition party to Labour is to its left and nationalist. That puts a premium on appealing to voters who are to Labour's left, puts left-wing policy ideas on the political agenda every time a minister enters the Assembly, and makes policy that looks 'English' an invitation to attack by Plaid Cymru. The result is that a Welsh Labour party shot through with devo-scepticism is led by a man, Rhodri Morgan, who says New Labour is nearing death (BBC News Online, 2006), and is famous for policies that claim to put 'clear red water' between Wales and England (Osmond, 2004). The complexity, though, is that the territorial and social fragmentation characteristic of Wales is replicated and exacerbated by an electoral system that created something like four-party politics in 2007. Labour is the largest party but it has hovered on the line between a majority and minority government and spends more time on the minority side. Conservatives, Plaid Cymru, and Liberal Democrats each have a different ideological and tactical relationship to Labour (and there are even arguments that they should join together in one of the more remarkable grand coalitions imaginable). This means that Labour is more secure in Wales than in Scotland over time (because it is likely to stay largest), less secure so far (because it has not had stable coalitions), more tactically free (because its problems surround it) but also more under threat. While appeals to Welsh leftist distinctiveness might head off losses to left, nationalist Plaid Cymru, it probably does little to win over Conservatives in a place on the borders like Chepstow, which is almost a suburb of Bristol. So far, Labour has mostly focused on winning and keeping left voters, a position that is more comfortable for a not-very-New Labour party and that directly contests its biggest rival, Plaid Cymru.

The Welsh policy community was, meanwhile, able to develop public health ideas and sell them. The reason is partly that Wales has a long tradition of public health thinking and a thread of creative thinking that runs through the work of NHS Wales in the 1980s and 1990s (when Wales was a pioneer in many aspects of health management) or that we see in the influence of the left-wing social thinker, researcher, and GP Julian Tudor Hart. First Minister Rhodri Morgan, speaking on the record in Cardiff on 2 December 2006,[11] quoted Tudor Hart's full statement of the 'inverse care law':

The availability of good medical care tends to vary inversely with the need for it in the population served. This inverse care law operates more completely where medical care is most exposed to market forces, and less so where such exposure is reduced (Tudor Hart, 1971).

Very few first-rank politicians cite Tudor Hart and as Tudor Hart noted at the time, none until then had quoted the statement in full, including its second sentence. The fact that a Labour First Minister says such things probably captures the distinctiveness of debate in Wales.

But Labour's tone in Wales also comes from its electoral situation. Consider Plaid Cymru's 2007 manifesto:

Our vision is of health services rooted in the heart of our communities, a health service that is as much about promoting wellbeing as it is about tackling illness, a health service that will ensure that the people of Wales, whatever their background and wherever they live have the opportunity to lead healthy and happy lives.

In other words, there is a good deal of consensus between the two biggest Welsh parties on the importance of public health. If anything, Plaid Cymru, which is generally to the left of Labour, is less interested in promoting public health and more interested in dealing with the various problems of the Welsh health services.

The force of public health argument in Welsh politics does not just come from its compatibility with a party disposed to the left under pressure from Plaid Cymru on its left. There are obvious partners in advocacy, above all in local government; the argument for 'joining up' in the interests of public health is also an argument for greater local government influence on various policy fields. Local government in Wales is powerful and a good partner in advocacy (Jeffery, 2006). And within medicine, there is not just a distinctive and little-known Welsh policy history (Greer, 2004; Michael and Webster, 2006) but there is also an unusual form of policy community – one with very few of the powerful health service and academic medical institutions that simultaneously lead, and deny oxygen to alternatives, in Scotland. Finally, Welsh devolution produced a distinctive new political class – for example, one that is almost gender equal. There was and is a sense of political experimentation in Welsh politics that makes it easier to question strong, old divisions such as that between the NHS and local government (Osmond, 2000; Rawlings, 2003b).

The result was that Wales, like Scotland, redirected health resources to answer health need almost immediately after devolution began, and it then went on to do something unprecedented: reorganise the NHS in order to foreground public health and health inequalities. This reorganisation took the form that fits well with a policy community interested in joining up services, reducing inequality, and promoting local government's interest, namely a sweeping restructuring that made the key NHS commissioning bodies (Local Health Boards) coterminous with and highly linked with local government. This has not worked particularly well; the travails of the Welsh health services in the last few years are (too) well publicised and at times threatened to discredit the whole idea of making public health a core concern of health policy overall, while it is always risky to expect organisational change to alter the hospital-dominated assumptive worlds of policymakers and bureaucracies (McClelland, 2002).

Meanwhile, inequalities proved intractable. Health inequalities often reflect inequalities of life chances and income in the broader society. Welsh policymakers recognised that in publication after publication, but had difficulty drawing conclusions that could translate into health policy. The result was a fairly steady retreat from their early policy statements, under pressure because of the much discussed problems of health services. It is always difficult to identify a specific point at which the wind shifted, but that was probably the appointment of a new health minister in January 2005 and the May 2005 strategy *Designed for Life* (Welsh Assembly Government, 2005) which focused the energies squarely on better managing NHS Wales, with a corresponding de-emphasis of the older strategies.

The new focus of scarce ministerial time on the management of health services came alongside shifts in the content of public health policy. Spring 2004 saw the launch of 'Health Challenge Wales', a package of public health policies (such as school nutrition programmes) and efforts to change lifestyle. It, too, has a concept from Julian Tudor Hart in it. But the concept, 'co-production' of health, is very different. It views health as a product jointly produced by patient and doctor (Tudor Hart, 1992). From a government point of view, it is much less ambitious and with not much effort turns into a lifestyle focus little different from the hectoring advertisements of England. The combination of *Designed for Life* and Health Challenge Wales was less of a change in policy direction than it was a change in policy effort. Failure to enunciate a convincing and effective public health strategy combined with pressure from health services, and the public health agenda ground to a halt. The problems were predictable: it is difficult to affect ministries outside health; social inequality is a major and tenacious phenomenon that is unlikely to be eliminated by a health policy; and hospitals are more politically salient than public health or health inequalities.

The reorganisation also created a National Public Health Service for Wales. This body moves public health out of the NHS and integrates public health protection across territorial levels; while creating such a unified service is in line with much Welsh political debate, it was precipitated by the reorganisation of English communicable disease control and creation of the Health Protection Agency in the wake of Getting Ahead of the Curve (Department of Health, 2002); something, urgently, had to be done with shared services once the English reorganisation began (Rowland, 2006). In principle it also creates a strong internal lobby for more public health policy in the future. While in core public health this probably gives Wales a better communicable disease control system than in more fragmented systems, its impact on other areas of policy is still difficult to detect.

England

English health politics is not about public health. Even when the Treasury-commissioned reports of businessman Derek Wanless highlighted the impossibility of the NHS persisting without improved public health (Wanless, 2002), and the government consequently produced a white paper (Department of Health, 2004), it was never clear how much political will lay behind the request for public health advocates to air their ideas. If English public health is to be improved, it seems that much of the 'full engagement' Wanless asks of the population will involve lifestyle choices rather than attacks on the wider determinants of poor public health.[12] Not all ideas serve politicians equally well in English politics, and the policy community reflects decades of politicians who thought their careers would be best served by lifestyle-focused, or no, public health policies.

This is because UK (English) politicians face an opposition that is to their right, and the swing voters are to their right. Labour can almost ignore voters on its left in England, while in Scotland and Wales it must be attentive to them. It is impossible, for example, to find a significant discussion of public health in recent Conservative general election manifestos or current policy documents (as of January 2007). But there is a long Conservative tradition of preferring lower taxes, less NHS spending, and more private finance. So Labour in England, uniquely, thinks that it must save the NHS by demonstrating to the public that it is good value for money (interviews, ministerial special advisors, September 2003, July 2006). The swing voters in Scotland and Wales, unlike those in England, are to the left of Labour and committed to the NHS in a way not thought to be the case in England. So, in England, policy focuses on demonstrating that the NHS is efficient, and shies away from public health policy or anything that seems like lifestyle authoritarianism. Consider party rhetoric again: Labour, in its 2005 manifesto, discussed public health firmly under the rubric of 'Healthy Choices' – explaining that 'people want to take responsibility for their own health outside the NHS as well as within it' (The Labour Party, 2005 ch. 4). This is a far cry from Labour's Scottish or Welsh policies and rhetoric.

The health policy community abets this; while there is a strong and intellectually credible public health policy community in England, it is relatively much less important than those responsible for and commenting upon health services. Health services enjoy an enormous infrastructure of academics, think tanks, journals, officials and journalists in England, and lively left-versus-right debates not found elsewhere. The dominance of the health services in public debates, which reflects the preoccupations of the

English policy community and politicians, also means that there is a very narrow scope for policies billed as public health. This means, for example, that a Deputy Chief Medical Officer claimed that 'social marketing' is key to the English approach (Adshead and Thorpe, 2007). Social marketing is an approach strikingly absent from the other devolved countries whereas the importation of market research to change individual (consumer) behaviour fits the tone of English politics and policy debates (for a fuller discussion of social marketing see French, this volume).

England's public health record is still relatively weak on health inequalities and even its record on lifestyle change is patch. The botched attempt to have a partial ban on smoking in public places is a prominent case of a public health policy that was watered down. This involved trying to ban smoking only in pubs that served food. It did give rise to the memorable statement by the then Secretary of State for Health, John Reid, that smoking was one of the few joys available to the poor (CNN.com, 2004). It was only after a difficult vote that Labour shifted to a complete ban on smoking in public places.

England has seen significant changes in the communicable disease control function. In the wake of the 2001 terrorist and anthrax attacks in the USA, the Chief Medical Officer (CMO) launched a review that led to the creation of the Health Protection Agency (HPA) in England. This undid the previous set of discrete organisations (such as the Public Health Laboratory Service) and instead concentrated the resources under Department of Health control into the new agency. The HPA, remarkably, has very little statutory support; when we trace out the responsibilities for much of health protection, it turns out that statutory responsibility still generally lies within the NHS, RDPHs and local government. What the HPA does have is resources, flexibility, and prestige. The reorganisation exacerbated an already absurd level of formal discontinuity; the last clear guidance on NHS responsibilities for communicable disease control dates from 1993. The English NHS has been reformed beyond recognition since then, but it is the basis on which parts of the English health system still attempt to operate (Rowland, 2006). The result is that England now has a sophisticated, prestige agency, the HPA, which has international and some all-UK functions (including running the Northern Irish surveillance and laboratory facilities), but which is often poorly integrated with the local health services. It is a testament, at least, to the dramatic changes that can come when an organisational entrepreneur (the Chief Medical Officer), a problem (terrorism preparedness), and politicians needing action (such as the government in 2002) come together.

Bright spots are actually in the UK's fiscal policy. Tax policy has become more progressive. In benefits policy there has also been modest improvement to a limited extent in work on social inclusion. Together they should, by any argument, improve public health, but are rarely or never presented as such. English policymakers and activists are less inclined, or less successful, to medicalise the quest for social justice. Social justice policies, in England, tend not to be presented primarily as public health policies.

Northern Ireland

Northern Ireland's institutional and political complexity does not just shape the (small) quantity of headline policymaking; it has also shaped a distinctive policy community, approach to public health policy, and set of institutions. Northern Irish politics demands very little policy because its party system is so firmly set around intra-unionist and intra-nationalist debates (it is only in Northern Ireland that policymakers argue that the victory of a 'save the local hospital' candidate, such as happened in Omagh, is a good thing because it suggests some non-sectarian electoral interest) (interview, Belfast, December 2006). The result has been that there is relatively little local policy argument; and the second-order result of the fractured politics was, of course, a civil breakdown so severe that direct rule ministers rather than anybody from Northern Ireland have been in government since 1970. What pressure there is for policy change tends to be diffuse, is not articulated in very helpful ways, and is very often focused around hospital services.

The Northern Irish health services and public health policy community have adapted to this situation. They have distinctive values, including a strong emphasis on neutrality in a war-torn environment (Campbell, 2007). They also have lived under a direct rule regime that put its emphasis on quiet. Unable to appeal for decisions and often saddled with poorly designed systems, they had great latitude as long as they created no problems for the minister.[13] This is what I have called 'permissive managerialism'.

'Permissive managerialism' and devolution combined had curious and very positive effects in Northern Ireland. An enterprising CMO and some colleagues were able to develop and to a large extent implement *Investing for Health* – which Donald Acheson called the best public health strategy published in English (Department of Health Social Services and Public Safety, 2002; Wilson and Oliver, 2007). The advocates for Investing for Health took advantage of the optimism with which devolution began to put through a comprehensive, non-legislative programme that brought together things departments already did, and tried to make them work together better through networks and changes to programmes that would create synergy. This was developed within the Northern Irish public sector, via civil service networks and much persuading. It is possible to identify the three determined officials who – almost alone – sold *Investing for Health* across the Northern Irish public sector (interview, retired official, Belfast, June 2006). Northern Ireland politicians were pleased to have a distinctive strategy developed in-house, and unlike direct rule ministers were willing to sign off on it. With that approval, the official machine and health services were able to start implementing it. The go-ahead, crucially, came from the devolved politicians, but otherwise it was a highly positive demonstration of what permissive managerialism could permit.

Permissive managerialism is also a poor description of Northern Ireland at the time of writing in 2006–2007. Northern Ireland's claim on the contemporary UK budget is, at bottom, its ability to create havoc. That capacity to create havoc is much diminished by the peace process, leaving the UK government free to think about Northern Ireland as a devolution policy issue rather than a war zone. Frustrated with both the slow progress of the 'peace process' and the expensive public services of Northern Ireland (at a time of tightening in the rest of the UK), it has ceased to treat Northern Ireland with its normal budgetary indulgence (high-ranking official, Belfast, December 2006). This is partly a strategy to force a restoration of devolution by making direct rule unattractive; it is also a simple application of the kinds of reorganisation and efficiency drives that have been very common in the rest of the UK government. This strategy dovetailed with the Review of Public Administration which was built into the Belfast Agreement (www.rpani.gov.uk). Devolution was suspended, but the Review continued, with support from a frustrated London and from many frustrated but wary managers and officials in Northern Ireland. The Review has not been a wholly happy experience; considerations of good public services and cost-cutting have been difficult to reconcile, as have been the low policy capacity of Northern Ireland in general with the demand for speedy change made intermittently by direct rule ministers. The immediate consequence was that of the 246 pages of the Review of Public Administration proposals, there was one paragraph on public health, which called for a single public health authority (Review of Public Administration, 2005; Wilson and Oliver, 2007). It should be no surprise that a project that was ultimately given its force by the UK Treasury and Westminster politicians would focus on administrative rationalisation in health services. In public health, the consequences remain largely unclear as of May 2007. Given the tendency of much public health to rely on informal networks, an especially strong tendency in small Northern Ireland, there is no reason to expect there will ever be a clear statement of 'how it works'.

Conclusion: A fragile future

The argument in this chapter is that the public health policy outcomes that we have seen with devolution are a consequence of the UK's post-devolution institutions and the differences in its policy communities and party systems. Appetite for public health policy, and the kind of public health policy that is adopted, varies with these political variables. The evidence base for smoking bans, social marketing, or a separate public health corps does not stop at borders; what does stop is the reach of policy advocates and the particular problems of any one set of politicians. There has, indeed, been some convergence, but we see that mostly in the Welsh Assembly Government's retreat from its most novel public health strategies after they simply failed to deliver political success or major policy results.

This means that the future of devolved policy is continued divergence. Even if Scotland is led by the SNP and the UK by the Conservatives, many of the voters on which those parties depend will be the same ones on whom Labour depended – the voters who swing between parties. This concentrates political minds and tends to focus attention on voters who might not be representatives of the country as a whole, but who can decide who governs. Those voters' references will loom large no matter who is in office. Likewise, policy communities change with governments, but not much. Professional analysts and advocates do not give up when the government changes. In the main they will continue to argue cases that are nationally specific although the particular political context may encourage greater or less participation of groups with particular views. The result is that while the public health trajectories might change, they are very unlikely to converge; comparing the position of Labour and each of its three rival parties in different devolved jurisdictions highlights the distinctive areas of consensus in each polity.

The problem is the fragility of the UK system, which might endanger experimentation while failing to coordinate when coordination is required. Intergovernmental relations and divergent politics are creating the system we have in 2007; they also contain the seeds of serious threats to both policies and the public health infrastructure. The UK, in public health policy as other areas, combines a permissive institutional structure that allows considerable policy divergence with polities that have deeply rooted political reasons to diverge. The result is a 'fragile divergence machine' (Greer, 2007). It is a divergence machine because of its combination of permissive legislation and political drives to diverge that produces very different policy. It is fragile because the institutions underpinning it are weak (Trench, forthcoming) and not necessarily capable of withstanding technical meddling or political assault. The result will be that public health policy is likely to have to begin to do what public health policymakers in other countries have long had to do: grapple with intergovernmental relations and institutions as necessary conditions for public health policies. Devolved politics forces some politicians to care more about public health, but a fragile system of intergovernmental relations poses a threat to the public health benefits of devolution.

Notes

1 Major works on devolution drawn upon include Rawlings (2003a), Trench (2001, 2005, 2007, 2008) and Hazell and Rawlings (2005).

2 In May 2007 the SNP became the largest party in the Scottish Parliament, and now operates a minority administration in the Scottish Government.

3 The nine standard regions are: East of England, East Midlands, Greater London, Northeast England, Northwest England, Southeast England, Southwest England,

West Midlands, and Yorkshire and Humberside. The Government Office for London has different roles because it must work with the elected Greater London Authority and Mayor of London. All the standard regions have larger populations than Northern Ireland or Wales.

4 The 'Southeast' standard region, a hornet's nest of health management problems in 2006, is divided into two Strategic Health Authorities.

5 This is one of the stronger answers to the 'West Lothian Question', i.e. the question of why Scottish MPs should vote on English health policy when English or Scottish MPs cannot vote on Scottish health policy: the case for devolved MPs voting on UK law is that the UK's role in devolved policies is important and cannot be eliminated. MPs, when they vote on the budget, and voters when they elect UK governments, are exercising a powerful influence on even devolved areas of Scottish or Welsh life.

6 For example: COBRA is a UK government committee, not an intergovernmental forum. There are no intergovernmental forums with the power to act. This means that devolved representation, during a crisis when time is short and a 'command and control' approach likely, would mean either (1) the highly unusual participation of devolved politicians in a UK government committee or (2) devolved representation through the Secretaries of State for Northern Ireland, Scotland, and Wales-UK politicians, all of them likely to be dividing their time with a bigger portfolio, and without automatic access to the administration, information, networks, and preferences of devolved politicians.

7 There are two major exceptions. One is that Scotland can vary income tax up or down by three per cent. It has not; Scotland's politicians are reluctant to raise taxes, and they know that lowering them while enjoying higher per-capita funding than England would produce a hurricane of English resentment. The other is local government – the devolution of local government, extensive in Scotland and Wales, includes the devolution of its financial instruments. Even if no devolved government changes local government finance, responsibilities can be offloaded onto it and rates when they want to.

8 Much of this is based on 2001–2003 interviews reported in Greer (2004), and 89 subsequent interviews with devolved health policymakers.

9 http://www.snp.org/policies/health, accessed 21 January 2007.

10 http://www.scottishlabour.org.uk/manifestosection12/ accessed 21 January 2007.

11 At the *New Statesman* devolution and health summit, Cardiff, National Assembly for Wales.

12 Highlighting the catastrophic financial consequences of poor health for the NHS is common across the UK, but only Gordon Brown's Treasury, in hiring Wanless, put it so clearly to the front as a justification for public health policy.

13 Consider the Western hospitals; managers and officials have been trying for almost 20 years to force decisionmakers to a well thought out solution to the hospital planning problems of London/Derry and Counties Fermanagh, and Tyrone. Neither direct rule nor devolved ministers wanted to make a decision, and a whole generation of managers lobbied for change but ran doomed and inefficient services as well as they could despite being convinced by the clinical and financial arguments that reconfiguration of some sort should happen.

References

F. Adshead and A. Thorpe, 'Public health in England', in S. Griffiths and D. Hunter (eds), *New Perspectives in Public Health* (Abingdon: Radcliffe, 2007), pp. 29–36.

BBC News Online, 'Morgan predicts end to new Labour', 1 December 2006, retrieved 1 December 2006.

D. Bell and A. Christie, 'Finance – The Barnett Formula: Nobody's Child?', in A. Trench (ed.), *The State of the Nations 2001: The Second Year of Devolution* (Thorverton: Imprint Academic, 2002), pp. 135–52.

P. Cairney, 'Using devolution to set the agenda: The smoking ban in Scotland', presented at the Political Studies Association, Leeds, 2005.

P. Calain, 'Exploring the international arena of global public health surveillance', *Health Policy and Planning*, 22:1 (2006) 2–12.

H. Campbell, '"Nothing about me, without me" NHS values past and future in Northern Ireland', in S. Greer and D. Rowland (eds), *Devolving Policy, Diverging Values? The Values of the United Kingdom's National Health Services* (London: Nuffield Trust, 2007), pp. 55–68.

CNN.com, 'Minister: smoking joy for poor', 9 June 2004, retrieved 16 January 2007.

Department of Health, Getting ahead of the curve: A strategy for combating infectious diseases including other aspects of health protection (London: Department of Health, 2002).

Department of Health, *Choosing Health: Making Healthy Choices Easier* (London: HM Stationary Office, 2004).

Department of Health, Annual Report (London: Department of Health, 2005).

Department of Health Social Services and Public Safety, Investing for Health (Belfast: Department of Health Social Services and Public Safety, 2002).

H. M. Dingwall, *A History of Scottish Medicine* (Edinburgh: Edinburgh University Press, 2003).

P. Donnelly, 'Public health in Scotland: the dividend of devolution', in S. Griffiths and D. Hunter (eds), *New Perspectives in Public Health* (Abingdon: Radcliffe, 2007), pp. 22–9.

J. C. Faber, 'The European Blood Directive: a new era of blood regulation has begun', *Transfusion Medicine*, 14 (2004) 257–73.

D. Fraser, 'Scotland "finding itself frozen out of Brussels"', *The Herald*, 22 January 2007.

S. L. Greer, 'The Fragile Divergence Machine: Citizenship, Policy Divergence, and Devolution', in A. Trench (ed.), *Devolution and Power in the United Kingdom* (Manchester: Manchester University Press, 2007), pp. 136–59.

S. L. Greer, *Territorial Politics and Health Policy: UK Health Policy in Comparative Perspective* (Manchester: Manchester University Press, 2004).

S. L. Greer, 'Why Do Good Politics Make Bad Health Policy?', in C. Sausman and S. Dawson (eds), *Future Health Organisations and Systems* (Basingstoke: Palgrave, 2005), pp. 105–28.

S. L. Greer, *Responding to Europe: Government, NHS and Stakeholder Responses to the EU Health Challenge* (London: The Nuffield Trust, 2006a).

S. L. Greer, 'A Very English Institution: Central and local in the English NHS', in R. Hazell (ed.), *The English Question* (Manchester: Manchester University Press, 2006b), pp. 194–219.

S. L. Greer, 'The Fragile Divergence Machine: Citizenship, policy divergence, and intergovernmental relations', in A. Trench (ed.), *Devolution and Power in the United Kingdom* (Manchester: Manchester University Press, 2008), pp. 139–59.

S. L. Greer and H. Jarman, *The Department of Health and the Civil Service* (London: The Nuffield Trust, 2006).

S. Griffiths and D. Hunter (eds), *New Perspectives in Public Health* (Abingdon: Radcliffe, 2007).

R. Hazell (ed.), *The State and the Nations: The First Year of Devolution in the United Kingdom* (Thorverton: Imprint Academic, 2000).

R. Hazell (ed.), *The State of the Nations 2003: The Third Year of Devolution in the United Kingdom* (Exeter: Imprint Academic, 2003).

R. Hazell, 'Introduction: What is the English Question?', in R. Hazell (ed.), *The English Question* (Manchester: Manchester University Press, 2006), pp. 1–23.

R. Hazell and R. Rawlings (eds), *Devolution, Law Making and the Constitution* (Exeter: Imprint Academic, 2005).

D. Heald and A. McLeod, 'Beyond Barnett? Financing Devolution', in J. Adams and P. Robinson (eds), *Devolution in Practice: Public Policy Differences Within the UK* (London: Institute for Public Policy Research, 2002), pp. 147–75.

House of Lords Select Committee on the Constitution, *Devolution: Inter-Institutional Relations in the United Kingdom* (London: HM Stationary Office, 2002).

D. J. Hunter, *Public Health Policy* (Cambridge: Polity, 2003).

J. Jamison, H. Legido-Quigley and M. McKee, 'Cross-border care in Ireland', in M. Rosenmöller, M. McKee and R. Baeten (eds), *Patient Mobility in the European Union: Learning from Experience* (Brussels: European Observatory on Health Systems and Policies, 2006), pp. 39–58.

C. Jeffery, 'Devolution and Local Government', *Publius*, 36:1 (2006) 57–74.

J. W. Kingdon, *Agendas, Alternatives, and Public Policies* (New York: HarperCollins, 1995).

S. McClelland, 'Health Policy in Wales – Distinctive of Derivative?', *Social Policy and Society*, 1:4 (2002) 325–33.

M. McKee and E. Mossialos, 'Health policy and European law: Closing the gaps', *Public Health*, 120:S1 (2006) 16–21.

I. McLean, *The Fiscal Crisis of the United Kingdom* (Basingstoke: Palgrave Macmillan, 2005).

P. Michael and C. Webster (eds), *Health and Society in Twentieth-Century Wales* (Cardiff: University of Wales, Board of Celtic Studies, 2006).

C. Nottingham, *The NHS in Scotland: The Legacy of the Past and the Prospect of the Future* (Aldershot: Ashgate, 2000).

J. Osmond, 'A Constitutional Convention by Other Means: The First Year of the National Assembly for Wales', in R. Hazell (ed.), *The State and the Nations* (Thorverton: Imprint Academic, 2000), pp. 37–78.

J. Osmond, 'From Corporate Body to Virtual Parliament: The Metamorphosis of the National Assembly for Wales', in R. Hazell (ed.), *The State of the Nations 2003: The Third Year of Devolution in the United Kingdom* (Exeter: Imprint Academic, 2003), pp. 13–48.

J. Osmond, 'Nation Building and the Assembly: The Emergence of a Welsh Civic Consciousness', in A. Trench (ed.), *Has Devolution Made a Difference? The State of the Nations 2004* (Exeter: Imprint Academic, 2004), pp. 43–78.

L. Paterson, A. Brown, J. Curtice, K. Hinds, D. McCrone, A. Park, K. Sproston and P. Surridge, *New Scotland, New Politics?* (Edinburgh: Polygon at Edinburgh University Press, 2001).

R. Rawlings, *Delineating Wales: Constitutional, Legal and Administrative Aspects of National Devolution* (Cardiff: University of Wales Press, 2003a).

R. Rawlings, 'Towards a Parliament: Three Faces of the National Assembly for Wales', in R. Wyn Jones (ed.), *Contemporary Wales*, Volume 15 (Cardiff: University of Wales Press, 2003b), pp. 1–18.

Review of Public Administration, *The Review of Public Administration in Northern Ireland – Further Consultation* (Belfast: Review of Public Administration – Northern Ireland, 2005).

D. Rowland, *Mapping Communicable Disease Control Administration in the UK* (London: Nuffield Trust, 2006).

M. Sandford, *The New Governance of the English Regions* (Basingstoke: Palgrave Macmillan, 2005).

G. Sartori, *Partidos y Sistemas de Partidos* (Madrid: Alianza Editorial, 1999[1986]).

Scottish Executive Health Department, *Improving Health in Scotland: The Challenge* (Edinburgh: Scottish Executive, 2003a).

Scottish Executive Health Department, *Partnership for Care: Scotland's Health White Paper* (Edinburgh: HM Stationary Office, 2003b).

C. Spry, 'Who Decides on Scotland's Health?', in G. Hassan (ed.), *Anatomy of the New Scotland: Power, Influence and Change* (Edinburgh: Mainstream, 2002), pp. 103–13.

C. Tannahill, 'Health and health policy', in G. Mooney and G. Scott (eds), *Exploring Social Policy in the 'New' Scotland* (Bristol: Policy, 2005), pp. 199–220.

The Labour Party, *Forward not Back: The Labour Party Manifesto 2005* (London: The Labour Party, 2005).

A. Trench, *The State of the Nations 2001: The First Year of Devolution in the United Kingdom* (Thorverton: Imprint Academic, 2001).

A. Trench (ed.), *The Dynamics of Devolution: The State of the Nations 2005* (Exeter: Imprint Academic, 2005).

A. Trench, 'The Government of Wales Act 1006: The Next Steps in Devolution for Wales', *Public Law*, (2006) 687–96.

A. Trench (ed.), *State of the Nations 2008* (Exeter: Imprint Academic, 2008).

A. Trench (ed.), *Devolution and Power in the United Kingdom* (Manchester: Manchester University Press, 2007).

J. Tudor Hart, 'The Inverse Care Law', *The Lancet*, 1:7696 (1971) 405–12.

J. Tudor Hart, 'Two Paths for Medical Practice', *The Lancet*, 340 (1992) 772–4.

D. Wanless, *Securing our Future Health: Taking a Long-Term View* (London: HM Treasury, 2002).

Welsh Assembly Government, *Designed for Life: A World-Class Health Service for Wales* (Cardiff: Welsh Assembly Government, 2005).

R. Wilford, *Aspects of the Belfast Agreement* (Oxford: Oxford University Press, 2001).

R. Wilford and R. Wilson, 'Northern Ireland: Valedictory?', in R. Hazell (ed.), *The State of the Nations 2003: The Third Year of Devolution in the United Kingdom* (Exeter: Imprint Academic, 2003), pp. 79–118.

R. Wilson, *Northern Ireland: What's Going Wrong* (London: The Constitution Unit, 2003).

R. Wilson and Q. Oliver, *A Picture of Health? Tacking Health Inequalities in Northern Ireland* (Belfast: Democratic Dialogue/Stratagem, 2007).

R. Wilson and R. A. Wilford, 'Northern Ireland: Renascent?', in A. Trench (ed.), *Has Devolution Made a Difference? The State of the Nations 2004* (Exeter: Imprint, 2004), pp. 79–120.

K. J. Woods and D. Carter (eds), *Scotland's Health and Health Services* (London: TSO, 2003).

N. Zahariadis, *Markets, States, and Public Policy: Privatization in Britain and France* (Ann Arbor: University of Michigan Press, 1995).

2

International Public Health – The Future Place of Primary Care*

Jenny Amery and Stephen Gillam

Introduction

Most preventable deaths occur in poor countries. Poor people carry the greatest burden from communicable diseases including AIDS, TB and malaria, particularly in Africa. However, non-communicable chronic conditions, once regarded as diseases of affluence, are increasing in poor countries (World Health Organisation, 2005b). The changing burden of disease implies changing models of service delivery. Reducing income poverty through economic development will improve health status, but poor people also need access to effective, affordable, preventive and curative health services, including essential medicines. Primary care services have an essential role to play in future global health.

In 1978 at Alma Ata, primary health care was declared to be the key to delivering 'health for all' by the year 2000. Primary health care was to be 'based on practical, scientifically sound and socially acceptable methods and technology made universally accessible through people's full participation and at a cost that the community and country can afford' (World Health Organisation, 1978). The social and political goals of those epochal declarations – acknowledging as they did the social and economic determinants of health – were subsequently diluted. The failure in most countries to provide even selective packages of low cost primary care, coupled with the proliferation of 'vertical' initiatives to address specific global health problems, hastened its eclipse. Primary health care merited little mention in the Millennium Declaration of 2000.[1]

In this chapter we argue the case to bring the focus back onto primary care in the interests of global public health in future. We begin the chapter by examining the changing global burden of disease and outlining how it should be addressed. We go on to consider the implications of burden of disease for health systems in future, and reassert the particular contribution primary care can make towards reducing this burden and ensuring greater equity of health outcomes in future. Since this chapter was written, the 2008 World Health

---

*This chapter was received for publication in Winter 2006.

Report has supported the crucial role of primary health care in strengthening countries' health systems to respond to their citizens' health needs and the global health challenges of the future (World Health Organisation, 2008).

1   The global burden of disease

The premature deaths and preventable ill-health of millions of poor people present a major challenge now and in the future. Figure 2.1 shows the relative burden of disease by different regions of the world in 2002. It shows the inequality across regions, and the high burden of communicable disease in Sub-saharan Africa and South Asia. The implications for appropriate priorities and interventions are outlined below.

Communicable diseases

Communicable diseases remain, and will remain, a major cause of ill-health and death in poor countries, despite advances in vaccine development, diagnosis and available treatment. Figure 2.1 shows that in middle and low-income countries communicable diseases account for over 60 per cent of disease burden, compared to about 30 per cent in the low-income countries of South Asia, and an even greater burden in Sub-Saharan Africa. Most of this disease burden is from malaria, HIV, TB, and 'neglected' tropical diseases such as Leishmanisasis, Trypanosomiasis and Schistosomiasis. Globally, there are two million deaths each year from TB and one million from malaria. An estimated 33 million people worldwide were living with HIV at the end of 2007. Overall, the HIV incidence rate is thought to have peaked in the late 1990s,

Figure 2.1   Burden of disease in DALYs[2] per 100,000 population due to four broad disease categories by region

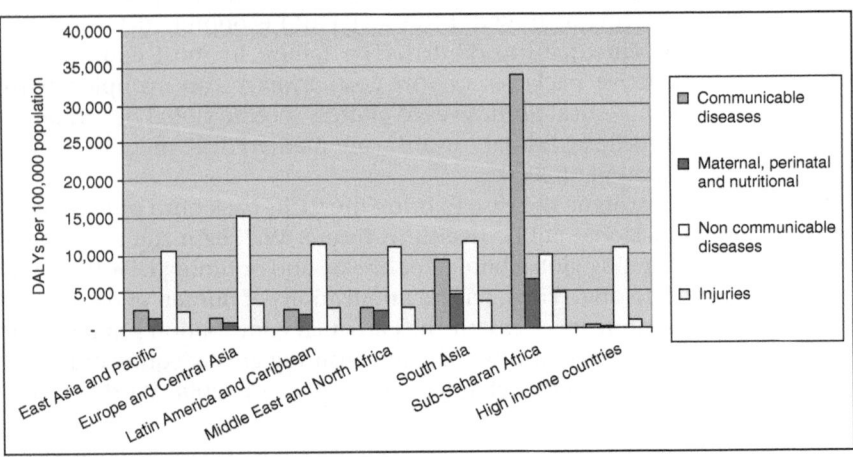

Source: WHO Global Burden of Disease data for 2002

and stabilised, although the incidence continues to rise in some countries. Sub-Saharan Africa has 10 per cent of the world's population and more than 60 per cent of all those living with HIV. Women are disproportionately affected. Even where new infections are decreasing, the lag time between infection and death means the burden of disease will remain high for years to come (UNAIDS, 2008). Communicable disease will remain a significant challenge in future, with AIDS a major cause of death globally. New diseases such as SARS will emerge, and a further pandemic of influenza is likely.

Reproductive and child health

Overall, the lifetime risk of maternal death for a woman in high-income countries is 1 in 4000. In middle-income countries it is 1 in 61, and in low-income countries 1 in 17 (AbouZahr and Wardlaw, 2003). This is the largest disparity in health outcome between the richest and poorest countries. Most of these deaths could be prevented if interventions, already known, were available to all women. These include access to family planning methods and safe abortion, to skilled attendants at the time of delivery, and to 24-hour emergency obstetric care, because most life-threatening complications such as post-partum haemorrhage cannot be predicted (Campbell and Graham, 2006). Women's health can also be improved through better access to family planning and other reproductive health services. Progress has been made in some countries but more needs to be done. For example, about one third of pregnancies worldwide each year (80 million) are unwanted or unplanned. This reflects an unmet need for family planning worldwide, and ongoing concerns about how to ensure the future supply of contraceptive methods to those who need them (Cleland *et al.*, 2006). Accessible primary health care is part of the solution. Many of the other issues which impact on reproductive health fall outside the health arena – women's empowerment, literacy, and poverty, for example. These cannot be speedily tackled as they require new policies and in some cases legislation, but they are known to be effective. A recent impact evaluation in Bangladesh showed that a child born to a mother with primary education is around 20 per cent less likely to die than a child born to a mother with no education; increasing to 80 per cent for women with secondary education. Girls' education is more cost effective, for example, than rural electrification. Rural electrification reduced the probability of deaths to those under five years of age, but at a cost of US$20,000 per death averted (World Bank, 2005).

Maternal health is linked with child health, but there are fundamental differences in effective approaches to addressing them. While successful approaches to child health improvement involve delivery of services as close to the community as possible (Bryce *et al.*, 2003), the reduction of maternal mortality is associated with access to hospital-based interventions for life-threatening complications around the time of delivery (World Bank, 2003). Good maternal health requires functioning health services at community and hospital levels, and effective referral systems between them. It is therefore considered an important marker of a functioning health system (United Nations, 2005).

Despite falling death rates in many countries, and an anticipated decline in infant mortality rates, approximately 10.8 million children die each year. Of these deaths, 90 per cent occur in only 42 countries. In poorer countries, serious illnesses commonly occur sequentially or concurrently before death. For example, measles is often complicated by pneumonia or diarrhoea. Underweight and micronutrient deficiencies decrease host defences, and malnutrition is estimated to contribute to about 60 per cent of avoidable childhood deaths (Black, 2003). Three-quarters of all child deaths in sub-Saharan Africa and in South Asia are from acute respiratory infections, diarrhoeal diseases, perinatal conditions, measles and malaria.

The interventions to prevent these deaths are well researched. They mostly require 'low tech' interventions delivered or supported through primary health systems. These include preventive interventions such as the promotion of exclusive breastfeeding for the first six months and appropriate complementary feeding, the use of insecticide treated bed nets to prevent malaria, clean delivery and specific neonatal care. The treatment interventions include oral rehydration therapy for diarrhoeal diseases, antibiotics for sepsis, antibiotics for pneumonia, antimalarials, zinc supplementation to reduce the morbidity and mortality from diarrhoea, and others (Jones, 2003). These are likely to remain important interventions in future and should be developed.

Integrated management of childhood illnesses (IMCI) is a strategy for improving child health through the combined delivery of a set of cost-effective interventions. It began with a set of clinical guidelines to manage a sick child at a health facility, and expanded to include household, community, and referral interventions. Despite the challenges and constraints to implementation, IMCI remains a promising approach to integrating primary health care (Bryce *et al.*, 2005), one that can be adapted to local circumstances in future. For example, an estimated 1.1 million newborn deaths occur annually in India – about 28 per cent of the world's total. Two major adaptations have been made to the IMCI model there: integrated management of neonatal illness, and a focus on early home visits for all newborns. Results from pilot districts in India are awaited (Lawn *et al.*, 2006).

Non-communicable disease and injury

Of increasing importance to future global health are non-communicable diseases. Rates of obesity, diabetes and ischaemic heart disease are rising, and rates of chronic disease are projected to become more significant in all countries by 2030 (Mathers and Loncar, 2006), increasing by 56 per cent globally from 2002. When countries are grouped by per person income, chronic diseases are projected to be the leading cause of death in all income groups in 2015 (Strong *et al.*, 2005). In 2003 the estimated world prevalence of diabetes in people aged 30 to 79 was 5.1 per cent, or 141 million people. By

2025 this is projected to rise to 6.3 per cent or 332 million people, of which no less than 264 million will be in developing countries (Disease Control Priorities Project, 2007a). This places an additional burden on health systems. In low-income countries road traffic accidents are expected to cause proportionately more deaths by 2030, becoming the seventh leading cause of death (Ameratunga, 2006).

Factors contributing to the changing pattern of disease include international migration, rapid rural-to-urban migration in most poor countries, and changing family structures (Disease Control Priorities Project, 2007b). Robust public health measures in sectors other than health are required to address the key risk factors of nutrition, smoking, unsafe sex, and the growing epidemic of injury and death from road traffic accidents (Ameratunga, 2006). In the next section we set out the prerequisites for future public health gain, including economic and political organisation, as well as elements of the health system.

2 Prerequisites for future health gain

Economic growth

The number of people living in poverty globally is falling, but at current rates of poverty reduction, there will still be 617 million people living on the equivalent of less than a dollar a day by 2015 (World Bank, 2006). Orthodox economic arguments highlight the need for macroeconomic growth to reduce levels of poverty, but there are increasing concerns about 'jobless' growth, with millions of poor people remaining at the margins of society. Debt relief and fairer trade with access to markets for poorer countries require action from rich country governments. More predictable aid would enable countries to fund sustainable five to ten year health plans and invest in well-trained workforces. Greater investment is needed in the development of new technologies: for example, better diagnostics, medicines and vaccines for HIV, TB and malaria. But none of these will make a significant difference without strong health services: accessible to poor people and staffed by well-trained, supervised, motivated and adequately rewarded health workers. Countries like Sri Lanka have shown that the health of the population can be improved to the level of many developed countries with modest macroeconomic growth and public investment in health services (Rannan-Eliya, 2001). Low-income countries where significant improvements have taken place in the health of the population without high or rapidly rising incomes also include Costa Rica, Cuba and Kerala State in India. Priority support for community level health facilities and staff have characterised these 'high achievers'.

Inequality, social inclusion and equity

The widening economic inequalities within and between countries are exacerbated by new patterns of communication and consumption, rapid urbanisation and concomitant degradation of the environment. The accompanying economic and demographic changes affect working conditions, learning environments, and family patterns – the social and physical fabric of communities. Against this background, many countries have signed up under the aegis of the WHO to the Bangkok Charter (World Health Organisation, 2005a). This identifies actions, commitments and pledges required to address the determinants of health. Key principles are:

- globalisation as a positive force for health improvement
- promoting health as a core government responsibility
- health promotion as good corporate responsibility
- environments empowering individuals and communities to improve health
- regulation and legislation to protect citizens and promote their health.

Signatories recognise the requirement for investment and partnership across governments, international organisations, civil society, and the private sector. This approach moves the debate from the global market as the enemy of good health and the corporate sector as unengaged, to recognising that new models of joint working are needed. It requires new approaches to improve health that embrace a range of stakeholders whose priorities may differ – but they too need careful evaluation.

One challenge to successful implementation is that hitherto, certain population groups have worse health outcomes and are persistently excluded from access to health services because of their ethnicity, caste, gender, religion or other characteristics. For example, in India infant mortality rates for scheduled castes and tribes are significantly higher than those of the rest of the population (World Bank, 2004). For geographically remote and isolated populations it may cost more to deliver cost-effective interventions than in accessible, more densely populated areas. Well trained, multi-skilled primary care workers can bring effective services to such populations, but only if this is given political priority and adequate funding.

Good health system governance

Effective health systems will also require effective governance. Much poor performance in terms of health service delivery is due to weaknesses in institutions, budgeting and public expenditure management (Grindle, 2002). Governments should be held to account for maintaining fiscal discipline, ensuring resources are spent in line with stated priorities, are not lost through corruption or mismanagement, and are used to achieve maximum impact on health outcomes. Making information more accessible and promoting transparency in fees, budgets and expenditure enable corruption to be tackled more easily, but there are often strong forces at work to avoid such transparency. Citizens' voices in budget allocations (Brazil), budget monitoring (South Africa) and budget auditing (Rajasthan, Northern India) have enabled local people to influence the use of public funds (World Development Report, 2004). The 2005 Commission for Africa Report concluded that without progress in improving governance, all other reforms would have limited impact (Commission for Africa, 2005). Given the plurality of most health economies, improved governance is crucially important in the private and voluntary sectors as well as in public systems.

Adequate funding

Better governance can improve resource allocation, but one of the reasons for low health service coverage and poor health outcomes is low expenditure on health per capita. The Commission on Macroeconomics and Health calculated that US$34 per capita in 2002 prices was needed to provide a basic package of services to address the main causes of ill-health and premature death in low-income countries (World Health Organisation, 2002). (The package comprised many of the same components of primary care defined at Alma Ata.) This would require an additional US$40 to 52 billion by 2015 and would save some eight million lives each year. In 2000 African countries pledged in Abuja, Nigeria to increase funding for health from around 8 per cent on average to 15 per cent of their budgets but few have achieved that level to date. Inadequate action on these commitments has been attributed to the lack of accountability of governments, costly debt servicing, and poor tracking systems for government resources (Action Aid, 2005). However, some countries are attaining measurably better levels of service coverage with lower levels of expenditure. For example, Sri Lanka has remarkably good health outcomes and its public sector spends only $US15 per capita on health; investment is in more cost-effective interventions with greater efficiency of spend. This is due in part to the equitable allocation of resources for health and a judicious mix of skilled health personnel (Levine *et al.*, 2004).

Adequate staffing

Adequate numbers of well-trained, motivated health workers are essential for effective service delivery. Many countries face a deep crisis in staffing their health services, resulting from chronic under-investment in staff and health systems (World Health Organisation, 2006). This is exacerbated by the burden of AIDS, especially in southern African countries. There, the health services are overwhelmed with AIDS patients, and the capacity of health services to cope is further limited because of illness and death from AIDS among health workers and their families. Staff shortages are also made worse by low-income countries subsidising high-income ones by supplying them with trained staff through outward migration. From Africa the net outflow is equivalent to about US$500 million a year (World Health Organisation, 2006). Changes to international recruitment practice may help to manage the flow of migrants in future, but migration is the result of low pay, lack of career prospects and poor working conditions in 'source' countries, as well as high-income 'destination' countries' inability to train and meet their own workforce requirements (World Health Organisation, 2006).

Coherent national health policy and priorities

There is a trend toward vertical health programmes focusing on specific disease areas. Current examples of vertical programmes include those addressing polio eradication, AIDS, TB, malaria, and childhood immunisation. There are over 70 global health partnerships and initiatives addressing diseases or other specific health needs, many with private-public financing. This is in addition to the multilateral development agencies working in health, notably the EC, World Bank, Regional Development Banks, UN technical agencies such as WHO, UNICEF, UNFPA, UNAIDS, private entities such as the Bill and Melinda Gates Foundation, and many bilateral donors.

Targeted programmes raise the profile of specific health conditions, mobilise additional resources, and often deliver short-term results against specific targets. The global eradication of smallpox was a major success, but efforts to eradicate malaria since the 1960s have notably failed, and eradication is no longer a goal. Vertical approaches divert human and financial resources, and can undermine and weaken other health initiatives, despite achieving their own specific objectives. There is increasing concern that they may undermine broader health service delivery, through duplication of effort, distortion of national health plans and budgets, and particularly through diversion of scarce trained staff. Vertical programmes tend to focus on a single disease, often neglecting the multiple needs of each patient. Vertical approaches address one disease or issue at a time, and are controlled by experts. When health systems are extremely weak, such as post conflict or when governments lack legitimacy or capacity to fund or provide any meaningful services, vertical programmes delivered initially by the UN or NGOs, may be the best way to provide services. The burgeoning of top-down programmes challenges many countries' capacity to address agreed national priorities, and to coordinate the work of different donors. It is important that efforts are made in parallel to (re)build public health systems in future, and not weaken them further.

Better information for managing performance and assessing effectiveness

The Millennium Development Goals (MDGs) collectively address the different dimensions of poverty and health.[3] There are a number of weaknesses inherent in the goals. For example, the MDG indicators measure average progress for a country, but do not reflect inequalities or widening gaps creating potential to leave poorer people further behind in future. Monitoring data in countries need to be disaggregated to reflect relative progress on health outcomes amongst the poorest and excluded groups. The framing of numerical targets has focused attention, but risks a technocratic, top-down approach to the complex challenges facing different countries and cultures (United Nations, 2006). Governments and international organisations do not always use the same data sources or definitions. Furthermore, progress towards the health-related millennium development goals and respective indicators is limited by poor information, incomplete vital registration of births and deaths, and poor quality data. There is an urgent need, therefore, for better data systems to guide results-based performance monitoring, better disaggregation to allow analysis of equity and distributional issues, and improved capture of health service quality measures. The management of chronic diseases increasingly calls for longitudinal patient records, which require a very different approach to the activity-based record systems most commonly used.

The processes of target-setting expose further knowledge gaps. Notably, only 10 per cent of the annual $70 billion spent on global health research targets the diseases responsible for 90 per cent of the world's health problems (Labonte and Spiegel, 2003). In addition to increased global investment, new ways of stimulating research into the diseases of poverty, and the development of commodities including vaccines, diagnostics and medicines are required. Evaluative research is urgently needed on the best way of delivering health interventions: to better understand what works and why.

Strong public health services

To maximise their benefit, health resources must be reallocated towards more cost-effective services, poorer geographical regions within countries, and services that are used by poor people. Effective policies, well implemented,

---

Box 2.1   Core public health functions

These include:
- Collection and dissemination of evidence for public health policies
- Public health regulation and enforcement
- Pharmaceutical policy regulation and enforcement
- Epidemiological and behavioural surveillance for risk factors of disease
- Prevention and control of disease
- Health promotion
- Inter-sectoral action for improving health
- Monitoring and evaluation of public health policy
- Development of human resources and capacity for public health

Source: Adapted from A. Wagstaff and M. Claeson, 2004.

can greatly improve the health of poor people, as illustrated by the examples of Sri Lanka and Kerala State in India. The HIV epidemic and emergence of new diseases such as SARS have highlighted the crucial role of governments in strengthening and maintaining core public health functions (Wagstaff and Claeson, 2004). Essential aspects of a successful core public health function are set out in Box 2.1, and include many of the prerequisites for health gain already discussed.

Population health is improved by the existence of a well-functioning district health system comprising first contact primary care, community services (e.g. midwifery, pharmacy) and first-referral (district) hospitals. This organisational and service unit is fundamental to effective health care provision, and failure to recognise the interrelationship between component levels has had high health costs and resulted in great inefficiency (Doherty and Govender, 2004). In developing countries, factors such as geographic and financial inaccessibility, limited funds and staff, erratic drug supply, and non-functioning equipment often mean that the services offered at the primary care level are disappointingly limited in their range, coverage, and effect. Primary care has been neglected as a strategic priority, yet provides a conduit through which many of resources for health can flow. What do we mean by primary care and how can this first level be strengthened?

Strong primary care

The Alma Ata Declaration of 1978 rejected the vertical approach to disease management and called on governments to tackle common underlying causes of ill-health, by building sustainable health care systems, locally-based and locally controlled (World Health Organisation, 1978). Emphasis was given to people's participation in health. Reviewing European primary care, Boerma (2006) has emphasised the benefits of strong primary care in developing teamwork and collaboration which helps smooth the interface with secondary care and increase patient responsiveness. In addition, screening, monitoring and follow up can only be effectively carried out by the coordinated efforts of various professional groups on the basis of the population they serve. The difficulty of transposing health systems across international boundaries is widely acknowledged, but evidence from high-income countries can be applied to the developing world (and vice versa). The World Bank has estimated that the primary care level could potentially deal with up to 90 per cent of health care demands and that only 10 per cent of care needs require the services and skills typically associated with hospitals (World Bank, 1994). Primary health care is considered below in terms of its role as provider and coordinator of other care.

Care provision

Low- and middle-income countries, like high-income ones, face a future of increasing prevalence of non-communicable illness. This shift has already led to the coexistence of persisting infectious disease, nutrition and reproductive health problems alongside emerging non-communicable disease and related risk factors (such as hypertension, obesity, diabetes, stroke, and cardiovascular disease). The challenge this transition poses to the provision of primary care is considerable. For the most part, existing health systems are oriented to maternal and child health and the management of acute illness. Thus developing primary care services appropriate to future needs will require extending the reach and capacity of primary acute care systems (presently oriented to episodic care) to accommodate the need for effective systems of long-term care and monitoring.

There are a number of reasons why, and ways in which, primary care should be developed in this way. Not only does the primary care level constitute the first point of patient or family contact, it is also a critical base for extending care to communities and vulnerable groups. Outreach services may focus on individual preventive measures (such as immunisation, vitamin A, or oral rehydration therapy) or community-wide health-promoting efforts (such as education on child nutrition or adult diets and exercise). Increasingly, home-based care for chronic conditions, such as HIV and AIDS and post-stroke rehabilitation, can be expected to feature in outreach services. These services depend substantially on community support and mechanisms for identifying, training and supporting village or community health workers. Adequate resources have to be allocated along with new service responsibilities, and local political institutions must be functional and accountable to the population (Wagstaff and Claeson, 2004).

Care coordination

Primary care, as a level of care, is thus a key interface that links, on the one hand, ambulatory care with hospital and specialty services and, on the other, individual clinical care with community-wide or population-wide health, nutrition and family planning programmes. Acting as the fulcrum of

---

Box 2.2   Two successful programmes

National programmes such as the Lady Health Workers in Pakistan's National Family Planning and Primary Care Programme, or the Auxiliary Nurse Midwives and ASHAs (Accredited Social and Health Activists) in India's National Rural Health Mission, aim to train and support enough community health workers to provide a range of reproductive, child, maternal and other health services and health promotion and preventive interventions, to a defined catchment population at village level. These initiatives have the potential to provide continuity of care and basic management of chronic diseases. These health workers depend crucially on a functioning referral system for their patients to access more complex care when required (Government of India, 2005; Government of Pakistan, 2007).

a comprehensive care and support system, development of primary care requires that local management teams plan services for their defined catchment communities (Jha and Mills, 2002). Two successful programmes are described in Box 2.2 as examples.

This coordinating function provides a major economic justification for primary care: evidence suggests that health systems which are primary care oriented are more likely to deliver better health outcomes, lower costs and greater public satisfaction (Macinko *et al.*, 2003). However, achieving these benefits is not inevitable. Our analysis identifies six key challenges for primary care services to achieve better public health in future. The focus is on poor countries, but the messages apply equally to policies directed to those who are poor and disadvantaged in rich countries.

Six challenges for primary care to deliver public health in future

1. What kind of primary care is affordable and appropriate in different settings?

No single model of primary health care will be universally applicable. A major challenge is to establish the most effective combinations or clusters of interventions that can target multiple conditions and risk factors affecting key community groups (children, women, and older adults, for example) and which are appropriately adapted to local epidemiological, economic, and sociocultural contexts. Clustering interventions achieves comprehensiveness while at the same time acknowledging resource constraints. For example, community-oriented primary care (COPC) seeks to integrate public health practice by delivering primary care to defined communities on the basis of assessed health needs (Mullan and Epstein, 2002). COPC remains a powerful, enduring concept but its protagonists have made little mark beyond developing countries (see Box 2.3).

Intervention clusters are likely to include IMCI (integrated management of childhood illnesses); maternal and reproductive health services; clinic and community-based management of tuberculosis, HIV/AIDS, and sexually transmitted infections; malaria management; management of hypertension, other cardiovascular risk factors, and – increasingly – stroke and cardiovascular disease; and mental illness and substance abuse.

The UK has traditionally been regarded as boasting some of the best primary care services in the developed world; to these in large measure has been attributed the relative efficiency of the National Health Service. Ironically, moves to create a market for these services with the encouragement of large private sector providers may fragment health care (Hill *et al.*, 2007). Experience from North America suggests that, for example, parcelling up the care of chronic diseases between different commercial companies principally concerned to increase profit margins results in less efficient (higher transaction costs) and more inequitable (excluding patients at higher risk) care (Weiner *et al.*, 2002).

2. How can equity goals be promoted?

One well-attested form of differential access to care is the so called 'inverse prevention' effect whereby communities most at risk of ill-health tend to experience the least satisfactory access to the full range of preventive services (Acheson Report, 1998). User charges for primary care have been repeatedly shown to deter those most likely to benefit from preventive activities (NHS Centre for Reviews and Dissemination, 2000). Indeed, one way to address this is to provide financial incentives for poorer people to visit services. The conditional cash transfer schemes in Mexico have improved health outcomes for a large number of poor people (Skoufis, 2005). Other methods of demand-side financing where money or vouchers are given to the poorest people to increase access to particular services such as maternity care, are being piloted in many countries (Standing, 2004). Other ways to improve equitable access include the monitoring of service delivery and health outcomes by separate population groups, and provision of incentives to service providers to deliver services to these groups.

3. How can the workforce be developed and retained?

The creation of dynamic health teams at the primary level is one of the greatest requirements for scaling up effective primary care. Public health competencies, especially as they relate to the management of chronic disease, are of particular importance to the 21st Century global health care workforce (World Health Organisation, 2005b). At the same time, one of the most challenging constraints is to overcome the loss of motivation and sense of resignation of the great body of primary care workers who work in under-staffed settings; who lack consistent, quality support; and who have grown accustomed to a norm of inadequate service delivery (Narasimhan *et al.*, 2004). In most developing countries primary care roles are regarded as low status, less valued than hospital medicine by both the public and policymakers. Only high level political commitment, adequate governance and funding will raise the status of primary care and attract suitable workers to it. Ironically, poor countries which emulated training standards of the industrialised countries, such as Ghana, have been most vulnerable to poaching by them (Blanchet *et al.*, 2003).

4. How can the rhetoric of patient and public involvement be made a reality?

In many poor countries even the rhetoric of greater patient and public involvement in health is absent. Julian Tudor Hart, an eloquent exponent of COPC in the Welsh mining village where he practised, long ago argued for the need to look in a new way at the relationship between doctors and patients as 'co-producers of health' and develop alliances between health workers and the public in defence of health (Tudor Hart, 1988). Public health is likely to improve when health services meet community expectations and treat patients in a dignified manner. In addition, primary-level facilities can be used as a community resource (providing communal meeting places, for example) and primary care services can contribute support to neighbourhood sports and community development activities.

The diffusion of new technologies may provide greater scope for self-care amongst some groups in developing countries, as is anticipated in the high-income countries. Escalating rates of cell phone connectivity in India will transform access to information and health services in rural India, for example (Muir Gray, 1999).

5. How can low-income countries increase their capacity to obtain and use health information?
A basic longitudinal record for monitoring child development and reproductive health events is needed universally by primary care service providers. Such records are also essential to manage chronic diseases effectively, to follow symptoms, biochemical and other test results, and the impact of treatment over time.

Tanzania Essential Health Interventions Project (TEHIP) (see Box 2.3), and related experience, make clear that delivery of effective primary care requires a greatly stepped-up capacity to provide an evidence base that is founded on local disease and risk factor burdens, the performance of local health services, client use of public as well as private and traditional services, and (where appropriate) the costs of providing care. Effective use of such information can profoundly enhance the ability of the health system to deliver on its core service functions, target high-risk and vulnerable groups,

---

Box 2.3   Tanzania Essential Health Interventions Project
Community-oriented primary care underpins the Tanzanian Essential Health Interventions Program (TEHIP), 1997–2004. TEHIP has tested how and to what extent evidence can guide planning of the health sector at district level in order to improve technical and allocative efficiency (de Savigny *et al.*, 2002). A dynamic process of using high-quality local information, coupled with local problem solving, planning, and ownership, was central to appropriate decisionmaking and consequent implementation. New analytic tools were devised that would help focus resource allocation on the major 'intervention-addressable' disease burdens. The net effect of decentralised funding, together with a mutually reinforcing series of planning, management, and capacity-development inputs, was an increase in resources for cost-effective interventions addressing the largest shares of the preventable local burden of disease; an increase in the use of government health services; and a decrease in mortality in infants, children under five, adolescents, and adults. This was achieved with relatively limited resources.

assess coverage in service provision, and gauge health effects. Moreover, such information is vital to establishing the dimensions of the local disease burden that should be managed at the primary care level (Bellagio Study Group on Child Survival, 2003).

6. How can the evidence base be extended?
The empirical evidence with regard to large-scale and routine primary care programmes is scant (Doherty and Govender, 2004). There is plenty of evidence for cost-effective interventions that could vastly improve maternal and child health, for example, but less evidence on how to ensure that these services, when delivered in resource-poor settings, reach the most vulnerable populations to lasting effect (Victora *et al.*, 2004).

Whether primary care has an impact on health has much to do with the quality and effectiveness of the services provided, but also how the service is delivered, whether it is perceived as relevant to people's immediate needs, and whether it is affordable and culturally acceptable. Thus evidence gathered in high-income countries, may be less useful in countries with less developed health systems. Evaluations are required of new forms of organising primary care services in specific locations (in particular, balancing persisting acute needs with the growing need for chronic care, or establishing the skill mix that is most effective in particular settings). To date, a community-focused operational research agenda has been neglected in favour of the evidence base for individual interventions. Such research is complex because it is context-specific and dependent on local capacity and commitment.

Conclusion

Adequate delivery of services at the primary care level is fundamental to effective functioning of health systems if they are not going to be overwhelmed by the emerging epidemics of chronic and non-communicable diseases which will add to the current burden of communicable disease. However, for the most part, primary care systems in low- and middle-income countries have yet to receive the sustained attention and resources that their importance warrants. Early efforts at primary care expansion in the late 1970s and early 1980s were overtaken in many parts of the developing world by economic crisis, sharp reductions in public spending, political instability, and emerging disease. Essential packages based on cost-effectiveness criteria have been criticised for their largely disease-oriented and top down approach. In most poor countries even these limited versions of general primary care remain incompletely applied and largely unaffordable.

Primary care amounts to more than a simple summation of individual technological interventions. Its power resides in linking different disciplines, integrating different elements of disease management, stressing early prevention and the maintenance of health. Effective general primary care that responds to the rapid health transitions under way in all socioeconomic contexts offers the potential for major health and, hence, development gains that provide good value for money and enhance equity. Critical make-or-break points include increased financial investments paralleled by sustained investment in human resources (principally the strengthening of local staff capacity, including supportive management – and the encouragement of innovation in services development). Far greater attention is needed to improving delivery and service quality, monitoring service coverage, improving access by vulnerable groups and establishing constructive partnerships with local communities. Developing effective, sustainable primary care systems is a major challenge for those active in the policy and practice of public health.

Notes

1 The largest ever gathering of heads of state in September 2000 in New York adopted the Millennium Declaration which was then translated into a roadmap. The eight goals in the section on development and poverty eradication are known collectively as the Millennium Development Goals. They build on agreements made at major UN conferences in the 1990s and represent commitments to tackle poverty, hunger, ill-health, gender inequality, lack of education, lack of access to clean water, environmental degradation, and the need for global partnerships for development. Goals 4, 5 and 6 are, respectively, to reduce child mortality, improve maternal health, and combat HIV and AIDS and other diseases.

2 Disability Adjusted Life Year (DALY) is a measure of the burden of ill-health that takes into account both reduced life expectancy and quality of life. It is widely used internationally despite limitations. Values vary widely according to discount rates and weighting of different age groups used. Relatively poor data are available for some countries and conditions, but no better alternative measure has yet been agreed.

3 Millennium Developments Goals to be achieved by 2015
    • Halve extreme poverty and hunger
      1.2 billion people still live on less than $1 a day. But 43 countries, with more than 60 per cent of the world's people, have already met or are on track to meet the goal of cutting hunger in half by 2015.
    • Achieve universal primary education
      113 million children do not attend school, but this goal is within reach:
      Empower women and promote equality between women and men
      Two-thirds of the world's illiterate people are women, and 80 per cent of its refugees are women and children. Since the 1997 Microcredit Summit, progress has been made in reaching and empowering poor women, nearly 19 million in 2000 alone.
    • Reduce under-five mortality by two-thirds
      11 million young children die every year, but that number is down from 15 million in 1980.
    • Reduce maternal mortality by three-quarters
      In the developing world, the risk of dying in childbirth is one in 48. But virtually all countries now have safe motherhood programmes and are poised for progress.

- Reverse the spread of diseases, especially HIV/AIDS and malaria
  AIDS and other diseases have erased a generation of development gains in some countries in Africa. Countries like Brazil, Senegal, Thailand and Uganda have shown that the HIV epidemic can be slowed and reversed.
- Ensure environmental sustainability
  More than one billion people still lack access to safe drinking water; however, during the 1990s, nearly one billion people gained access to safe water and as many to sanitation.
- Create a global partnership for development, with targets for aid, trade and debt relief. Too many developing countries are spending more on debt service than on social services. New aid commitments made in the first half of 2002 alone, though, reached an additional $12 billion per year by 2006.

References

C. AbouZahr and T. Wardlaw, 'Maternal Mortality in 2000: Estimates developed by WHO, UNICEF and UNFPA' (2003), cited in Department for International Development, Reducing maternal deaths: evidence and action (London: DFID, 2004).

D. Acheson, Independent Inquiry into Inequalities in Health Report (London: HM Stationary Office, 1998).

Action Aid, Four years after Abuja: more action required on spending commitments (London: Action Aid, 2005).

S. Ameratunga, M. Hijar and R. Norton, 'Road traffic injuries: confronting disparities to address a global health priority', *The Lancet*, 367:9521 (2006) 1533–40.

Bellagio Study Group on Child Survival, 'Knowledge into action for child survival', *The Lancet*, 362: 9380 (2003) 323–7.

R. E. Black, S. S. Morris and J. Bryce, 'Where and why are 10 million children dying every year?' *The Lancet*, 361:9376 (2003) 2226–34.

N. Blanchet, G. Dussault and B. Liese, The human resource crisis in health services (Washington DC: World Bank, 2003).

W. Boerma, 'Public health in the driving seat', in R. Saltman and A. Rico (eds), *European Observatory on Health Systems and Policy* (Copenhagen: World Health Organisation, 2006).

J. Bryce, S. el Arifeen, G. Pariyo, C. Lanata, D. Gwatkin and J. P. Habicht, 'Reducing child mortality: can public health deliver?', *The Lancet*, 362:9378 (2003) 159–64.

J. Bryce, C. G. Victora and J. P. Habicht, R. E. Black and R. W Scherpbier, on behalf of the MCE-IMCI Technical Advisors, 'Programmatic pathways to child survival: results of a multi-country evaluation of integrated management of childhood illness', *Health Policy Planning*, 20 (2005) i5–i17.

O. Campbell, W. Graham, on behalf of the Lancet Maternal Survival Series steering group, 'Strategies for reducing maternal mortality: getting on with what works', *The Lancet*, 368:9543 (2006) 1284–99.

J. Cleland, S. Bernstein and A. Ezeh, A. Faundes, A. Glasier and J. Innis, 'Family planning: the unfinished agenda', *The Lancet*, 368:9549 (2006) 1810–27.

Commission for Africa, Our Common Future: Report of the Commission for Africa (London: Commission for Africa, 2005).

D. de Savigny, H. Kasale, C. Mbuya, G. Munna, L. Mgalula, A. Mzige and G. Reid, Tanzania Essential Health Interventions Project: TEHIP Interventions – An Overview (Dar es Salaam, Tanzania: Ministry of Health, 2002).

Disease Control Priorities Project, Diabetes: The Pandemic and Potential Solutions (Washington DC: World Bank, 2007a).

Disease Control Priorities Project, *Disease Control Priorities in Developing Countries*, 2nd edn (Washington DC: World Bank, 2007b).

J. Doherty and R. Govender, The Cost-Effectiveness of Primary Care Services in Developing Countries: A Review of the International Literature. Working Paper No 37 (Washington DC: Disease Control Priorities Project, 2004).

Government of India, Ministry of Health and Family Welfare, National Rural Health Mission: Framework for Implementation 2005–2012 (New Delhi: Government of India, 2005).

Government of Pakistan, Ministry of Health, National Programme for Family Planning and Primary Health Care, Annual Report 2005–06 (Government of Pakistan, 2007).

M. Grindle, Good Enough Governance: Poverty Reduction and Reform in Developing Countries (Cambridge: Kennedy School of Government, Harvard University, 2002).

A. Hill, S. Griffiths and S. Gillam, '*Public Health and Primary Care: Partners in Population Health* (Oxford: Oxford University Press, 2007).

P. Jha and A. Mills, Improving Health Outcomes of the Poor: The Report of Working Group 5 of the Commission on Macroeconomics and Health (Geneva: World Health Organisation, 2002).

G. Jones, R. W. Steketee, R. E. Black, Z. A. Bhutta and S. S. Morris, 'How many child deaths can we prevent this year?', *The Lancet*, 362:9377 (2003) 65–71.

R. Labonte and J. Spiegel, 'Setting global health research priorities', *British Medical Journal*, 326 (2003) 722–3.

J. Lawn, J. Zupan, G. Begkoyian and R. Knippenberg, 'Newborn Survival', in D. T. Jamison, J. G. Breman, A. R. Measham, G. Alleyne, M. Claeson, D. B. Evans, P. Jha, A. Mills and P. Musgrove (eds), *Disease Control Priorities in Developing Countries*, 2nd edn (New York: Oxford University Press, 2006), pp. 531–50.

R. Levine and the 'What works' working group, with M. Kinder, *Millions Saved: Proven Successes in Global Health* (Washington DC: Center for Global Development, Peterson Institute, 2004).

J. Macinko, B. Starfield and L. Shi, 'The contribution of primary care systems to health outcomes within organization for economic cooperation and development (OECD) countries, 1970–1998', *Health Services Research*, 38:3 (2003) 831–65.

C. D. Mathers and D. Loncar, 'Projections of Global Mortality and Burden of Disease from 2002 to 2030', *PLoS Medicine*, 3:11 (2006), 442.

J. A. Muir Gray, 'Postmodern medicine', *The Lancet*, 354:9189 (1999) 1550–2.

F. Mullan and L. Epstein, 'Community-oriented primary care: new relevance in a changing world', *American Journal of Public Health*, 92:11 (2002) 1748–55.

V. Narasimhan, H. Brown, A. Pablos-Mendez, A., O. Adams, G. Dussault, G. Elzinga, A. Nordstrom, D. Habte, M. Jacobs, G. Solimano, N. Sewankambo, S. Wibulpolprasert, T. Evans and L. Chen, 'Responding to the global human resource crisis', *The Lancet*, 363:9419 (2004) 1469–72.

NHS Centre for Reviews and Dissemination, Evidence from Systematic Reviews of the Research Relevant to Implementing the 'Wider Public Health' Agenda (York: University of York, NHS Centre for Reviews and Dissemination, 2000).

R. P. Rannan-Eliya, 'Strategies for Improving the Health of the Poor – The Sri Lanka Experience' (Colombo, Sri Lanka: Health Policy Programme, Institute of Policy Studies, 2001).

E. Skoufis, Progressa and its Impact on the Welfare of Rural Households in Mexico: Research Report 139 (Washington DC: International Food Policy Research Institute, 2005).

H. Standing, Understanding the 'demand side' in Service Delivery (London: DFID Health Systems Resource Centre, 2004).

K. Strong, C. Mathers, S. Leeder and R. Beaglehole, 'Preventing chronic disease: how many lives can we save?', *The Lancet*, 366: 9496 (2005) 1578–82.

J. Tudor Hart, *A New Kind of Doctor* (London: Merlin Press, 1988).

UNAIDS, *'Report of the Global AIDS Epidemic'* (Geneva: UNAIDS, 2008).

United Nations, 'Who's Got the Power? Transforming Health Systems for Women and Children: Task Force on Child Health and Maternal Health' (New York: United Nations, 2005).

United Nations, 'The Millennium Development Goals Report' (New York: United Nations, 2006).

Victora, C., Hanson, K., Bryce, J. and Vaughan, J. (2004) 'Achieving universal coverage with health interventions', *The Lancet*, 364:9444 (2004) 1541–8.

A. Wagstaff and M. Claeson, 'The Millennium Development Goals for Health: Rising to the Challenges' (Washington DC: World Bank, 2004).

J. Weiner, R. Lewis and S. Gillam, 'US Managed Care and PCTs: Lessons for a small island from a lost continent' (London: King's Fund, 2002).

World Bank, 'Better Health in Africa: Experience and Lessons Learned' (Washington DC, World Bank, 1994).

World Bank, Investing in maternal health: 'Learning from Malaysia and Sri Lanka' (Washington DC: World Bank, 2003).

World Bank, 'Attaining the Millennium Development Goals in India' (Washington DC: World Bank, 2004).

World Bank, 'Maintaining the momentum to 2015? An impact evaluation of interventions to improve maternal and child health and nutrition in Bangladesh' (Washington DC: World Bank, 2005).

World Bank, 'Global Economic Prospects' (Washington DC: World Bank, 2006).

World Development Report, 'Making services work for poor people' (Washington DC: World Bank, 2004).

World Health Organisation, 'Primary Health Care. Report of the International Conference on Primary Health Care', Alma-Ata, USSR (Geneva: World Health Organisation, 1978).

World Health Organisation, 'Macroeconomics and Health: Investing in Health for Economic Development. Report of the Commission on Macroecomics and Health' (Geneva: World Health Organisation, 2002).

World Health Organisation, Bangkok Charter (Geneva: WHO, 2005a).

World Health Organisation, 'Preparing a Workforce for the 21st Century: The Challenge of Chronic Conditions' (Geneva: World Health Organisation, 2005b).

World Health Organisation, 'World Health Report: Working Together for Health' (Geneva: World Health Organisation, 2006).

World Health Organisation, 'World Health Report: Primary Health Care now more than ever' (Geneva: World Health Organisation, 2008).

3
Improving Public Health: Balancing Between Poles

Sue Atkinson

Success in improving the public's health depends upon all those involved understanding the need to balance their thoughts and actions between poles which pull in different directions, and yet which both need to be satisfied. This need for balance is seen in the tension between a reliance on the rationally based methods of scientific enquiry and evidence and a focus on the art of emotionally and intuitively based forms of explanation and action; between a focus on delivery through the NHS and delivery through cross-sectoral collaboration, extending way beyond the NHS; between a focus on individual behaviour and a focus on social determinants of health; and between a focus on improving the health of the population as a whole and on reducing the inequalities in health between different sections of the population.

This chapter, in three sections, opens with a consideration of the necessity for policy to navigate seemingly opposing poles and to lose sight of neither end. The chapter then asks questions of available evidence as a basis for identifying promising avenues for improvement. The third section looks to the future of comprehensive public health policies and partnership working and the implications for national service and research organisations, public health professionals, health and other organisations, and regional and local partners.

1   Public health on a see-saw: Balancing between poles

Science and art

Public Health is both science and art. The science is the epidemiology, statistics, sociology and evidence of what works, whilst the art is knowing how to take opportunities and use the systems that are in place to make a difference. The real skill is in the balance between the poles. Whilst they are often presented as 'either/ors', the contention is that they must be viewed as 'both/ands' if public health is to be improved.

Focus on delivery through the NHS and through cross-sectoral collaboration

The approach to public health in the NHS is to apply public health skills to identify population needs for health services and provide evidence for effectiveness of clinical and service interventions. Working with Local Authorities through a cross-sectoral, collaborative approach recognises the wider health impacts of, for example, housing, transport, or the environment. The truth is that public health practitioners must be effective in all of these domains. To be healthy, people need access to efficient and effective preventative and ameliorative health services, and they also need to improve and maintain their health, which will be more affected by their lifestyle. In turn, many factors which influence lifestyle, such as education, employment, environment, housing and transport are 'provided' or influenced by statutory and governmental agencies other than health services (Dahlgren and Whitehead, 1991).

To be effective in all domains, public health practitioners need to bring their skills to bear both within the NHS and within wider institutional contexts. This is currently achieved locally by Directors of Public Health (DPHs) holding joint appointments between the NHS and Local Authority, even though some appointments are more 'joint' than others and not all DPHs have the support to maximise their effectiveness across both spheres. While there will never be a single 'best place' for public health practitioners, they must be flexibly ready to work in and with different domains.

Focus on individual lifestyle and social determinants

Townsend (1979), the Black Report (1980), the government commissioned The Health Divide (Whitehead, 1987) and the Acheson Report (1998) demonstrated the relationships between health, socioeconomic status and various health determinants. A Treasury commissioned report (Wanless, 2004) identified the need for greater focus on prevention and 'public health' issues, encouraging the population to a 'fully engaged' scenario. This Wanless 'upstream prevention' route to NHS financial viability in the next 20 years focused on individuals, their lifestyles, and social determinants. In a recent review Wanless reported disappointment at the lack of effective action thus far (Ham, 2007).

The interrelationship between individual behaviour and the various factors that impact on health and wellbeing is captured in Dahlgren and Whitehead's (1991) social model of public health (see Figure 3.1).

The concentric semicircles represent the various layers of 'influence' on the individual at the centre. The inner layer identifies individual lifestyle factors, such as smoking, healthy food and physical activity. The sequential outer layers include public services, living and working conditions and the outermost layer the socioeconomic, cultural and environmental conditions. All layers have influence on the others and 'determine' whether

Figure 3.1   The main determinants of health

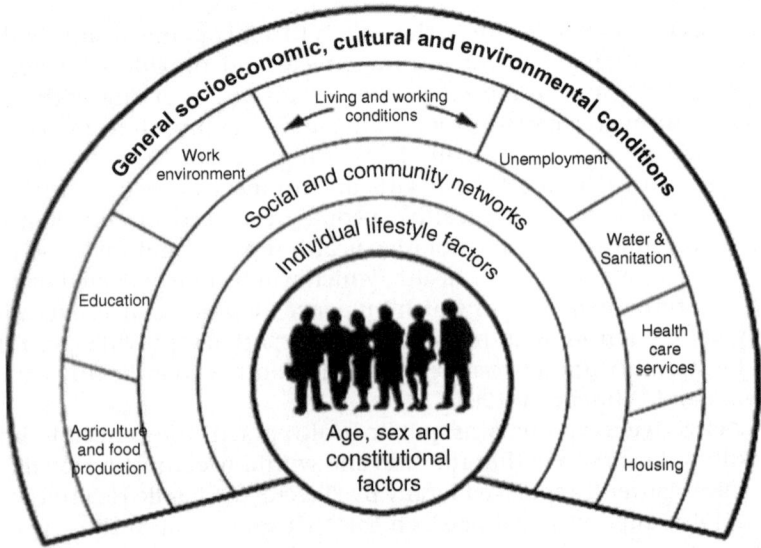

Source: From G. Dahlgren and M. Whitehead, Policies and strategies to promote social equity in health (Institute for Futures Studies, Stockholm, 1991)

any individual is likely to adopt a healthier lifestyle. Individuals are not in a position to adopt healthier lifestyles unless the outer layers enable and encourage relevant choices.

To take an example, more than 50 per cent of the UK population is over-weight or obese, and the number continues to increase, including among children. The question is what has influenced this increase and hence what must be done to reverse the trend. At the simplest level, the issue is about the balance of food (calorie) intake and physical activity. If individuals take in more calories than they exert then they will gain weight as fat. However this disguises what has caused the imbalance. Such factors include the avail-ability of 'fast' food with higher calorie values and fat content, the econ-omic pressures that cause families to have less time for cooking, or children's inability to play outside and use up energy in physical activity because of faster traffic, loss of green spaces and fear of crime. These wider social factors lie in the outer layers of influence, representing the social determinants of health, and need to be addressed if a difference is to be made in individual behaviours and lifestyles.

In terms of making a difference to people's health, simple messages about healthy eating and taking more exercise will not be enough. The right envi-ronment, including economic and other incentives, needs to be provided to enable people to build more physical activity into their daily lives and make healthy choices about what they eat. They also need to have the skills and knowledge to eat and cook properly. Understanding and enhancing health requires a population focus, with research and policy action directed at the societies to which individuals belong (Tarlov, 1996).

Target inequalities or whole populations

Three broad policy approaches have been identified to lessen health inequalities (Graham, 2000): 1) improving the health of disadvantaged groups, 2) closing the gap between those in the poorest social circumstances and better off groups and 3) addressing the entire health gradient, i.e. the association between socioeconomic position and health across the whole population. Each approach has advantages and disadvantages, but the last is the most comprehensive, is underpinned by the value of 'equity' and is least likely to cause perverse consequences. Graham (2000) argues that these three approaches are complementary and not mutually exclusive; each can build on the other in sequence. To be successful, however, all three require action on social determinants in the outer rings of Dahlgren and Whitehead's diagram. It has been demonstrated by modelling in London that adoption of either of the first two approaches alone at a local level will not achieve desired targets for reducing inequalities; instead, a comprehensive cross-sector London-wide approach would be needed (Fitzpatrick *et al.*, 2004). Unfortunately, this is counterintuitive to those who are running specific Primary Care Trusts (PCTs) and Local Authorities who only have a responsibility for their population. In the recent governmental review of the Greater London Authority's powers (UK Parliament, 2007), the mayor has been given the responsibility to develop a strategy on health inequalities in partnership with the Regional Director of Public Health (his Health Advisor), the NHS and other relevant partners. It is to be hoped that this may encourage a more London-wide approach, with all the individual organisations across London working together to achieve change.

The illustrations above all give the same message: public health needs to work both in the NHS and local government while addressing both individual lifestyle and social determinants of health and focusing on both disadvantaged communities and the whole population. Public health policy and practice is about achieving a balance between poles that, although constantly in tension, must be seen as interdependent and each requiring sustained attention.

Regardless of the focus of approach, however, and whatever interventions are put in place, one of the basic questions is what evidence is there for what works.

2 What works? Creating and using evidence

There is a large and growing body of evidence in public health on individual behaviours (such as smoking and taking exercise), social and community influences (such as social integration and working conditions), wider social determinants (such as housing) and socioeconomic factors (such as poverty and employment) (Wilkinson and Marmot, 2003). The breadth of potential interventions presents a major challenge in knowledge management and translational research if the research designs are to be fit for purpose and the results of research are to impact on policy and practice.

There is a huge body of discussion about the performance of the NHS in securing translation of the results of clinical research into everyday practice (Haynes and Haines, 1998). The challenges are magnified when one turns to evidence-based public health policy. Obstacles include the need for multi-agency collaboration and the reality of the relatively short timescales which preoccupy politicians. The development and implementation of an effective public health intervention is likely to take longer than one electoral cycle. Cross-European work undertaken on alcohol in young people by Megapoles – a network of public health in the capital cities of Europe – demonstrated that most of the cities that had policies on alcohol had not based them on the research evidence of what makes a difference (Ranzetta *et al.*, 2003). Beyond the need for quick results there is also the power of other interests; for example, Nuthall (2006) judges the power of the drinks industry to be such that it was able to 'water down' the recent EU alcohol plan.

Nonetheless, attempts are being made to harness and collate available public health evidence. The National Institute for Clinical Excellence (NICE) focused in its early years on clinical interventions and cost-effectiveness, but in 2005 it changed its name to the National Institute for Health and Clinical Excellence and its mission to provide 'national guidance on promoting good health and preventing and treating ill health', hence the review of evidence in public health topics was included in its remit. NICE has embarked on two streams of work on public health – one on 'interventions' and one on longer-term 'programmes'. The 'interventions' work focuses on defined specific interventions to improve public health such as 'preventing STI and reducing the rate of under-18 conceptions, especially among vulnerable and at risk groups' or 'promoting the mental wellbeing of children in primary schools', whilst the 'programmes' work is focused on wider comprehensive programmes to improve health such as 'the promotion and creation of physical environments that support increased levels of physical activity' (see Chalkidou *et al.*, this volume; www.nice.org.uk).

Rigorous processes are applied to intervention and programme streams of work, including evidence reviews and cost-effectiveness evaluations. Ensuing guidance from NICE is expected to be adopted by the NHS and monitored by the Health Care Commission, but as the public's health is affected by considerably more than just the NHS, NICE guidance can and is being directed at other bodies such as schools, Local Authorities, workplaces and housing bodies. We have yet to see if NICE guidance will be implemented outside the health sector, whether NICE has any powers to require such bodies to adopt their guidance and what mechanisms there may be to encourage the adoption of evidence.

There is no guarantee, for example, that schools will be willing or able to adopt NICE guidance on 'promoting the mental wellbeing of children in primary schools'. Schools are complex organisations whose primary responsibility is educating children and young people, and which have many targets for educational attainment set directly by the Department for Children, Schools and Families. Schools may well recognise that emotional wellbeing, mental health, disadvantage and behavioural problems may be significant factors in relation to children's attainment, and that the guidance from NICE would provide good advice on cost effective interventions. While the focus of a school is not mental health (or even mental wellbeing), schools may be interested in the question of how they can improve their students' educational attainment through improvements in their health. Thus, conscious of a limited capacity to focus efforts on the health of their pupils, school may want a more general set of answers, which would cover all health aspects, including mental wellbeing, healthy eating, healthy physical activity and specific behaviours relating to sex, drugs and alcohol. While it is vital that schools are involved in any broader programme, however, it would be naïve to expect a schools-based programme alone to solve problems of young people's health.

Research questions, therefore, need to address the broader needs of society and non-health organisations, if those organisations are expected to act on that research. This requires a more complex multidisciplinary research approach, which could provide answers on 'what works' from a variety of organisations' perspectives.

Within the narrower purview of the NHS, the Wanless report (2004), *Choosing Health* (2004) and *Our Health, Our Care, Our Say* (2006), directed attention to health improvement and prevention and to the delivery of appropriate health services in the community, outside of hospitals. Commissioning these services in England is the province of PCTs. PCTs are charged with making decisions about the package of preventive and other services which can be delivered safely and cost-effectively in community settings for maximum health gain. Specific NICE guidance on, for example, smoking or sexual health, should inform services commissioned, but they will not address the more complex commissioning questions.

NICE's guidance is frequently supported by systematic reviews undertaken by the Cochrane collaboration (www.cochrane.org), which also develops protocols on health care, and includes public health issues within its remit. Development of its Public Health electronic library is underway. A more recent addition developed along similar lines with similar methodologies, is the Campbell Collaboration (www.campbellcollaboration.org), which offers reviews of evidence on social, behavioural and educational areas including crime and criminal justice. Both of these collaborations and their libraries offer collations of the available evidence on multiple public health topics, but they also tend to focus on specific issues rather than on complex interactions. These review bodies draw on international research in order to maximise the evidence available. However, there may be cultural differences between countries in regard to what works in social and public health arenas, whereas this is much less likely to be an issue in purely medical/clinical interventions. A certain intervention on public health judged successful in one country might not fit with the cultural norms of other countries such that its implementation there might not yield the predicted positive effects. For example, there is evidence from the US that Life Skills Training in schools used to address alcohol and drug abuse has some success, but there is no evidence that such an approach will work within the UK, with the very different attitudes to alcohol consumption in the two countries (Botvin *et al.*, 1994). However, the strength of these research collaborations, especially those specifically focused on non-health organisations, serves to strengthen the potential for evidence-based interventions being adopted by non-health organisations.

The nature of the research evidence, however, as well as the complexity and diversity of organisations involved in implementing change to improve the public's health, means that even these collaborative approaches only partially support public health policy and practice.

Health is very sensitive to the social circumstances in which people live – the social determinants of health (Wilkinson and Marmot, 2003). For example, people who are less well off have substantially shorter life expectancies and more illness than the rich. In London there is a difference of six years in male life expectancy across the capital between different geographic areas (Barer *et al.*, 2002, 2004). Whilst those at the bottom of the social ladder run approximately twice the risk of serious illness and early death as those at the top, there is also a clear social gradient. Disadvantage, in the form of few assets, poor education, insecure employment and/or poor housing, tends to concentrate in the same people and have a cumulative effect.

For each of these social determinants there is evidence of impact on health, from which policy implications can be drawn. For example, stress and lack of control over work and home are known to have powerful effects on health (Marmot and Stansfeld, 2002), hence the policy implications that schools, workplaces and institutions need to give people not only material and social security, but also a sense of belonging, being valued and participating in decisionmaking.

Translating the policy implications into practical steps that each school, workplace and institution can deliver is the next step. It is here that the art of public health may need to come into play to identify whether there are opportunities to build evidence into practice within, say, the workplace, and the policy implications for such change at a national, regional or local level.

Evidence alone does not ensure policy impact. Taking transport as an example, it is known that increasing walking, cycling and public transport can promote health through greater physical activity, reducing fatal accidents, reducing air pollution and increasing social contacts (Soderland *et al.*, 1996). Further research indicates that creating more roads encourages more car use (McCarthy, 1999). From this there are clear transport policy implications for health – which include increasing cycling and walking paths, improving public transport and finding incentives for businesses and individuals to reduce their car use. Health evidence has influenced transport policies in some circumstances; for example in London, the Mayor and Greater London Authority, who hold responsibility for the London Transport Strategy, are also charged with 'improving Londoner's health' (UK Parliament, 1999). This provided an opportunity to undertake a health impact assessment on the Mayoral strategies to ensure health was taken into account (Mindell *et al.*, forthcoming). The health impact assessment undertaken on the draft London Transport Strategy enabled a reconsideration of the strategy to increase its inclusion of walking and cycling (Mindell *et al.*, 2004). Similarly, early deaths due to pollution were part of the evidence driving the successful London Congestion Charge policy (Watkiss *et al.*, 2002). New evidence of increased risk of heart attack and stroke as a result of pollution (Miller *et al.*, 2007) would strengthen the evidence in support this policy. However, whilst there are such examples of where health evidence has influenced and changed policies, there remains a considerable effort to be made on the part of public health practitioners at all levels to ensure that evidence on health and social determinants is utilised appropriately and systematically to inform policy at all levels and in all relevant fields (Mindell *et al.*, forthcoming).

Evidence exists of the relationship between health and social determinants and hence policy implications can be drawn for each individual social determinant (Wilkinson and Marmot, 2003). However, it is not apparent how these policy implications may interact with each other in addressing several social determinants at the same time, and therefore what the overall policy implications may be. An example exists in urban development and health. Evidence exists that links many of the components of urban health, e.g. housing, planning, green spaces, transport links, civic amenities and integrated employment (Kawachi and Berkman, 2003; McCarthy and Ferguson, 1999; Hanlon *et al.*, 2006; Maas, 2006), to improved health outcomes (Box 3.1), but it may not be known how to bring these about. For example, while past research has demonstrated the health benefits of green space, new research is beginning to identify the possible mechanisms by which this greater health is achieved – whether through improved air quality, stress reduction, increased activity, etc. (De Vries, 2006).

However, the questions asked by urban developers (even if they are willing to accept that there is good evidence that green spaces should be built into

---

Box 3.1　Desirable outcomes of healthy urban developments

- Housing – affordable and health improving (e.g. reducing damp)
- Configuration – social integration and inclusion
- Transport – integrated, accessible, public and active (e.g. encouraging walking and cycling)
- Social and Community infrastructure – schools/libraries/leisure/sports integrated with health services delivery
- Healthy food – private and community food gardens, agriculture, markets, shops, easy access
- Lighting – safety and reducing crime
- Green spaces – access, leisure, exercise, clean air
- Health provision – whole spectrum, modern, integrated with other infrastructure
- Local employment and skills – short-term and long-term, in public and private sector

---

developments) are much more practical questions, such as what size and shape of green space, how much is needed and whether it could be vertical (climbing greenery rather than horizontal gardens), how accessible must it be and what the implications are for community safety and crime rates. The available evidence from research studies may not provide the answers needed to put it into practice. A different approach to research questions, combining research from multiple disciplines, may be needed to achieve the practical desired outcome.

In relation to urban development and health, the issue – and the art of public health – is to decide whether synergy with other agendas provides an adequate opportunity for improving public health. Would a minimum or zero carbon development, including carbon reduction in terms of housing, transport, etc. give the same outcomes for health, and thus be a 'good enough' mechanism to achieve change for public health? The science is incomplete but the art may provide the right outcome.

A further consideration in relation to social determinants is whether the range of determinants commonly used and researched are still the most relevant. Social determinants of health are dynamic, changing over time and place. Should 'new' social determinants be considered? For example, the growing impact of corporate practices (such as marketing to the most deprived) can be considered influential on individual behaviour. Research has shown corporations to have a powerful effect on public health through the production, marketing and sale of food, alcohol, tobacco, automotives and firearms (Freudenberg, 2006). Although some researchers argue that corporate behaviour is an important social determinant (Freudenberg and Galea, 2007), it is only now being considered in the wider social determinants debate. Another example is the impact of changes in information technology, which can both enable health and other kinds of information to reach people quickly and improve health care efficiency. However, it can also risk exacerbating disparities by disseminating these technologies inequitably (Gibbons, 2005).

3 The future: Comprehensive public health policies and partnership working

It can be seen that to improve public health, change needs to be affected at the individual, community, professional and policy levels – individuals change their behaviour, but communities and policies affect social determinants and hence 'enable' those individuals to change their behaviour. Some evidence exists, but it does not yet give a comprehensive action plan, even for the NHS, and certainly not for other organisations, such as schools. Some factors are influenced locally and some at regional, national and international levels, and public health policies need to span across all levels. Healthy food is important to the individual, but just giving out information and imploring people to eat healthily is unlikely to have much impact. Policies need to influence all of the layers in the Dahlgren and Whitehead diagram (see Figure 3.1) to ensure that healthy food is available and accessible through such measures as preventing poor estates only having expensive and 'processed' foods available, educating in home economics and cooking skills, providing healthy school and workplace meals, ensuring that junk food is not advertised, ensuring people have adequate incomes and are in employment so they may purchase healthy food, and designing farming and food policies to encourage locally available produce. The challenge of improving the public's health is hugely ambitious.

The complex and cross-sectoral nature of public health means that working partnerships between levels and agencies is crucial to achieving change. Failure to act in a coherent partnership will make health inequalities worse and may deter individuals from making healthy choices. This has been seen in smoking policies over the past 20 years. The health promotion messages in the 1970's and 80's exhorting the public to stop smoking were rightly based on the available evidence about the effects of tobacco on health. However, the approach focused only on campaigns and health promotion material. None of the wider social determinants that have been shown to influence whether people are able to make the choice to stop smoking were addressed. The outcome was a widening of the inequalities in health as a result of smoking, due to the fact that those in higher socio-economic groups were more likely to be able to act on this information, whilst those in lower socioeconomic groups were not. Such was the effect that, in a study published in 2007, smoking in managerial and professional groups stood at 16 per cent whilst 34 per cent of people in routine and manual occupations still smoked (Action on Smoking and Health, 2007). Health inequalities were worsened by policy messages on health promotion, which focused on an individual's lifestyle and behaviour, to the neglect of considering the wider social determinants of behaviour. The current anti-smoking strategy includes a wider policy to ban smoking in public places, which evidence has shown to be one of the most compelling methods to encourage and enable people from all socioeconomic groups to quit.

There is now a growing recognition of the importance of partnership involvement in health improvement and this is starting to be captured formally in England in the new Local Area Agreements (LAAs) between Local Authorities and their partners, including PCTs, police, local business and the third and voluntary sector. Many LAAs now include health improvement targets and focus on the partners working together to improve health, attracting new government resources to the area by achieving specific targets. Similarly, the white paper on local government (Department of Communities and Local Government, 2006) recognises the importance that local government can make to the many aspects of health improvement and local engagement. The development of joint DPHs across PCTs and Local Authorities is in recognition of the importance of the need for partnerships. Parallel partnership arrangements between local government and health are also being developed in the devolved nations of the UK. For example, Glasgow has recently appointed a joint DPH across the health authority and the City government. This enables a focus on such priorities as housing and worklessness, which will improve health through work, not just with the NHS, but also with wider cross-sectoral collaborations. These various examples illustrate a range of public health issues and their impact on individuals' lives. They demonstrate that some evidence is available and collated on individual topics, but that the evidence is often not available to answer the big questions on prevention that are of key importance to people both within the health service and in other organisations. They also indicate the salience of individual behaviour and lifestyle on the health of the individual. However, more importantly, they demonstrate that this is not achieved by imploring individuals to change. Partnership working at all levels to ensure that policies encourage and enable an environment and other factors that are right for individuals to improve their health, must be the responsibility of those who are responsible for policy-making. Public health practice is a combination of the science of evidence and the art of achieving change using the evidence.

What lessons can be learned from this analysis of public health as at the intersection of competing yet complimentary pressures? It requires close collaboration between agencies and a flexibility of outlook which can comprehend the need to focus simultaneously on the individual and the community; on the whole population and on those most disadvantaged within it; on individual behaviour and social determinants; and on scientific evidence and the 'art' of understanding human behaviour and how to take the opportunities and use the systems presented to make change happen in complex organisations.

Implications for the Department of Health and interdepartmental working

For national health policy, the clearest implication is that to affect change in the population's health, an approach that both addresses individual needs and embraces broader policies to support individuals to adopt healthier lifestyles is paramount. Without these two complementary approaches, the risk is that – as happened with health promotion on smoking – inequalities will widen as a result of 'individual' approaches that neglect the influence of wider social determinants. Similarly, attempts at government-wide cross-sector working on inequalities (Department of Health, 2003) must be supported and protected from the natural inclination for departments to work in silos.

At a national level, ministers and government departments have control of broader government policies to address the social influences that impact on health. The Chief Medical Officer, in the early 2000s, took an important step by positioning each RDPH across England to work directly with one other government department. This meant that for the first time, there was a recognised senior public health expert with a specific remit to work with government departments including Transport, the Home Office, Department of Environment, Food and Rural Affairs (Defra), Department for Children, Schools and Families, and Office of the Deputy Prime Minister, now Department for Communities and Local Government (DCLG). The experience of RDPHs was such that they brought a broad knowledge of public health to these departments at a senior level. In many cases the joint work developed and the knowledge gained by the other government departments about health issues and impacts in relation to their policies has been significant. For example, planning for health improvement and services has been integrated into 'Sustainable Communities' policies of DCLG, health aspects of sustainability and food policies being led by Defra have been incorporated, and many of the children's and young people's policies led by DfES include health aspects. The Council for Science and Technology's report, *Health Impacts – A Strategy across Government* (2006), identified the importance of cross-departmental collaboration continuing. The challenge for RPHGs and RDPH will come from priority setting in times of scarce resources and an urgency to address issues arising within the NHS.

Implications for national R&D and knowledge management

Nationally, there are good mechanisms to collate and to disseminate available evidence through Cochrane and Campbell collaborations and through NICE. However, merely collating the available evidence is not adequate and there is a need for better mechanisms for identifying key research questions within this complex field of public health, not just from the perspective of health services, but also from other organisations' perspectives. Emphasis needs to be given to the translation of results from within and beyond the NHS and related central departments to schools, workplaces and community organisations, and to the practicalities of implementation. Multidisciplinarity is essential, as is a research paradigm which acknowledges the place of social determinants and the complex interplay between those different social determinants.

Moreover, since social determinants of health are dynamic, changing over time and place, it is important to address new drivers of health and health disparities, such as corporate practices and information technology, as well as all aspects of current social determinants, like marriage and partnership configurations and flexible working. Researchers need to find ways to address these 'newer' social determinants with more etiological and intervention research.

Implications for public health organisations and professionals

Efficient and effective knowledge management systems – sourcing, integrating and delivering – requires action from public health organisations and professionals. How is the limited capacity and capability of public health organisations, further diminished by repeated re-organisations, able to utilise the best available scientific evidence, but also have the knowledge and skills to undertake an integrated approach to public health practice by using opportunities and mechanisms, such as new commissioning processes within the NHS, to deliver improved public health? Local DPHs are delivering locally with small teams, often expected to have expertise in all aspects of public health, including smoking, housing, clinical effectiveness, transport, screening, pandemic flu, inequalities and so on to an endless list.

The challenge nationally, regionally and locally is to find whether there are common agendas and hence synergies between the social determinants for health improvement and other drivers which will provide a 'good enough' fix for improving health. For example, there are government moves to encourage social enterprises; at the same time, government could encourage these organisations to improve their employees' health by increasing their control over their own work (Sustainable Development Commission, 2007). Likewise, there is potential synergy between the sustainability and climate change agenda and healthy urban development (Sustainable Development Commission, 2007).

Implications for health sector organisations

Wanless (2004) identified the importance of shifting the focus of health services to prevention and health improvement. This was echoed in the

Choosing Health initiatives. In times when finances are particularly squeezed, extra efforts need to be applied to sustain this broader approach. A different model of the health service, embracing health improvement as well as treatment and care, and effective, financially beneficial health promotion elements like reducing smoking prior to elective operative procedures (London Health Observatory, 2006), needs to be implemented as part of new commissioning mechanisms. In this way, the health system will follow Wanless' counsel that we improve health in order to have a financially viable health service in the future.

Implications for non-health agencies

NICE guidance is starting to include recommendations to non-health organisations. For this partnership to be effective, attention needs to be paid to the incentive structure operational at institutional and managerial levels, and to the rest of the interacting agencies' agendas. Trying to find ways to answer the most pressing questions posed by both health and non-health organisations is a challenge, in terms of research questions and methodologies, for NICE and academics.

Implications for regional and local partners

At a regional and local level, public health practitioners need opportunities, levers and mechanisms, which will vary from place to place, in order to address health improvement and inequalities using both individual approaches and the relevant social determinants. Programmes to support individuals to adopt healthy lifestyles are important, but enabling these healthy lifestyles to be adopted by wider policy action on such aspects as economics, housing and education is necessary to achieve change. Partnership working is key to making this happen and practitioners need to use formal mechanisms, such as LAAs and joint DPH appointments, but also use the informal mechanisms of social influence. There is no 'one size fits all' model and the skill of public health is to bring together both the balance of evidence and how to make it happen in practice, using opportunities that arise, by 'piggybacking' health onto other agendas, for example, as well as systematic mechanisms, such as applying health impact assessments routinely within organisations.

Whilst it may be tempting to review the public health system, the nature of achieving change in public health is such that it can only be achieved by finding balance in the process of working across boundaries. There is no one 'right place' for public health. There is much to be said, especially following repeated reorganisations within the NHS, for now allowing a period of stability in order to encourage public health practitioners and their partners to get on with the job. If further change is afoot, then let there be some pilots to gather evidence around new models and ensure that they are an improvement on the existing structural arrangements rather than pursuing wholesale change once again.

Conclusions

Public health policy and practice is a balancing act, requiring the utilisation of scientific evidence from research and analysis and the art of knowing how and when to apply it in practice to complex and integrated problems. Whilst much debate is spent on the dualism of public health, with protagonists making the case for each side, it can be seen that to improve the public's health, both of the various polar positions need to be addressed at once. The efforts that are expended on debating the pros and cons of the various polar positions would be better spent on public health delivery. There is no one right answer and no simple solution. Public health is a complex amalgam of science and art that needs to be addressed by complex mechanisms.

References

D. Acheson, *Independent Inquiry into Inequalities in Health* (London: HM Stationary Office, 1998).

Action on Smoking and Health, *Smoking Statistics: who smokes and how much* (London: Action on Smoking and Health, 2007).

R. Barer, G. Marshall, J. Fitzpatrick, L. Cragg and B. Jacobson, *Health in London Report* (London: London Health Commission, 2002).

R. Barer, J. Fitzpatrick and C. Traore, *Health in London Report* (London: London Health Commission, 2004).

D. Black, J. Morris, C. Smith and P. Townsend, *Inequalities in Health: Report of a working party* (London: Department of Health and Social Security, 1980).

G. J. Botvin, S. P. Schinke, J. A. Epstein and T. Diaz, 'Effectiveness of culturally focused and generic skills training approaches to alcohol and drug abuse prevention among minority youths', *Psychology of Addictive Behaviours*, 8:2 (1994) 116–27.

Council for Science and Technology, *Health Impacts – A Strategy across Government* (London: Council for Science and Technology, 2006).

G. Dahlgren and M. Whitehead, *Policies and strategies to promote social equity in health* (Stockholm: Institute for Futures, 1991).

Department of Communities and Local Government, *Strong and prosperous communities* (London: Department of Communities and Local Government, 2006).

Department of Health, *Tackling Health Inequalities: a programme for action* (London: Department of Health, 2003).

Department of Health, *Choosing Health: making healthier choices easier* (London: Department of Health, 2004).

Department of Health, *Our Health, Our Care, Our Say: a new direction for community services* (London: Department of Health, 2006).

S. De Vries, 'Possible mechanisms behind the relationship between green spaces and health, and their implications', 5th International Conference on Urban Health, Amsterdam, 2006.

J. Fitzpatrick, D. Hofman and B. Jacobson, *The London Health Forecast: can London's health divide be reduced?* (London: London Health Observatory, 2004).

N. Freudenberg, 'The impact of corporate practices on the health of cities: implications for health promotion', 5th International Conference on Urban Health, Amsterdam, 2006.

N. Freudenberg and S. Galea, 'Corporate practices as a social determinant', in S. Galea (ed.), *Macrosocial Determinants of Health* (New York: Springer, 2007).

C. Gibbons, 'A Historical Overview of Health Disparities and the Potential of eHealth Solutions', *Journal of Medical Internet Research*, 7:5 (2005) e50.

H. Graham, 'The challenge of health inequalities', in H. Graham (ed.), *Understanding Health Inequalities* (Buckingham: Open University Press, 2000), pp. 3–21.

C. Ham, 'The Wanless Review: slow progress on public health may need more health spending', *British Medical Journal*, 335 (2007) 572–3.

P. Hanlon, D. Walsh and B. Whyte, *Let Glasgow Flourish* (Glasgow: Glasgow Centre for Population Health, 2006).

B. Haynes and A. Haines, 'Getting research into practice: barriers and bridges to evidence based clinical practice', *British Medical Journal*, 317:7153 (1998) 273–6.

I. Kawachi and L. Berkman (eds), *Neighborhoods and Health* (Oxford: Oxford University Press, 2003).

London Health Observatory, *Stop before the op: a briefing on the short term benefits of preoperative Smoking Cessation in London* (London: London Health Observatory and Smokefree London, 2006).

J. Maas, 'Green space health and feeling of social safety', 5th International Conference on Urban Health, Amsterdam, 2006.

M. G. Marmot and S. A. Stansfeld, *Stress and heart disease* (London: British Medical Journal Books, 2002).

M. McCarthy, 'Transport and health', in M. G. Marmot and R. Wilkinson (eds), *The Social Determinants of Health* (Oxford: Oxford University Press, 1999) pp. 132–54.

M. McCarthy and J. Ferguson, *Environment and Health in London* (London: King's Fund, 1999).

K. A. Miller, D. S. Siscovick, L. Sheppard, K. Shepherd, J. H. Sullivan, G. L. Anderson and J. D. Kaufman, 'Long-Term Exposure to Air Pollution and Incidence of Cardiovascular Events in Women', *New England Journal of Medicine*, 356:5 (2007) 447–58.

J. Mindell, C. Bowen, N. Herriot and S. Atkinson, *Health Impact Assessment as a Public Health Tool in Regional Strategy Development* (Quebec: Telescope, forthcoming).

J. Mindell, L. Sheridan, M. Joffe, H. Samson-Barry and S. Atkinson, 'HIA as an agent of policy change: Improving the health impacts of the Mayor of London's draft transport strategy', *Journal of Epidemiology and Community Health*, 58 (2004) 169–74.

K. Nuthall, 'Europe waters down alcohol plan', *Environmental Health News*, 21:44 (2006) 4.

L. Ranzetta, J. Fitzpatrick and F. Seljmani, *Megapoles: Young People and Alcohol* (London: Greater London Authority, 2003).

N. Soderland, J. Ferguson and M. McCarthy, *Transport in London and the Implications for Health* (London: The Health of Londoner's Project, 1996).

Sustainable Development Commission, *Healthy Futures 6: The natural environment, health and wellbeing* (London: Sustainable Development Commission, 2007).

A. R. Tarlov, 'Social determinants of health: the sociobiological translation', in D. Blane, E. Brunner and R. Wilkinson (eds), *Health and Social Organisation: Towards a Health Policy for the 21st Century* (New York: Routledge, 1996), pp. 71–93.

P. Townsend, *Poverty in the United Kingdom: A Survey of Household Resources and Standards of Living* (London: Penguin Books and Allen Lane, 1979).

UK Parliament, *Greater London Authority Act 1999* (London: HM Stationary Office, 1999).

UK Parliament, *Greater London Authority Act 2007* (London: HM Stationary Office, 2007).

D. Wanless, *Securing Good Health for the Whole Population: final report* (London: HM Treasury, 2004).

P. Watkiss, C. Brand, F. Hurley, A. Pilkington, J. Mindell, M. Joffe and R. Anderson, *On the Move* (London: NHS Executive London, 2002).

M. Whitehead, *The Health Divide* (London: Health Education Council, 1987).

R. Wilkinson and M. G. Marmot (eds), *Social Determinants of Health: The Solid Facts*, 2nd edition (Copenhagen: World Health Organisation, Europe, 2003).

4
Social Marketing: Putting the Public, Not Professionals, at the Heart of Public Health; Don't Rain on my Parade!

Jeff French

Introduction

The Wanless reviews (2002, 2004) made it clear that approaches to improving population health that were in effect at the time were not working, reaffirming the conclusion reached by the Review of the Health Select Committee (2001) that the public health system of England at the turn of the 21st century was not fit for purpose and that 'more of the same will not deliver the health improvement targets that the government has set out'. The thesis of this paper is that current approaches to public health improvement, with a focus on behaviour change, are still rooted in a mindset of benign paternalism that is discordant with the focus on joint responsibility and co-delivery of health improvement. This disjuncture, coupled with a fractured and weak public health system, makes it clear that a fundamental reappraisal of how our efforts to improve health are organised and delivered needs to be undertaken. The chapter argues that social marketing (SM) will become the dominant paradigm for delivering public health improvement services and service improvement across the NHS because it closely mirrors governments' and citizens' policy values and philosophy of delivering public service interventions from a citizen-focused perspective and because it is an approach that is rooted in a philosophy of practice that emphasises systematic planning, a focus on value for money and return on investment.

A key commitment set out in *Choosing Health* (Department of Health, 2004) was to develop a more personalised and choice-based approach to the promotion of health, and to review how better to help people live healthier lives. This commitment was reemphasised in the recent *Our Health, Our Care, Our Say* white paper (Department of Health, 2006a) and *Health Challenge England* (Department of Health, 2007a). The policy focus on choice and on joint responsibility between the state and individuals are key drivers for the wider public sector reform agenda of the early 21st century (Prime Minister's Strategy Unit, 2006). It represents a fundamental shift in thinking about how to further improve both public services and population health.

Policy context

New paternalism and new individualism

During the 20th century the state's influence on the lives and health of populations grew in significance. The introduction of policies and legislation, universal education, universal suffrage, the establishment of new health and social services and professional groups to provide them have had a large impact on the prevention of disease and the promotion of better health. It can be argued however that this 'big state' approach has now moved past its zenith. We may be at the beginning of a new phase in civic development, one that seeks to place the citizen as consumer at the centre of attempts to maintain and further improve health (Prime Minister's Strategy Unit, 2007). Governments are often paternalistic; part of their function is to ensure that citizens are protected and have environments in which they can flourish. However, paternalism can take many forms. The hallmark of new paternalism is a focus not only on tackling the determinants of ill-health and punishing 'bad' behaviour, but also on incentivising positive choices and creating the conditions in which people feel able to and want to make healthy choices for their own and their families' benefit.

New paternalism locates responsibility with individuals, providers of public services, and private organisations to create the environments and the social norms in which healthy choices can be made. Specifically the responsibility of those delivering public services is to place the needs and wishes of individuals at the centre of their planning and provision. This rests on a new understanding of the individual and the role of the state. Rather than 'blaming the victim' (Ryan, 1976), or what could be called 'old individualism', new individualism is about blaming service or product providers for failing to deliver what citizens require so that they can live the healthy and self-actualising lives that they demand. Individuals not only have the right to expect that services will be geared up to meet their needs but also have the responsibility within their sphere of influence to do all they can to protect their own health and to contribute to the development of wider social movement for health and wellbeing.

Let the people be heard

Eighty-nine per cent of people agree that individuals are responsible for their own health and 93 per cent agree that parents are more responsible than anyone else for their children's health (Kings Fund, 2004), whereas only 33 per cent of people think that the government has a key role to play in promoting health and less than four per cent believe that it has the most important role (OfCom and NOP, 2005). Eighty-four per cent of parents feel they are most responsible for ensuring that their children eat a healthy diet, only seven per cent believe that the government is the most responsible, and less than three per cent believe that food retailers are the most responsible (Jebb, Steer and Holmes, 2007). There is evidence of significant public demand for health information (Department of Health, 2004), but also strong support for state action to promote the health of the public (Lent and Arend, 2004). While people want public service professionals to make key judgements and give advice, they also want to be empowered to influence this process (Ipsos MORI, 2007). This evidence suggests that public health interventions must in the future understand and engage people in delivering solutions. We need to recognise that policy that treats people as passive recipients of professionally determined solutions and simple exhortations to change behaviour will probably not bring about the large population level change that is required to improve health.

What we need instead is a concerted shift towards a more coordinated, sustained, and evidence and intelligence-based[1] approach built on a deep understanding of the issues that impact people's lives. This effort needs to be focused simultaneously upstream, in-stream and downstream. Upstream policy is that which is designed to address the determinants of health, while in-stream actions and policy help people to cope with poor health and adverse conditions and downstream efforts are those public health interventions which are designed to help people change behaviour to improve health.[2] As argued by Paul Corrigan (Warwick Institute of Governance and Public Management, 2004), public health's primary focus on the determinants of health to the exclusion of other explanations:

...explains too much and leaves no dialectic for the importance of individual agency. The concept has to be reconsidered in the light of the fact that we now live in a world of consumption – a place where more people are able to have many more 'consumption experiences', or choices, than were available in previous eras. People enjoy consumption and the sense of being in control that it brings them. In these circumstances determining factors make a less powerful impact and the concept of external determining factors is itself less acceptable to people. Public Health cannot stand outside this world of consumption experience.

We do, of course, know that those with more power and resources can be more in charge of their consumption experiences and also have more choices. These disparities in choice and control are some of the reasons for health inequalities (Wilkinson and Marmot, 2003). However less choice and less power are not the same as no choice and no power. It is also well understood that choice systems are usually the most efficient way to distribute resources, but that they can favour the better off and the more articulate (Giddens, 2003). However, it is also known that universal systems can advantage the better off and articulate in many circumstances (Lent and Arend, 2004). The government's solution to this conundrum has been articulated by John Reid at the 2004 Faculty of Public Health seminar: 'Of course men and women have free will. But they don't exercise that willpower in the same circumstances as each other, or in circumstances of their own choosing. That is the central realistic point we have to address' (Reid, 2004). Creating an environment of maximum choice for the majority requires the coordinated application of legislation to address health determinants, education to inform and empower people, and a focus on markets to influence the behaviour of both individuals and organisations. In this way we can shift to a more balanced view of the locus of power, from what Rothschild (2001) calls the 'apparent power' of government to the 'actual power' of individuals. We need to recognise the fact that both governments and individuals have power and responsibilities and that a public health strategy must explicitly acknowledge this.

It's not what you do it's the way that you do it

Attaining the kind of huge behavioural shift that Wanless called for (2004) will require an equally significant shift in the way public health is practised and a significant shift in current approaches to the coordination of government activities directed to enhancing health behaviour. What we know is that our current approaches are not working at a sufficient rate in most areas to achieve the scale of health improvement set out in government targets or to slow and ultimately reverse growing health inequalities (Department of Health, 2006b).

We have invested too often in short-term projects at the expense of inte- grated long-term programmes of action (NCC, 2006). Across government there are numerous short-lived campaigns such as, for example, Home Office and local police knife amnesty campaigns. The campaign which began on 24 May 2006, running for five weeks until 30 June 2006, has not been credited with having any significant effect on knife carrying by young men (Centre for Crime and Justice Studies, 2006).

We have looked in vain for 'the' answer through a stilted and inappropriate use of *a priori* scientific reasoning and evidence gathering, drawing only on published papers in peer reviewed journals and in so doing screening out 95 per cent or more of what we know is available. A more effective approach to policy is based on using *a posteriori* reasoning that facilitates access to the deep pool of tacit knowledge and understanding built up over many years by communities, individuals and practitioners, together with systematic reviews of what has been published. In this way we can develop not only evidence-based policy but also intelligence-based policy.

When seeking to help individuals to change their health-related behaviour we have focused too much on simple approaches to behaviour change that place sole responsibility at the door of individuals (NCC, 2006). Whilst we have developed impressive data gathering systems related to mortality, morbidity and health sector utilisation we have invested much less in developing a deep understanding of the wants, fears, needs, motivations, and barriers people face that either enhance or detract from their ability to live healthy lives (Department of Health, 2006c). In short we are fantastic at counting the sick and the dead but much less adept at understanding the living.

Further weaknesses in our current approach are evident in a focus on investing too much responsibility for improving health in small and diminishing teams of specialist public health practitioners. These teams are staffed by people drawn from a narrow range of feeder professions who are not equipped or enabled through legislation to exercise sufficient power to act as effective leaders across all those sectors that need to contribute to improving health.

In recent years our public health effort has been informed by three mantras: the need to focus on upstream determinants of health, the need to engage and develop communities, and to a lesser extent the need for good health information (Department of Health, 1998). This conception of the problem

Figure 4.1   Tools of behaviour management 2006

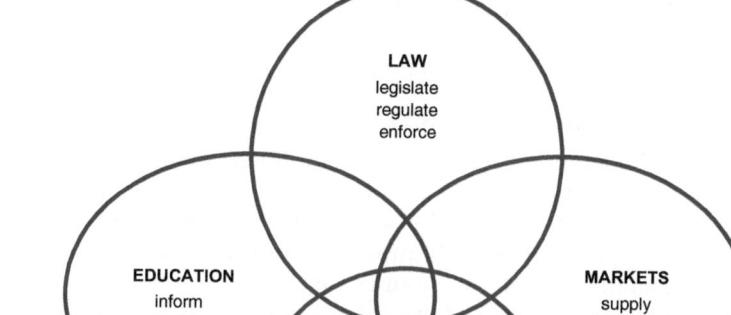

Law/enforcement/regulation: a body of rules and action prescribed by controlling authority and having binding force
Education: informs, persuades and creates awareness about benefits and develops skills for change
Markets: influences behaviour through consumer choice focused on mutually beneficial exchange
Civics: state and other collectively funded goods and services provided to support mutually agreed social priorities

Source: National Social Marketing Centre@

and consequent solutions is not wrong, simply incomplete. As Rothschild (1999: 24) states, 'Current public health behaviour management relies heavily on education and law while neglecting the underlying philosophy of marketing and exchange'.

All liberal democratic free market societies have four basic tools that can be used to deliver a better life experience for citizens: the law, education, civic services, and markets, as means of managing behaviour change. These are illustrated in Figure 4.1.

Each tool has its strengths and weaknesses, but all four tools are needed to build an integrated health improvement strategy. However, there has been insufficient congruence between the use of these tools for the promotion of health and very little focus on the highly influential tool of markets. There has been a failure to recognise that in a market and consumer dominated society the law, education and the provision of public services are becoming less influential. A focus on law and education also indicates a failure to recognise that the state actually has diminishing power to influence citizens through these means in the face of mass literacy, mass wealth, multimedia mass communication, low absolute poverty and increased consumer demands.

The rising star of social marketing (SM)

The close ideological alignment between SM and liberal democratic imperatives makes it an ideal match for selection by governments as a preferred approach for public health intervention and strategy development. SM is a highly systematic approach to health improvement that sets out unambiguous success criteria in terms of behaviour change. In this respect, SM stands in stark contrast to many public health interventions which demonstrate weak planning systems and poor evaluation (HDA, 2002; HDA, 2004; HDA, 2005). SM will also be attractive to government because of its emphasis on developing deep customer insight, empowering choice, and population segmentation in delivering interventions to respond to a diversity of needs (Prime Minister's Strategy Unit, 2007).

Defining social marketing

The term 'social marketing' was used for the first time by Philip Kotler and Gerald Zaltman (1971). There has been a lively debate about definitions and practice but it has recently been defined for the purposes of the National Social Marketing Strategy as:

> ...the systematic application of marketing concepts and techniques alongside other approaches to achieve specific behavioural goals for social good (NCC, 2006: 4).

SM has a number of defining principles and concepts. It is focused on enabling, encouraging and supporting voluntary behaviour change amongst

Figure 4.2   The Social Marketing Customer Triangle

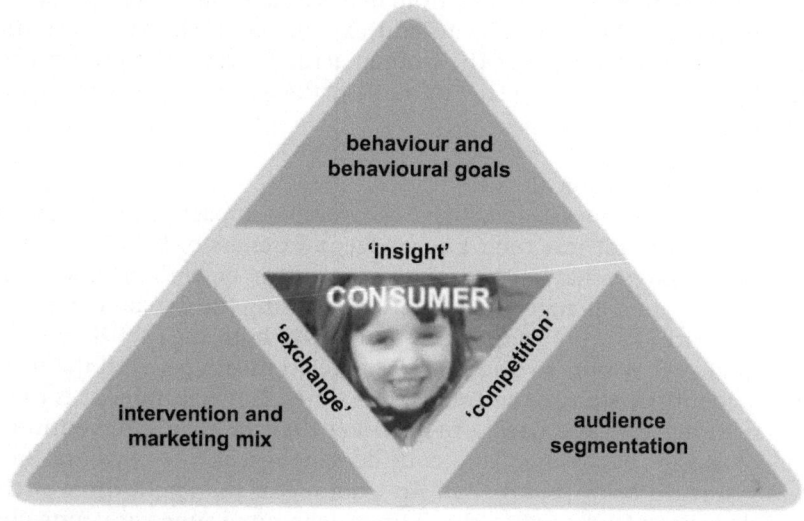

'customer triangle' © nsmc

Source: NSMC 2006@

specific audiences, and the reengineering of services and systems to support and facilitate this change.

Social marketing's key features

SM is based on a number of core principles which are captured diagrammatically in Figure 4.2. The 'Social Marketing customer triangle' is a simple device to help highlight seven core principles, starting with the customer or consumer placed at the centre. A brief explanation of each of these seven follows, with examples of projects which help illustrate the principle. Not all SM interventions can be expected to demonstrate all the principles (Andreasen, 2002), but many do and therefore overlap.

1.   People at the centre
SM begins and ends with a focus on the individual, within their social context. The main concern is to ensure that all interventions are based around and directly respond to the needs and wants of the person, rather than the person having to fit around the needs of the service or intervention. SM always starts with seeking to understand 'where the person is at now' rather than 'where someone might think they are or should be'. This helps avoid the tendency to start crafting messages or interventions before a real understanding of the issue is reached. For example, a smoking cessation programme for pregnant women in Sunderland is a good illustration of how a highly effective SM intervention was developed from such

a people-centred approach (Lowry *et al.*, 2004). This project undertook focus groups with women, mainly from deprived areas and social groups, to help understand their attitudes to and experience of smoking cessation in order to understand where the women actually were. The project then redesigned and offered services to address the barriers the women had identified.

2. Clear behavioural goals

SM is driven by a concern to achieve measurable impacts on what people actually do, and not just their knowledge, awareness or beliefs about an issue. Establishing behavioural goals requires going beyond the traditional focus on behaviour change and instead recognising the dynamic nature of behaviour within a whole population. It looks at both the positive and the problematic behaviours to understand the relationship between them and looks to identify patterns and trends over time and what influences these. A behavioural goals approach also describes the aim of an intervention in terms of specific behaviours, and considers manageable behavioural steps towards a main behavioural goal. An example of the application of this principle is Food Dudes, a healthy eating programme aimed at young children which sets out clear and measurable behavioural goals and measures itself against these (www.fooddudes.co.uk). Food Dudes aimed to increase children's consumption of fruits and vegetables, by combining availability in schools with positive social models and rewards to the children who tried the fruits and vegetables. At follow-up, the positive effects of the programme were reflected in greater consumption, more variety in what was consumed and where (Bangor Food and Activity Research Unit).

3. Developing insight

SM is driven by actionable insights that are able to provide a practical steer for the selection and development of interventions once the issue is understood from the perspective of the audience. An actionable insight is a proposition for a course of action that can be tested, derived by professional judgement based on streams of both research data and knowledge of the evidence base for interventions. To develop such insight means moving beyond traditional information and intelligence (e.g. demographic or epidemiological data) to look more closely at why people behave in the way that they do. Consideration is given to the possible influences and influencers on behaviour, and specifically what people think, feel, and believe. Importance is placed on considering those factors within and outside an individual's control. For example, a mouth and bowel cancer SM initiative aimed at encouraging early attendance began by developing insight about what would move and motivate people to report early. This investment resulted in a highly effective programme (Eadie and Cohen, 2007).

4. The exchange

A central concept of SM is that of 'exchange.' The theory of exchange has its roots in economics, psychology and sociological theory. Exchange recognises that if people are going to change their behaviour or collectively work for social change they need to believe that the reward for such action is worth the price paid. The price paid is the financial, emotional and time cost of taking part in any change programme. SM puts a strong emphasis on understanding what is to be 'offered' to the intended audience, in terms of the payback or reward, based upon what they value and consider important. It also requires an appreciation of the full cost to the audience of accepting the offer, which may include money, time, effort, social consequences, etc. The aim is to maximise the potential offer and its value to the audience, while minimising all the costs of adopting, maintaining or changing a particular behaviour. This involves considering ways to increase incentives and remove barriers to the positive behaviour, while doing the opposite for the negative or problematic behaviour. For example, MacAskill and colleagues (2002) suggest that the benefits of stopping smoking that offset the benefits of smoking for many people are seen to reside in issues other than their own health, such as financial worries and concerns for their children's health. Examples of people facing similar lives who have given up smoking and who feel good can also be used to design services to help individuals change their habits. The Sunderland smoking project designed a catalogue-style magazine showing the women what they could buy with the money if they gave up smoking (Robinson, 2006).

5. The competition

SM uses the concept of competition to examine all the factors that compete for people's attention and willingness or ability to adopt a desired behaviour. It looks at both external and internal competition (National Social Marketing Centre, 2007). External competition can include those directly promoting potentially negative behaviours but can also include other potentially positive influences that might be seeking to gain the attention of the same audience. Internal competition includes the power of pleasure, enjoyment, risk taking, habit and addiction that can directly affect a person's behaviour. For example, the 2000 Florida Truth campaign, a youth-focused anti tobacco campaign (www.protectthetruth.org), rather than taking an ill-health approach to smoking prevention, built a programme around youth combating the tobacco industry's efforts to recruit young people to smoke. Truth focused on exposing the deliberate manipulation tactics employed by the tobacco industry by designing adverts that challenged the validity and honesty of the industry's statements. This example represented a form of competitor action that led to substantial falls in tobacco use (Social Marketing Institute, 2007).

6.   Segmentation

SM uses a developed segmentation approach which recognises different publics. This goes beyond traditional 'targeting' approaches commonly used in marketing, that may focus on demographic characteristics or epidemiological data, by considering alternative ways that people can be grouped and profiled. In particular, it examines how different people view and act and what moves and motivates them. This is often referred to as psychographic research, which focuses on lifestyle preferences and issues around identity – for example, activities, interests, opinions, and current behaviours. It ensures interventions can be tailored to people's differing needs. For example, the 2001 Australian Where's your head at? illicit drugs programme in Australia developed different programmes for different groups of young people (www.drugs.health.gov.au). In its scoping phase, the campaign used market research to determine the different segments of young people who displayed varying degrees of risk of initiating illicit drug use, and had different needs and motivations toward its use. Recognising this, three complementary strategy streams were designed to address the different sub-groups – lower risk, thrill seekers and reality swappers – with positive reinforcement between the three streams. A further example from a project in the US aimed at reducing the risk of cardiovascular disease within the Hispanic population identified six population sub-groups, each of which required a slightly different message (Williams and Flora, 1995). Powell *et al.* (2007) note the potential of geodemographic analysis, with the aid of the MOSAIC UK database, to identify the characteristics of households 'at risk'. Segmentation and insight support the development of tailored responses and can help to increase the efficiency and effectiveness of public health interventions.

7.   Intervention mix and marketing mix

SM recognises that in any given situation there are a range of intervention options or approaches that could be used to achieve a particular goal with different groups of people. As single interventions are generally less effective than multi-level interventions, the issue is also to consider the relative balance or mix between interventions or approaches selected. Where this is done at the strategic level it is commonly referred to as the 'intervention mix', while at the level of a dedicated SM campaign the term 'marketing mix' (i.e. that mix of interventions aimed at supporting the desired behaviour change) is more common. A good example of such an approach is the national tobacco control campaign in England. Go Smoke Free 2000 uses a sustained approach and a wide range of interventions to reduce smoking (www.gosmokefree.co.uk). These include cessation services run alongside a national ban on smoking in public. Borrowing from traditional marketing models, thinking about intervention mixes brings useful attention to the 'p' of policy, which can help support individual behaviour change. Go

Smoke Free also makes use of the marketing mix, by offering different 'products', at the right 'price' (addressing costs and sacrifices, as well as savings), in different 'places' (online, by telephone, through primary care facilities), which are promoted appropriately (though integrated media advertisements, online, through primary care practices).

How Social Marketing can be used and applied

SM can be used to inform and assist policy formulation, strategy development, and related implementation and delivery, including service development and design. When considering how SM might be able to assist work, it is useful to make a distinction between using it strategically and using it operationally.

SM concepts and principles may be used strategically to ensure that a strong customer focus directly informs the identification and selection of appropriate interventions. For example, the 2000 Road Crew SM programme run by the State of Wisconsin in the US focused on preventing alcohol-related road deaths and accidents and demonstrated that taking a customer focus can lead to new and highly effective forms of intervention that are readily taken up. In the case of Wisconsin, drinkers voluntarily switched from attempting to drive their cars after a night drinking to a limousine taxi service that took them to and home from bars. Road Crew was built on a deep understanding of what motivated men to drink and drive and equally what would help them change behaviour, i.e. the 'exchange' discussed above. Road Crew provided a service that was a convenient, low cost alternative to driving that also enhanced the social drinking experience of the target audience (Wisconsin Department of Transportation).

Operational SM is undertaken as a planned process and worked through systematically to achieve specific behavioural goals. Critical to this process is the initial scoping stage, which examines and assesses issues. Scoping also provides the focus for subsequent development and evaluation. For example, the 2006 obesity programme in England has used SM principles to scope and develop its approach (MRC Human Research Nutrition and Department of Health, 2007).

Developing Social Marketing in the UK in the future

A strong tradition of the systematic application of SM principles has not developed in the UK to the extent that it has in the US, Canada or Australia, even though some of the individual central principles and techniques have been applied in the mainstream of health promotion interventions without the label of SM being attached to them. Its relative lack of influence within policy circles, academic institutions or amongst practitioners is probably due to a number of factors.

Public health practice in the UK is highly regulated and codified by powerful professional groups who determine not only what constitutes public health's arena of concern but also what effective practice is, what competencies are important, and which are preeminent. The dominance of the medical public health paradigm in the UK, focused as it is on disease surveillance and prevention, has led to a situation in which the contributions of fields of practice outside the traditional expertise of medical public health (epidemiology and infection disease control) have been relegated to subordinate positions. Thus, health promotion, health communication, community development, as well as SM, have not received the prominence that evidence suggests they warrant (International Union for Health Promotion and Education, 2000).

SM may also have failed to develop significantly in the UK due to a general antithesis towards 'markets' and marketing philosophy by public health practitioners. Many public health academics, policy lobbyists and practitioners have long argued that prevention and treatment of disease should be viewed by all governments as their primary duty. In so doing, the avoidance of disease is positioned as the driving force and the ultimate goal of the world's economic and political systems (WHO, 2005). Smith *et al.*, for example, have advocated that health actually constitutes the most important form of 'global public good' (2003: 4). Conceived in this way, public health as traditionally portrayed represents a radical socialist position calling for no less than a global, political and economic reorientation.

For those public health practitioners of this persuasion, the goal of society is not the promotion of individual freedom, collective prosperity or the accumulation of wealth. In fact in this construction, markets and capitalism are part of the problem rather than being part of the solution to improving health. Controlling disease is seen as the first and most important social activity, and the key indicator of social progress. This 'collective paternalistic' stance stands in stark contrast to an approach to health promotion taken by many governments who view public health as one consideration in creating the circumstances in which people can exercise the freedom to lead the kind of life they want and to enjoy it to the fullest extent possible without doing harm to others. The control of disease is thus one factor that is weighed alongside other markers of what constitutes a happy and vibrant society (White, Dolan and Peasgood, 2006).

SM's development in the UK has been further slowed by the dominance of what can be called the 'campaign paradigm', or social advertising approach, to public health over the last forty years. This paradigm is characterised by an over-reliance on awareness and information-focused social advertising 'campaigns', to the exclusion of other forms of health promotion intervention. There are a number of drivers for this paradigm including the perceived need by politicians to be seen to be taking action on public health issues, and a lack of understanding and knowledge about what health communication programmes can and cannot deliver.

Some common criticisms of Social Marketing

SM can be accused of placing undue responsibility on individuals to solve public health problems (Maibach and Holtgrave, 1995). If a programme focuses solely on the willingness and ability of individuals to adopt a certain type of behaviour, it is argued that it can place an inordinate amount of responsibility on individuals. However, when developing SM programmes, it is widely accepted that it is also necessary to address the social, political or physical barriers that enable or inhibit individual health behaviour. It should also be remembered that SM principles can be applied to inform the decisions and actions of socioeconomic and political decisionmakers and service providers. SM has the potential to be a key tool for convincing decisionmakers and individuals who are in a position to influence overall health determinants and risk conditions to make significant changes, as in for example, the 2000 Perth Travel Smart metropolitan transport strategy. The strategy has set the direction for transport for 35 years in Perth, Australia, based on extensive user research and clear behavioural goals to model travel demand management as part of the transport solutions (http://www.dpi.wa.gov.au/ travelsmart).

SM can also be accused of being used to manipulate public opinion and behaviour (Grier and Bryant, 2005). The issue of manipulation is one of a number of ethical issues that face all forms of public health interventions, not just those applying a SM approach. SM does not seek to manipulate people against their will; rather it responds to their wants and needs by crafting interventions that understand and use these drivers for achieving positive outcomes for individuals and communities. The issue of who defines positive outcomes is obviously crucial. Ideally, positive outcomes are ones that have broad popular support and for which public sector organisations have a mandate from the public to pursue.

In this way, SM uses principles and techniques that seek to understand the links between the motives of individuals, their desired behaviour and the environment that either supports or hinders positive health choices being made. Any type of underhand manipulation in the form of promoting untruths or any form of coercion is obviously just as unacceptable in SM as in any other field. In terms of the wider ethical debate, it may be argued that in some circumstances coercion is justified to protect public health. All countries have a number of public health laws that restrict freedoms for the common good. In these situations there is nearly always general popular support for such interventions. People are usually prepared to have their freedoms restricted if they agree there is sufficient level of threat and there are proven interventions that can reduce such threats.

Conclusion

SM offers a methodology and philosophy that fully embraces the importance of markets, choice and mutual responsibility for health. At a time of declining trust in civic institutions, fragmentation of society and rising consumerism, SM offers a public health response for engaging with markets as a dynamic force for health improvement rather than viewing markets and consumerism as part of the problem. SM also offers a way to balance the rights of individuals and the rights of wider society through the exercise of free, but not unrestricted, choice, and the provision of incentives to behave in a way that maximises personal advantage and the health and wellbeing of the wider society.

With the publication of the national Social Marketing Review (NCC, 2006) and the English Government's acceptance of its recommendations (Department of Health, 2006c) and its subsequent publication of Ambitions for Health (2008), the challenge for public health is now clear. There is a need to embrace the principles of SM and to start to ensure that deep insight about why people believe and act as they do, and what can be done to help them change in ways that benefit their overall health and wellbeing, sits at the core of public health practice. Public health practitioners will need to invest time and effort in developing their understanding of SM principles and techniques so that they can become champions for the communities they serve. Developing deep contextual understanding about communities through gathering market research data and other forms of user data will enhance public health practitioners' understanding and empathy with the people in those communities.

Public health practitioners, like their marketing counterparts in the private sector, will need to ensure that all interventions start from a clear identification of what will help people, rather than with a purely professionally defined solution. Authentic SM is not about telling people what to do and making them do it, but the art of understanding what will help people to make choices which lead to healthier lives. In short, we have to learn how to make healthy choices fun, easy and popular and not be seen as agents of a nanny state who rain on people's parades.

Notes

1   Evidence alone is never the only stream of intelligence used to make policy strategy or operational decisions. Intelligence also includes information sources such as epidemiology, service uptake data, demographic data, competition analysis, horizon scanning, market research data, knowledge, attitude and behavioural data. These data sources, along with evidence, are mediated by the need for policy coherence and understanding of political imperatives, and are ideally also informed by impact assessments and cost benefit studies or modelling (Department of Health, 2007b).

2   There is a need to simultaneously focus upstream in policy terms on the determinants and risk conditions that impact people's health whilst at the same time focusing in-stream on how people can be helped to cope with the socioeconomic circumstances that they find themselves in. It is also necessary to focus on what has often been termed as downstream health promotion targeted at empowering and enabling people to protect their health (Whitehead, 1989).

References

A. R. Andreasen, 'Marketing Social Marketing in the social change marketplace', *Journal of Public Policy and Marketing*, 21:1 (2002) 3–13.

Bangor Food and Activity Research Unit, 'Increasing Children's Consumption of Fruit and Vegetables', School of Psychology, University of Wales, Aberystwyth (accessed 7 May 2007).

Centre for Crime and Justice Studies, *Knife crime: ineffective reactions to a distracting problem: A review of evidence and policy* (London: Centre for Crime and Justice Studies, 2006).

Department of Health, *Information for health: an information strategy for the modern NHS 1998–2005* (London: Department of Health, 1998).

Department of Health, *Better Information, Better Choice, Better Health* (London: Department of Health, 2004).

Department of Health, *Choosing Health* (London: HM Stationary Office, 2004).

Department of Health, *Our Health, Our Care, Our Say* (London: HM Stationary Office, 2006a).

Department of Health, *Tackling Health Inequalities: Status Report on the Department of Health* (London: Department of Health, 2006b).

Department of Health, *Informing Healthier Choices: Consultation* (London: Department of Health, 2006c).

Department of Health, *Programme for Action – Update of Headline Indicators* (London: Department of Health, 2007).

Department of Health, *Health Challenge England* (London: Department of Health, 2007a).

Department of Health, *Better policy-making: Plans for a system of policy governance* (London: Department of Health, 2007b). First report of the DMB Policy Committee April.

Department of Health, *Ambitions for Health* (London: Department of Health, 2008).

D. Eadie and L. Cohen, 'A marketing strategy to increase awareness of oral and bowel cancer', in G. Hastings (ed.), *Social Marketing: Why Should the Devil have all the Best Tunes?* (Oxford: Butterworth-Heinemann, 2007), pp. 236–44.

A. Giddens, *Neoprogressivism: The Progressive Manifesto* (Cambridge: Polity, 2003).

S. Grier and C. A. Bryant, 'Social Marketing in public health', *Annual Review of Public Health*, 26 (2005) 319–39.

Health Development Agency, *A review of evaluation in community-based art for health activity in the UK* (London: Health Development Agency, 2002).

Health Development Agency, *Evaluation of community-level interventions for health improvement: a review of experience in the UK* (London: Health Development Agency, 2004).

Health Development Agency, *Evaluation resources for community food projects* (London: Health Development Agency, 2005).

Health Select Committee, *Review of Public Health: Report Two* (London: House of Commons, 2001).

International Union for Health Promotion and Education, *The evidence of health promotion effectiveness: A report for the European Commission* (Paris: International Union for Health Promotion and Education, 2000).

Ipsos MORI, *Policy Review Citizens Forum: Emerging Conclusions* (London/Harrow: Ipsos MORI, 2007).

S. Jebb, T. Steer, and C. Holmes, *The Healthy Living Social Marketing Initiative: A Review of the Evidence* (Cambridge: MRC Human Nutrition Research, 2007). Figures quoted by permission from Project Rainbow Co-operative Group.

P. Kotler and G. Zaltman, 'Social Marketing: an approach to planned social change', *Journal of Marketing*, 35 (1971) 3–12.

A. Lent and N. Arend, *Making Choices. How Can Choice Improve Local Public Services?* (London: New Local Government Network, 2004).

R. J. Lowry, S. Hardy, C. Jordan and G. Wayman, 'Using Social Marketing to increase referrals of pregnant smokers to smoking cessation services; a success story', *Public Health*, 118:4 (2004) 239–43.

S. MacAskill, M. Stead, A. M. MacKintosh and G. Hastings, '"You cannae just take cigarettes away from somebody and no' gie them something back": Can Social Marketing help solve the problem of low-income smoking?', *Social Marketing Quarterly*, 8:1 (2002) 19–34.

E. Maibach and D. R. Holtgrave, 'Advances in public health communication', *Annual Review of Public Health*, 16 (1995) 219–38.

National Social Marketing Centre, *Social marketing works!* (London: National Social Marketing Centre, 2007).

National Consumer Council, *It's our health: Realising the potential of effective social marketing: Independent review findings and recommendations* (London: National Consumer Council, 2006).

OfCom and NOP, *Survey into Public Views on the Promotion of Health* (London: NOP, 2005).

Opinion Leader Research, *Public Attitudes to Public Health Policy* (London: Kings Fund, 2004).

J. Powell, A. Tapp, J. Arme and M. Farr, 'Primary care professionals and social marketing of health in neighbourhoods: a case study approach to identify, target and communicate with "at risk" populations', *Primary Health Care Research & Development*, 8 (2007) 22–35.

Prime Ministers Strategy Unit, *The UK Government's Approach to Public Service Reform* (London: Cabinet Office, 2006).

Prime Minister's Strategy Unit, *Building on Progress: Public Services:* HM Government Policy Review (London: Cabinet Office, 2007).

J. Reid, Speech to the Faculty of Public Health (London: Royal Society of Medicine, 10 June 2004).

F. Robinson, 'Targeting preventable ill health', *Practice Nurse*, 32:10 (2006) 10–12.

M. Rothschild, 'Ethical Considerations in the Use of Marketing for the Management of Public Health and Social Issues', in A. Andreasen (ed.), *Ethics in Social Marketing* (Washington DC: Georgetown University Press, 2001), pp. 17–38.

M. Rothschild, 'Carrots, stick and promises: a conceptual framework for the management of public health and social behaviours', *Journal of Marketing*, 63 (1999) 24–37.

E. Ryan, *Blaming the Victim* (New York: Vintage Books, 1976).

R. Smith, R. Beaglehole, D. Woodward and N. Drager (eds), *Global Public Goods for Health* (Oxford: Oxford University Press, 2003).

Social Marketing Institute, 'Success Stories – Florida "Truth" Campaign', http://www.social-marketing.org/success/cs-floridatruth.html (accessed 8 October 2007).

Warwick Institute of Governance and Public Management, 'An Evening with Professor Paul Corrigan, Special Advisor to the Health Secretary John Reid', Warwick Business School, 27 October 2004.

D. Wanless, *Securing Our Future Health: Taking a Long-term View* (London: HM Treasury, 2002).

D. Wanless, *Securing Good Health for the Whole Population* (London: HM Treasury, 2004).

M. White, O. Dolan and T. Peasgood, *Final report for DEFRA Review of research on the influences on personal well-being and application to policy making* (Sheffield: Tanaka Business School, Imperial College London and Centre for Well-being in Public Policy, University of Sheffield, 2006).

M. Whitehead, *Swimming up stream* (London: Kings Fund, 1989).

World Health Organisation, *The Bangkok Charter for Health Promotion in a Globalized World* (Geneva: World Health Organisation, 2005).

R. Wilkinson and M. Marmot, *Social Determinants of Health: The Solid Facts*, 2nd edn (London: World Health Organisation, 2003).

Wisconsin Department of Transportation, 'Statistical and Technical Reports', http://www.dot.wisconsin.gov/library/publications/format/reports.htm (accessed 3 October 2007).

Part II
Influencing Outcomes

5
Promoting Healthy Behaviour: Evidence from Psychology

Laura Corbett

Introduction

Health is a nation's fundamental form of wealth: it is indispensable to a productive economy and is the basis of individual capacity. Ensuring the conditions conducive to population health is the purpose of public health. In this way, public health serves as both a body of knowledge and a domain of practice. During the 19th century, public health relied on such technical and scientific advancements as improved sanitation and sewage systems to tame filth and contagion in order to improve life expectancy and population wellbeing. However, coherent public health governance in Europe only emerged in response to the cholera pandemics and the population needs of rapid urban expansion, when tides of people fled the countryside in pursuit of the opportunities afforded by the Industrial Revolution. Epidemiology came to dominate public health during the mid-19th century and remains influential in contemporary public health. However, its positivist orientation proves dissatisfying, for it lacks the capacity to consider the psychological and social contributors to health. Yet moving beyond the limitations of this epidemiological orientation demands that health issues no longer be individualised and detached from their psychological and social context. To this end, epidemiology is being forced to share the stage with an approach to public health which understands that the sources of and solutions to poor health are multidimensional and that successful policy will result only if public health pays attention to the biological, psychological and social determinants of health.

In the biomedical model, illness is understood as a deviation from the biological norm that emanates from within the individual. In this way, biomedicine decontextualises disease from its social, cultural and political determinants. Conversely, psychosocial models consider health to be a product of the complex interactions between individual attributes, social and economic agents and the physical environment. Translated into practice, this philosophical shift in public health becomes the health promotion model of intervention, where individual needs, motivations and barriers are considered to create a climate conducive to healthy social and behavioural change. Yet when moving from individuals to populations, the psychosocial approach often relies on the precarious necessities of dense social networks and increased social cohesion to improve population health. This position is precarious not only because social networks can be both constructive and coercive but because a narrow understanding of social cohesion defined as informal social relations enervates its practical application by public health (Lynch *et al.*, 2003).

Nevertheless, public health governance is sufficiently convinced of the ability of health promotion to improve population health that it regards the role of health promotion as pivotal to state efforts advocating healthy behaviours. In conjunction with the practices of its voluntary and private-sector counterparts, the Department of Health (2004, 2005) delivers messages seeking to expand the collective awareness of health risks using information thought sufficient to inspire healthful behaviour change. Yet this dependence on information dissemination betrays a dependence on cognitive models of rational risk-assessment, exhibiting a partiality to paradigms of human behaviour that circumscribe programme success. It is thus imperative that any serious public health effort to affect healthy behaviour change appreciate all the ingredients necessary to create an auspicious intervention.

With its wide theoretical repertoire, health psychology can benefit health promotion by elucidating how social and psychological forces shape health attitudes, values, beliefs and action. To its credit, social psychological theory defies biomedicine's territorial domain by considering the range of social conditions and environmental contexts that shape health (Mittelmark, 1999), thereby flouting biomedicine's individualising inclinations. Social psychological frameworks address: behaviour intentions; environmental impediments to behaviour change; individual competencies: outcome expectations: behavioural norms: personal standards: mood; and self-confidence (Elder *et al.*, 1998), with results derived from a strong research tradition addressing issues of persuasion and compliance.

Given the limited success of lifestyle prescriptions (see Frohlich and Potvin, 1999; Lupton, 1994), it is increasingly apparent that effective public health initiatives require problem-structuring paradigms that extend beyond the individual to recognise the wider social, cultural and political context. If health promotion has any chance of achieving behaviour change, the evidence suggests that it must be comprehensive in its approach in targeting all levels of responsibility, from the individual to society. In the name of health promotion, an approach that appreciates the individual in context and interventions derived from tested theories is crucial to realising population health.

Achieving the objective of health promotion necessitates that public health be equipped with the main psychological theories promoting health. To this end, this chapter begins with a consideration of Attribution Theory, the Health Belief Model, the Transtheoretical Model, the Theory of Reasoned Action and Social Cognitive Theory. Moving from premise to praxis, this theoretical introduction is followed by a discussion of efficacious health promotion interventions chosen to illustrate how successful interventions advance from theory to inquiry, from individually-focused interventions to community-orientated policies. The examples are primarily drawn from North America, reflecting a dearth of theory-led interventions in the UK. According to the evidence amassed, improving the effectiveness of cessation or prevention initiatives demands a comprehensive approach that incorporates mass communications, empowerment and skills development, community enrichment and healthy public policy. Issues for future application and research are considered in the discussion.

Psychological theories

Attribution Theory

Heider (1958), the father of Attribution Theory, argued that people need to believe that the social world is predictable and controllable. Later, Kelley (1967, 1972) extended Heider's work in explaining how information translates into causal explanations used to satisfy causal queries. According to Kelley (1972), attribution formation is influenced by distinctiveness, consensus, consistency over time and consistency over modality: Distinctiveness explains whether an individual's behaviour is characteristic of the individual irrespective of context; consensus considers whether the behaviour adheres to conventions; and consistency addresses whether the behaviour remains fixed across time and place. How these components are combined dictates whether behaviours are ascribed to internal traits or to external sources.

Applying Attribution Theory to the problem of why someone struggles to adopt healthier eating requires answers to three attributional questions:

1. Is there consistency; for example is eating vegetables usually a problem for this person?
2. Is there distinctiveness; is the problem with vegetables in general or only with squash and beets in particular?
3. Is there consensus; do others also resist eating more vegetables?

If the individual alone consistently struggles with vegetables then our attribution is more likely to identify the problem as an internal, dispositional matter rather than as an external, situational force. Thus, in relation to health promotion, Attribution Theory suggests that an individual's capacity to adopt new attitudes, beliefs or behaviours depends on whether their attributions are internally or externally oriented.

In part, the appeal of Attribution Theory to health promoters comes from its simplicity. Indeed, its successful application demands only two ingredients: One, that it be introduced in circumstances where people are looking to explain a situation, such as individuals seeking to understand their poor health. Two, that explanations for these events be found in internal attributions, with illness being attributed to lifestyle practices rather than to environmental factors. In essence, the effective implementation of Attribution Theory encourages health promotion efforts to prompt internal attributions, thereby setting the stage for individual behaviour change.

Depending on what individuals attribute their health status to, the decided attribute may significantly influence how health promoters approach health promotion. Efforts commonly used to modify misguided attributions include the use of role models, reinforcement techniques and authoritative persuasion. However, these approaches are ineffectual unless individuals aspire to improved health. In such cases, incentives may be necessary to surmount the hurdle of indifference. For instance, in studying the post-programme exercise motivation and adherence levels of cancer survivors, results revealed that programme exercise, perceived success, expected success and affective reactions were significant predictors of post-programme exercise (Courneya *et al.*, 2004). Quality of life post-programme and changes in physical fitness were related to perceived success, suggesting that Attribution Theory may be successfully used to understand the exercise patterns of cancer survivors following a programme intervention. The important issue for health promoters is that the external impetuses driving behaviour change are not inherently negative. Instead, external rewards and punishments can prove effective if individuals ascribe their meriting of external rewards to internal attributes. Otherwise, the external agent is unlikely to generate long-term, internally-driven behaviour change.

Health Belief Model

According to the Health Belief Model, five key descriptors determine our response to illness:

1. Our perceived susceptibility to the disease.
2. The perceived severity of the disease, with perceived severity wielding a greater influence over behaviour than actual severity.

Together, perceived susceptibility and perceived severity comprise the perceived threat of the disease, determining our behavioural response.

3. The perceived benefits from the behaviours generating health benefits.
4. The perceived barriers to preventive actions, such as the time and effort required. If we believe that the benefits of a preventive behaviour exceed its costs, this belief increases the probability of a behavioural response.

5. Perceived efficacy, meaning the self-assessment of our ability to successfully adopt the targeted behaviour.

These five descriptors were later joined by a sixth – cues to action, which
recognised that the desired behaviour may not emerge without prompting
from internal or external cues (Becker *et al.*, 1977).

Evidence suggests that action prompts can aid in predicting health
behaviours, with external prompts such as information being particularly
important. In fact, according to the Health Belief Model, information is the
basis for modifying beliefs with the ultimate objective of ensuring future
healthy behaviour. Employing the Health Behaviour Model demands that
health promoters establish a connection between risky behaviours and disease
outcomes, that they emphasise the gravity of disease and that they devise
preventive behaviours that are relatively easy to perform. For example, in
an assessment of the influence that causal health attributions and coping
mechanisms have on the quality of life in end-stage renal disease patients,
it was proposed that problem-focused coping, an internally-oriented health
locus of control and an externally-oriented medical locus of control
ensured a better quality of life in patients (Pucheu *et al.*, 2004). Findings
from this study suggest that the patients' physical quality of life enjoys
enhanced protection when they strongly believe that their behaviour
influences their health and that the patients' psychological quality of life is
lessened when the illness is perceived as less controllable, thus necessitating emotion-oriented coping.

When health promoters adopt the role of messenger, there is an assumption about the audience's ability to learn and acquire the skills necessary
to perform the proposed health behaviour. However, health promoters
increasingly understand that information will not necessarily be absorbed and
assimilated on presentation. Indeed, recognising that this underlying assumption may be limiting, health promoters often prefer the role of social marketer
in seeking to ensure that information is presented in a manner that is sufficiently persuasive and motivating so as to encourage individuals to adopt
or maintain the healthy behaviour. In this way the information is made
digestible by being broken down into manageable units, with connections
drawn between new information and established knowledge and the message
itself being made easier to grasp and recall (Manning, 1997). Yet there is an
assumption of population health literacy held by both the messenger and the
social marketing approaches to health promotion, an assumption that is misguided given the considerable gap in health literacy exacerbating existing
health and care divides between the richest and poorest segments of society.

The Health Belief Model is a common tool in the health promotion arsenal,
not least because it has survived considerable theoretical scrutiny. In a review
of literature employing the Health Belief Model in relation to various health
and screening behaviours, Janz and Becker (1984) documented substantial

support for the Health Belief Model, with 'perceived barriers' serving as the most prominent predictor of behaviour change. In the social marketing context, Lefebvre (2000) identified three applications of the Health Belief Model as integral to health promotion initiatives. The first application finds the Health Belief Model particularly pertinent to populations who are at risk but do not consider themselves so. In response, the use of fear- or anxiety-driven messages aims to increase the sense of the perceived threat to at-risk, in-denial populations. The second application finds the 'barriers' and 'benefits' features of the Health Belief Model familiar to social marketing initiatives, notably in relation to price and placement selections designed to increase the benefits and reduce the costs of new behaviours. The third application either patently or tacitly incorporates the 'cues to action' feature of the Health Belief Model in social marketing programmes, stimulating a latent readiness to act and stirring overt behaviour.

For example, consider the application of the Health Belief Model to dietary practices. Abood *et al.* (2003) analysed the efficacy of a worksite nutrition education intervention using the Health Belief Model to promote healthy dietary behaviours in order to diminish the risk for cardiovascular disease and cancer. Results not only revealed that the perceived benefits of healthy nutriment and nutrition cognition increased among participants, but that the treatment group significantly reduced their consumption of total calories, fat, saturated fat, and cholesterol. In another application of the Health Belief Model to nutrition, researchers attempted to increase the consumption of whole grains by older Americans (Ellis *et al.*, 2005). The programme addressed each component of the Health Belief Model not only through information but also by using taste-testing to conquer any ingrained aversions, teaching participants how to incorporate whole grains into their diet and how to read nutrition labels. Later, the programme's efforts were fortified through recipes and tip sheets that were provided to ensure continued message reinforcement at home. According to the results participants increased their consumption of whole grains, their knowledge about whole grains and their adherence to the belief that whole grains would decrease their risk of disease. However, it bears mentioning that since the Health Belief Model was initially devised to address simple health behaviours, its application must incorporate the concept of self-efficacy to ensure the maintenance of behaviour change. This makes the Health Belief Model most relevant when designing the motivational component of behaviour change interventions.

Transtheoretical Model

The Transtheoretical Model, more commonly known as the 'Stages of Change' model, is another favourite of health promoters. The model depicts individuals proceeding through a five-stage progression of cognitive processing and behavioural patterns (Prochaska and DiClemente, 1984), from precontemplation, contemplation, preparation and action to maintenance or relapse.

During the precontemplation phase the possibility of change has yet to surface, be it because of ignorance, denial or demoralisation. During the contemplation stage, the possibility of change materialises, though it is no more than a possibility and there is no consideration of how change could be realised. Effectively targeting contemplative individuals demands increasing their knowledge, emphasising the threat and proposing efficacious alternatives. The preparation stage is distinguished by both contemplation and preparation coming to the fore. During the action stage, efforts from the preparation stage are realised, which makes fostering competence and goal-setting imperative. Finally, it is in the maintenance stage that behavioural modification is deemed entrenched. In relapse stage, individuals find themselves in the position of revisiting one of the previous stages of change when they abandon the healthy learned behaviour in favour of the familiar unhealthy behaviour. Indeed, the possibility of relapse acknowledges that despite its linear presentation, advancement through the stages is not necessarily linear nor is behaviour change absolute since both are dynamic processes.

Recognising the non-linear nature of behavioural change often proves useful when designing health promotion interventions. For instance, consider the application of the Stages of Change Model to substance misuse. To determine the predictive ability of the precontemplation stage, Callaghan and colleagues (2005) surmised that precontemplative adolescents would be more prone to abandon a residential inpatient substance-abuse programme than would other attendees. According to the results, the precontemplation subscale predicted patient treatment withdrawal while precontemplative patients proved more likely to prematurely abandon addiction treatment. Equipped with this knowledge, programmes can use the Transtheoretical Model to identify and address those incoming patients who are most likely to struggle to fulfil the necessary treatment protocol.

Increasingly, the evidence suggests that people advance from one stage of the Transtheoretical Model to the next when the advantages of behaviour change outnumber the impediments (Prochaska and Velicer, 1997; Rhonda *et al.*, 2001). Essentially, the ratio of benefits-to-barriers determines later behaviour suggesting that interventions aiming to move individuals from the precontemplation to the contemplation stage should emphasise the benefits upfront and address the barriers down the line (Ganiats and Sieber, 2000). For instance, the value that people assign to a particular health outcome – say physical fitness – may significantly shape how they perceive the ascribed benefits associated with that health outcome – say increased energy and endurance. Thus, exercise programmes emphasising the benefits of physical activity that emerge within the first six months may prove more motivating than those emphasising the health benefits expected over the subsequent five years, thereby promoting the benefits associated with short-term health gains rather than decreasing the barriers to change.

An important feature of the Transtheoretical Model is its message that there are few members in any target audience who are primed for an action-driven initiative, necessitating a greater emphasis on advancing individuals from the early stages of the change trajectory. Indeed, the Transtheoretical Model recognises the importance of matching interventions to cognitive-behavioural stages, in turn ensuring more effective health promotion strategies (Rhonda *et al.*, 2001). For instance, those in the exercise contemplation stage stand to benefit from an increased awareness of the gains associated with exercise while those in the remaining stages are best served by specific information on how to increase physical activity (Kloek *et al.*, 2006). This approach recognises that different stages of change are distinguished by distinct 'processing patterns' (Prochaska and Velicer, 1997). The processes of change within the Transtheoretical Model are the independent variables that foist individuals between stages and that, by extension, offer useful guides to health promotion interventions. Ten processes in particular are bolstered by empirical validation (Prochaska and DiClemente, 1984; Prochaska *et al.*, 1988), with the precontemplation and contemplation stages best served by the experiential processes of context reassessment,[1] consciousness-raising[2] and self-reassessment.[3] Alternatively, those in the action and maintenance phases are best served by such behavioural processes as contingency management,[4] counter-conditioning[5] and stimulus control.[6] These findings highlight the importance of pairing the intervention with the individual's current stage of change to ensure an effective behaviour transformation.

For instance, consider the review by Prochaska and Velicer (1997) of 12 studies assessing how personal 'pros and cons' fluctuate according to the stage achieved within the Transtheoretical Model. Up to and including the precontemplation stage, the number of 'cons' dwarf the number of 'pros'. However, on reaching the contemplation stage the number of 'pros' begins to surpass the number of 'cons'. Ascending from contemplation to action requires that the number of 'cons' diminish while the 'pros' remain steady or even make modest gains. Given the dance between 'pros and cons' across the stages, Prochaska and Velicer argue that the 'pros' must increase at twice the rate as the 'cons' decline in order to shift an individual from precontemplation into action. Indeed, this proposal is reminiscent of loss aversion in Prospect Theory where our preference for avoiding loss supersedes our interest in securing gains, with some studies suggesting that losses are twice as psychologically powerful as are gains (Kahneman and Tversky, 1979). Translated into practice, this formula recommends that twice as much effort be expended in increasing the benefits of change as is devoted to minimising the perceived costs and barriers in the name of health promotion.

Theory of Reasoned Action

The Theory of Reasoned Action emphasises the concept of behavioural intention, with intentions derived from: individual behavioural outcome expectancies; attitudes toward the behaviour; and the normative beliefs held about what influential others would do in the relevant situation (Elder *et al.*, 1998). From this perspective, the most direct relationship exists between intentions and actions, with intentions increasing the probability of action.

In the Reasoned Action model, attitudes serve as efficient instruments to assess situations. On occasions when we must react quickly, attitudes allow our feelings to guide our response (Sanbonmatsu and Fazio, 1990). However, the theory is more complicated than a linear association between attitudes and actions. Rather, intentions are determined both by attitudes and by subjective norms (Ajzen and Fishbein, 1980): attitudes indicate how individuals feel about performing the preventive behaviour while subjective norms are the perceived social influences around the behaviour. So, the ingredients determining a beneficial behavioural response are the positive feelings towards the behaviour and the social pressures to behave accordingly. The other half of the model is comprised of perceived consequences and the influence of significant others. More specifically, perceived consequences prove most influential on attitudes when the consequences are readily recalled while significant others prove most influential on subjective norms when we are eager to please.

Since the Theory of Reasoned Action first emerged, Ajzen (1985) appended perceived control as an influence on intentions, operating alongside attitudes and subjective norms. Perceived control pertains to intentions to act, with intentions buttressed by perceived personal control over the behaviour. By adding perceived control to the Theory of Reasoned Action, it became clear that voluntary control is variable, prompting Ajzen (1985) to christen the expanded theory the Theory of Planned Behaviour. Essentially, the Theory of Reasoned Action concerns behaviour within the realm of individual control while the Theory of Planned Behaviour incorporates actions, objectives and outcomes over which individuals exhibit limited control.

While the Theory of Reasoned Action and the Theory of Planned Behaviour are familiar to health promotion initiatives, their efficacy is often attenuated by partial applications. For instance, while subjective norms and references receive considerable attention by health promoters, this emphasis comes at the expense of considering how to shift attitudes in favour of healthy behaviours (Lefebvre, 2000). As an exception, the '5 A Day for Better Health' study by Sutton and colleagues (1995) discovered that the target audience of those who reported eating two to three servings of fruits and vegetables a day and who were trying to increase their level of consumption considered those who consumed five servings of fruits and vegetables daily in two ways. On the one hand, they were viewed as more sensible, disciplined, healthy, wholesome and fit and on the other hand they were deemed less capable, dependable, gentle and friendly than themselves. Incorporating the model in its entirety enabled health promoters to develop materials that combined the target's positive self-perceptions with their positive perceptions of people who consume five fruits and vegetables daily.

Social Cognitive Theory

In order to address behaviour modification, Social Cognitive Theory (Bandura, 1977) offers intervention strategies which recognise the dynamic, continuous interplay between personal characteristics, individual behaviour and the wider social context. According to Social Cognitive Theory, three factors influence the probability that one will adopt a healthy behaviour: self-efficacy; personal goals; and outcome expectancies. Having incorporated concepts and practices from cognitive, behavioural and emotional models of behaviour modification, Social Cognitive Theory employs a broad assortment of constructs, including: reciprocal determinism; behavioural capacity; expectations; self-efficacy; observational learning; and reinforcements. Social Cognitive Theory pivots on the notion of self-efficacy as instrumental to behaviour change, offering various strategies to boost self-efficacy such as: establishing incremental goals; drafting behaviour contracts with contingent rewards; and implementing self-monitoring and reinforcement techniques.

Yet despite the strength of Social Cognitive Theory as a comprehensive, constructive approach to behaviour modification, its inclusiveness and intricacy hamper efforts to define and measure its theoretical constructs. Moreover, Social Cognitive Theory suffers from analytical incongruity with analyses emphasising observational learning and self-efficacy to the exclusion of their companion constructs. Such analytical selectivity comes at the expense of an understanding of how all of the theoretical components jointly interact, a limitation that is prevalent in applications of health psychology theory to health promotion initiatives.

Putting theory into practice, Allison and Keller (2004) assessed the influence of self-efficacy on physical activity among seniors following a cardiac event. Operating within an experimental framework, two of the three groups were subject to one of two supportive telephone protocols: one being self-efficacy coaching, the other being attention control. Results revealed a robust association between self-efficacy and physical activity during post-cardiac rehabilitation in contrast to the attention control approach, with findings most pronounced for 'increased physical activity' and 'self-efficacy for physical activity'. Thus when telephone communication involved coaching to bolster self-efficacy, the results indicated improved self-efficacy and physical activity levels to the benefit of post-cardiac rehabilitation. As such, while the self-efficacy approach failed to exhibit a direct effect on the perceived level of physical activity capacity as predicted by the authors, in its place emerged an indirect interaction effect on the distance walked and the physical activity self-confidence of post-cardiac seniors.

Evidence in action: the keys to success

No community context permits a structured, controlled environment from which to consider whether or how particular health promotion interventions affect attitudes and behaviours. Moreover, few health promotion programmes proceed without complementary initiatives, challenging efforts to isolate the health-enhancing determinant. Nevertheless, there are examples of efficacious interventions that operate as exemplars when developing future strategies. Most notable in this regard are smoking interventions, though many of the lessons learned from smoking cessation initiatives have served health promotion in other areas. The following examples describe promising interventions which hinge on a number of key factors that prove imperative to success.

Concerns peaked during the 1970s about the possibility of widespread smoking among adolescents, despite a broad understanding of nicotine's deleterious effects on health. In response, Evans and colleagues (1978) designed the first significant application of social psychological principles to a preventive intervention. Dubbed the Social Psychological Deterrents of Smoking in Schools Project, the initiative implemented and evaluated an intervention equipping seventh-graders with techniques to resist peer pressure to smoke, parental smoking models and media messages glorifying smoking. Since children tend to consider the negative consequences of smoking at a temporal distance, efforts also sought to stress the immediate physiological consequences of smoking. Indebted to the Social Influence[7] model, this anti-smoking effort relied on Bandura's Social Cognitive Theory (1977) to explain acquired expectations and learned behaviours around smoking. Additional contributors also included Bandura's concept of self-efficacy (1982) along with the Transtheoretical Model (DiClemente *et al.*, 1991) to furnish seventh-grade students with effective skills to resist social pressures to smoke. Using videos as one medium, increased student awareness was achieved using same-sex, non-smoking peers to inform pupils about probable social pressure situations and to equip students with the necessary skills to resist smoking. In the classroom, students were introduced to the interim consequences of smoking and given the opportunity to practise their resistance techniques. Finally, the school itself was peppered with posters reinforcing the campaign's message. According to results from classroom surveys, the researchers discovered that few students had ever even considered smoking, a finding that was used to rectify erroneous norms which prompted young people to think that everyone smoked. From this ongoing study, findings indicated that students exposed to the prevention intervention were less likely to become smokers than were those in the reference groups (Evans, 1976, 1984; Evans *et al.*, 1981).

The Social Psychological Deterrents of Smoking in Schools Project marks the earliest of efforts to apply psychological techniques to tobacco prevention initiatives, inspiring much of the subsequent prevention research. Evidence has since confirmed that school-based prevention initiatives enjoy considerable success when using Social Influence and Life Skills practices[8] (Kumpfer *et al.*, 1997). A closer consideration of the Social Influence Approach finds that it embraces three primary techniques. One involves students learning social resistance techniques from teachers or peer leaders. A second attempts psychological vaccination, achieved by teaching students to analyse tobacco advertisements. The third embraces normative education, with individual defences against coercion fortified by arguments that undermine pressures to smoke (McGuire, 1964; Evans, 1976). The Social Influence Approach can take credit for decreasing the number of new smokers after the initial intervention by up to 50 per cent (Donaldson *et al.*, 1994; Ellickson and Bell, 1990; de Vries *et al.*, 2006), with declines evident among both sporadic, social smokers and regular, recurrent smokers. Benefits also accrue to participants of competence enhancement approaches (Botvin and Kantor, 2000; Gilchrist and Schinke, 1986; Botvin *et al.*, 1990), with reports of tobacco consumption declining by 40 and 75 per cent. Indeed, the Life Skills Training programme has proven successful in decreasing tobacco consumption by 56 to 66 per cent at the one year mark without reinforcement sessions (Botvin *et al.*, 1983). When reinforcement sessions were included in the Life Skills Training programme, smoking declined by 87 per cent (Botvin *et al.*, 1983). However, these successes must be qualified since smoking cessation results typically have a lifespan of three years if not followed-up by reinforcement (Pentz *et al.*, 1989).

Studying the effects of Social Influence initiatives, five characteristics emerge as contributors to effective school-based substance misuse programmes (Botvin *et al.*, 2000; Flynn *et al.*, 1992). These include:

1. Techniques to resist peer pressure.
2. Pursuits designed to foster self-esteem and self-empowerment coupled with stress-management skills.
3. Efforts to align social norms with health objectives.
4. Interactive components that engage students.
5. The inclusion of peers and positive role models in programme provision.

On a cautionary note, these successes are particular to interventions promoting healthy eating, physical activity and mental health, with applications beyond these areas in need of further analysis. On a more promising note, evidence exists to suggest that the outcomes of school-based interventions can be sustained by complementary community-based initiatives (Stewart-Brown, 2006).

School-based initiatives generate greater success when information dissemination is coupled with behaviour-based programmes addressing behavioural inclinations, intentions and abilities (Contento *et al.*, 1995). An example of an effective school-based initiative to improve healthy eating includes the following instructions: keep a personal inventory of what is consumed; determine food-related habits to identify problem behaviours; establish personal change goals; observe the desired behaviours modelled by peers and adults; support and motivate individual change; and enhance self-efficacy through skill development (Resnicow *et al.*, 1991; Lytle, 1995). However, achieving optimal results demands a supportive school context that provides healthy food choices, thereby transcending the traditional emphasis on school-based education to alter the nutritional content of school meals. Given that repeated exposure can shape a child's willingness to accept foods, as can the social affective environment where it is served (Eertmans *et al.*, 2001), schools can increase children's acceptance of healthy foods by ensuring dietary familiarity and support (Lytle, 1995). In 1997, the Colorado Nutrition Network piloted a social marketing campaign to promote healthy food choices among low-income Coloradans by targeting preschoolers in Head Start classrooms through a 'try new foods' initiative, using various nutrition education activities and repeated opportunities to taste 13 novel foods. Indeed, school programmes like Head Start that provide attending children with meals have demonstrated positive results in terms of children's familiarity and intake of healthy foods (Young *et al.*, 2004). Moreover, Head Start performance standards require that parent education programmes furnish parents with food preparation and nutrition skills, thereby boosting Head Start pupil programme gains (Story *et al.*, 2006).

In order to maximise their efficacy, health promotion interventions face the formidable task of changing the context in which individuals make choices. Expanding on strictly school-based efforts, the Midwestern Prevention Project (MPP) is considered one of the more effective community-based substance misuse programmes. First implemented in 1984 in Kansas City and later transposed to Indianapolis in 1987 (Chou *et al.*, 1998), the initiative demanded that five steps be introduced sequentially. Step one disseminates promotional advertisements through the mass media to introduce each programme phase. Step two introduces the school-based intervention, inspired by a combination of the Social Influence and Social Competence Models[9] and presented by trained teachers and peer leaders to students in grades six and seven. Step three involves the parental component using parent-principal meetings and parent-child communication training. Step four coordinates and coaches coordinated and coached community leaders to establish action groups. Step five draws on such policy changes as declaring schools to be drug-free zones and increasing taxes on alcohol. Evaluations at both one year and three year

intervals following the introduction of these five steps by the MPP initiative found that consumption of alcohol, tobacco and cannabis all diminished among students. For our purposes, it is worth noting that the
success of this programme is in part attributed to the inclusion of such
psychological tools as Social Influence, Diffusion of Innovation,[10] mass
communication[11] and empowerment[12] schemes.

In order to bolster their efficacy, community-based programmes typically
combine mass communication techniques with school-based initiatives.
For instance, when the two approaches were combined to combat adolescent smoking, students exhibited a more consistent decrease in smoking
than did students exposed only to school-based programmes (Wakefield
and Chaloupka, 2000). In a similar prevention programme targeting adolescent girls, results indicated a 40 per cent decline in the weekly smoking rate
of girls aged 14 to 16 who were subjected to a combined media and school-
based intervention (Worden *et al.*, 1996). Encouragingly, these results per-
sisted at the two year follow-up mark.

Overall, initiatives employing mass communications and community-based
approaches have generated more striking and persistent results in adolescents
and youth when compared with efforts confined to the school or the family
(Wakefield and Chaloupka, 2000; Worden *et al.*, 1996). Improving the effectiveness of cessation or prevention initiatives demands a comprehensive
approach incorporating mass communications, empowerment and skills
development, community enrichment and healthy public policy. Health promotion activities need to address the reality that many young people are regularly bombarded by forcible and formidable social influences that undermine
health promotion efforts including: poverty, parental neglect, substandard
schools, decaying cities and media messages normalising promiscuity, violence and substance misuse (Commers *et al.*, 2007). A comprehensive approach
to health promotion is therefore essential.

Efforts to advance population health make apparent the need for a wider
range of instruments to address broad problems – and policy tools provide
the broadest approach to health promotion. For instance, consider the
complementarity of three policy initiatives seeking to curb smoking
and substance misuse: the first approach establishes environments free
from tobacco, alcohol or drugs; the second approach inhibits access
to tobacco and alcohol; and the third approach raises the cost of smoking
and drinking through price hikes or tax increases. In studying the efficacy
of school policies on student substance use in Ontario it emerged that
pupils in schools embracing the broader range of policies reported less
alcohol consumption and less heavy drinking than did their counterparts
attending schools with minimal or modest policies in place (Glicksman
et al., 1999). Moreover, the effect of restricting substance use at school also
appears to ease the peer pressure on students to start smoking in the first
place.

To gauge the efficacy of school policies on student smoking in American schools, four policies concerning smoking prevalence rates were assessed (Pentz *et al.*, 1989). These included: whether smoking was prohibited on school property; whether smoking was prohibited near school premises; whether there was a closed school premise minimising chances to smoke near school grounds; and whether there was an official smoking prevention strategy in effect. Results revealed that schools implementing all four policies exhibited lower smoking prevalence rates than did schools embracing fewer than the full four. There is little doubt, therefore, that policy initiatives can suppress adolescents' substance use, particularly with young smokers who face the possibility of a hefty fine.

Ontario's tobacco strategy prohibits sales to minors, with the daily implementation of this initiative left to merchants. To discourage minors considering an illicit purchase, merchants are provided with signs indicating that tobacco will not be sold to minors. However, as profit motives can dissuade merchants from adhering to this law, ongoing inspections are necessary to ensure that merchants serve as enforcers. Those failing to uphold the ordinance must answer to health department officers and complete a merchant instruction course. Follow-up compliance assessments suggest that these instruction sessions effectively discourage future tobacco sales to minors. Indeed, Ontario is but one of the many examples documenting the deterring effect that access prevention has on adolescent smoking prevalence rates (Ahmad, 2005; Chen and Forster, 2006).

One particularly effective programme worth noting is the Tobacco Policy Options for Prevention (TROP) initiative implemented in 14 Minnesota communities (Forster *et al.*, 1998). The objectives of this initiative were fourfold: to raise the relevance of smoking as an issue among minors within the designated communities; to modify local regulations in a manner which increased the efficacy of tobacco restrictions to minors; to alter merchant and adult responses to the access of tobacco by minors; and to implement tobacco sale prohibition statutes. From the randomised community studies it emerged that efforts to implement these objectives tempered the growth in rates of daily smoking in addition to there being fewer cigarette purchases among teens in the TROP groups when compared with their control group counterparts. Comparable interventions have enjoyed similar successes in diminishing alcohol use and misuse in adolescents (Komro and Toomey, 2002; Milne *et al.* 2007).

Legislation requires that tobacco retailers contribute to health promotion by eliminating sales to minors, a demand also made of servers. Yet, while enforcement checks deter sales of tobacco and alcohol, the enforcement effect decays after three months suggesting the need for regular reinforcement (Wagenaar *et al.*, 2005). But beyond legislation alone, even greater gains have been made using an environmental policy approach that sought to: mobilise the community in support of the 'Preventing Alcohol Trauma:

A Community Trial' initiative; ensure responsible alcohol service; increase the enforcement efficiency of drink-driving; reduce the availability of alcohol to minors; and use municipal levers to control the number and density of outlets offering alcohol (Holder, 2000). Results revealed that the initiative diminished alcohol-related vehicle accidents, lowered alcohol sales to minors, increased the responsible alcohol serving practices of bars and restaurants and bolstered community support for and awareness of alcohol problems.

Other health promotion interventions benefiting from site-specific interventions place their emphasis on nutritious consumption. For instance, consider those healthy eating programmes that have ventured out into the community to implement effective supermarket initiatives (see Glanz and Yaroch, 2004), the most common of which provides nutrient information, shelf labelling and in-store promotions. Overall, effective interventions in the area of healthy consumption are distinguished by a broad ambit that incorporates environmental controls, mass media campaigns and policy implementation. One broad, albeit blunt, policy instrument is taxation, a tool that has proved particularly effective in diminishing tobacco and alcohol consumption. Across the board, the evidence identifies a link between cigarette price increases and tobacco consumption decreases (Rivara *et al.*, 2004; Ross *et al.*, 2005). The favoured formula estimates that for every 10 per cent price increase there is a 3-4 per cent decrease in tobacco use (Farrelly *et al.*, 1998). In terms of adolescent smoking, declining tobacco consumption is most pronounced among those facing a substantial price increase, suggesting that taxation is an effective instrument with which to mount a sustained suppression of tobacco consumption in adolescents (Ross *et al.*, 2005). Yet the effects of taxation are not confined to tobacco since taxes exhibit a comparable effect on alcohol consumption (Chaloupka, 2003), with heavy drinking among adolescents waning following the institution of a tax increase (Hollingworth *et al.*, 2006). Moreover, the effect of taxation is even more pronounced on tobacco and alcohol consumption in adults (Bourne *et al.*, 1994; Toomey and Wagenaar, 1999), with modest tax increases proving a greater disincentive to adult smoking than to youth smoking. Indeed, American public health and policy officials consider tobacco taxation to be their most potent smoking deterrent (Pierce-Lavin and Gellar, 1998; Lantz *et al.*, 2000).

Yet for taxation to be most effective, it must be part of a comprehensive preventive initiative. For instance, consider the diversion of tobacco tax gains to smoking cessation programmes in California and Massachusetts, a move that prompted further declines in each state's tobacco consumption patterns (Al-Delaimy *et al.*, 2007; Koh, 2002; Messer *et al.*, 2007; Robbins *et al.*, 2002). However, the most pronounced results from anti-smoking interventions remain attributable to school-based tobacco prevention initiatives (Centre for Disease Control, 2001; Moore *et al.*, 2001). To their credit, school-based prevention programmes have not been constrained by directives to superimpose a standardised approach across individual schools. Instead, effective approaches appreciate the importance of adapting to group smoking norms and student characteristics, providing a targeted response that is reinforced by societal prevention and taxation. When considered in relation to alcohol consumption, taxes similarly succeed in suppressing alcohol use while reducing such deleterious by-products as car fatalities (Toomey and Wagenaar, 1999) and public aggression (Holder *et al.*, 2000).

Turning to efforts emphasising healthy consumption, healthy eating interventions in the American workplace have proved increasingly popular of late. What in part explains this popularity is that the worksite comes equipped with possible contextual interventions, social support and the social influence needed to embrace healthy habits. Efforts targeting the workplace rely on a blend of competition, individual and collective goal-setting and management reinforcement. Effective workplace interventions are characterised by: the inclusion of all employees; the broad circulation of printed information or self-help initiatives; the application of incentives; public demonstrations of engagement and commitment; contextual modifications to suit healthy objectives; and employee involvement in planning and executing the initiative (Rogers and Glantz, 1991; Contento *et al.*, 1995). From a review of health promotion interventions encouraging healthy eating, it emerges that efficacious interventions in schools, workplaces, primary care and community settings are distinguished by (Roe *et al.*, 1997):

- An emphasis on diet or diet plus exercise rather than broadening the scope to address a range of risk factors.
- An application of behavioural theories and objectives, moving beyond the mere provision of information.
- The arrangement of personal contacts with participants either individually or in small groups using active participation and behaviour modification techniques.
- A degree of intervention personalisation in response to participants' individual traits and context.
- Changes to the local environment to support healthy eating, such as offerings in local shops and restaurants.

Discussion

The mark of a successful intervention is the inclusion of individual, social and contextual change initiatives. From an individual perspective, the crucial psychological components of healthy behaviour are perceived impediments and self-efficacy. From a social perspective, social support is fundamental to any effort striving for healthy behaviour change. From a contextual perspective, effective interventions recognise the importance of mass media campaigns and policy implementation. As interventions spanning the triad are greater than the sum of each part, initiatives must bridge the intervention spectrum in order to reap the potential synergistic effects for population health.

The rationale behind recruiting health psychology to devise healthy public policy finds three arguments in its favour (Mittelmark, 1999). First, rather than policymaking being understood as rational, methodical and objective, the inclusion of psychology allows policymaking to be appreciated as a normative and dynamic endeavour, with policy efforts subject to external forces and decisionmaking not limited to the confines of fact (Walt, 1994). Moreover, policymaking strives to achieve social influence through persuasion and compromise, tools that draw sustenance from social psychological findings. Second, the contribution of health psychology to preventive efforts in a variety of domains – some of which are reviewed here – suggests that health psychology can improve the practice of policymaking through the application of psychological findings. Third, with increasing recognition of the value generated by interdisciplinary works, psychology has much to contribute to policymaking in concert with sociology and political science, which hitherto have dominated the field. Yet to increase the contribution of health psychology to public health, health psychology must abandon the sterility of the laboratory in order to study social processes in practice.

Indeed, there are a number of challenges to advancing an evidence-based public health agenda. For instance, while evidence increasingly documents successful psychologically-informed interventions benefiting health, rarely are these results translated into health promotion practice. This disconnect is not particular to promotion or prevention practices in health but is characteristic of health care itself (Committee on Quality, 2001). For instance, evidence-based diabetes management offers guidance on thwarting complication-generating results that are both important and efficient (Joyner *et al.*, 1997). Yet despite the existence of such evidence-based directives there is little indication of their practical application, particularly when considering lifestyle education and behavioural concerns (Woolf and Atkins, 2001). Explanations for this continuing dissociation between research and routine include: insufficient time; a lack of training and resources; an absence of feedback and incentives; and weak systemic and structural efforts to realise research gains (Green, 2001).

Further contributing to this division is the rationale behind psychological research. In favouring a linear, standardised progression, researchers adhere to a formula where determining intervention efficacy in controlled settings often comes at the expense of establishing intervention efficacy in population-based contexts. As a solution, Glasgow and colleagues (2003) propose that assessments of both efficacy and effectiveness answer four questions about whether an intervention succeeds in: connecting with many people, particularly those who stand to gain the most; adapting to a variety of contexts; translating coherently at the hands of different implementers equipped with varying degree of instruction and competence; and generating enduring results that can be inexpensively reproduced.

There are also issues concerning what is measured and how. Improving the measurement of health promotion interventions necessitates a greater emphasis on qualitative evaluative techniques, countering the common perception of qualitative approaches as struggling to achieve validity and reliability. This is not to say that quantitative methods should be abandoned, nor that quantitative efforts are satisfactory as they stand. For instance, take the practice of discounting the future. Psychologists have demonstrated that people typically prefer a present reward over a future reward of equivalent value, just as people prefer to postpone a punishment rather than receive an immediate punishment of equal weight (Frederick, 2006). Discounting involves adjusting for this time preference. Health economists use discounting in their economic assessments, haggling over what the discount rate should be. However, discounting proves particularly problematic in terms of prevention and promotion programmes, for while the costs incurred by prevention programmes are immediate, health outcomes emerge over time, leaving the benefits to fall outside any cost-benefit analysis (Ganiats and Sieber, 2000). A full-valued present dollar expenditure juxtaposed against discounted future health benefits generates ratios objectionable to most decisionmakers. As such, evidence of health promotion interventions being cost-effective remains questionable. Some of the ways in which the National Institute for Health and Clinical Excellence is addressing this in England are covered in the chapter by Chalkidou *et al.* in this volume.

In order to redress the limited ability of the current evidence to address health inequalities, four shortcomings must be considered when evaluating health promoting interventions (Green, 2001). The first must recognise the distinction between what are heralded as 'best practices' in research and what works to meet the needs of disadvantaged populations in practice. The second must address the dissociation between research feeding 'best practices' and how best to translate those practices to reach targeted communities. The third involves rebalancing the disproportionate success of individual behaviour change among the more affluent and educated with the more modest gains among the less affluent, less educated and less socially-engaged. The fourth demands bridging the distance between academia-driven research controlled by the investigator and the contribution of local practitioners, community groups, agencies and governments to ensure that university research meaningfully serves local needs.

While prevention interventions have succeeded in modifying behaviours, these successes often prove difficult to sustain (Glasgow *et al.*, 1999). Irrespective of whether the intervention focus is on individuals or groups, the continued success of health promotion initiatives requires that interventions span multiple levels, take direction from established behaviour change approaches and consider the willingness of participants to change (Prochaska and Velicer, 1997). Moreover, it bears reiterating that any success achieved by health promoting efforts will be constrained without confronting the structural or relational impediments to change.

Conclusions

The paradox of health promotion is that the benefits of preventive measures accrue to the collective more so than to individual participants (Jenkins, 2003). Yet in their quest for rigorous evidence to demonstrate the efficacy of preventive interventions, evaluations of health promotion initiatives are constrained by their confinement to individuals in laboratories, clinics and classrooms. These circumscribed settings deviate from the breadth and complexity of the social systems in which mass health promotion campaigns are conducted and in which individual risks are taken. Moreover, research in pursuit of a single best theory or practice ensuring efficacious health promotion is not only fallacious but futile given the variability among and the proportion of confounding variables that contribute to any singular context, much less the inherent variability found within any target audience.

Moving beyond the divide between the one-size-fits-all approach to health promotion and specialised approaches to intervention design and implementation, Green (2001) distinguishes between what health promotion research can deliver – a generalisable process for planning – and what it cannot – a specific plan. Thus health psychology can be used to help identify approaches to community engagement, techniques for determining the needs and situation of the community, the means of gauging resources, approaches to planning programmes and tools for ensuring that needs, resources and circumstances encounter the appropriate interventions. Therefore, in the future 'best practice' should mean a diagnostic tool that establishes what practitioners and policymakers need to identify and invest in target communities. This strategy links community capacity and needs with the appropriate mechanisms for ensuring that health promotion interventions succeed in addressing local needs.

The essence of policymaking is achieving social influence. Achieving social influence relies on persuasion, decisionmaking, compromise and shifting people's attitudes, all of which may be found in applications of psychological theories to health promotion. While no model is perfect, this review offers some indications of the significant contribution that health psychology can make to the success of future policy.

Notes

1 Context reassessment: Heightened awareness about the influence that unhealthy behaviour has on one's environment.
2 Consciousness raising: Discovering and learning new information that supports healthy behaviour change.

3 Self-reassessment: A reevaluation of one's cognitions and emotions, particularly in relation to the problem behaviour.

4 Contingency management: The rewarding of positive behavioural changes.

5 Counterconditioning: The substitution of unhealthy behaviours with positive alternatives.

6 Stimulus control: Anticipatory efforts that are made to ensure that individuals can cope with, avoid or remove negative stimuli that may trigger a relapse.

7 Social Influence Theory was born of the recognition that social factors are significant contributors to the initiation and early stages of drug use, with the media, peers and family considered socially influential. The original research on Social Influence was conducted by Evans and colleagues (Evans, 1976; Evans *et al.*, 1978) in relation to adolescent cigarette smoking. From there, Evans devised and tested a unique approach to tobacco, alcohol and narcotic prevention that is notable not only because it was the first approach to engender behaviour modification, but because it introduced many of the components that remain integral to the more effectual drug abuse prevention programmes (Botvin, 1996).

8 Life Skills Training is a tobacco, alcohol, and drug abuse (primarily marijuana) prevention programme for use with students between the ages of 11 and 14. This three-year programme equips adolescents with the motivation and skills to defy peer and media pressures to use drugs, cultivates personal self-management skills and general social skills and champions anti-drug norms (see Botvin *et al.*, 2003).

9 Social Competence Theory is understood not only as *having* thoughts, feelings and behaviours but as *having the capacity* to assimilate these for the purpose of performing social functions and achieving outcomes valued in the designated context and culture (Topping *et al.*, 2000). For instance, in the school setting the requisite functions and outcomes include mastering the assigned curriculum, satisfying concurrent personal social and emotional needs and acquiring transferable skills and attitudes that are relevant in a wider context.

10 *Diffusion of Innovation Theory* concerns the dissemination of novel ideas, products and practices throughout an organisation, community or society, or between societies. According to Rogers, diffusing innovations is 'the process by which an innovation is communicated through certain channels over time among the members of a social system' (1995, page 5). When applied in health promotion, diffusion of innovation requires a multifaceted, multilevel approach.

11 *Mass communication* refers to the dissemination of messages devised by gatekeepers to a broad audience via print, visual and audio mediums (Gamble and Gamble, 2006).

12 *Empowerment* efforts seek to increase the capacity of individuals to make choices and to translate those choices into actions and outcomes, with the ultimate objective being to master their own lives and achieve a critical appreciation of their environment (Zimmerman *et al.*, 1992).

References

D. A. Abood, D. R. Black and D. Feral, 'Nutrition education worksite intervention for university staff: Application of the Health Belief Model', *Journal of Nutrition Education and Behavior*, 35:5 (2003) 260–7.

S. Ahmad, 'Closing the youth access gap: The projected health benefits and cost savings of a national policy to raise the legal smoking age to 21 in the United States', *Health Policy*, 75:1 (2005) 74–84.

I. Ajzen, 'From intention to action: a theory of planned behavior', in J. Kuhl and J. Beckman (eds), *Action-Control: From Cognition to Behavior* (Heidelberg: Springer, 1985).

I. Ajzen and M. Fishbein, *Understanding Attitudes and Predicting Social Behavior* (Englewood Cliffs, NJ: Prentice-Hall, 1980).

W. K. Al-Delaimy, J. P. Pierce, K. Messer, M. M. White, D. R. Trinidad and E. A. Gilpin, 'The California Tobacco Control Program's effect on adult smokers: (2) Daily cigarette consumption level', *Tobacco Control*, 16:2 (2007) 91–5.

M. J. Allison and C. Keller, 'Self-efficacy intervention effect on physical activity in older adults', *Western Journal of Nursing Research*, 26:1 (2004) 31–46.

A. Bandura, *Social Learning Theory* (Englewood Cliffs, NJ: Prentice Hall, 1977).

A. Bandura, 'Self-efficacy mechanisms in human agency', *American Psychologist*, 37:2 (1982) 122–47.

M. H. Becker, D. P. Haefner and L. A. Maiman, 'The health belief model in the prediction of dietary compliance: a field experiment', *Journal of Health and Social Behaviour*, 18:4 (1977) 348–66.

G. J. Botvin, 'Preventing Drug Abuse through the Schools: Intervention Programs that Work', *National Conference on Drug Abuse Prevention Research: Presentations, Papers and Recommendations* (Washington, D.C.: National Institute on Drug Abuse 1996), pp. 43–56.

G. J. Botvin, E. Baker, L. Dusenbury, E. M. Botvin and T. Diaz, 'Long-term follow-up results of a randomized drug abuse prevention trial in a white middle-class population', *Journal of the American Medical Association*, 273:14 (1995) 1106–12.

G. L. Botvin, E. Baker, L. Dusenbury, S. Tortu and E. M. Botvin, 'Preventing adolescent drug abuse through a multimodal cognitive-behavioral approach: Results of a 3-year study', *Journal of Consulting and Clinical Psychology*, 58:4 (1990) 437–46.

G. L. Botvin, L. Dusenbury, E. Baker, S. James-Ortiz, E. M. Botvin and J. Kerner, 'Smoking prevention among urban minority youth: Assessing effects on outcome and mediating variables', *Health Psychology*, 11:5 (1992) 290–9.

G. J. Botvin, K. W. Griffin, T. Diaz, L. M. Scheier, C. Williams and J. A. Epstein, 'Long-term follow-up data from a randomized control trial of a school population', *Addictive Behaviors*, 25:5 (2000) 769–74.

G. J. Botvin, K. W. Griffin, E. Paul, E. and A. P. Macaulay, 'Preventing tobacco and alcohol use among elementary school students through Life Skills Training', *Journal of Child & Adolescent Substance Abuse*, 12:4 (2003) 1–17.

G. J. Botvin and L. W. Kantor, 'Preventing alcohol and tobacco use through life skills training', *Alcohol Research and Health*, 24:4 (2000) 250–7.

G. J. Botvin, N. Renick and E. Baker, 'The effects of scheduling format and booster sessions on a broad-spectrum psychosocial approach to smoking prevention', *Journal of Behavioral Medicine*, 6:4 (1983) 359–79.

D. Bourne, L. W. Freni, P. Fisher, C. O'Connor, J. Lloyd and D. G. Bal, 'The effect of raising state and federal tobacco taxes', *Journal of Family Practice*, 38:3 (1994) 300–2.

S. L. Buka and I. J. Birdthistle, 'Long-term effects of a community-wide alcohol server training intervention', *Journal of Studies in Alcohol*, 60:1 (1999) 27–36.

R. C. Callaghan, A. Hathaway, J. A. Cunningham, L. C. Vettese, S. Wyatt and L. Taylor, 'Does stage-of-change predict dropout in a culturally diverse sample of adolescents admitted to inpatient substance-abuse treatment? A test of the Transtheoretical Model', *Addictive Behaviours*, 30:9 (2005) 1834–47.

Center for Disease Control, 'Effectiveness of school-based programs as a component of a statewide tobacco control initiative – Oregon, 1999–2000', *Morbidity and Mortality Weekly Report*, 50:31 (2001) 663–6.

F. J. Chaloupka, 'The Effects of Price on Alcohol Use, Abuse, and Their Consequences', in R. J. Bonnie and M. E. O'Connell (eds), *Reducing Underage Drinking: A Collective Responsibility* (Washington, DC: Institute of Medicine of the National Academies, The National Academies Press, 2003), pp. 541–64.

V. Chen and J. L. Forster, 'The Long-Term Effect of Local Policies to Restrict Retail Sale of Tobacco to Youth', *Nicotine and Tobacco Research*, 8:3 (2006), 371–7.

C. P. Chou, S. Montgomery, M. A. Pentz, L. A. Rohrbach, C. A. Johnson, B. R. Flay and D. P. MacKinnon, 'Effects of a community-based prevention program in decreasing drug use in high risk adolescents', *American Journal of Public Health*, 88:6 (1998) 944–8.

M. J. Commers, N. Gottlieb and G. Kok, 'How to change environmental conditions for health', *Health Promotion International*, 22:1 (2007) 80–7.

Committee on Quality Health Care in America, *Crossing the Quality Chasm: A New Health System for the 21st Century* (Washington, DC: National Academy Press, 2001).

I. Contento, G. I. Balch, Y. L. Bronner, L. A. Lytle, S. K. Maloney, C. M. Oslon and S. S. Swadner, 'The effectiveness of nutrition education and implementations for nutrition education policy, programs, and research: a review of research', *Journal of Nutrition Education*, 27:6 (1995) 277–418.

K. Courneya, R. Segal, R. Reid, L. Jones, S. Malone, P. Venner, M. Parliament, C. Scott, H. Quinney and G. Wells, 'Three independent factors predicted adherence in a randomized controlled trial of resistance exercise training among prostate cancer survivors', *Journal of Clinical Epidemiology*, 57:6 (2004) 571–9.

H. de Vries, F. Dijk, J. Wetzels, A. Mudde, S. Kremers, C. Ariza, P. D. Vitória, A. Fielder, K. Holm, K. Janssen, R. Lehtovuori and M. Candel, 'The European Smoking prevention Framework Approach (ESFA): effects after 24 and 30 months', *Health Education Research*, 21:1 (2006) 116–32.

Department of Health, *Choosing Health: Making Healthier Choices Easier* (London: HM Stationary Office, 2004).

Department of Health, *Choosing Better Oral Health: An Oral Health Plan for England* (London: HM Stationary Office, 2005).

Department of Human Services, *Health Promotion Strategies for Community Health Services: An Evidence-Based Planning Framework for Nutrition, Physical Activity and Healthy Weight* (Victoria, Australia: Public Health Division, 1998).

C. C. DiClemente, S. K. Fairhurst, M. M. Velasquez, J. O. Prochaska, W. F. Velicer and J. S. Rossi, 'The process of smoking cessation: An analysis of precontemplation, contemplation and preparation stages of change', *Journal of Consulting and Clinical Psychology*, 59:2 (1991) 295–304.

S. I. Donaldson, J. W. Graham and W. B. Hansen, 'Testing the generalizability of intervening mechanism theories: Understanding the effects of adolescent drug use prevention interventions', *Journal of Behavioral Medicine*, 17:2 (1994) 195–216.

A. Eertmans, F. Baeyens and O. Van den Bergh, 'Food likes and their relative importance in human eating behavior: review and preliminary suggestions for health promotion', *Health Education Research*, 16:4 (2001) 443–56.

J. P. Elder, J. X. Apadaca, D. Parra-Medina and M. L. Z. de Nuncio, 'Strategies for Health Promotion', in S. Loue (ed.), *Handbook of Immigrant Health* (New York: Plenum Press, 1998), pp. 567–86.

P. L. Ellickson and R. M. Bell, *Prospects for Preventing Drug Abuse among Young Adolescents* (Santa Monica, CA: Rand Publication Series, 1990).

J. Ellis, M. A. Johnson, J. G. Fischer and J. L. Hargrove, 'Nutrition and health education intervention for whole grain foods in the Georgia Older Americans Nutrition Program', *Journal of Nutrition for the Elderly*, 24:3 (2005) 67–83.

K. M. Emmons, 'Behavioral and social science contributions to the health of adults in the United States', in B. D. Smedley and S. L. Syme (eds), *Promoting Health: Intervention Strategies from Social and Behavioral Research* (Washington, D.C: Committee on Capitalizing on Social and Behavioral Research to Improve the Public's Health, National Academy Press, 2001), pp. 254–321.

R. I. Evans, 'Smoking in children: Developing a social psychological strategy of deterrence', *Preventive Medicine*, 5:1 (1976) 122–7.

R. I. Evans, 'A social inoculation strategy to deter smoking in adolescents', in J. D. Matarazzo, S. M. Weiss, J. A. Herd, N. E. Miller and S. M. Weiss (eds), *Behavioral Health: A Handbook of Health Enhancement and Disease Prevention* (New York: J. Wiley and Sons, 1984), pp. 765–74.

R. I. Evans, R. M. Rozelle, S. E. Maxwell, B. E. Raines, C. A. Dill, T. J. Guthrie, A. H. Henderson, P. C. Hill, 'Social modeling films to deter smoking in adolescents: Results of a three-year field investigation', *Journal of Applied Psychology*, 66:4 (1981) 399–414.

R. I. Evans, R. M. Rozelle, M. B. Mittelmark, W. B. Hansen, A. L. Bane and J. Havis, 'Deterring the onset of smoking in children: knowledge of immediate physiological effects and coping with peer pressure, media pressure, and parental modeling', *Journal of Applied Social Psychology*, 8:2 (1978) 126–36.

M. C. Farrelly, J. W. Bray and Office on Smoking and Health, 'Response to increases in cigarette prices by race/ethnicity, income and age groups – US, 1976–1993', *Morbidity and Mortality Weekly Report*, 47:29 (1998) 605–9.

B. S. Flynn, J. K. Worden, R. H. Secker-Walker, G. J. Bader, B. M. Gellerand, M. C. Costanza, 'Prevention of cigarette smoking through mass media intervention and school programs', *American Journal of Public Health*, 82:6 (1992) 827–34.

J. L. Forster, D. M. Murray, M. Wolfson, T. M. Blaine, A. C. Wagenaar and D. J. Hennrikus, 'The effects of community policies to reduce youth access to tobacco', *American Journal of Public Health*, 88:8 (1998) 1193–8.

S. Frederick, 'Valuing future life and future lives: A framework for understanding discounting', *Journal of Economic Psychology*, 27:5 (2006) 667–80.

K. L. Frohlich and L. Potvin, 'Collective lifestyles as the target for health promotion', *Canadian Journal of Public Health*, 90:S1 (1999) 11–14.

M. Gamble and T. W. Gamble, *Communication Works*, 8th edn (New York: McGraw-Hill, 2006).

T. G. Ganiats and W. J. Sieber, 'Valuing future health in social policy and human health behaviour', in M. S. Jamner and D. Stokols (eds), *Promoting Human Wellness: New Frontiers for Research and Practice and Policy* (Los Angeles: University of California Press 2000), pp. 325–44.

L. D. Gilchrist and S. P. Schinke, 'Self-control skills for smoking prevention', *Addictive Behaviors*, 11:2 (1986) 169–74.

K. Glanz and A. L. Yaroch, 'Strategies for increasing fruit and vegetable intake in grocery stores and communities: policy, pricing, and environmental change', *Preventive Medicine*, 39:2 (2004) S75–S80.

R. E. Glasgow, E. Lichtenstein and A. C. Marcus, 'Why don't we see more translation of health promotion research to practice? Rethinking the efficacy-to-effectiveness transition', *American Journal of Public Health*, 93:8 (2003) 1261–7.

R. E. Glasgow, T. M. Vogt and S. M. Boles, 'Evaluating the public health impact of health promotion interventions: the RE-AIM framework', *American Journal of Public Health*, 89:9 (1999) 1322–7.

L. Glicksman, E. Adlaf, K. Allison and B. Newton-Taylor, 'School-based drug policies and student drug use: a test of impact. In Centre for Addiction and Mental Health, Best Advice; Alcohol and Drug Prevention Programs for Youth: What Works (Toronto: Centre for Addiction and Mental Health', 1999.

L. W. Green, 'From research to "best practices" in other settings and populations', *American Journal of Health Behavior*, 25:3 (2001) 165–78.

A. Harden, A. Oakley and S. Oliver, 'Peer-delivered health promotion for young people: a systematic review of different study designs', *Health Education Journal*, 60:4 (2001) 339–53.

F. Heider, *The Psychology of Interpersonal Relations* (New York: Wiley, 1958).

H. D. Holder, 'Community prevention of alcohol problems', *Addictive Behaviours*, 25:6 (2000) 843–59.

H. D. Holder, P. J. Gruenewald, W. R. Ponicki, A. J. Treno, J. W. Grube, R. F. Saltz, R. B. Voas, R. Reynolds, J. Davis, L. Sanchez, G. Gaumont and P. Roeper, 'Effect of community-based interventions on high-risk drinking and alcohol-related injuries', *Journal of the American Medical Association*, 284:18 (2000) 2341–7.

W. Hollingworth, B. E. Ebel, C. A. McCarty, M. M. Garrison, D. A. Christakis and F. P. Rivara, 'Prevention of deaths from harmful drinking in the United States: the potential effects of tax increases and advertising bans on young drinkers', *Journal of Studies on Alcohol*, 67:2 (2006) 300–8.

N. K. Janz and L. Becker, 'The health belief model: a decade later', *Health Education Quarterly*, 11:1 (1984) 1–47.

C. D. Jenkins, *Building Better Health: A Handbook of Behavioural Change* (Washington, D.C: PAHO, 2003).

L. Joyner, S. McNeeley and R. Kahn, 'ADA's provider recognition program', *HMO Practice*, 11:4 (1997) 168–70.

D. Kahneman and A. Tversky, 'Prospect theory: an analysis of decision under risk', *Econometrica*, 47:2 (1979) 263–91.

H. H. Kelley, 'Attribution theory in social psychology', in D. Levine (ed.), *Nebraska Symposium on Motivation* (Lincoln, NB: University of Nebraska Press, 1967), pp. 192–238.

H. H. Kelley, 'Attribution in social interaction', in E. E. Jones, D. E. Kanouse, H. H. Kelley, R. E. Nisbett, S. Valins, and B. Weiner (eds), *Attribution: Perceiving the Causes of Behaviour* (Morristown, NJ: General Learning Press, 1972), pp. 1–26.

G. C. Kloek, F. J. van Lenthe, P. W. van Nierop, C. T. Schrijvers and J. P. Mackenbach, 'Stages of change for moderate-intensity physical activity in deprived neighborhoods', *Preventive Medicine*, 43:4 (2006) 325–31.

S. A. Koblinsky, J. F. Guthrie and L. Lynch, 'Evaluation of a nutrition education program for Head Start parents', *Journal of Nutrition Education*, 24:1 (1992) 4–13.

H. K. Koh, 'Accomplishments of the Massachusetts Tobacco Control Program', *Tobacco Control*, 11:S2 (2002) ii1–ii3.

K. A. Komro and T. L. Toomey, 'Strategies to prevent underage drinking', *Alcohol Research and Health*, 26:1 (2002) 5–14.

K. Kumpfer, M. Williams and G. Baxley, *Drug Abuse Prevention for At-Risk Groups* (Rockville, MD: US Department of Health and Human Services, National Institute on Drug Abuse, 1997).

P. M. Lantz, P. D. Jacobson, K. E. Warner, J. Wasserman, H. A. Pollack, J. Berson, and A. Ahlstrom, 'Investing in youth tobacco control: a review of smoking prevention and control strategies', *Tobacco Control*, 9:1 (2000) 47–63.

R. C. Lefebvre, 'Theories and models in social marketing', in P. N. Bloom and G. T. Gundlach (eds), *Handbook of Marketing and Society* (Newbury Park, CA: Sage Publications, 2000), pp. 506–18.

D. Lister-Sharp, S. Chapman, S. Stewart-Brown and A. Sowden, 'Health promoting schools and health promotion in schools: two systematic reviews', *Health Technology Assessment*, 3:22 (1999) 1–207.

D. Lupton, 'Consumerism, commodity, culture and health promotion', *Health Promotion International*, 9:2 (1994) 111–18.

J. Lynch, G. Davey Smith, G. Kaplan and J. House, 'Income inequality and mortality: importance of health to individual income, psychosocial environment and material conditions', in R. Hofrichter (ed.), *Health and Social Justice* (New York: John Wiley, 2003). pp. 217–27.

L. A. Lytle, 'Nutrition education for school-aged children', *Journal of Nutrition Education*, 27:6 (1995) 298–311.

T. Manning, 'Interactive environments for promoting health', in R. L. Street, W. R. Gold and T. Manning (eds), *Health Promotion and Interactive Technology: Theoretical Applications and Future Directions* (Mahwah, NJ: Lawrence Erlbaum Associates, 1997). pp. 67–78.

W. J. McGuire, 'Inducing resistance to persuasion: some contemporary approaches', in L. Berkowitz (ed.), *Advances in Experimental Social Psychology*, Volume 1 (New York: McGraw-Hill, 1964), pp. 191–229.

K. Messer, J. P. Pierce, S. J. Zhu, A. M. Hartman, W. K. Al-Delaimy, D. R. Trinidad and E. A. Gilpin, 'The California Tobacco Control Program's effect on adult smokers: (1) Smoking cessation', *Tobacco Control*, 16:2 (2007) 85–9.

S. Milne, S. Greenaway, K. Conway and W. Henwood, 'What next? Sustaining a successful small-scale alcohol consumption harm minimization project', in *Substance Use and Misuse*, 42 (1995), 1933–4.

M. B. Mittelmark, 'The psychology of social influence and healthy public policy', *Preventive Medicine*, 29:6 (1999) S24–S29.

L. Moore, C. Roberts and C. Tudor-Smith, 'School smoking policies and smoking prevalence among adolescents: multilevel analysis of cross-sectional data from Wales', *Tobacco Control*, 10:2 (2001) 117–23.

C. T. Orleans, 'Promoting the maintenance of health behavior change; Recommendations for the next generation of research and practice', *Health Psychology*, 19:S1 (2000) 76–83.

M. A. Pentz, B. R. Branon, V. L. Charlin, E. J. Barrett, D. P. MacKinnon and B. R. Flay, 'The power of policy: the relationship of smoking policy to adolescent smoking', *American Journal of Public Health*, 79:7 (1989) 857–62.

D. E. Peterson, S. L. Zeger, P. L. Remington and H. A. Anderson, 'The effect of state cigarette tax increases on cigarette sales, 1955 to 1988', *American Journal of Public Health*, 82:1 (1992) 94–6.

C. L. Perry, S. H. Kelder and K. A. Komro, 'The social world of adolescents: family peers, schools and the community', in S. Millstein, A. Petersen, and E. Nightingale (eds), *Promoting the Health of Adolescents: New Directions for the Twenty-first Century* (New York: Oxford University Press, 1993), pp. 73–96.

C. Pierce-Lavin and A. C. Geller, 'Creating statewide tobacco control programs after passage of a tobacco tax', *Cancer*, 83:S12A (1998) 2659–65.

J. O. Prochaska and C. C. DiClemente, 'Self-change processes, self-efficacy and decisional balance across five stages of smoking cessation', in P. F. Epstein, P. N. Anderson and L. E. Mortenson (eds), *Advance in Cancer Control* (New York: Alan R. Liss, Inc., 1984), pp. 131–51.

J. O. Prochaska and W. F. Velicer, 'The Transtheoretical Model of health behavior change', *American Journal of Health Promotion*, 12:1 (1997) 38–48.

J. O. Prochaska, W. F. Velicer, C. C. DiClemente and J. L. Fava, 'Measuring the processes of change: Applications to the cessation of smoking', *Journal of Consulting and Clinical Psychology*, 56:4, 520–8.

S. Pucheu, S. M. Consoli, C. D'Auzac, P. Franc[,]ais and S. Issad, 'Do health causal attributions and coping strategies act as moderators of quality of life in peritoneal dialysis patients?', *Journal of Psychosomatic Research*, 56:3 (2004) 317–22.

K. Resnicow, D. Cross and E. Wynder, 'The role of comprehensive school-based interventions: the results of four Know Your Body studies', *Annals of the New York Academy of Science*, 623:1 (1991) 285–98.

F. P. Rivara, B. E. Ebel, M. M. Garrison, D. A. Christakis, S. E. Wiehe and D. T. Levy, 'Prevention of smoking-related deaths in the United States', *American Journal of Preventive Medicine*, 27:2 (2004) 118–25.

H. Robbins, M. Krakow and D. Warner, 'Adult smoking intervention programmes in Massachusetts: a comprehensive approach with promising results', *Tobacco Control*, 11:2 (2002) ii4–ii7.

T. Rogers and K. Glantz, 'Worksite nutrition programs: a review', in J. P. Mayer and J. K. David (eds), *Worksite Health Promotion: Needs, Approaches and Effectiveness* (Lansing; Michigan Department of Public Health, 1991), pp. 112–51.

L. Roe, P. Hunt, H. Bradshaw and M. Rayner, *Health Promotion Interventions to Promote Healthy Eating in the General Population: A Review* (London: Health Education Authority, 1997).

E. M. Rogers, *Diffusion of Innovations*, 4th edn (New York: Free Press, 1995).

G. Rhonda, P. Van Assema and J. Brug, 'Stages of change, psychological factors and awareness of physical activity levels in the Netherlands', *Health Promotion International*, 16:4 (2001) 305–14.

H. Ross, L. M. Powell, J. A. Tauras and F. J. Chaloupka, 'New evidence on youth smoking behavior based on experimental price increases', *Contemporary Economic Policy*, 23:2 (2005) 195–210.

D. M. Sanbonmatsu and R. H. Fazio, 'The role of attitudes in memory-based decision making', *Journal of Personality and Social Psychology*, 59:4 (1990) 614–22.

D. L. Snow, J. K. Tebes, M. W. Arthur and R. C. Tapasak, 'Two-year followup of a social-cognitive intervention to prevent substance use', *Journal of Drug Education*, 22:2 (1992) 101–14.

S. Stewart-Brown, *What Is the Evidence on School Health Promotion in Improving Health or Preventing Disease and, Specifically, What Is the Effectiveness of the Health Promoting Schools Approach?* (Copenhagen: WHO Regional Office for Europe's Health Evidence Network, 2006).

M. Story, K. M. Kaphingst and S. French, 'The role of child care settings in obesity prevention', *Future of Children*, 16:1 (2006) 143–68.

S. M. Sutton, G. I. Balch and R. C. Lefebvre, 'Strategic questions for consumer-based health communication', *Public Health Reports*, 110:6 (1995) 725–33.

S. L. Syme, 'Community participation, empowerment and health: development of a wellness guide by California', in M. S. Jamner and D. Stokols (eds), *Promoting Human Wellness: New Frontiers for Research and Practice and Policy* (Los Angeles: University of California Press, 2000), pp. 78–98.

T. L. Toomey and A. C. Wagenaar, 'Policy options for prevention: the case of alcohol', *Journal of Public Health Policy*, 20:2 (1999) 192–213.

K. J. Topping, W. G. Bremner E. A. Holmes, 'Social competence: The social construction of the concept', in R. Bar-On and J. D. A. Parker (eds), *The Handbook of Emotional Intelligence: Theory, Development, Assessment, and Application at Home, School, and in the Workplace* (San Francisco: Jossey-Bass, 2000), pp. 28–39.

J. Townsend, P. Roderick and J. Cooper, 'Cigarette smoking by socioeconomic group, sex and age: effects of price, income, and health publicity', *British Medical Journal*, 309:6959 (1994) 923–7.

A. C. Wagenaar, T. L. Toomey and D. Erickson, 'Preventing youth access to alcohol: outcomes from a multi-community time-series trial', *Addiction*, 100:3 (2005) 335–45.

M. Wakefield and F. Chaloupka, 'Effectiveness of comprehensive tobacco control programmes in reducing teenage smoking in the USA', *Tobacco Control*, 9 (2000) 177–86.

G. Walt, *Health Policy: An Introduction to Process and Power* (London: Zed Books, 1994).

S. H. Woolf and D. Atkins, 'The evolving role of prevention in health care contributions of the US Preventive Services Task Force', *American Journal of Preventive Medicine*, 20:S3 (2001) 13–20.

J. K. Worden, B. S. Flynn, L. J. Solomon, R. H. Secker-Walker, G. J. Badger and J. H. Carpenter, 'Using mass media to prevent cigarette smoking among adolescent girls', *Health Education Quarterly*, 23:4 (1996) 453–68.

L. Young, J. Anderson, L. Beckstrom, L. Bellows and S. L. Johnson, 'Using social marketing principles to guide the development of a nutrition education initiative for preschool-aged children', *Journal of Nutrition Education and Behavior*, 36:5 (2004) 250–7.

M. A. Zimmerman, B. A. Israel, A. Schulz, B. Checkoway, 'Further explorations in empowerment theory: An empirical analysis of psychological empowerment', *American Journal of Community Psychology*, 20:6 (1992) 707–27.

Table 5.1 Summary of studies reviewed in Chapter 5

Author	Date	Location	Intervention	Outcome
Abood, Black & Feral	2003	USA	This work employed components of the Health Belief Model to determine if modifications to dietary habits would diminish fat and cholesterol intake.	There were significant increases in the perceived benefits of healthy consumption and nutrition knowledge among treatment participants. The treatment group also exhibited a significant decrease in total calories, fat, saturated fat, and cholesterol consumed.
Al-Delaimy, Pierce, Messer, White, Trinidad & Gilpin	2007	USA	This study considered age-specific consumption patterns among daily smokers in three states with differing tobacco control initiatives based on cigarette pricing and tobacco-control programmes.	The overall trend was declining cigarette consumption across all age groups in all states between 1992 and 2002, save for the oldest respondents in the tobacco growing state. Declines were most marked in average daily tobacco consumption in daily Californian smokers aged 35 and older. From their findings, the authors conclude that the California Tobacco Control Program coincided with significant decreases in cigarette consumption among daily smokers aged 35 years or older, which they predict should generate future declines in tobacco-related health effects.

Table 5.1 Summary of studies reviewed in Chapter 5 – *continued*

Author	Date	Location	Intervention	Outcome
Allison & Keller	2004	USA	This work considered the influence of a self-efficacy intervention (one of two supportive telephone protocols) on the self-efficacy and physical activity of older adults following a cardiac event.	Overall, the self-efficacy intervention revealed greater physical activity when contrasted with the attention control intervention. Although the self-efficacy intervention did not exhibit a direct effect on the level of self-efficacy in physical activity as anticipated, there was an indirect interaction effect on distance walked and physical activity confidence.
Botvin, Baker, Dusenbury, Tortu & Botvin	1990	USA	Using a randomised block approach, this study subjected schools to one of three treatments: 1) a prevention programme offering formal provider instruction and implementation feedback; 2) a prevention programme with videotaped provider instruction and no feedback; and 3) no treatment.	According to the results, significant prevention effects emerged for cigarette smoking, marijuana use, and heavy alcohol consumption. Prevention effects also surfaced for normative expectations and knowledge concerning substance misuse, interpersonal skills, and communication skills.
Botvin, Griffin, Diaz, Scheier, Williams & Epstein	2000	USA	The researchers conducted a large-scale randomised prevention trial to gauge the extent to which participation in a cognitive-behavioural skills-training prevention programme diminished drug misuse when compared with control groups. Schools were divided according to high, medium and low smoking prevalence, after which they were randomly assigned into the experimental	Findings suggest that the drug misuse prevention initiative targeting adolescents during middle school – along with the prevention approach considered here – can generate prevention effects that persist beyond high school graduation. According to the results, students undergoing the Life Skills Training prevention programme during middle school indicated less use

Table 5.1 Summary of studies reviewed in Chapter 5 – *continued*

Author	Date	Location	Intervention	Outcome
			or control conditions. Experimental subjects experienced a drug misuse prevention programme that involved a primary year of intervention in grade 7 followed by reinforcing interventions in the subsequent two years.	of illicit drugs than their control counterparts. Findings also suggest that illicit drug use can be curbed by targeting tobacco and alcohol consumption.
Botvin, Renick & Baker	1983	USA	This study assessed the efficacy of a psychosocial anti-smoking strategy for a 12 year old audience. Conducted by classroom teachers, it included a cognitive element concerned with the immediate consequences of cigarette smoking, a decisionmaking component, a relaxation-training component, a social skills training component and a self-improvement component. Also of interest were the comparative efficacy of two scheduling approaches and the contribution of reinforcement sessions in the year following programme completion.	From the results it emerged that the prevention programme cut new cigarette smoking in half by the end of the first year and by 55% by the end of the second year for the intensive format approach. New regular cigarette smoking was cut by 87% in the second year for students in the reinforcement condition. Significant changes consistent with non-smoking also appeared for several cognitive, attitudinal and personality variables.

Table 5.1 Summary of studies reviewed in Chapter 5 – *continued*

Author	Date	Location	Intervention	Outcome
Buka & Birdthistle	1999	USA	The emphasis here was on alcohol servers rather than drinkers, with community-wide interventions created to encourage responsible serving practices. The primary goal was to gauge any short- and long-term behaviour modifications in alcohol beverage servers who underwent the five hour 'Responsible Alcohol Service' training. Their approach favoured a prospective design to assess the self-reported health of participants on three occasions over five years, with a cross-sectional survey employed at the four year mark to contrast self-reported server behaviour in the target community with control communities.	Fifteen months post-training, trainees reported significantly more of the desired serving behaviour than did comparative control servers. Though the positive effects of server training faded over time, responsible serving behaviour at the four year mark remained higher than at pretraining levels. Results were most pronounced for servers characterised by fewer years serving experience, wait-persons, younger servers and servers who worked in establishments that lacked written policies regarding serving practices.
Callaghan, Hathaway, Cunningham, Vettese, Wyatt & Taylor	2005	Canada	Two techniques were employed to analyse the predictive utility of the Transtheoretical Model with adolescents in an inpatient substance-misuse treatment programme. One approach employed a hierarchical logistic regression model of attrition, demographic variables, and components of the Addiction Severity Index. The other approach used a chi-square analysis that tested the proposed link between stage of change and attrition status.	According to the results, the best predictive model of programme attrition was found among participants in the precontemplation stage.

Table 5.1 Summary of studies reviewed in Chapter 5 – *continued*

Author	Date	Location	Intervention	Outcome
Chou, Montgomery, Pentz, Rohrbach, Johnson, Flay & MacKinnon	1998	USA	This study considered an experimental, community-based substance misuse prevention programme for adolescents. Participants were either designated to a drug misuse prevention programme based on the Social Influence model or to a health-education-as-usual control. Of interest was the affect of the experimental Social Influence condition on the substance use of baseline users.	At the 3.5 year follow-up, this primary prevention programme discovered diminished drug use in users ages 11 and 12. Overall, a conservative assessment finds the programme responsible for decreases in misuse, particularly with cigarettes and alcohol. As has been found elsewhere in the literature, the effect sizes were modest for cigarettes and alcohol use and medial for marijuana. From this, the authors conclude that a primary prevention programmes based on the Social Influence model can affect non-users at baseline as well as those who have started using drugs.
Courneya, Segal, Reid, Jones, Malone, Venner, Parliament, Scott, Quinney & Wells	2004	Canada	This study addressed the predictors of adherence to (resistance) exercise training in prostate cancer survivors receiving androgen deprivation therapy.	While exercise adherence in the trial was stable, it was not optimal. Adherence was an outcome measure comprised of social cognitive, quality of life, behavioural, fitness and demographic variables. Three independent predictors of adherence in particular explained 20.4% of the variance: exercise stage of change, age and intention.

Table 5.1 Summary of studies reviewed in Chapter 5 – *continued*

Author	Date	Location	Intervention	Outcome
de Vries, Dijk, Wetzels, Mudde, Kremers, Ariza, Vitória, Fielder, Holm, Janssen, Lehtovuori & Candel	2006	Portugal, Finland, Spain, The Netherlands, Denmark, UK	During the first intervention year (1998–1999), a school-based programme provided information on Social Influence processes and training in refusal skills. As peer-led programmes were unusual in the participating countries, teachers were responsible for delivering the information. Classroom lessons continued during the second and third years of the study, while the school, parental and out-of-school initiatives were advanced.	Significant results existed for the non-smoking objective at 24 and 30 months after the pretest, and for social self-efficacy after 30 months. In Portugal, significant effects on cognitions emerged at 24 and 30 months on all indicators save for situational self-efficacy at 30 months. While significant effects surfaced in Portugal for the cognitions, and less so for Spain and Denmark, relatively modest effect sizes and insignificant changes were found in Finland, The Netherlands and the UK, prompting questions as to whether the initiatives were sufficiently powerful to modify the cognitions of smoking. With regard to the behavioural effects, the results demonstrated that 2.5 years after the initiation of the study, the project generated a marginal, significant effect where 23.4% of the initial non-smokers from the control group had become weekly smokers compared to 21.9% in the experimental group, representing a 6% suppression of smoking in the experimental group.

Table 5.1 Summary of studies reviewed in Chapter 5 – *continued*

Author	Date	Location	Intervention	Outcome
Donaldson, Graham & Hansen	1994	USA	The objective of this study was to assess the intervening mechanism in two programme models for averting adolescent drug use. More specifically, the authors considered the importance of normative education versus fostering skills to resist peer pressure in order to prevent alcohol, tobacco and marijuana consumption. The normative education approach sought to instill beliefs in conventional norms among students, specifically that substance use among their peers was less likely than they thought and that it was generally frowned upon by their peer group. The resistance skills training sought to foster skills in students to resist social pressures, in particular to identify and resist social pressure and to be assertive in peer interactions. Outcomes from the two approaches were compared with a programme offering normative education and resistance training and a programme that only provided information about substance use.	Findings suggest that both normative education and resistance training stirred the targeted causal processes. While beliefs about the prevalence and acceptability of substance use tempered the effects of normative education on future adolescent substance use, resistance skills failed to significantly predict future drug use. Moreover, these findings were virtually identical across sex, ethnicity, context (public versus private school students), substance (alcohol, cigarettes, and marijuana) and levels of risk, not to mention being durable across time. From this, the authors conclude that the effectiveness of Social Influence-based prevention programmes may be attributable to their ability to encourage social norms that curb an adolescent's social motivation to consume alcohol, cigarettes and marijuana.

Table 5.1 Summary of studies reviewed in Chapter 5 – *continued*

Author	Date	Location	Intervention	Outcome
Evans, Rozelle, Maxwell, Raines, Dill, Guthrie, Henderson & Hill	1981 1976, 1984	USA	These initiatives implemented and evaluated an intervention furnishing seventh-graders with the tools to resist pressure to smoke, parental smoking models and media messages glorifying smoking. Since children consider the negative consequences of smoking to be at some distance, the intervention also stressed the immediate physiological effects of smoking.	From the results, researchers discovered that few students had ever even considered smoking, a finding that redressed erroneous norms that encouraged young people to believe that all of their peers smoke. From this ongoing study, the finding has been that students exposed to the prevention intervention were less likely to become smokers than were those in the reference group.
Flynn, Solomon, Secker-Walker, Badger & Carpenter	1996	USA	This work considers a mass media anti-smoking initiative aimed at adolescent girls at heightened risk for smoking. Pupils were initially surveyed in grades 4–6 and annually over the subsequent four years. In the intervention group, students on entering grades 5–7 were subject to the four year media intervention and a school programme in two designated communities. In the control groups, students were only subject to the school programme.	Results reveal a 40% reduction in weekly smoking for those girls in grades 8–10 subject to the media and school interventions when compared with just the school programme. With smoking behaviour effects persisting through to grades 10–12, this suggests that mass media interventions targeting specific audience segments can decrease substance use behaviour in those segments.

Table 5.1 Summary of studies reviewed in Chapter 5 – *continued*

Author	Date	Location	Intervention	Outcome
Flynn, Worden, Secker-Walker, Badger, Geller & Costanza	1992	USA	This study sought to gauge the influence of a mass media intervention in furthering the efficacy of school cigarette anti-smoking programmes. Students in one pair of communities encountered media interventions and school programmes joined by common educational goals. Students in the matched pair of communities only encountered the school programme.	Results reveal significant decreases in self-reported smoking for the media plus school group. 'Weekly smoking' declined by 41%, 'cigarettes smoked yesterday' declined by 34% and 'cigarettes smoked over the past week' fell by 35%. Comparatively speaking, tobacco consumption patterns remained consistent for those outside of the intervention perimeter. According to the authors, these results illustrate that mass media interventions can effectively prevent smoking among adolescents providing that they are targeted and share educational objectives with school-based initiatives.
Gilchrist & Schinke	1986	USA	Both self-control and placebo sessions provided introductions and programme overviews, reviews of previous sessions and homework assignments. All subjects were exposed to films illustrating the physiological consequences of smoking and peer testimonials about the disadvantages of smoking. Subjects in the self-control condition were taught to identify stress and to use specific cognitive and behavioural techniques	Results suggest the relative efficacy of self-control skills in preventing smoking with early adolescents. More specifically, 15 months following the initial intervention, fewer self-control skills participants reported smoking one or more cigarettes in the preceding week in contrast with placebo and control condition subjects. Self-control skills – including self-instruction, self-reinforcement, problem-solving, and

Table 5.1 Summary of studies reviewed in Chapter 5 – *continued*

Author	Date	Location	Intervention	Outcome
			to counter negative feelings. Programme leaders modelled skill use and subjects practised skills in role plays and homework assignments. Subjects then learned communication, self-instruction, self-reinforcement, and problem solving skills. Leaders taught communication skills while subjects applied self-instruction and problem solving skills by working on group problem-solving exercises. All sessions in the placebo intervention addressed factual information and attitudes about smoking and health, with the goal being to reinforce subjects' attitudes toward smoking as a health risk.	communication skills – exhibited a positive effect with study subjects. By the post-test stage, self-control subjects and placebo participants were comparable in their health knowledge, intentions to smoke, and cigarette use. At a 15-month follow-up stage, self-control subjects indicated smoking fewer cigarettes than their placebo and control counterparts.
Holder, Gruenewald, Ponicki, Treno, Grube, Saltz, Voas, Reynolds, Davis, Sanchez, Gaumont & Roeper	2000	USA	The study format was a longitudinal recurrent time series of matched interventions in three communities over the course of four years. The interventions pursued five objectives: 1) fomenting community mobilisation; 2) ensuring responsible beverage service; 3) curbing underage drinking by limiting alcohol accessibility; 4) heightening local enforcement of drink driving laws; and	According to the population surveys, self-reported alcohol consumption per drinking occasion declined 6% from 1.37 to 1.29 drinks. Those indicating 'having had too much to drink' declined 49% from 0.43 to 0.22 times over a six month interval. Self-reported driving when 'over the legal limit' also decreased by 51% (0.77 versus 0.38 times) over a six month interval in the intervention groups. Traffic data revealed that evening injury

Table 5.1   Summary of studies reviewed in Chapter 5 – *continued*

Author	Date	Location	Intervention	Outcome
			5) circumscribing access to alcohol through zoning. Results were gathered from monthly telephone surveys of randomly selected participants in the intervention and comparison sites, traffic data on motor vehicle crashes and emergency department surveys.	crashes declined by 10% and crashes in which the driver had been drinking declined by 6% among intervention participants. Further, assault injuries observed in emergency departments declined by 43% in the intervention communities while all hospitalized assault injuries declined by 2%. From this, the authors conclude that a coordinated, comprehensive, community-based intervention can decrease high-risk drinking and alcohol-related injuries from vehicle accidents and physical aggression.
Messer, Pierce, Zhu, Hartman, Al-Delaimy, Trinidad & Gilpin	2007	USA	This study conducted a comparative retroactive assessment of the influence exerted by tobacco-control programmes, the cost of cigarettes and social norms about tobacco on smoking incidence in three states.	Nationally, long-term smoking rates declined by 25% during the 1980s while averaging a decrease of 3.4% annually during the 1990s. Cessation increased across all age groups, most notably by more than 40% among smokers aged 20–34. For smokers less than 50 years old, higher cigarette prices were correlated with higher quitting rates. Overall, comprehensive tobacco-control programmes exhibited a greater association with cessation success than did high cigarette prices alone, although both effects were confined to younger adults.

Table 5.1 Summary of studies reviewed in Chapter 5 – *continued*

Author	Date	Location	Intervention	Outcome
Moore, Roberts & Tudor-Smith	2001	UK	Survey responses were collected from teachers and students aged 15–16 years at 55 secondary schools in Wales in order to determine self-reported smoking behaviour. Participant responses were complimented by data gathered on the content and enforcement of school smoking policies.	Prevalence of both daily and weekly smoking was lower in schools where student smoking restrictions enjoyed blanket enforcement, with both daily and weekly smoking being inversely related to the strength of smoking policy provision. Schools that actively enforced pupil smoking policies exhibited a significantly smaller incidence of daily and weekly student smoking. Results suggested an association between policy strength, policy enforcement and smoking prevalence among pupils. Findings support the wider introduction of actively enforced comprehensive smoking policies in secondary schools.
Murray, Wolfson, Blaine, Wagenaar & Hennrikus	1998	USA	Participating communities enlisted in a 32-month community-organising initiative to mobilise citizens and engage the community in such activities as modifying ordinances, changing merchant policies and practices and tackling enforcement responses to reduce youth access to tobacco. Results were determined from before-and-after student survey responses and from attempts to purchase cigarettes in all retail outlets in participating communities.	Not only did participating communities authorise a comprehensive youth access ordinance, but increases in adolescent daily smoking in participating communities were tempered relative to control communities. Moreover, while successful cigarette purchases modestly decreased in participating communities during the study period, this difference was not statistically significant. The study suggests that policies devised to diminish youth access to tobacco can have a significant effect on adolescent smoking rates.

6
Embedding Public Health Policy in the Social Context: Sexual Behaviour and Perceptions of Risk

Zoë Slote Morris and Sandra Dawson

Introduction

Public health is directed towards improving the health of populations, rather than treating the diseases of individuals. Current English policy is set out in *Choosing Health: Making Healthier Choices Easier* (Department of Health, 2004) and focuses on individual behaviour change premised on a particular understanding of risk. A risk is defined by the World Health Organisation (2002) as 'the probability of an adverse outcome, or a factor that raises this probability' and can be used to refer to an endogenous or exogenous factor which is associated with an elevated chance of disease. *Choosing Health* focuses on 'life-style' risks. These include smoking, alcohol use, obesity and sexual health, and it is on the latter that this chapter focuses.

Targets for improving sexual health are seen in terms of reducing the occurrence of teenage pregnancy and sexually transmitted infections (Department of Health, 2004). These goals run counter to the results of more permissive sexual mores and practice: declining age of first intercourse, increasing numbers of lifetime partners, increasing incidence of concurrent relationships and increasing prevalence in sexually transmitted infections (Cassell *et al.*, 2006a). It is estimated that one-third of people in England remain sexually active while they wait for their Genitourinary Medicine (GUM) appointment (Moore, 2006). At the end of 2005, approximately 63,500 adults were living with HIV in the UK, of which about 32 per cent were unaware of their infection and likely to continue to have sex (British Medical Association, 2007). Further, it is said that sexual health services are in crisis (BBC, 2005; Health Service Journal, 2006; Moore, 2006).

This chapter aims to provide insight into why current policy cannot be expected to make significant improvements in sexual health if it continues with a simplistic interpretation of risk, and to offer some examples of interventions which could be used to guide policymaking in future. Our focus is on interventions designed to address behaviour change and health promotion, rather than treatment and communicable disease control. Where possible, studies from the UK are cited, although there are few published examples of successful UK interventions.

Risk

A risk approach to public health assumes that risks are knowable and manageable and that people are risk averse (Green, 1997). Managing risk is framed accordingly as an individual's public duty (Petersen, 1997) and those who place themselves and others at risk (of infection for example) are seen as irrational and irresponsible (Crawford, 1977; Crawford, 1994). There are, however, several challenges to this model which are germane to future policy. How people interpret information about risks (lay understanding of health and illness), how individuals manage risk within wider social and cultural structures and relationships, whether people are risk averse, and how individuals react to risk (risk compensation and reactance) all potentially disrupt this simple choice equation.

Interpreting risk

Lay epidemiology, that is 'routine observations of cases of illness and death in personal networks and the public arena', is used by individuals to interpret official guidance around risk (Pill and Stott, 1982; Warwick *et al.*, 1988). It is common for people to have a good knowledge of the risks of disease, but to assume that the risks are relevant to other people and not themselves (Davison *et al.*, 1992).

Social identity frames individuals' interpretation of who is at risk. Warwick *et al.* (1988) found, in a sample of young people's beliefs in two communities in England, that AIDS was seen as something from which particular groups of people were at risk. 'They' were people who were not like 'us': – 'gay men, injecting drug users, prostitutes, and those who were "promiscuous"' (Warwick *et al.*, 1988). Young gay men who do not practice safe sex often associate AIDS with older men and thus believe themselves to not be at risk (Crossley, 2004). Many studies describe men who engage in homosexual acts but who do not identify as homosexual, and therefore do not necessarily see themselves as 'at risk' (Warwick *et al.*, 1988). People we know are generally seen as safer sexual partners (Lear, 1995), as are those who look 'safe' and 'clean' (Marston and King, 2006).

Roberts and Kennedy (2006), citing Haglund (2003), note that some people who engage in sexual activity other than vaginal sex consider themselves to be abstinent, and are therefore unlikely to interpret risks as policymakers plan. Individuals' self-assessed risks are often lower than the assessments of professionals (Ward *et al.*, 2005b; Roberts and Kennedy, 2006).

Managing risk

It does not follow that understanding risk will lead to the management of risk. There are a number of aspects to this.

In assessing personal risk, individuals take account of a range of determinants, including some that are seen to fall outside the control of individuals (East, 2002), such as chance and luck (Rhodes and Cusick, 2002; Warwick et al., 1988). Rhodes and Cusick's (2002) UK study of how people with the HIV virus continued to engage in unprotected sex knowing that it put others at risk found that people explained their behaviour in a number of ways which involved denying agency and responsibility for managing risk: being drunk, overcome with desire, or being unable to stop condoms breaking.

Some threats to health do lie beyond the control of individuals and cannot therefore be managed. Blanc's (2001) review of power in sexual relationships uncovers violence and coercion, lack of choice about when, how and why women have sex, and a lack of control over how women might chose to use contraceptives. Much of the global incidence of STI is associated with economic dependency (Fenton, 2004) and sex work. Blanc's review relates mostly to the developing world but violence and coercion are features in UK society.[1] Moreover, Rhodes and Cusick (2000) report how some of their sample of HIV positive people in England used their 'powerlessness' as a justification for practicing unsafe sex.

An individual's capacity to manage risk also depends on the social norms and expectations which restrict their choices (Boyer et al., 2000; Crosby et al., 2000; Doljanac and Zimmerman, 1998; Millstein and Moscicki, 1995). The 'double-standard' is a recurring theme in studies undertaken in many countries (Warwick et al., 1988), in which men are still expected to engage in lots of sex with a number of partners whereas the same behaviour in women earns them a 'reputation' (Marston and King, 2006). Male desires are seen as 'unstoppable' which women are obliged to meet (Mitchell and Wellings, 1998; Rhodes and Cusick, 2002; Shoveller et al., 2004). These beliefs influence subsequent behaviour (Browne and Minichiello, 1994). Gavey et al.'s (2001) sample of women in New Zealand admitted to being so deeply imbued with these beliefs that they continued to engage in sex even when they knew they did not want to.

Sexual health is also influenced by the location of encounters. Stanley (2005) compared the experiences of young people in a seaside town and a rural area, and found that the carnival atmosphere of the seaside, with its transient communities and focus on 'having a good time', made everyday drinking and casual, unprotected sex commonplace. Roberts and Kennedy (2006) make a similar point about US college students, who see 'partying' as an essential feature of college life.

Condoms are not neutral technologies, but are attached to social meanings, most of which are negative (Roberts and Kennedy 2006; Warwick *et al.*, 1988), and vary by context. There is some evidence that women appear reluctant to buy or introduce condom use because it marks them off as 'slags' (Stanley, 2005; Rhodes and Cusick, 2002). Condom use is predicted by the nature and length of a relationship (Aalsma *et al.*, 2006) and whether the partner is a friend or is unknown. Condom use is perceived to represent a lack of trust within relationships (Flowers *et al.*, 1997; Marston and King, 2006; Rhodes and Cusick, 2002). Condoms are also associated with diminished sexual pleasure, and therefore rejected from use (Gavey *et al.*, 2001; Rhodes and Cusick, 2002; Roberts and Kennedy, 2006).

A final challenge in managing risk is that, within this social context, condom use depends on negotiation (Wight, 1992). Rhodes and Cusick found that not asking about HIV status was taken as tacit agreement not to use condoms (2002). Understandings need to be established through communication, and research shows how little partners talk about sex (Aggleton *et al.*, 1999; Blanc, 2001). Indeed, Marston and King (2006) note how people's sexual partners will often be deliberately ambiguous. Mitchell and Wellings (1998) study of young people in England who had sex 'out of the blue' did so in silence and did not talk about it afterwards either. There are a number of explanations for this. Lack of communication before intercourse serves to conceal 'a past' (important for women in particular), to protect self-esteem (Wight, 1992) and to help manage rejection (Marston and King, 2006). Adelman (1992) has also argued that discussion of condom use brings in the 'mundane' which is resisted in the context of 'passion'. When sex follows alcohol or drug use, discussion and negotiation are more difficult (Lear, 1995; Rhodes and Cusick, 2002).

Risk aversion

A number of factors undermine the assumption that individuals are risk averse. Risk-taking can be viewed positively (Mitchell and Wellings, 1998). Richens *et al.* (2000) argue that condom use has limited effect at the population level as those people who use them are more likely to be risk averse and therefore add little to the overall risk. Different people value different things, so defining and evaluating risk is not an objective function. Rhodes and Cusick (2002) found that some HIV positive respondents questioned the 'worth of death avoidance' in deciding not to practice safe sex. They also describe how HIV positive people still choose to have unprotected sex as they identify a trade-off between 'relationship safety' and 'viral danger' amongst people who know they are HIV positive. Love and intimacy are seen as essential aspects of relationship survival and these are symbolised through unprotected sex worth the risk of infection (Smith *et al.*, 1997; Gavey *et al.*, 2001; Crossley, 2001, 2004; Rhodes and Cusick, 2002).

Reactance

There is evidence to suggest that people will embrace risky behaviour to maintain independence. For example, Crossley (2004) uses the concept of reactance (Brehm, 1966) to explain why some gay men continue to engage in unprotected anal intercourse (UAI), knowing that it puts them at risk of disease. Crossley, suggesting that historically 'transgression' and 'resistance' has defined gay culture, argues that rebellion and resistance continue to be dominant cultural values, which manifest themselves through risky sexual practices now that sex between men has become more widely accepted. Because unprotected sex is forbidden it is also appealing (Billig, 1999), and sexual practices may become a part of individuals' identity (Halkitis and Parsons, 2003; Parsons and Bimbi, 2007). Central to reactance is resisting being told what to do (Gough and Conner, 2006). It involves trading greater independence, even if only perceived independence, for worse health (Whitehead and Russell, 2004; Fogarty and Youngs, 2000; Fogarty, 1997) and an expression of choice, independence and self-reliance.

Risk compensation

A final challenge to this simple model of risk calculation is that of risk compensation, where individuals behave in ways that are different but do not reduce overall risk. For example, it has been suggested that seat belt use increases risky driving (Lardelli-Claret *et al.*, 2003). Cassell *et al.* (2006b) have suggested that a focus on the technological aspects of HIV infection reduces people's perception of risk and thus discourages them from adopting preventive behaviours. A common reason given for engaging in risky sex by gay men in England is their view of AIDS not as a life-threatening disease, but a chronic condition to be managed (Crossley, 2004; Flowers *et al.*, 1997).

Whilst it is well known that condom use can contribute to reducing the transmission of HIV, Cassell *et al.* (2006b) also argue that the perception of condom use reducing risk leads to inconsistent use, and may even encourage a greater number of partners (Richens *et al.*, 2000). For example, evidence from the National Survey of Sexual Attitudes and Lifestyles (Johnson *et al.*, 2001) suggest that, whilst more people were using condoms in 2000 than in 1990, this offset increases in the number of sexual partners, as well as increases in risky practices.

Contextualising risk

A number of factors are associated with sexual risks, therefore; the blame can seldom be laid on individuals' ignorance alone. DiClemente *et al.* (2005) call for a 'socioecological' response to prevention and control of the STIs which takes account of the extra-individual factors that predict risk – relationships, community and society.

Whilst these can be seen as a series of concentric circles with the individual at the centre, they overlap and feedback from one another; poverty is both a societal, community and individual property. For example, Shoveller *et al.* (2004) argue that individuals' 'choices' have to be considered in the context of the interrelationships between social structures (for example, gender, social class and geographical location) and their individual agency. The assertiveness required for women to negotiate condom use is at odds with received notions of femininity, and this conflict may reduce their ability to manage their individual risk (Gavey *et al.*, 2001). Understanding the individual within their social context is therefore essential to understanding individual risk management. This realisation can be helpful in designing more effective policy in future.

Intervention types

A number of approaches are available to policymakers to help individuals change their behaviour. Individual interventions seek to modify individual behaviour in a one-to-one setting, often between a professional and client. Group level interventions aim to modify individual behaviour in a group setting, and can attempt to secure additional benefits through group support and peer influence. Community interventions hope to alter community norms, as well as individual behaviours (Herbst *et al.*, 2007). They are typically found to be more successful and achieve wider impact and sustainability (Herbst *et al.*, 2007; van Empelen *et al.*, 2003).

Interventions can also include an 'empowerment' element, and these approaches are most commonly focused at the community level. 'A community empowerment intervention seeks to effect community-wide change in health-related behaviour by organising communities to define their health problems, to identify the determinants of those problems, and to engage in effective individual and collective action to change those determinants' (Beeker *et al.*, 1998). These interventions normally aim to change attitudes by encouraging participants to recognise that their individual beliefs are part of wider circumstances, and to develop the skills to challenge existing structures (Beeker *et al.*, 1998; Wallerstein and Sanchezmerki, 1994).

Structural interventions are those 'that work by altering the context in which health is produced or reproduced...[and which] locate the source of public-health problems in factors in the social, economic and political environments that shape and constrain individual, community, and societal health outcomes' (Rhodes *et al.*, 2005). Structural interventions are distal, or 'upstream' (Bonell *et al.*, 2006). So-called 'broad-school' definitions include interventions that strive for macro-social changes – those that redistribute power and resources, and alter major institutions, legal systems and policies – and meso-social change – changes to social networks, community norms, local health systems and local physical environments. In this there is some overlap within community approaches. 'Narrow-school' interventions, on the other hand, address only macro-social change.

In practice, most interventions which address structural issues take a broad-school approach. They recognise that individual risk cannot be uncoupled from social and political context – it is 'extra-individual' – but that individuals can be supported to change. Fenton (2004), for example, argues the importance of addressing poverty in countering AIDS, but counsels against taking a 'fatalistic attitude in which little can be done until some utopian poverty-free ideal can be achieved'. The figure featured in Chapter 3 (p. 60) illustrates these individual/social interactions.

The paper now turns to an examination of policy interventions which aim, in various ways, to change individual behaviour either as individuals or as collections of individuals in communities.

Policy interventions

Interventions aimed at the reinterpretation of risk

Where policy interventions aim to tackle issues around the interpretation of sexual risk, they need to address individuals' tendency to see risk as something germane to 'others' rather than 'themselves' and to 'this practice' rather than 'that person'. Thus, for example, different approaches to reduce their risks may need to be made to the same men, depending on whether the focus is on their risky sexual behaviour with women or men (Amirkhanian *et al.*, 2001).

One solution is to attach healthy behaviours to practices with positive meanings. For example, Philpott (2006) describe how (male) transsexual sex workers in India use female condoms to 'express their femininity'. Another solution is to design messages with which individuals can identify and which they can internalise. In practice, designing messages that influence behaviour requires understanding the users and tailoring information for them (Ellis and Grey, 2004; Philpott *et al.*, 2006; Rietmeijer, 2006; Wellings *et al.*, 2006; Ward *et al.*, 2005a). For example, Scholes *et al.* (2003) describe an American project using a computer-generated self-help magazine which was individually tailored based on risk survey responses. Women participating in the study reported higher rates of condom use, more comfort with talking about and carrying condoms and higher self-efficacy.

Many examples of successful interventions in the US undertook considerable consultation with target audiences when putting together the mass media element of their programme (Kegeles *et al.*, 1996; Ross *et al.*, 2004; Sikkema, 2005) to ensure messages were salient to their intended audience. In the successful Mpowerment programme, a community-based HIV prevention intervention for gay men in the US, a number of media channels were used, and it was found that men with different risk profiles responded to different media and messages (Kegeles *et al.*, 1999).

Improving individuals' ability to interpret risk in the sexual health context also means challenging their assumptions of who is 'safe'. Earlier attempts have included informational approaches, but we have not been able to find convincing evidence of these being effective. Policy strategies that require individuals to make judgements about the risk that others pose are likely to be less successful than those which seek to diffuse new practices across wider communities. Given that alcohol and drug use are associated with greater sexual risk-taking (Stanley, 2005), interventions designed to reduce intoxication may also help individuals reinterpret their approach to risk (Cohen *et al.*, 2006).

Managing risk

Information to help individuals manage risk is often conveyed through media campaigns. Evidence suggests that mass media campaigns have limited effect (Hausser and Michaud, 1994), but can be useful in providing a supportive social environment for individual behaviour change. To be effective, information must be tailored and targeted, clear and basic (Ellis and Grey, 2004; Wellings *et al.*, 2006), and aimed specifically at reducing risk (Robin *et al.*, 2004). For example, Traeen (1992) explains the failure of a Norwegian campaign to promote condom use as a result of its message being about sex and love, rather than HIV.

In addition to providing them with sufficient levels of information, there are four basic challenges involved in helping individuals to manage risk. First, individuals need to be persuaded that they can manage risk. Second, ways need to be found to support those who cannot manage risk on their own. Third, social norms around sex, and condom use in particular, need to be addressed. Fourth, communication needs to be improved. The majority of interventions attempt to address the final two challenges, though the first two are equally critical and all four will now be discussed.

First, managing risk has to appear feasible if it is not to be dismissed out of hand. Campaigns are also more likely to succeed in supporting individual behaviour change when the behaviour change is about risk reduction and not abstinence (Ellis and Grey, 2004). Philpott *et al.* (2006) argue that 'safe sex' and 'pleasurable sex' appear in opposition in health promotion, and if pleasure is the primary driving force behind engaging in sexual activity, materials need to reflect this. The Mpowerment programme ran group discussions designed to eroticise 'safe sex' (Kegeles *et al.*, 1996).

Interventions which go beyond information and develop skills also appear to help individuals manage risk. A number of US HIV interventions that produced positive behaviour changes sought to develop communication, negotiation and assertiveness skills (Cohen *et al.*, 1991, 1992; Gomez *et al.*, 1999; Kelly *et al.*, 1989; Sikkema, 2005; Jemmott *et al.*, 1992), condom use skills (DiClemente and Wingood, 1995; Kegeles *et al.*, 1996) and relationship skills (Kelly *et al.*, 1989; Sikkema, 2005). The opportunity to rehearse skills and role play are a common feature of effective interventions (Boyer *et al.*, 1997; Cohen *et al.*, 2002; Jemmott *et al.*, 1992; Kelly *et al.*, 1994).

For example, in the Mpowerment project, participants were provided with the opportunity to practice condom use on models, and to come up with strategies designed to orchestrate safer sex (Kegeles *et al.*, 1996). The men were also given opportunities to practice their sexual negotiation skills in role plays. Between baseline and follow-up the proportion of men who engaged in unprotected sex fell overall, with a greater reduction in unprotected sex with boyfriends rather than casual partners – where the majority of unprotected sex takes place.

Successful interventions also seek to increase self-efficacy and resilience (Gomez *et al.*, 1999; Rietmeijer, 2006; Robin *et al.*, 2004), as such interventions can help challenge people's fatalism and perceived lack of agency. Gomez *et al.* (1999) describe a US intervention designed to reduce a group of Latina women's vulnerability to HIV infection. Based around a grass-roots community group, one element of the programme was a series of peer-supported programmes to increase their self-esteem. At intake 42 per cent of the women reported having used a condom at some time, and 21 per cent in the last encounter. At follow-up six months later, these figures were 48 per cent and 26 per cent respectively. Statistically significant improvements were shown to their sexual communication comfort, traditional gender roles and sexual comfort.

RESPECT, a US intervention aimed at increasing safe-sex, was designed to increase self-efficacy, as well as change social norms to promote condom use, reduce numbers of partners, and increase discussion of HIV/STI testing with partners (Rietmeijer, 2006). One evaluation comparing RESPECT with two traditional 'didactic' programmes found significant differences (Kamb *et al.*, 1998). At three and six month follow-up those in the RESPECT intervention group reported significantly higher condom use, and at 12 months significantly lower incidence of STI.

Loss of agency through drug and alcohol use is also relevant to individuals' abilities to manage risk. A number of US programmes aimed at improving individual sexual decisionmaking attempt to reduce participants' rates of having sex whilst intoxicated (Ross *et al.*, 2004), but this relies on the individual to change several behaviours. Strategies that attempt to reduce levels of intoxication in society may prove more fruitful.

A second challenge for interventions to reduce risk is when individuals cannot manage risk, perhaps as a result of violence, coercion, or economic dependence. Across the world economic disadvantage is associated with greater sexual risk, including commercial sex work, higher rates of STIs (Parker *et al.*, 2000; Fenton, 2004), and higher levels of sexual abuse (Blanc, 2001; Petersen *et al.*, 2005). Economic and gender disadvantage overlap. Addressing these issues is likely to rely on more structural policy interventions which address these broad issues. Examples of policy interventions in this domain are mainly from the developing world.

Parker *et al.* (2000) cite a Kenyan project which gave female commercial sex workers a business start-up fund (mostly used to sell fruit and vegetables or crafts) and business training, alongside education on safe-sex. Participants reported a decline in their number of sexual partners, increased condom use, and an increase in wellbeing associated with no longer having to sell sex.

Pronyk (2006) describes a women's microfinance project in South Africa, coupled with skills-based gender and HIV training, aimed at reducing intimate-partner violence and improving sexual health. However, early evaluations found a reduction in reported partner violence, but little effect on sexual behaviour. Petersen's (2005) work on intimate-partner violence in South Africa shows how deep seated attitudes are, and how unlikely they are to be changed by individual women whatever their levels of personal self-efficacy.

A third challenge to managing risk are the social norms that surround sex. These include gender differences in the social expectations around numbers of partners and the importance of male pleasure, and condom use. Changing community norms to reduce risky behaviour and promote healthier behaviour is an important aspect of interventions which appear to have achieved behaviour change (Ellis and Grey, 2004; Johnson *et al.*, 2006; Robin *et al.*, 2004; Wellings *et al.*, 2006).

Many of the programmes discussed above attempt to change attitudes, as well as build self-efficacy and develop skills (Gomez *et al.*, 1999; Kegeles *et al.*, 1999). For example, the US youth programme *Be Proud! Be Responsible!* challenges beliefs which influence risky behaviour. The programme focused on hedonism (including the role of condoms in diminishing pleasure) and partner-reaction belief (that partners will respond negatively to condom use). At three-month follow-up the intervention groups reported lower frequency of sex, reduced number of partners, reduced number of female partners they believed to have other male partners, increased condom use, and reduced anal sex (Jemmott *et al.*, 1992).

The success of these programmes depends on their attempts to alter community values rather than just individuals. Many effective interventions make a virtue of social pressure and have used social networks to disseminate messages which attempt to change norms (Kegeles *et al.*, 1999; Kegeles *et al.*, 1996; Kelly *et al.*, 2006; Parkhurst and Lush, 2004; Santelli *et al.*, 1995; Sikkema, 2005). Parkhurst and Lush (2004) attribute a significant part of Uganda's success in managing HIV prevention to the use of existing social networks and organisations to disseminate messages, working with community networks including churches and community groups, in which each group was forced to develop their own particular response. One cohort study suggests a decline in men reporting two or more concurrent partners from 43 per cent to 12 per cent between 1987 and 1992 (Konde-Lule, 1993, 1995). Stoneburner and Low-Beer (2004) conclude that 'despite limited resources, Uganda has shown a 70 per cent decline in HIV prevalence since the early 1990s, linked to a 60 per cent reduction in casual sex'.

In Uganda the community approach came largely out of necessity, in the absence of a public health and health care infrastructure (Parkhurst and Lush, 2004), but such an approach can also be planned into an intervention. The *Mpowerment* (Kegeles *et al.*, 1996; Kegeles *et al.*, 1999) project materials and activities were designed by participants in the project, and a peer network approach was used to provide outreach. Kegeles *et al.* (1999) put some of the success of the project down to the 'ownership' by the target group and their desire for a sense of community. Policymakers will also be pleased to hear that using peer outreach workers also made the project economical to run.

Kelly *et al.* (2006) report a study using a social network intervention to reach a socially marginalised, but high risk, group of Roma men in Bulgaria. The intervention used social network leaders as trained advisors and advocates for members of their peer group. Members of 55 social networks were recruited to the study, which included a control group who received standard individual counselling from a professional. At 12 month follow-up the intervention group showed significantly higher knowledge of AIDS, more positive attitudes to condom use and more intention to reduce risks. Moreover, STIs had been treated at baseline, and at the follow-up the intervention groups showed lower rates of infection of gonorrhoea and syphilis, though no difference in chlamydia. Kelly *et al.* attribute the positive outcomes of the study to the use of the social network design in a community where distrust of outside authorities was high, and where advice and information from social leaders was considered to carry more weight.

Fourth, communication and relationship skills can assist individuals to communicate with their sexual partners, and to challenge social norms. This can be achieved through role play, by assertiveness training and by developing negotiation skills. Better still, however, would be interventions which change community norms and behaviours, and thus place less demand on an individual's ability to communicate and negotiate around norms which do not support safe sexual behaviour.

Intervention responses to risk aversion, reactance and risk compensation

The majority of interventions address some aspects of risk management, but do not always deal well with risk aversion, reactance, or risk compensation.

For example, risk compensation can start to be addressed through the provision of information which recasts AIDS as more than a chronic condition with a technical solution, or that reinforces the message of limiting the numbers of sexual partners people have. The provision of any information seems more likely to succeed where it developed following the principles set out above, such as being tailored, targeted, and based on deep understanding of the intended audience. To be successful, messages intended for individuals resistant to being told what to do need to present new behaviours as reflecting individual choice and independence. Peer work seems particularly pertinent in the context of reactance.

Community interventions which change social attitudes seem a hopeful route forward. In the context of risk aversion, the perceived trade-off between using condoms to protect against disease and not using condoms to preserve trust and intimacy can only be addressed by attaching new meanings to condom use, such as that loving someone means protecting them from disease. Unsafe sex might become less attractive if finding partners willing to engage in unprotected sex became more difficult because of wider attitudes and expectations, that is if interventions are successful in shifting social norms and practices at the community level.

One aspect of risk aversion relates to death avoidance. It is plausible that structural interventions that improve individuals' overall wellbeing could thereby encourage people to take fewer risks, as well as giving them the means to do so. Ross *et al.* (2004) report how a high risk African-American community in Houston, Texas, attributed risky sexual practices to disadvantage, lack of recreational opportunity, boredom and the related substance abuse.

One interesting feature of the Mpowerment project was that it understood the importance of the social for the client groups, and recognised that few appropriate social opportunities existed in the communities (Eugene, Oregon and Santa Barbara, California). It therefore created new social opportunities, setting up a drop-in centre and sponsoring a number of activities from dances to hikes to which participants were invited to bring friends. By this means the project was able to attract young gay men to places where they could take part in the project. It provided a focus point for the educational aspects of the programme, and also gave greater scope for capturing the potential of peer influence.

Policy may be most successful when it is able to change behaviour without requiring individuals to calculate risk or choose alternative actions. Manipulation of the built environment is also a potential tool for policymakers seeking to change norms and individual behaviour. For example, Blake *et al.* (2003) noted that young people are more likely to have used condoms in their most recent sexual encounter where condoms are available in schools (Furstenberg, Jr. *et al.*, 1997; Guttmacher *et al.*, 1997).

Legal interventions can also be used to attempt behaviour change, and promote health. Parker *et al.* (2000) describe the success of the 100% Condom Program in Thailand. The state supplied condoms free of charge to sex establishments, even though condoms are illegal. If clients refuse to use a condom, services are withheld. The policy is enforced through local monitoring and sanctions on providers.

The success of such an approach depends on all sex workers complying, and the positive results from Thailand are contrasted with a similar approach in Bombay where workers and madams have been more concerned about losing business than ensuring condom-use (Bhave *et al.*, 1995). Such an approach may not be the best lever for changing population behaviour in other countries therefore. In another context, there is little evidence in the UK that the legal age of consent deters sexual activity amongst young people below that age (Collier and Blake, 2006). Thus, policymakers will need to draw on a deep understanding of client groups and a range of policy tools to seek changes in sexual behaviour.

Conclusion

Supporting future sexual health appears to be a great, but important policy challenge (BMA, 2007). Whilst pursuing improvement policymakers find themselves in an unenviable situation of increasing rates in risky behaviour alongside inadequate treatment services.

Our focus has been on behaviour change, rather than controlling infection. Finding evidence of interventions that support individual behaviour change has been difficult. Moreover, for every example of an intervention that produced a positive effect, there are counter-examples of programmes that did not. Parkhurst and Lush (2004) note that 'many different approaches [to behaviour change interventions] have been shown to achieve some limited positive results, but none stands out as particularly effective'.

In future policymakers need not be paralysed by lack of evidence (Yach *et al.*, 2005). There are positive examples of interventions to be found in the literature, and there is a degree of consensus about what effective interventions should look like (Wellings *et al.*, 2006). One important feature of success appears to be that interventions are multifaceted. Many projects illustrate the importance of using a number of approaches simultaneously (Kegeles *et al.*, 1996; Kegeles *et al.*, 1999; Parkhurst and Lush, 2004; Ross *et al.*, 2004), as different people respond to different types of messages located in different places; and because changing norms at community level are essential to reinforcing and sustaining change at the individual level. Thus, for example, more positive attitudes to condom use can be translated into behaviour change more successfully if condoms are more easily available for use (Cohen *et al.*, 1991; Cohen *et al.*, 1992; Kegeles *et al.*, 1999; Ross *et al.*, 2004).

Successful interventions also engage with communities (Ward *et al.*, 2005a). This has a number of benefits, including providing insight into a particular community's beliefs, norms, expectations and barriers to change, but also providing an additional unpaid workforce who can engage in outreach activities. They also attempt to alter the physical environment in which the risk behaviour is performed in order to change incentive structures and to help take responsibility away from the individual.

Interventions should also attempt to shift social behaviours of communities by indirect means. For example, policies which aim to reduce alcohol use and drug use might prove fruitful ways forward as risky behaviours tend to cluster, and unprotected sex is often associated with intoxication. Policies designed to address socioeconomic and gender inequalities could also be expected to yield a decline in risky behaviours such as selling sex (Caceres, 2002). While it is plausible that interventions should thus aim to address the determinants of risk, there is little evidence of successful interventions which meet the rigourous evaluation standards of NICE (Ellis and Grey, 2004). Arguably this is because it is easier to develop interventions that increase the self-esteem of women and improve their comfort with talking about sex (Gomez *et al.*, 1999), than it is to alter the more general, deeply embedded constraints which force women into dependent or vulnerable roles (Jacob *et al.*, 2006; Petersen *et al.*, 2005). It may also mean the evaluation criteria are too narrow to reflect what public health interventions are trying to achieve.

Lack of data should not prevent attempts to address economic and gender inequalities in future as these factors are likely to take many years to change. Hitherto, the interventions most successful in changing individual behaviour have been guided by psychological theory (Ellis and Grey, 2004; Robin *et al.*, 2004; Wellings *et al.*, 2006), and thus a fruitful line of enquiry may be to design interventions to change societies around sociological theory.

While it is important to put existing data to good use, if social and political context is important, then one major concern must be the lack of evidence from the UK. Many of the studies reported on UK populations were not successful, including sex education in Scotland (Henderson *et al.*, 2007), and community-interventions targeted at gay men in Scotland (Flowers *et al.*, 2002) and male sex workers in England (Ziersch *et al.*, 2000).

It is not that risk cannot be calculated and managed, but that this cannot be done by individuals alone. Policies must be based on a knowledge of socially constructed and socially experienced lifestyles. We hope that our review of the evidence will contribute towards improving understanding of ways to conceive better, more effective policy in future. The evidence shows that some things work for some people some of the time, and that the key to success is likely to lie in combining a variety of focused interventions concurrently, designed around a good understanding of people within their social community context and led by them.

Note

1   The 2000 British Crime Survey reported that 0.9 per cent of women aged 16 to 59 said that they had been subject to sexual victimisation in the past year, most often by partners (Myhill and Allen, 2002).

References

M. C. Aalsma, J. D. Fortenberry, M. A. Sayegh and D. P. Orr, 'Family and Friend Closeness to Adolescent Sexual Partners in Relationship to Condom Use', *Journal of Adolescent Health*, 38 (2006), 173–8.

M. B. Adelman, 'Sustaining Passion: Eroticism and Safe-Sex Talk', *Archives of Sexual Behaviour*, 21 (1992), 481–94.

P. Aggleton, K. Rivers and S. Scott, *Use of the Female Condom: Gender Relations and Sexual Negotiation* (Geneva: UNAIDS, 1999).

Y. A. Amirkhanian, J. A. Kelly, A. V. Kirsanova, W. DiFranceisco, R. A. Khoursine, A. V. Semenov, V. N. Rozmanova, 'Patterns of HIV Risk Behavior in a Large Community Sample of Russian Men Who Have Sex with Men: An Emerging Epidemic', *AIDS*, 15 (2001), 407–12.

C. Beeker, C. Guenther-Grey and Raj, 'Community Empowerment Paradigm Drift and the Primary Prevention of HIV/Aids', *Social Science & Medicine*, 46 (1998), 831–42.

G. Bhave, C. P. Lindan, E. S. Hudes, S. Desai, U. Wagle, S. P. Tripathi and J. S. Mandel, 'Impact of an Intervention on HIV, Sexually-Transmitted Diseases, and Condom Use Among Sex Workers in Bombay, India', *AIDS*, 9 (1995), S21–S30.

M. Billig, *Freudian Repression: Conversation Creating the Unconscious* (Cambridge: Cambridge University Press, 1999).

S. M. Blake, R. Ledsky, C. Goodenow, R. Sawyer, D. Lohrmann and R. Windsor, 'Condom Availability Programs in Massachusetts High Schools: Relationships with Condom Use and Sexual Behavior', *American Journal of Public Health*, 93 (2003), 955–63.

A. K. Blanc, 'The Effect of Power in Sexual Relationships on Sexual and Reproductive Health: An Examination of the Evidence', *Studies in Family Planning*, 32 (2001), 189–213.

C. Bonell, J. Hargreaves, V. Strange, P. Pronyk and J. Porter, 'Should Structural Interventions Be Evaluated Using RCTs? The Case of HIV Prevention', *Social Science & Medicine*, 63 (2006), 1135–42.

C. B. Boyer, D. C. Barrett and T. A. Peterman, 'Sexually Transmitted Disease (STD) and HIV Risk in Heterosexual Adults Attending a Public STD Clinic: Evaluation of a Randomized Controlled Behavioral Risk-Reduction Intervention Trial', *AIDS*, 11 (1997), 359–67.

C. B. Boyer, M. Shafer, C. J. Wibbelsman, D. Seeberg, E. Teitle and N. Lovell, 'Associations of Sociodemographic, Psychosocial, and Behavioral Factors with Sexual Risk and Sexually Transmitted Diseases in Teen Clinic Patients', *Journal of Adolescent Health*, 27 (2000), 102–11.

J. W. Brehm, *A Theory of Psychological Reactance* (New York: Academic Press, 1966).

British Broadcasting Corporation, 'Britain in Sexual Health "Crisis"', http://news.bbc.co.uk/1/hi/programmes/panorama/4339264.stm, 14 October 2005.

British Medical Association, *Sexually Transmitted Infections: An Update from Board of Science*, January 2007, http://www.bma.org.uk/ap.nsf/Content/stiupd07, accessed 24 August 2007.

J. Browne and V. Minichiello, 'The Condom – Why More People Don't Put It On', *Sociology of Health & Illness*, 16 (1994), 229–51.

C. F. Caceres, 'HIV among Gay and Other Men Who Have Sex with Men in Latin America and the Caribbean: A Hidden Epidemic?' *AIDS*, 16 (2002), S23–S33.

J. A. Cassell, C. H. Mercer, L. Sutcliffe, I. Petersen, A. Islam, M. G. Brook, J. D. Ross, G. R. Kinghorn, I. Simms, G. Hughes, A. Majeed, J. M. Stephenson, A. M. Johnson and A. C. Hayward, 'Trends in Sexually Transmitted Infections in General Practice 1990–2000: Population Based Study Using Data from the UK General Practice Research Database', *British Medical Journal*, 332 (2006a), 332–4.

M. M. Cassell, D. T. Halperin, J. D. Shelton and D. Stanton, 'Risk Compensation: The Achilles' Heel Of Innovations in HIV Prevention?', *British Medical Journal*, 332 (2006b), 605–7.

D. Cohen, C. Dent and D. Mackinnon, 'Condom Skills Education and Sexually-Transmitted Disease Reinfection', *Journal of Sex Research*, 28 (1991), 139–44.

D. A. Cohen, D. P. Mackinnon, C. Dent, H. R. C. Mason and E. Sullivan, 'Group-Counselling at STD Clinics to Promote Use of Condoms', *Public Health Reports*, 107 (1992), 727–31.

D. A. Cohen, S. Y. Wu and T. A. Farley, 'Structural Interventions to Prevent HIV/ Sexually Transmitted Disease: Are They Cost-Effective for Women in the Southern United States?', *Sexually Transmitted Diseases*, 33 (2006), S46–S49.

J. Collier and H. Blake, 'Sexual and Reproductive Health in Pregnant Teenagers Presenting for Antenatal Care or for Termination', *Current Paediatrics*, 16 (2006), 211–15.

R. Crawford, 'You Are Dangerous to Your Health – Ideology and Politics of Victim Blaming', *International Journal of Health Services*, 7 (1977), 663–80.

R. Crawford, 'The Boundaries of the Self and the Unhealthy Other: Reflections on Health, Culture and Aids', *Social Science & Medicine*, 38 (1994), 1347–65.

R. A. Crosby, R. J. Ciclemente, G. M. Wingood, C. Sionean, B. Cobb and K. Harrington, 'Correlates of Unprotected Vaginal Sex among African American Female Teens: The Importance of Relationship Dynamics', *Archives of Pediatrics & Adolescent Medicine*, 154 (2000), 893–9.

M. L. Crossley, 'Making Sense of "Barebacking": Gay Men's Narratives, Unsafe Sex and the "Resistance Habitus"', *British Journal of Social Psychology*, 43 (2004), 225–44.

C. Davison, S. Frankel and G. D. Smith, 'The Limits of Life-Style: Reassessing Fatalism in the Popular Culture of Illness Prevention', *Social Science & Medicine*, 34 (1992), 675–85.

Department of Health, *Choosing Health: Making Healthier Choices Easier*, Cm 6374 (London: Department of Health, 2004).

R. J. DiClemente, L. F. Salazar, R. A. Crosby and S. L. Rosenthal, 'Prevention and Control of Sexually Transmitted Infections among Adolescents: The Importance of a Socio-Ecological Perspective – a Commentary', *Public Health*, 119 (2005), 825–36.

R. J. DiClemente and G. M. Wingood, 'A Randomized Controlled Trial of an HIV Sexual Risk-Reduction Intervention for Young African-American Women', *Journal of the American Medical Association*, 274 (1995), 1271–6.

R. F. Doljanac and M. A. Zimmerman, 'Psychosocial Factors and High-Risk Sexual Behaviour: Race Differences among Urban Adolescents', *Journal of Behavioral Medicine*, 21 (1998), 451–67.

L. East, 'Regenerating Health in Communities: Voices from the Inner City', *Critical Social Policy*, 22 (2002), 147–73.

S. Ellis and A. Grey, *Prevention of Sexually Transmitted Infections (STIs): A Review of Reviews into the Effectiveness of Non-Clinical Interventions* (London: Health Development Agency, 2004).

L. Fenton, 'Preventing HIV/AIDS through Poverty Reduction: The Only Sustainable Solution?', *Lancet*, 364 (2004), 1186–7.

P. Flowers, G. J. Hart, L. M. Williamson, J. S. Frankis and G. J. Der, 'Does Bar-Based, Peer-Led Sexual Health Promotion Have a Community-Level Effect Amongst Gay Men in Scotland?', *International Journal of STD & AIDS*, 13 (2002), 102–8.

P. Flowers, J. A. Smith, P. Sheeran and N. Beail, 'Health and Romance: Understanding Unprotected Sex in Relationships between Gay Men', *British Journal of Health Psychology*, 2 (1997), 73–86.

J. S. Fogarty, 'Reactance Theory and Patient Noncompliance', *Social Science & Medicine*, 45 (1997), 1277–88.

J. S. Fogarty and G. A. Youngs, 'Psychological Reactance as a Factor in Patient Noncompliance with Medication Taking: A Field Experiment', *Journal of Applied Social Psychology*, 30 (2000), 2365–91.

F. F. Furstenberg Jr, L. M. Geitz, J. O. Teitler and C. C. Weiss, 'Does Condom Availability Make a Difference? An Evaluation of Philadelphia's Health Resource Centers', *Family Planning Perspective*, 29 (1997), 123–7.

N. Gavey, K. Mcphillips and M. Doherty, '"If It's Not on, It's Not On" – or Is It? Discursive Constraints on Women's Condom Use', *Gender & Society*, 15 (2001), 917–34.

C. A. Gomez, M. Hernandez and B. Faigeles, 'Sex in the New World: An Empowerment Model for HIV Prevention in Latina Immigrant Women', *Health Education & Behavior*, 26 (1999), 200–12.

B. Gough and M. Conner, 'Barriers to Healthy Eating Amongst Men: A Qualitative Analysis', *Social Science & Medicine*, 62 (2006), 387–95.

J. Green, *Risk and Misfortune: The Social Construction of Accidents* (London: UCL Press, 1997).

S. Guttmacher, L. Lieberman, D. Ward, N. Freudenberg, A. Radosh and D. D. Jarlais, 'Condom Availability in New York City Public High Schools: Relationships to Condom Use and Sexual Behavior', *American Journal of Public Health*, 87 (1997), 1427–33.

K. Haglund, 'Sexually Abstinent African American Adolescent Females' Descriptions of Abstinence', *Journal of Nursing Scholarship*, 35 (2003), 231.

P. N. Halkitis and J. T. Parsons, 'Intentional Unsafe Sex (Barebacking) among HIV-Positive Gay Men Who Seek Sexual Partners on the Internet', *AIDS Care-Psychological and Socio-Medical Aspects of AIDS/HIV*, 15 (2003), 367–78.

D. Hausser P. A. Michaud, 'Does a Condom-Promoting Strategy (the Swiss-Stop-AIDS-Campaign) Modify Sexual-Behavior Among Adolescents', *Pediatrics*, 93 (1994), 580–5.

Health Service Journal, 'Sexual Health. Slow Rise on Access Target', *Health Service Journal*, 16 March 2006.

M. Henderson, D. Wight, G. M. Raab, C. Abraham, A. Parkes, S. Scott and G. Hart, 'Impact of a Theoretically Based Sex Education Programme (Share) Delivered by Teachers on NHS Registered Conceptions and Terminations: Final Results of Cluster Randomised Trial', *British Medical Journal*, 334 (2007), 133–6.

J. H. Herbst, C. Beeker, A. Mathew, T. Mcnally, W. F. Passin, L. S. Kay, N. Crepaz, C. M. Lyles, P. Briss, S. Chattopadhyay, R. L. Johnson, 'The Effectiveness of Individual-, Group-, and Community-Level HIV Behavioral Risk-Reduction Interventions for Adult Men Who Have Sex with Men: A Systematic Review', *American Journal of Preventive Medicine*, 32 (2007), S38–S67.

M. E. Jacob, S. Abraham, S. Surya, S. Minz, D. Singh, V. J. Abraham, J. Prasad, K. George, A. Kuruvilla and K. S. Jacob, 'A Community Health Programme in Rural Tamil Nadu, India: The Need for Gender Justice for Women', *Reproductive Health Matters*, 14 (2006), 101–8.

J. B. Jemmott, L. S. Jemmott and G. T. Fong, 'Reductions in HIV Risk-Associated Behaviors among Black Male Adolescents: Effects of an AIDS Prevention Initiative', *American Journal of Public Health*, 82 (1992), 372–7.

A. M. Johnson, C. H. Mercer, B. Erens, A. J. Copas, S. Mcmanus, K. Wellings, K. A. Fenton, C. Korovessis, W. Macdowall, K. Nanchahal, S. Purdon and J. Field, 'Sexual Behaviour in Britain: Partnerships, Practices, and HIV Risk Behaviours', *The Lancet*, 358 (2001), 1835–42.

W. D. Johnson, L. V. Hedges and R. M. Diaz, *Interventions to Modify Sexual Risk Behaviours for Preventing HIV Infection in Men Who Have Sex with Men* (Review) (London: Cochrane Collaboration/John Wiley & Sons Ltd, 2006).

M. L. Kamb, M. Fishbein, J. M. Douglas, F. Rhodes, J. Rogers, G. Bolan, J. Zenilman, T. Hoxworth, C. K. Malotte, M. Iatesta, C. Kent, A. Lentz, S. Graziano, R. H. Byers and T. A. Peterman, 'Efficacy of Risk-Reduction Counseling to Prevent Human Immunodeficiency Virus and Sexually Transmitted Diseases – a Randomized Controlled Trial', *Journal of the American Medical Association*, 280 (1998), 1161–7.

S. M. Kegeles, R. B. Hays and T. J. Coates, 'The Mpowerment Project: A Community-Level HIV Prevention Intervention for Young Gay Men', *American Journal of Public Health*, 86 (1996), 1129–36.

S. M. Kegeles, R. B. Hays, L. M. Pollack and T. J. Coates, 'Mobilizing Young Gay and Bisexual Men for HIV Prevention: A Two-Community Study', *AIDS*, 13 (1999), 1753–62.

J. A. Kelly, Y. A. Amirkhanian, E. Kabakchieva, S. Vassileva, T. L. Mcauliffe, W. J. DiFranceisco, R. Antonova, E. Petrova, B. Vassilev, R. A. Khoursine, B. Dimitrov, 'Prevention of HIV and Sexually Transmitted Diseases in High Risk Social Networks of Young Roma (Gypsy) Men in Bulgaria: Randomised Controlled Trial', *British Medical Journal*, 333 (2006), 1098–100.

J. A. Kelly, D. A. Murphy, C. D. Washington, T. S. Wilson, J. J. Koob, D. R. Davis, G. Ledezma and B. Davantes, 'The Effects of HIV AIDS Intervention Groups for High-Risk Women in Urban Clinics', *American Journal of Public Health*, 84 (1994), 1918–22.

J. A. Kelly, J. S. St Lawrence, H. V. Hood and T. L. Brasfield, 'Behavioral Intervention to Reduce AIDS Risk Activities', *Journal of Consulting and Clinical Psychology*, 57 (1989), 60–7.

J. K. Konde-Lule, 'The Social and Demographic Impact of AIDS in a Rural Ugandan Community: Results of a 5 Year Follow up Study, 1987–92', Population Association of Uganda Annual Conference (Kampala, Uganda, 1993).

J. K. Konde-Lule, 'The Declining HIV Serprevalence in Uganda: What Evidence?', *Health Transition Review*, 5 (1995), 27–33.

P. Lardelli-Claret, J. D. Luna-Del-Castillo, J. J. Jimenez-Moleon, M. Garcia-Martin, A. Bueno-Cavanillas and R. Galvez-Vargas, 'Risk Compensation Theory and Voluntary Helmet Use by Cyclists in Spain', *Injury Prevention*, 9 (2003), 128–32.

D. Lear, 'Sexual Communication in the Age of AIDS: The Construction of Risk and Trust among Young Adults', *Social Science & Medicine*, 41 (1995), 1311–23.

C. Marston and E. King, 'Factors That Shape Young People's Sexual Behaviour: A Systematic Review', *Lancet*, 368 (2006), 1581–6.

S. G. Millstein and A. Moscicki, 'Sexually Transmitted Disease in Female Adolescents: Effects of Psychosocial Factors and High Risk Behaviors', *Journal of Adolescent Health*, 17 (1995), 83–90.

K. Mitchell and K. Wellings, 'First Sexual Intercourse: Anticipation and Communication. Interviews with Young People in England', *Journal of Adolescence*, 21 (1998), 717–26.

A. Moore, 'Sexual Health. Watford Memo Says Meeting 48-Hour Target Is an Impossibility. Service "Collapse" Warning', *Health Service Journal*, 13 July 2006, 8.

A. Myhill and J. Allen, *Rape and Sexual Assault of Women: the Extent and Nature of the Problem* (London: Home Office, 2002).

R. G. Parker, D. Easton and C. H. Klein, 'Structural Barriers and Facilitators in HIV Prevention: A Review of International Research', *AIDS*, 14 (2000), S22–S32.

J. O. Parkhurst and L. Lush, 'The Political Environment of HIV: Lessons from a Comparison of Uganda and South Africa', *Social Science & Medicine*, 59 (2004), 1913–24.

J. T. Parsons and D. S. Bimbi, 'Intentional Unprotected Anal Intercourse among Men Who Have Sex with Men: Barebacking – from Behavior to Identity', *AIDS and Behavior*, 11 (2007), 277–87.

I. Petersen, A. Bhana and M. Mckay, 'Sexual Violence and Youth in South Africa: The Need for Community-Based Prevention Interventions', *Child Abuse & Neglect*, 29 (2005), 1233–48.

A. Petersen, *Risk, Governance and the New Public Health* (London: Routledge, 1997).

A. Philpott, W. Knerr and V. Boydell, 'Pleasure and Prevention: When Good Sex Is Safer Sex', *Reproductive Health Matters*, 14 (2006), 23–31.

R. Pill and N. C. Stott, 'Concepts of Illness Causation and Responsibility: Some Preliminary Data from a Sample of Working Class Mothers', *Social Science & Medicine*, 16 (1982), 43–52.

P. M. Pronyk, J. R. Hargreaves, J. C. Kim, L. A. Morison, G. Phetla, C. Watts, J. Busza and J. D. H. Porter, 'Effect of a Structural Intervention for the Prevention of Intimate-Partner Violence and HIV in Rural South Africa: A Cluster Randomised Trial', *The Lancet*, 368 (2006), 1973–83.

T. Rhodes and L. Cusick, 'Love and Intimacy in Relationship Risk Management: HIV Positive People and Their Sexual Partners', *Sociology of Health & Illness*, 22 (2000), 1–26.

T. Rhodes and L. Cusick, 'Accounting for Unprotected Sex: Stories of Agency and Acceptability', *Social Science & Medicine*, 55 (2002), 211–26.

T. Rhodes, M. Singer, P. Bourgois, S. R. Friedman and S. A. Strathdee, 'The Social Structural Production of HIV Risk among Injecting Drug Users', *Social Science & Medicine*, 61 (2005), 1026–44.

J. Richens, J. Imrie and A. Copas, 'Condoms and Seat Belts: The Parallels and the Lessons', *The Lancet*, 355 (2000), 400–3.

C. A. Rietmeijer, 'Risk Reduction Counselling for Prevention of Sexually Transmitted Infections: How It Works and How to Make It Work', *Sexually Transmitted Infections*, 83 (2006), 2–9.

S. T. Roberts and B. L. Kennedy, 'Why Are Young College Women Not Using Condoms? Their Perceived Risk, Drug Use, and Developmental Vulnerability May Provide Important Clues to Sexual Risk', *Archives of Psychiatric Nursing*, (2006) 20, 32–40.

L. Robin, P. Dittus, D. Whitaker, R. Crosby, K. Ethier, J. Mezoff, P. H. Ches, K. Miller and K. Pappas-Deluca, 'Behavioral Interventions to Reduce Incidence of HIV, STD, and Pregnancy among Adolescents: A Decade in Review', *Journal of Adolescent Health*, 34 (2004), 3–26.

M. W. Ross, N. S. Chatterjee and L. Leonard, 'A Community Level Syphilis Prevention Programme: Outcome Data from a Controlled Trial', *Sexually Transmitted Infections*, 80 (2004), 100–4.

J. S. Santelli, D. D. Celentano, C. Rozsenich, A. D. Crump, M. V. Davis, M. Polacsek, M. Augustyn, J. Rolf, A. L. McAlister and L. Burwell, 'Interim Outcomes for a Community-Based Program to Prevent Perinatal HIV Transmission', *AIDS Education and Prevention*, 7 (1995), 210–20.

D. Scholes, C. M. McBride, L. Grothaus, D. Civic, L. E. Ichikawa, L. J. Fish and K. S. H. Yarnall, 'A Tailored Minimal Self-Help Intervention to Promote Condom Use in Young Women: Results from a Randomized Trial', *AIDS*, 17 (2003), 1547–56.

J. A. Shoveller, J. L. Johnson, D. B. Langille and T. Mitchell, 'Socio-Cultural Influences on Young People's Sexual Development', *Social Science & Medicine*, 59 (2004), 445–65.

K. J. Sikkema, 'HIV Prevention among Women in Low-Income Housing Developments: Issues and Intervention Outcomes in a Place-Based Randomized Controlled Trial', *Annals of the American Academy of Political and Social Science*, 599 (2005), 52–70.

J. Smith, P. Flowers and M. Osborn, *Interpretative Phenomenological Analysis and the Psychology of Health and Illness* (London: Routledge, 1997).

N. Stanley, 'Thrills and Spills: Young People's Sexual Behaviour and Attitudes in Seaside and Rural Areas', *Health, Risk & Society*, 7 (2005), 337–48.

R. L. Stoneburner and D. Low-Beer, 'Population-Level HIV Declines and Behavioral Risk Avoidance in Uganda', *Science*, 304 (2004), 714–18.

B. Traeen, 'Learning from Norwegian Experience – Attempts to Mobilize the Youth Culture to Fight the AIDS Epidemic', *AIDS Education and Prevention*, Suppl. S, FAL (1992), 43–56.

P. Van Empelen, G. Kok, N. M. C. Van Kesteren, B. Van Den Borne, A. E. R. Bos and H. P. Schaalma, 'Effective Methods to Change Sex-Risk among Drug Users: A Review of Psychosocial Interventions', *Social Science & Medicine*, 57 (2003), 1593–608.

N. Wallerstein and V. Sanchezmerki, 'Freirian-Praxis in Health-Education – Research Results from an Adolescent Prevention Program', *Health Education Research*, 9 (1994), 105–18.

D. J. Ward, B. Rowe, H. Pattison, R. S. Taylor and K. W. Radcliffe, 'Reducing the Risk of Sexually Transmitted Infections in Genitourinary Medicine Clinic Patients: A Systematic Review and Meta-Analysis of Behavioural Interventions', *Sexually Transmitted Infections*, 81 (2005a), 386–93.

H. Ward, C. H. Mercer, K. Wellings, K. Fenton, B. Erens, A. Copas and A. M. Johnson, 'Who Pays for Sex? An Analysis of the Increasing Prevalence of Female Commercial Sex Contacts among Men in Britain', *Sexually Transmitted Infections*, 81 (2005b), 467–71.

I. Warwick, P. Aggleton and H. Homans, 'Constructing Common Sense – Young People's Beliefs About AIDS', *Sociology of Health & Illness*, 10 (1988), 213–33.

K. Wellings, M. Collumbien, E. Slaymaker, S. Singh, Z. Hodges, D. Patel and N. Bajos, 'Sexual Behaviour in Context: A Global Perspective', *Lancet*, 368 (2006), 1706–28.

D. Whitehead and G. Russell, 'How Effective Are Health Education Programmes Resistance, Reactance, Rationality and Risk? Recommendations for Effective Practice', *International Journal of Nursing Studies*, 41 (2004), 163–72.

D. Wight, 'Impediments to Safer Heterosexual Sex – a Review of Research with Young People', *AIDS Care-Psychological and Socio-Medical Aspects of AIDS/HIV*, 4 (1992), 11–23.

World Health Organization, *The World Health Report 2002: Reducing Risks, Promoting Healthy Life* (Geneva: WHO, 2002).

D. Yach, M. McKee, A. D. Lopez and T. Novotny, 'Improving Diet and Physical Activity: 12 Lessons from Controlling Tobacco Smoking', *British Medical Journal*, 330 (2005), 898–900.

A. Ziersch, J. Gaffney and D. R. Tomlinson, 'STI Prevention and the Male Sex Industry in London: Evaluating a Pilot Peer Education Programme', *Sexually Transmitted Infections*, 76 (2000), 447–53.

7
In Sickness and in Health? Dynamics of Health and Cohabitation in the United Kingdom

Martin Karlsson, Les Mayhew and Ben Rickayzen

1. Introduction

Most developed countries' populations are ageing rapidly with consequent implications for public spending on long-term care (LTC), pensions and health care. The UK dependency ratio (the number of retired people per 100 people of working age) is projected to increase from 24 today to 38 in 2040. Although substantial, the increase is lower than in many other countries. In Japan, for instance, the ratio is projected to increase from 30 today to 65 in 2040 (United Nations, 2002).

Such demographic changes are expected to have a significant impact on the demand for LTC. Most consumers of LTC are over age 80; for example, in England, almost 80 per cent of care home inhabitants belong to this age group (Bajekal, 2002). Since increasing life expectancy causes this group to grow at a faster rate than the general retired population, there is concern that the demographic burden could make the current system of financing LTC unsustainable. Indeed, in the UK, there is already a trend towards concentrating resources only on individuals with severe disability (Karlsson *et al.*, 2004).

Still, relatively little is known about long-term trends and the determinants of the disablement process. One important issue that has not yet been resolved is the long-term trends in healthy life expectancy and disabled life expectancy. Three competing hypotheses have been proposed. The most optimistic one, suggesting a compression of morbidity, was proposed by Fries (1980). According to this perspective, adult life expectancy is approaching its biological limit so that if disability spells can be postponed to higher ages the result will be an overall reduction in the time spent disabled. By contrast, Gruenberg (1977) suggested an expansion of morbidity based on the argument that the observed decline in mortality was mainly due to falling accident rates. The third hypothesis was proposed by Manton (1987) according to whom the development in mortality and morbidity is a combination of the two, which could lead to an expansion of the time spent in good health as well as the time spent in disability.

Official statistics, however, are surprisingly inconclusive as to which of the three hypotheses prevails in reality (Bone *et al.*, 1995, Bebbington and Darton, 1996, Bebbington and Comas-Herrera, 2000). In general, results seem to be sensitive to the definition of disability (activities of daily living (ADLs) or limiting long-standing illness) as well as to the severity of disability taken into account. Despite this ambiguity in the statistics, the long-term trends have important implications for the future funding of long-term care. In a long-term projection model, Karlsson *et al.* (2006) find that an optimistic scenario ('compression of morbidity') implies some two million disabled older people fewer than the most pessimistic scenario ('expansion of morbidity'). In the pessimistic scenario, the element of the tax rate necessary to finance formal long-term care would have to increase by around 80 per cent of its present level, whereas virtually no increase would be necessary in the optimistic scenario. Similar differences arise in the supply of and demand for informal care (that is, unpaid care provided by spouses, children or other members of the local community): with an optimistic scenario, there is virtually no shortfall of informal carers in the next few decades, whereas the pessimistic scenario leads to a serious deficit of informal care that will eventually strain public finances.

This paper focuses on one particular aspect of the disablement process, namely the effects of cohabitation on disability. In this paper, 'cohabitation' is broadly defined to include all types of cohabitation between partners – including married couples. Cohabitation is of particular importance for several reasons. Firstly, cohabitation is strongly correlated with health (a relationship which seems to be stronger for higher ages; Lillard and Panis, 1996) and it is of great interest to know whether this correlation reflects a causal effect – so that changing cohabitation patterns would have implications for health – or merely reflects self-selection into and out of cohabitation (that is, people who cohabit are healthier at the outset). Separating causation and correlation leads to a host of methodological challenges that will be discussed below.

Secondly, knowing the relationship between cohabitation and disability is important for analysing the implications of ageing for long-term care. Informal care comprises a substantial part of total long-term care resources and around 75 per cent of all LTC recipients receive informal care (Karlsson *et al.*, 2006). It is a common concern that there may be a shortage of informal carers if certain discernible trends carry on in the future. These trends are, *inter alia*, the increase in single person households, the rising number of childless older people and the increase in the proportion of females in paid employment. It should be noted, however, that there are some trends that could be expected to countervail these threats to informal care provision. These could include, for instance, a decreasing age at which people retire, together with an improvement in health among younger retirees. This scenario implies that there will be a larger pool of able retirees available in the future to provide informal care; however, the opposite could also apply with an increasing state pension age. Another factor could be changing social values leading to increased male participation in this traditionally female activity.

One good source of information on informal care is the General Household Survey, which offers comparisons over time between different cohorts. Previous research (Pickard, 2002) shows that, as expected, the composition of informal care provision has changed markedly over the last 15 years. There has been a marked drop in the provision of informal care coming from outside the household, whereas the proportion of people providing care within their own household has remained more or less constant. Overall, there has been a significant decrease in the number of people providing care to parents or parents-in-law, whereas the provision of care to spouses has increased significantly.

In this paper, we make use of all available waves of the British Household Panel Survey (BHPS) data in order to study the determinants of disability and cohabitation of males over time. We focus on men since, according to Wilson and Oswald (2005) for example, health effects of cohabitation are more pronounced for men. Our research has three main aims. Firstly, we want to analyse the effects of cohabitation on disability. Secondly, we consider time trends in disability and cohabitation jointly to explore relationships between the two. Thirdly, we examine socioeconomic differences – as captured by educational attainment – in disability. Educational attainment is particularly important in this context because it is very convenient as a socioeconomic indicator as it normally remains constant over most of the life course. Moreover, it is a well established result in health economics and epidemiology that education is an important factor in explaining socioeconomic differences in health (cf. Fuchs, 2004). Finally, empirical studies of marital matching indicate that education is an important aspect of a person's 'marriageability' (Wong, 2003). Hence, excluding education might lead to an overestimation of the importance of cohabitation status for health.

There are two main methodological challenges. The first one is that we seek to estimate a dynamic model, where previous disability and cohabitation status influence current disability and cohabitation status. Secondly, we seek to distinguish causation from correlation in the relationship between cohabitation and disability. This requires using simulation techniques that allow for systematic differences between cohabiting and non-cohabiting individuals which are not discernible in the data. For instance, it might be that healthier people are considered more attractive, and our method is one way to correct for this type of reverse causality.

There is little previous empirical research in the field. Brown (2000) performed a simple empirical analysis of the National Survey of Families and Households (waves 87–88), estimating the effects of cohabitation and relationship characteristics, allowing for self-selection into cohabitation, on psychological wellbeing. Brown found no evidence of self-selection, but observed that simple cohabitation is less beneficial to psychological health than marriage. The main explanation seems to be poorer relationship quality in cohabitation relationships.

Cheung (2000) looked at cohabitation and mortality amongst British women. Analysing the Health and Lifestyle Survey, Cox regressions were used in order to allow for self-selection into cohabitation. This is one of few studies allowing for reverse causality from health to marital status (that is, people being healthy having a higher propensity to be married). Having adjusted for age and marital selection factors, being single was significantly associated with higher mortality, but being divorced or widowed was not. Another study that tries to compensate for reverse causation is Goldman *et al.* (1995). They analyse marital status, health and mortality amongst older people, controlling for baseline health (that is, before a change in marital status), socioeconomic status and social networks. The main finding was that marriage affects mortality only for men, and that the effect is modest. Widowed men were more likely to be disabled, whereas single women are actually healthier than their married counterparts.

Finally, Lillard and Panis (1996) use a simultaneous equations approach to estimate the relationship between health, marital status and mortality, with instrumental variables to account for the reverse causality problem. One of their hypotheses is that the selection effect has a 'demand side' (that is, healthy people are more attractive) and a 'supply side' (that is, unhealthy people have more to gain from marriage as social norms prescribe couples staying together when one becomes ill), and they find indications of both: the observable, or explained, part of health status tends to be negatively correlated with marriage, whereas the unobservable, or unexplained part is positively correlated. That is, if the good health status is attributable to personal characteristics, it tends to reduce the propensity to get married, whereas the propensity goes up for a person whose good health is not attributable to personal characteristics. For example, this result would imply that adverse health effects from unemployment (an observable characteristic) are connected with an increased chance of being married, whereas the opposite holds for individual variations in health that cannot be explained by such personal characteristics. The paper by Lillard and Panis represents the most rigorous attempt to take the reverse causality issue into account; however, the models estimated do not allow for random changes over time in the dependent variable, or autocorrelation (that is, that these random changes are persistent once they occur).

A good overview of the empirical research to date is provided by Wilson and Oswald (2005). After reviewing a great number of articles on the relationship between cohabitation and health – psychological, physical and mortality – they identify the following general conclusions:

- Marriage reduces the risk of psychological illness
- Marriage tends to increase life expectancy

- Marriage makes people healthier and happier
- Men tend to gain more from the advantageous effects of marriage
- There is not only a 'guardian effect' (that is, changes in risk behaviours) – marriage seems to have other positive effects on health as well
- The quality of the relationship is important

There is, therefore, still a paucity of research into the issue of cohabitation and health, both theoretical and empirical. Another reason for exploring the relationship of cohabitation on marriage is that much of the research undertaken so far relates to marriage, as opposed to cohabitation. With continuing upward trends in unmarried cohabitating likely to be more important to future health, it is the objective of this paper to shed some light on the empirical relationship, using econometric techniques that have previously not been applied to the issue. The chapter is organised as follows. Section 2 outlines the methodological approach and describes the dataset; Section 3 presents the results and Section 4 concludes.

2 Methodological approach

2.1 The dataset

Our analysis uses the first 12 waves of the British Household Panel Survey (1991–2002). In this subsection, we define the variables used and report the treatment of missing values. In our regressions, we include all 1540 male individuals who were older than 50 in the start year. For the descriptive analysis in subsection 3.1, we provide information on all 3159 permanent members of the panel (males and females) who were older than 50 in the start year in the analysis.

2.1.1 Variables

The variables used for estimation are presented in Table 7.1.

Table 7.1 Definition of variables in estimating relationship between cohabitation and health

Variable	Definition
A	Age (Calendar year minus birth year)
E1	University Degree
E2	Teaching/Nursing Qualifications
E3	A Levels
E4	O Levels or equivalent
C	Individual married or cohabiting
H	Health limits daily activities

The definitions are mostly obvious, but the health variable H requires some further explanation. It is based on information as to whether the individual is alive in a certain year or not (for dead individuals, the variable takes on the value H=4). For survivors, we use the questions concerning whether the health status of the respondent limits daily activities. The categories allowed for in these questions are roughly equivalent to Activities of Daily Living.[1] As is common in long-term care insurance underwriting, we assume that 'moderate disability' (H=2) corresponds to having failed two activities, and 'severe disability' (H=3) corresponds to having failed three or more activities. Respondents who report that their health limits at most one daily activity are coded as healthy (H=1). A further note should be the suppression of the education category E5, which does not have any of the qualifications mentioned in categories E1–E4. Hence, this is the group with the lowest level of educational attainment, and it includes people who left school without O-levels.

2.1.2   Treatment of missing values

Missing variable values are a particular problem in this work, since excluding individuals with missing observations is not an option as it would bias the mortality rates. In general, some 2–3 per cent of observations were missing. Some of these were quite easy to impute from earlier or later observations: for instance; somebody who has a university degree in a certain year will have a university degree in any subsequent year.

In a second step, we assumed that if an individual has the same cohabitation status or health status in the two years either side of a missing observation, we assume that the missing observation had the same value as the two surrounding ones. This seems reasonable given how slowly health and cohabitation status may change,[2] but it might be problematic since it would bias the estimates if there is a substantial probability of two transitions occurring over that time period. Given, however, the low number of missing observations of this kind, the impact on the parameter estimates must be relatively low.

For all observations that were still missing after this exercise, we simply assumed that they belong to the most common categories (that is, cohabitation, healthy and no education). Although this approach can be problematic, it would be equally problematic to make imputations based on variables used in the estimations. Further, it can again be argued that the small number of missing cases will mean that this practice has a limited impact on the results.

2.2   Data analysis

2.2.1   Maximum simulated likelihood

Our econometric model includes two estimating equations; one for cohabitation and one for health. We follow closely the estimation technique taken by Börsch-Supan *et al.* (1993) and adapt it to our problem. Firstly, we allow for unobserved person-specific attributes in both cohabitation and health. In other words, we do not assume that all differences in health trajectories are attributable to observable characteristics (age, gender, education) but we exploit the longitudinal character of the dataset to allow for systematic differences between individuals which emerge from the analysis.

Disability status varies over time, but it also has an important, time-invariant component reflecting the fact that some people are 'structurally' healthier than others. This unobserved heterogeneity may be due to a large number of factors, some of which might not even be measurable. For instance, systematic differences in intelligence, environment, cultural norms or genetic predisposition, could all have a permanent effect on health. Similarly, concerning cohabitation status, it can be assumed that some people are 'structurally' more likely to be in a relationship than others, even after controlling for observable characteristics such as sex and education. This might be to do with, for example, intelligence, religious beliefs, region or mental health. Furthermore, if there is selection into marriage based on health (or variables correlated with health) we would expect the person-specific attributes of the two estimating equations to be correlated as well.

Ignoring this unobserved heterogeneity would give us a biased estimate of the true relationship between the variables in our model. However, our simulation-based approach allows us to incorporate unobserved heterogeneity in the model, without having to define to which of the factors mentioned above it is attributable. Hence, our approach could also be seen as a test of whether these individual attributes are important, or whether controlling for observable factors only would be sufficient.

Moreover, not all unobserved differences can be captured by components which do not vary over time. Hence, we also allow for time-varying disturbances, which are potentially correlated across the equations and potentially exhibiting autoregression, meaning that there is persistence in unobservable characteristics. We give a more detailed account of the assumptions in the Appendix.

2.2.2   Estimating equations

We now define the two estimating equations and then investigate the error structure more closely. The health variable is discrete and takes on four different values: healthy, moderately disabled, severely disabled, and dead. Hence, we choose to estimate an ordered probit model. This involves a latent, unbounded and continuous health variable H_t^*:

$$(1) \quad H_t^* = \delta_1 E_t + \delta_2 A_t + \delta_3 A_t^2 + \delta_4 A_t^3 + \delta_5 A_t^4 + \delta_6 \hat{C}_t + \delta_7 \hat{C}_{t-1} + \delta_8 \hat{H}_{t-1} + \delta_9 t \, \varepsilon_t^H$$

where E_t is education, A_t is the age^3 in year t, δ_9 captures a linear time trend, C_t and C_{t-1} represent the cohabitation status in the current and the previous period, respectively, and (with a slight abuse of notation[4]) H_{t-1} refers to whether the individual was moderately or severely disabled in the previous year. Our model allows for state dependence in both dependent variables, in that disability and cohabitation status in the previous year also influence current disability.

Then, just as in the standard model, the actual state of disability is defined according to a switching function:

$$(2)\ \hat{H}_t = \begin{cases} 1 & if & H_t^* \geq \alpha_1 \\ 2 & if & \alpha_1 < H_t^* \geq \alpha_2 \\ 3 & if & \alpha_2 < H_t^* \geq \alpha_3 \\ 4 & if & \alpha_3 < H_t^* \end{cases}$$

where the values of H_t, ranging from 1 to 4, correspond to healthy, moderately disabled, severely disabled and dead, respectively and the alphas are cut-off points defining the limit between the various health states. Needless to say, death is treated as an absorbing state, meaning that no recovery from death is possible.

For cohabitation status, we estimate a binomial probit. Hence, the latent function is:

$$(3)\ C_t^* = c + \beta_1 E_t + \beta_2 A_t + \beta_3 A_t^2 + \beta_4 A_t^3 + \beta_5 A_t^4 + \beta_7 \hat{C}_{t-1} + \beta_8 \hat{H}_{t-1} + \beta_9 t + \varepsilon_t^C$$

where c is a constant, and the rest of the independent variables are the same as in equation (1) above. The switching function is then

$$(4)\ \hat{C}_t = \begin{cases} 1 & if \\ 0 & otherwise \end{cases} C_t^* \geq 0$$

Further details on the estimation approach are provided in the Appendix.

3 Results and discussion

In this section, we present some descriptive statistics, parameter estimates for the regressions described in subsection 2.2.2, and some discussion of the implications of the results. Our model estimates can also, however, be used to simulate survival curves for different subsections of the populations, as demonstrated in Karlsson *et al.* (2007a).

3.1 Descriptive statistics

Table 7.2 shows the main variable of interest – disability – and how it evolves with age. We have defined disability in accordance with our estimation model. Table 7.2 shows the positive association between disability and age.

For instance, among people in their fifties, fewer than 10 per cent are disabled, whereas at the highest ages, almost half of the population is either moderately or severely disabled. In the remainder of this paper, we use the term 'healthy' to mean a person who has no, or a very low, level of disability.

Table 7.2   Health status (ADLs) by age, 1991
(Males and females. Number of individuals; percentage in italics).

Age	Healthy	Moderate	Severe	Total
<60	952	29	47	1,028
	92.61%	2.82%	4.57%	100.00%
60–69	911	55	56	1,022
	89.14%	5.38%	5.48%	100.00%
70–79	639	52	85	776
	82.35%	6.70%	10.95%	100.00%
80–89	219	28	56	303
	72.28%	9.24%	18.48%	100.00%
90+	15	4	10	29
	51.72%	13.79%	34.48%	100.00%
Total	2,736	168	254	3,158
	86.64%	5.32%	8.04%	100.00%

Next, we look at the role of cohabitation. In Table 7.3, we cross-tabulate the initial wave by health status and cohabitation status. The two seem to be strongly correlated; a person not cohabiting is 50 per cent more likely to be disabled as a person who is cohabiting.

Table 7.3   Health status (ADLs) by cohabitation status, 1991

Cohabit	Healthy	Moderate	Severe	Total
No	1,818	89	117	2,024
	89.82%	4.40%	5.78%	100.00%
Yes	918	79	137	1,134
	80.95%	6.97%	12.08%	100.00%
Total	2,736	168	254	3,158
	86.64%	5.32%	8.04%	100.00%

Table 7.4 shows time trends. We cross-tabulate the cohabitation status in 1991 with health status in 1996. People who were cohabiting in 1991 had a higher chance of being alive and healthy in 1996. The mortality rate, in particular, seems to be high for non-cohabiting people when compared to cohabiting people.

Table 7.4   Health status 1996 (ADLs) by cohabitation status, 1991

Cohabit	Healthy	Moderate	Severe	Dead	Total
No	739	60	194	141	1,134
	65.2	5.3	17.1	12.4	100.0
Yes	1,539	79	256	151	2,025
	76.0	3.9	12.6	7.5	100.0
Total	2,278	139	450	292	3,159
	72.1	4.4	14.2	9.2	100.0

Table 7.5 shows cross-tabulations for education with health status in 1996. The education variable reflects the self reported educational attainment, where for simplicity we have merged the educated categories into one single group corresponding to an educational level of at least a GCSE (or its predecessors: GCE, Higher School Certificate etc.). As expected, a higher educational attainment is correlated with better health. The effect of education seems to be particularly strong for moderate disability, where the prevalence amongst non-educated people is more than twice as high as the corresponding figure for educated people.

Table 7.5   Health status 1996 (ADLs) by educational attainment, (GCSE + equivalent) 1991

Education	Healthy	Moderate	Severe	Dead	Total
No	1,443	113	338	227	2,121
	68.0	5.3	15.9	10.7	100.0
Yes	835	26	112	65	1,038
	80.4	2.5	10.8	6.3	100.0
Total	2,278	139	450	292	3,159
	72.1	4.4	14.2	9.2	100.0

Whilst providing useful insight into the relationship between cohabitation and health, these analyses do not take into account factors such as age, time trends and any systematic differences between groups and hence the need for our estimation approach.

3.2   Parameter estimates

Estimation results for cohabitation are presented in Table 7.6. In the table, the first group of variables are the exogenous variables (that is, determined outside the model) which include a constant, age, education and a time trend. Education seems to have very little explanatory power for the cohabitation variable (as can be seen by the high p values for the variables Edu2–4). The age estimates (Age, Age^2 etc.) are individually insignificant but taken as a group they are significant, which reflects the fact that the probability of cohabitation is declining with age, but at a non-linear rate. As expected, there is a negative time trend in cohabitation which is weakly significant.

The next group of variables represent state dependence; that is, how the cohabitation and health states in the previous year affect cohabitation in the current year. The label C_{t-1} refers to the cohabitation status in the previous year, and 'Moderate$_{t-1}$' and 'Severe$_{t-1}$' refer to whether the individual was moderately or severely disabled in the previous year. There seems to be very strong state dependence in the cohabitation variable, and some albeit weaker effects of previous disability on current cohabitation.

Parameters σ^{hc}, ω^{hc}, ω^{cc} and ρ_1 refer to the structure of the error terms. We explain their interpretation in the Appendix. They measure to which extent changes to health and cohabitation, which cannot be attributed to the independent variables, are correlated over time or between the two estimating equations.

In this part, we find evidence of assortative mating into cohabitation (i.e., a positive correlation in the health status of partners), as demonstrated by the negative coefficient estimated for the ω^{hc} parameter. The implication is that people predisposed to be unhealthy are also less likely to be cohabiting. On the other hand, as indicated above, the results also suggest that there is an adverse selection effect in cohabitation (that is, people with disabilities have stronger incentives to remain with their partners, as the positive estimates for 'Moderate$_{t-1}$' and 'Severe$_{t-1}$' indicate), since the occurrence of disability increases the probability of staying in the cohabitation state. However, this result is statistically not very significant.

Furthermore, we estimate a positive coefficient for the σ^{hc} parameter, implying that the changes in unobserved differences between people actually exhibit a negative correlation between cohabitation and health. This has a similar interpretation to the ω^{hc} parameter since it also measures the degree of non-causal correlation between cohabitation and health. In this case, the parameter measures how the correlation evolves due to shocks that occur over time. In other words, this finding suggests that people who experience adverse shocks to their health are more likely to stay in their relationship. This is to be contrasted with the previous finding of a positive correlation between cohabitation and health in fixed unobservables (as captured by ω^{hc}).

In general, our results suggest that the relationship between cohabitation and health is not straightforward: people who are generally healthy seem to have higher chances of finding a partner, but once people are cohabiting, it seems that the occurrence of disability increases the chances of staying together. Whereas the causal effect of disability is not significant (although the positive effect of moderate disability is almost significant at the 10 per cent level), the significant estimate of parameter σ^{hc} suggests that adverse health shocks are associated with increased probability of cohabitation. This finding suggests that we have observed the 'supply side' effect discussed by Lillard and Panis (1996).

In summary: increasing age, increasing education level, and being disabled does not predict cohabitation. Cohabiting previously is positively associated with cohabitation now, as is having had an adverse health shock. Being 'structurally' predisposed to poorer health or not cohabiting are both associated with less likelihood of cohabiting.

Table 7.6　Estimation results, cohabitation. Males

Variable	Coefficient	Std Error	T Stat	P Value
Constant	−0.01	0.31	−0.05	0.96
Age	−0.23	0.16	−1.41	0.16
Age^2	0.37	0.30	1.19	0.24
Age^3	0.01	0.01	0.85	0.40
Age^4	−0.20	0.17	−1.20	0.23
Edu2	0.59	0.43	1.38	0.17
Edu3	0.33	0.60	0.54	0.59
Edu4	−0.33	0.23	−1.42	0.16
C_{t-1}	4.46	0.33	13.68	0.00
$Moderate_{t-1}$	0.67	0.42	1.62	0.11
$Severe_{t-1}$	0.12	0.31	0.40	0.69
Year	−0.08	0.04	−1.93	0.05
σ^{hc}	0.44	0.09	5.03	0.00
ω^{cc}	0.04	0.07	0.66	0.51
ω^{hc}	−0.24	0.10	−2.35	0.02
ρ_1	−0.31	0.11	−2.90	0.00
Loglik	−811.06			
$Loglik_0$	−1,974.50			
Pseudo R^2	0.59			
N	7,986			

In Table 7.7, we present parameter estimates for the disability variable.

Again, the first group of variables are the exogenous factors such as age and education. The age parameters also tend to be insignificant, but they are jointly significant; hence, health is declining with age but at a non-linear rate, and again, we find that the education level of the individual has low explanatory power (as can be seen by the high p values of the variables Edu2–4).

Table 7.7   Estimation results, health. Males.

Variable	Coefficient	Std Error	T Stat	P Value
Age	−0.0450	0.0494	−0.9117	0.362
Age^2	−0.0003	0.0019	−0.1431	0.886
Age^3	0.0005	0.0030	0.1555	0.876
Age^4	0.0480	0.0238	2.0160	0.044
Edu2	−0.1806	0.2677	−0.6746	0.500
Edu3	−0.1456	0.5527	−0.2633	0.792
Edu4	0.1382	0.2697	0.5125	0.608
Year	0.0565	0.0211	2.6804	0.007
C_t	−2.3147	0.3298	−7.0172	0.000
C_{t-1}	1.8693	0.2882	6.4873	0.000
Moderate$_{t-1}$	0.8199	.01934	4.2386	0.000
Severe$_{t-1}$	0.9866	0.1925	5.1258	0.000
σ^{hc}	0.4427	0.0880	5.0330	0.000
ω^{hh}	0.6666	0.2189	3.0449	0.002
ω^{hc}	−0.2371	0.1008	−2.5326	0.019
ρ_2	−0.1838	0.0949	−1.9374	0.053

The next set of estimates represents state dependence; that is, the degree to which previous cohabitation and health states influence current disability. These parameter estimates provide many interesting insights. Firstly, we notice that cohabitation has a very strong (and strongly significant) effect on health (C_t is significant even at the 1 per cent level). However, the effect of losing a partner is even stronger, and is comparable to the effect of an onset of severe disability in the previous year. In order to see this, notice that the net effect of cohabitation for a person who was cohabiting in both periods is equal to −0.44 (that is, 1.87–2.31) whereas for a person who had a partner and lost him or her in the last year has a net effect of 1.87 (this is, again, the parameter estimate for C_{t-1}; remember that a higher value implies higher degree of disability). Thus, in comparison to a person who does not suffer bereavement,[5] the adverse health effects are substantial and indeed seem to be even greater than the effect of previous severe disability (variable Severe$_{t-1}$ has parameter estimate 0.99). Hence, the cohabitation state clearly has a strong impact on health, even after unobserved heterogeneity has been accounted for.

Furthermore, we find that there is strong and statistically significant state dependence in the disability variable; being moderately disabled ('Moderate$_{t-1}$') reduces future health prospects substantially (which is captured by a point estimate of 0.82 in the table), and the effect of severe disability ('Severe$_{t-1}$') is slightly higher (point estimate 0.99). We also find that the time trend is towards worse health, as demonstrated by the positive parameter estimate of the year variable. This is at odds with the general increase in life expectancy that has been observed in the UK as in many other countries. This result has two possible interpretations. One possibility is that the increases in life expectancy which have been observed in the UK population are due to changes in the independent variables we are studying. This would imply that younger cohorts have higher levels of education and different family structures than older cohorts. However, given that the explanatory value of education is limited according to our results, and given the development towards less stable family structures, this explanation seems unlikely.

An alternative interpretation is that the model used here simplifies too much. It might not be appropriate to assume that the cut-off values between different disability states (and death) – that is, α_1, α_2 and α_3 – are constant over time. Indeed, data for the development of healthy life expectancy (HLE) over the last few decades suggest that a substantial proportion of the gains in life expectancy are spent in moderate disability, whereas the time spent in severe disability has tended to decrease. This might in turn be due to improvements in medical technology. If this is the case, the three cut-off values might well be diverging over time and this is then the effect picked up by the time coefficient estimated here. This explanation would imply that an individual with given characteristics and age would have greater chances of being healthy the later he was born (thus representing a cohort effect). Thus it remains an issue for future research to analyse whether the boundaries between the healthy state, disability, and death diverge over time.

Finally, we find that unobserved systematic differences between people are very significant in explaining the dynamics of health. Unobserved heterogeneity (parameter ω^{hh}, point estimate 0.67 in Table 7.7) accounts for a substantial share of the variation in the data. This result can be interpreted as follows. Consider the variation in health which cannot be explained by differences in age, educational attainment or cohabitation status. Our estimates suggest that around 40 per cent of this residual variation is due to inequalities (of any kind), whereas 60 per cent is purely random.

Again, we can conclude that causal effects from education seem to be dominated by variation in these types of unobserved characteristics. This also helps us to understand why the education variables come out insignificant: educated people are not healthier because they are educated, but because they are healthier from the outset. This is a finding which is very relevant for policy.

4 Conclusions

The main challenge to the future of the UK long-term care system is not dealing with general trends in health, but ensuring that there will be enough informal carers to take care of those in need. Karlsson *et al.* (2006)

suggest that there might be a shortfall of up to 40 per cent of the informal care needed if the trends in the next three to four decades are unfavourable. Since the vast majority of disabled older people only receive informal care, this would put a considerable strain on public finances if the care instead became formal.

This research has indicated that there is a simple association between cohabitation and health but that this relation becomes more complicated if health at the outset (before cohabitation) and also during cohabitation is taken into account. We found evidence of assortative mating into cohabitation; that is, people with better health prospects seem to be more likely to be cohabiting, but we also found that disabled people are more likely to remain with their cohabitation partner. This could imply that people in good health are considered to be more attractive at the outset, but it also indicates that adverse changes in health actually increase the probability of remaining in a relationship.

Whether this effect is due to social norms concerning the duties of a partner or behavioural changes of the individual becoming disabled (branded the 'supply side effect' by Lillard and Panis, 1996), remains an issue for future research. Likewise, it is of interest to speculate to what extent this effect remains even in times when the volatility of relationships increases and people's commitment to their partners has a tendency to diminish, and as social attitudes change. Earlier research on marriage suggests that the quality of the relationship is significant to health (Wilson and Oswald, 2005). We also found that cohabitation has a strong direct effect on health which remains even after unobserved differences between people have been allowed for. This might be one reason why disabled people are more likely to remain with their partner. Conversely, losing one's partner in the last year seems to have an even stronger, negative effect on health that is comparable in magnitude to becoming severely disabled. This may suggest that there is a role for more counselling services to deal with bereavement issues.

The dataset we are using is a very rich source of information, following a representative sample of the UK population over a very long period of time. Yet, there are some limitations in the data as well as in our approach. Firstly, the disability variable we are using is self-reported disability. Self-reported health measures can always be questioned on the basis that there might be individual differences in reporting behaviour. On the other hand, self-reported health has been shown to be closely connected with more 'objective' health measures and provide a very good predictor of mortality (cf. Hernández-Quevedo *et al.*, 2005). A further problem with the data is that the BHPS does not include people living in institutions. This is, of course, particularly relevant in our analysis of disability, since individuals moving into institutional care will be excluded. To some extent, our panel data approach alleviates this problem, but it would be useful to assess the degree of attrition bias in future research.

The findings with regard to cohabitation have several important implications from a public policy standpoint since a world in which people did not cohabit would also be a more expensive world from a tax payer's standpoint. Health care, long-term care, social care and the social security system of paying benefits would all be significantly affected. The fact that social care costs will likely increase when older people live on their own is not a new finding, but that their health and therefore care needs could be affected raises significant policy issues to the extent that institutions and the tax benefit system treat people as couples rather than as individuals. Hence one could draw the conclusion that policies which give financial and social inducements to live alone – such as policies in the Scandinavian countries (cf. Karlsson *et al.*, 2007b) – could have unforeseen consequences in these regards but also wider implications for housing and raising families.

These conclusions are, of course, speculative and more research is needed. Firstly the analysis should be extended to include females. It is likely that females exhibit different dynamics in their disability and cohabitation paths than males, and it is a plausible hypothesis that cohabitation and bereavement have different effects on women than on men. Furthermore, it would be useful to get a better understanding of how the health states of spouses are interrelated. The assortative mating argument suggests that the health status of spouses should be positively correlated. Our sample gives some indications for this to be the case. For instance, in the first wave there are 2490 couples for which the health states of both spouses are recorded. Out of these, 1764 were couples where both spouses reported the same health status (for simplicity, we merged all disabled states into one). This means that a healthy person has an 89 per cent chance of living together with another healthy person, whereas the probability of a disabled person living with a healthy person is only 53 per cent.

7.1 Appendix 7.1: The estimation strategy

In this appendix we give some further details on how the parameters of the model have been estimated, with particular focus on the modelling of unobserved heterogeneity.

Modelling unobserved heterogeneity

In order to ensure that the estimated causal effects of age, education and cohabitation are not confounded with systematic differences between individuals, we allow for a very general structure in the error terms. The various parameters estimated in this part can be summarised as:

- Fixed individual attributes: some individuals are more likely than others to be disabled, and there is some variation in the propensity to be cohabiting as well. These effects, or rather their variances, are captured by the parameters ω^{hh} (disability) and ω^{cc} (cohabitation) below. A high value of ω^{hh} implies that a great share of the variation in disability is attributable to unobserved structural differences which are unrelated to the independent variables.

- Correlation in unobservables: this effect, represented by the parameter ω^{hc} below, measures the degree to which people who are structurally predisposed to be unhealthy are also more likely to be cohabiting. This is an important parameter since it captures systematic differences between people which would otherwise (wrongly) be identified as a causal effect of cohabitation on health. A high value of ω^{hc} implies that a great deal of the observed correlation between disability and cohabitation is due to people being different at the outset and not due to causation.

- Correlation in shocks: This parameter, denoted σ^{hc}, captures how random shocks to health and cohabitation are correlated. Hence, this parameter is similar to the 'correlation in unobservables' parameter above, with the difference that the correlation refers to temporary effects and not structural characteristics of the individual. If this variable is significant, there are factors not captured by the independent variables that influence both disability and cohabitation. Again, disregarding this effect would lead to an overestimation of the causal effect of cohabitation on health.

- Autocorrelation: This effect, represented by parameters ρ_1 and ρ_2 below, shows to what extent shocks to health and cohabitation are persistent over time. These do not have an obvious interpretation but are necessary once we allow for persistence (that is, state dependence) in the dependent variables since otherwise the coefficients would be biased. Bertrand *et al.* (2004) have shown that as soon as there is persistence in the dependent variables, a causal effect will be picked up even when there is none unless autocorrelation is allowed for.

Discussion

We estimate the model outlined in equations (1) and (3) using maximum likelihood. However, given that the two dependent variables are both limited – taking on discrete values only – estimating a dynamic model with the type of error structures we have outlined above poses some challenges. The main problem is that the likelihood function attains so many dimensions that it becomes intractable.

However, maximum simulated likelihood offers a solution to this problem. The idea of this estimator is to draw several series of error terms which are consistent with the data actually observed. We employ an algorithm proposed by Geweke (1989). In short, it means that we draw a series of numbers from a uniform distribution and then transform them (in a straightforward application of the integral transform theorem) into a truncated normal variable that fits the observed data. In terms of the cut-off point in the equation (2), the simulated error terms must be such that each individual ends up in the disability category actually observed in the data. The Geweke algorithm produces unbiased estimates of the parameters, and once it has been implemented, standard maximum likelihood techniques can be used to estimate the model.

In general, the simulation estimator produces consistent estimates of the parameters of the econometric model. Furthermore, Börsch-Supan and Hajivassiliou (1993) find that for 20 simulations per observation, the simulation bias is negligible. Hence, the estimator seems to be appropriate for our purposes.

There is, however, one practical problem related to the assumption of persistence in the two dependent variables. This problem has to do with the treatment of initial observations, as a simple estimation along the lines outlined above would be based on the erroneous assumption that the system is in equilibrium in the first period. This will lead to inconsistent estimates. Two different approaches have been suggested to remedy this problem. The first one, proposed by Heckman (1981), is to estimate the initial conditions separately and allow for any type of correlation pattern between the initial conditions and any subsequent condition. An alternative to this is provided by Wooldridge (2000) who proposes modelling the distribution of the heterogeneity conditional on the initial condition and any time varying regressors that may be present. Doing this does not require internal consistency with the underlying statistical model nor does it require computations that are as involved as the Heckman (1981) method, but it does require additional distributional assumptions.

Unfortunately, none of these approaches will be useful for our purposes. Heckman's approach increases the number of parameters to be estimated substantially, and given the size of the dataset this becomes a hopeless task. With Wooldridge's method, we are left with the problem that most variables used for estimation, apart from age and the dependent variables themselves, tend to be time-dependent. Hence, using that approach would prevent us from estimating the parameters of interest.

The initial condition problem decreases with the number of waves in the panel, however. Since we have many waves at our disposal, the problem is likely to be relatively small in our case. Furthermore, since we are focusing on older people in the population, it could be argued that the model should be close to equilibrium once their conditions are being recorded in the BHPS.

Notes

1 Activities of daily living are activities related to personal care and include bathing or showering, dressing, getting in or out of bed or a chair, using the toilet, and eating.

2 In our sample, 4.7 per cent of individuals change their cohabitation status year on year and 12.7 per cent change their health status.

3 We need to go as far as the 4th power since other specifications tend to have health improving at extreme ages.
4 The previous health status is actually captured by two dummies, Moderate$_{t-1}$ and Severe$_{t-1}$ which for simplicity have been summarised as one (i.e. H_{t-1}) in equation (1).
5 Our estimates rely on the assumption that dissolution of the relationship has the same effect on health irrespective of the reason for the dissolution (whether bereavement, divorce or separation). However, amongst males aged 50 and over, the single most common reason for dissolution of relationships is bereavement, accounting for 82 per cent of all transitions out of cohabitation. Hence, we interpret our parameter estimates as measuring the effect of bereavement although they are actually an average for all types of transitions out of cohabitation.

References

M. Bajekal, *Care Homes and their Residents* (London: HM Stationery Office, 2002).

A. C. Bebbington and R. A. Darton, *Healthy life expectancy in England and Wales: recent evidence*, PSSRU Discussion Paper 1205 (1996).

A. Bebbington and A. Comas-Herrera, *Healthy Life Expectancy: Trends to 1998, and the Implications for Long Term Care Costs*, PSSRU Discussion Paper 1695 (London School of Economics, 2000).

M. Bertrand, E. Duflo and S. Mullainathan, 'How much should we trust differences in-differences estimates?', *Quarterly Journal of Economics*, 119:1 (2004) 249–75.

M. Bone, A. C. Bebbington, C. Jagger, K. Morgan and G. Nicolaas, *Health expectancy and its uses* (London: HM Stationary Office, 1995).

A. Börsch-Supan and V. A. Hajivassiliou, 'Smooth unbiased multivariate probability simulators for maximum likelihood estimation of limited dependent variables models', *Journal of Econometrics*, 58:3 (1993) 347–68.

S. L. Brown, 'The effect of union type on psychological wellbeing: depression cohabitants versus marrieds', *Journal of Health and Social Behaviour*, 41:3 (2000) 241–55.

Y. B. Cheung, 'Marital status and mortality in British women: a longitudinal study', *International Journal of Epidemiology*, 29:1 (2000) 93–9.

J. Fries, 'Aging, Natural Death and the Compression of Morbidity', *New England Journal of Medicine*, 303:3 (1980) 130–5.

V. R. Fuchs, 'Reflections on the socio-economic correlates of health', *Journal of Health Economics*, 23:4 (2004) 629–36.

J. Geweke, Efficient Simulation from the Multivariate Normal Distribution Subject to Linear Inequality Constraints and the Evaluation of Constraint Probabilities (Durham, NC: Duke University, Mimeo, 1989).

N. Goldman, S. Korenman and R. Weinstein, 'Marital status and health among the elderly', *Social Science and Medicine*, 40:12 (1995) 1717–30.

E. M. Gruenberg, 'The failures of success', *Milbank Memorial Foundation Quarterly/Health and Society*, 55 (1977) 3–24.

J. J. Heckman, 'The incidential parameters problem and the problem of initial conditions in estimating a discrete-time data stochastic process', in C. F. Manski and D. McFadden (eds), *Structural Analysis of Discrete Data with Econometric Applications* (Cambridge, MA: MIT Press, 1981), pp. 179–95.

C. Hernandez-Quevedo, A. Jones and N. Rice, Reporting bias and heterogeneity in self-assessed health: evidence from the British Household Panel Survey (York: Health Econometrics and Data Group (HEDG) Working Paper 05/04, 2005).

M. Karlsson, L. Mayhew, R. Plumb and B. Rickayzen, An International Comparison of Long-Term Care Arrangements: An Investigation into the Equity, Efficiency and

Sustainability of the Long-Term Care Systems in Germany, Japan, Sweden, the United Kingdom and the United States (London: Internal Research Paper, Cass Business School, City University, 2004).

M. Karlsson, L. Mayhew and B. Rickayzen, 'Future costs for long-term care. Cost projections for long-term care for older people in the United Kingdom', *Health Policy*, 75:2 (2006) 187–213.

M. Karlsson, L. Mayhew and B. Rickayzen, In Sickness and in Health? Dynamics of Health and Cohabitation in the United Kingdom (London: Internal Research Paper, Cass Business School, City University, 2007a).

M. Karlsson, L. Mayhew and B. Rickayzen, 'Long term care financing in four OECD countries: fiscal burden and distributive effects', *Health Policy*, 80:1 (2007b) 107–34.

L. A. Lillard and C. W. A. Panis, 'Marital status and mortality: the role of health', *Demography*, 33:3 (1996) 313–27.

K. G. Manton, 'Response to "an introduction to the compression of morbidity"', *Gerontologica Perspecta*, 1 (1987) 23–30.

L. Pickard, 'The decline of intensive intergenerational care of older people in Great Britain, 1985–1995', in *Population Trends* (London, Office for National Statistics, 2002).

United Nations Population Database (2002), *World Population Prospects*, 'The 2006 Revision Population Database', retrieved from http://esa.un.org/unpp/ March 2007.

C. M. Wilson and A. J. Oswald, How does marriage affect physical and psychological health? A survey of the longitudinal evidence (Warwick: University of Warwick, IZA Discussion Paper No. 1619, 2005).

Linda Wong, 'Structural estimation of marriage models', *Journal of Labor Economics*, 21:3 (2003) 699–727.

J. Wooldridge, The initial conditions problem in dynamic nonlinear panel data models with unobserved heterogeneity (Ann Arbor: University of Michigan, Mimeo, 2000).

8
Successful Ageing: A Useful Concept for the Future?

Yvonne Doyle, Martyn Sherriff and Martin McKee

Introduction

Since the 1950s, countries of the developed world have experienced increases in life expectancy at advanced ages. Whereas in 1960 men could expect to live for 67.5 years and women for 73 years, in 2005 they could expect to live for 75.8 and 81 years, respectively (Visco, 2001). At the age of 80, men can expect to live for another 7.3 years and women for another 8.9 years.

An important question for policymakers and individuals alike is whether projected gains in longevity will be accompanied by increases in illness, disability, vulnerability and also service use. Some argue that there will be a compression of morbidity (Fries, 1980); others an increase in morbidity (Parker and Thorslund, 2007); and others still a concurrent decline in mortality and morbidity (Manton et al., 1997). In England, healthy life expectancy (that is, years of life free from limiting longstanding illness) is increasing over time – but not by as much as life expectancy itself (Bissett, 2002). However, no clear pattern emerges from the comparison of trends in life expectancy with healthy life expectancy in available cross-country data up to 2050 (Jacobzine, 2002). Healthy life expectancy is hard for demographers to calculate, as demographic factors alone are not sufficient to project potential future population patterns or needs. Other important drivers of healthy life expectancy include control of chronic disease, health behaviours, and changes in the prevalence of very frail individuals.

Studies suggest that it is not inevitable that physical or cognitive health declines with older age, and research over the last 35 years has shown intellectual gains until people reach their early 40s, with stability until their early 60s (Schaie, 2001). Decline is minimal until they reach their mid-70s. Intellectual performance is multi-dimensional, involving verbal ability, memory, reasoning and numerical skills. Verbal ability and memory are the last to deteriorate (Schaie, 2001). Although substantial changes appear to occur late in life, and then for those functions that are less central and practised, few individuals show global deficit by age 80. Yet cohort effects seem to matter, in that more recent generations of older people show lower levels of decline than earlier cohorts at the same age. This may be due to increased education or lifestyle opportunities, the ability of recent cohorts to take advantage of technological improvements, or compression of physical morbidity (Schaie, 1993).

US researchers contend that a range of variables within personal control are highly predictive of a good state of health at age 70 (Berkman, 1993). Examples include not smoking, 'mature psychological defences' such as no known mental illness in middle age, and the numbers of years in education (Vaillant, 1980). Sixty-five year olds who engage in regular physical activity have been shown to have lower 12 year mortality and service use and lower risk of respiratory disease, although this may reflect pre-existing disability at baseline (Vintners, 2001). It has been assumed that physiological pathways mediate the association between physical activity and reduced mortality. However, the activities of older people result in complex effects beyond mere physical fitness. Social activity is also associated with longevity and health (Baltes, 1993).

In examining why social, productive and physical activity are independently associated with lower 12 year mortality, it is hypothesised by researchers that psychosocial pathways mediate the health benefits of activity, and that meaningful social roles promote a sense of self-efficacy. The consequent stress reduction may enhance cellular and humoral immunity (Schaie, 1993; Vintners, 2001). This, along with rising public expectations and concerns about healthcare utilisation, has led to attempts to understand what constitutes 'successful ageing' and how it may be promoted in the population.

Current definitions of 'successful' ageing

The sporadic use of the term 'successful ageing' dates from the mid 1960s and initially described reducing morbidity and mortality, coming into widespread use in the 1980s. In 1987, Rowe and Kahn defined successful ageing as 1) low probability of disease and related disability, 2) high cognitive and physical function and 3) active engagement with life. In their model all three terms are relative and one may contribute to the others in a sequential manner (for instance, high function leading to active engagement). Successful ageing, according to them, goes beyond the mere potential to become engaged in activity; it involves social productivity. Activity is defined as 'productive' if it creates societal value, such as community work, whether or not it is reimbursed (Rowe and Kahn, 1987).

Rowe and Kahn have been criticised for proposing too narrow a concept of success. One study found that only between 9 and 19 per cent of people in the southern US satisfied all their criteria for successful ageing (Strawbridge *et al.*, 2002). If successful ageing is taken as minimal disruption of function despite signs of chronic disease, then the net widens to include up to 50 per cent of study populations (Strawbridge *et al.*, 2002). In addition, qualitative interviews indicate that people value wellbeing and social functioning more than physical and psycho-cognitive performance (Montross *et al.*, 2006).

Recently, the range of factors proposed in the literature has broadened to include some that are both more personalised and subjective, such as length of active life, measures of biological and psychological health, social competence and activity, economic wellbeing, and life satisfaction (Bowling and Iliffe, 2006; Von Faber *et al.*, 2001). For instance, although half the respondents in the Health Survey for England 2005 (Craig and Mindell, 2007) reported having some illness that limited their activities, only 13 per cent assessed their health as 'bad' or 'very bad'. One explanation might be that 'success' is a process of adaptive response, that of making the most of what one expects from old age. The addition of a subjective element could thus make the concept of successful ageing more useful. Because life satisfaction and social support have been shown to be independently associated with fewer demands on the health system (Roos and Havens, 1991), unravelling these strands is particularly relevant to policymakers interested in controlling healthcare costs, as well as promoting the wellbeing of their populations.

This chapter reports on a study which uses structural equation modelling (SEM) to examine whether a model of 'successful ageing' as proposed by Rowe and Kahn can be demonstrated in a population from the mainland of Britain, or whether another concept of successful ageing is needed. The implications of the findings for future policy are analysed in the discussion.

Method

The sample

The population used was that of the Health and Lifestyle Surveys (Cox, 1987; Cox, 1993). Although not specifically designed to measure the nature of ageing, the Health and Lifestyle Surveys ('HALS') are rich in variables of interest to researchers of ageing. They followed a cohort of 9003 subjects aged 16 years and over living in Britain, surveying them in 1984/5 ('HALS1'), and then again in 1991/2 ('HALS2') with additional questions about the intervening years. Both times, the subjects completed a face-to-face interview and a self-administered questionnaire, and were visited by a nurse, who measured clinical variables such as blood pressure.[1]

For our research, we lifted from this dataset all those aged 55 years and over who participated in both surveys. There were 3005 subjects aged 55 years and over in 1984. By 1991, 791 (26 per cent) had died and a further 22 per cent were not available for interview – mainly due to illness or infirmity.

Method of analysis

The analysis was designed first to test the conceptual model of Rowe and Kahn, and to then explore any other conceptual variables that seemed to contribute to 'successful ageing'. The method used for both of these tasks was structural equation modelling (SEM). Whereas the goal of general linear modelling (such as, for example, analysis of variance or regression analysis) is to model individual observations, the primary aim of SEM is to model covariance; that is, to identify the 'latent' variables – the variables which are theoretical and 'can only be determined to exist as a combination of other measurable variables' (Reisinger and Turner, 1999, p. 71) – that belong to a construct, here the construct of 'successful ageing'. The output of the model ('success') is also conceptual, meaning that it too only exists insofar as it is defined by measurable variables.

SEM proceeds through a series of iterative models in order to find those which best fit the data. Models can be changed with the removal or addition of different measurable (or 'manifest') variables in order to improve the fit of the model, thus revealing which matter most to the construct. In this way SEM was used to explore which of these, beyond those described by Rowe and Kahn, contributed most to successful ageing.

The data from the Archive were presented in Stata Version 9.2 (Stata-Corp, 2006) and were initially analysed in this package. For the HALS data, each case has a unique serial number on which it was possible to match data (for instance on follow-up) using the merge-match procedure in Stata. The basic descriptive data about each subject were extracted as well as a large range of variables of possible use within the models. The model was developed using the LISREL 8.80 programme (Joreskog, 1996). Prepared data were imported into PRELIS from Stata.

Principal component analysis was used to understand any new latent variables. Individual variable path relationships were estimated via the Robust Maximum Likelihood method. The Satorra Bentler Chi-Square was used to estimate the overall fit of the model with the wider population (Satorra and Bentler, 1994).

Measures

Because the first objective of this study was to test Rowe and Kahn's model of successful ageing, variables were selected from the HALS datasets to capture the three factors identified by Rowe and Kahn in their model: risk of disease, level of functioning and engagement with life. The data were all categorical and were re-coded to ensure answers associated with good outcomes were coded in the same direction, to aid interpretation of the model.

Risk of disease was captured by the following four 1984/5 variables: presence of limiting long-term illness, respiratory function, hypertension and smoking status.

Level of cognitive and physical function was captured in the data by the following two 1984/5 variables: self-reported handicap, and general health questionnaire (GHQ) score.

Of these, limiting long-term illness, GHQ score and respiratory function were combined to form the 'function and risk' input variable in the tested Rowe and Kahn model in the first stage of our study, whilst the rest were included as variables in an expanded model in the second stage.

Engagement with life was captured in the data by the following 1984/5 variables: amount of social/educational/voluntary activities undertaken, level of contact with others and physical activities/sports undertaken. All three formed the 'active engagement' input of the Rowe and Kahn model in the first stage of our study and were variables in the final model in the second stage.

The initial variables chosen do not represent a comprehensive list of all potential risk and disease measures, but the best useable 1984/5 data toward the purpose of approximating the Rowe and Kahn model. While originally included as 1984/5 variables in the model, body mass index, memory function, self-reported health and self-reported handicap either demonstrated very weak path relationships or (in the case of self-reported handicap) destabilised the model, and when they were eventually removed from the analysis the model statistics improved. Destabilisation meant that the model no longer fitted the data. The 1991/2 survey data provided both objective and subjective measures that could be tested as variables signifying successful ageing.

In the first stage of modelling, we assigned four variables to signify Rowe and Kahn's model of success. These were: own views about lifestyle, self-reported health in 1991/2, perceived level of physical activity compared with peer age group and ability to get out and about. Subsequently principal component analysis demonstrated two elements to success: a subjective and objective component. The subjective variables that clustered signified a 'confidence' factor; shown by the first three of the 'success' variables. The objective factor was about engagement with life in 1991/2 and was signified by whether one got out and about, combined with three other 1991/2 manifest variables: social, leisure and community activities undertaken, recent deterioration in health or hospitalisation and recent physical activity.

Other 1991/2 variables, including GHQ score, limiting long-term illness and physical handicap, either destabilised the model (in the case of GHQ score) or added little to it (because they overlapped closely with other variables such as deterioration in health), and so were removed.

The data for each indicator are assumed to be drawn from normal distributions within the elderly population, though moderate violations of this assumption would still allow modelling to occur.

Treatment of missing values

Because 'bootstrapping' is considered unsound in SEM, all cases with missing data were removed completely from the analysis. The size of the dataset was large enough to ensure that approximately 1600 subjects with complete longitudinal data were available for modelling.

It should be noted that those 1984/5 subjects who were unable to participate in the 1991/2 study due to death or disability differed in several respects from those who were able to do so. While two thirds of the latter group felt themselves to be in good health, just over half of the former group agreed. In particular, those who had died by the time of the 1991/2 survey had higher levels of disease and disability, smoked more, had fewer leisure and physical activities, and experienced less social contact with friends.

Results

In the first stage of this study, the purpose of the modelling was to ascertain whether a model would converge when combining data from 1984/5 and 1991/2. What emerged was a very simple model where a latent factor that combined function and risk in 1984/5 influenced active engagement in 1984/5, which in turn mediated success seven years later. Figure 8.1 shows this first converged model. Ellipses are used to denote latent variables (here, function and risk in 1984/5, active engagement in 1984/5, and

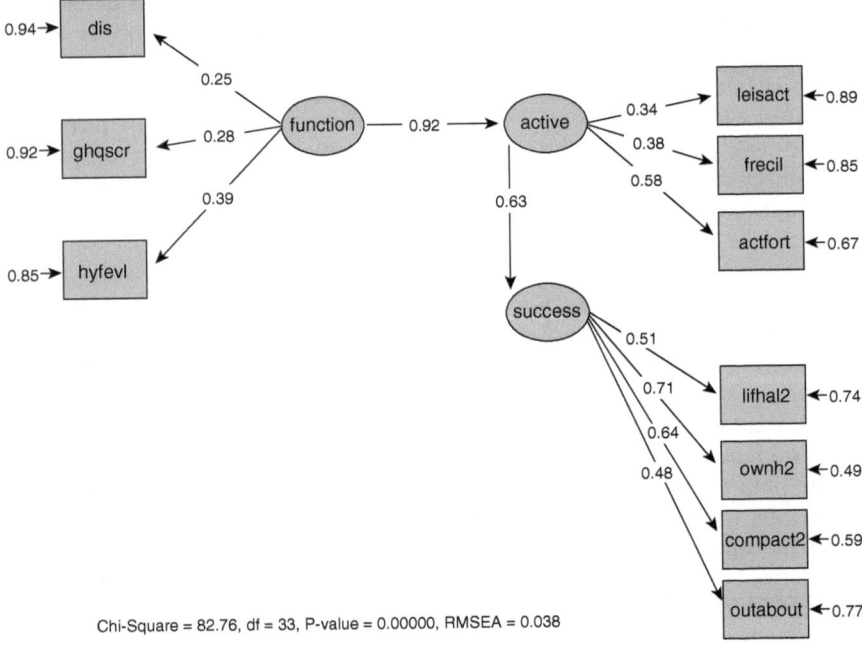

Figure 8.1   A simple converged model, unmodified

successful ageing), boxes indicate manifest variables, single-headed arrows indicate effects, and double-headed arrows indicate associations between variables. The rules for structural equation modelling state that in path analysis with latent variables, one factor loading for each factor (i.e. between an indicator and its factor) should be fixed at 1. This normalises the data, providing a unit of measurement for the (unmeasured) factor; in turn this provides a measure to which the remaining indicators can relate. These fixed paths in the model are indicated by the gray lines.

The manifest 1984/5 HALS1 variables were: limiting long-term illness (represented in Figures 8.1 and 8.2 as 'dis'), GHQ score ('ghqscr') and measured respiratory function ('hyfev1'), which all contributed to the latent variable, risk and function in 1984/5; and leisure activities and hobbies ('leisact'), visiting friends ('freci1') and recent physical activities ('actfort'), the three of which contributed to the latent variable, active engagement in 1984/5. The manifest 1991/2 HALS2 variables were: self-reported lifestyle in the seven years since 1984/5 ('lifhal2'), physical activities in comparison to one's peers ('compact2'), self-reported health ('ownh2') and getting out and about ('outabout'), all four of which together signified success as defined by Rowe and Kahn.

The Goodness of Fit Statistics are shown in Table 8.1 below, and explained in the appendix.

Table 8.1 Goodness of Fit Statistics for first converged model

χ^2	RMSEA	CFI	SRMR	Model AIC
82.76	0.038 90% Confidence Interval for RMSEA = (0.028; 0.048) P-Value for Test of Close Fit (RMSEA < 0.05) = 0.98	0.97	0.064	126.76

In the second stage, many different combinations of manifest variables were tried. Several combinations led to improved models. It became clear that these variables clustered in distinctive patterns, and principal component analysis identified two main components to the latent variable, successful ageing. The first was one's self-expressed view of health and physical competence. This 'how well I feel I am progressing' factor had an element of the comparative with one's age group peers. The other component related to recent activities and events in subjects' lives, like social activities, any recent illness or deterioration in a longstanding condition. This structural model supported a fuller set of variables from the 1984/5 data in the combined 'function and risk' and 'active engagement' domains as well.

Figure 8.2 shows the second model. The model was developed on a randomly selected 50 per cent of the combined HALS1 and HALS2 dataset (not just those able to complete the HALS2 survey). The same model converged on the other 50 per cent of the data subsequently. This model is a better fit to the data than the first model, and it also has been modified to provide a non-significant χ^2, which is a desirable result in SEM. This means that, with relatively few modifications, the model in this sub-population is not different from the wider population and thus this model has potential utility in explaining the hypothesis it is testing: the nature of successful ageing in a British population, in a model proposed by Rowe and Kahn.

In addition to the manifest variables used in the first model, the new model accommodated several additional ones: past history of hypertension in 1984/5 ('pastds9' in Figure 8.2) and present smoking status in 1984/5 ('regfag'), which, in addition to the three manifest variables from the first model, contributed to the latent variable, risk and function; and leisure activities and hobbies in 1991/2 ('leisact2'), recent hospitalisation or deterioration in long-term illness in 1991/2 ('hlthcnd1') and recent physical

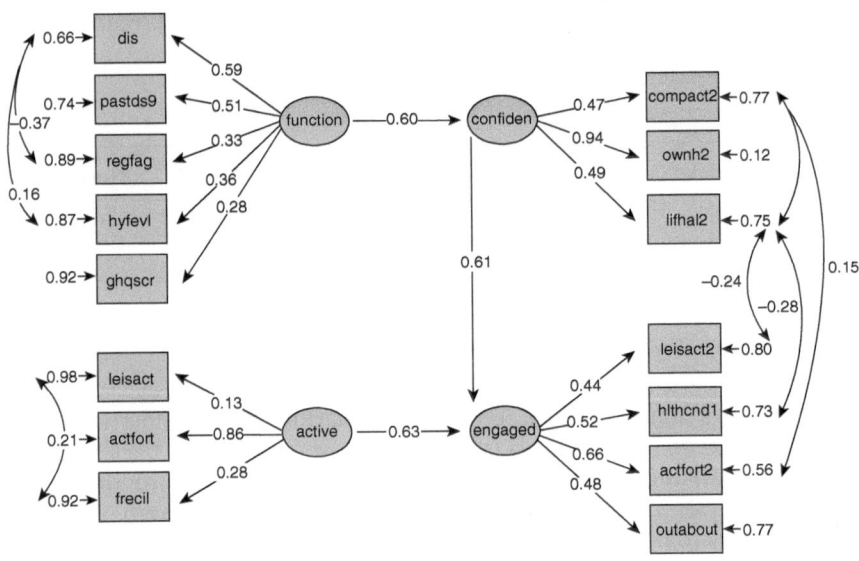

Random 50% sample. Chi-Square=90.53, df=76, P-value=0.12216, RMSEA=0.021

Figure 8.2   The first model with new latent variables for success, in a randomly selected 50 per cent sample of data, and modified to give a non-significant Chi Square

activities in 1991/2 ('actfort2'), which contributed to the latent variable, engagement with life in 1991/2, in addition to getting out and about in 1991/2, which was part of successful ageing in the first model.

The Goodness of Fit Statistics are shown in Table 8.2 below, and explained in the appendix.

The structure of this model was such that both function/risk and active engagement in 1984/5 influenced components of success in 1991/2.

Table 8.2   Goodness of Fit Statistics for first model with new latent variables for success

χ^2	RMSEA	CFI	SRMR	AIC
90.53	0.021 90% Confidence Interval for RMSEA = (0.0; 0.038) P-Value for Test of Close Fit (RMSEA < 0.05) = 1.00	0.99	0.078	181.67

The relationship between the factors in the structure was moderately strong, and all their two sided t-values were significant at the 0.01 level. The ultimate expression of success was active engagement with life in 1991/2, which was mediated by confidence in one's health and abilities in 1991/2 and previous social and physical activities in 1984/5.

Although several other structures were tested, none both converged and gave such a good rendering of the outcome of engagement with life. The possibility that engagement with life in 1991/2 influenced confidence in oneself was also tested – in other words, that confidence was the final outcome of success. This model had a poor fit, and the structural equations indicated poor or statistically implausible relationships between the factors as well.

There were also some strong relationships in the measurement model. These included in 1984/5: long-term illness, hypertension and function/risk; recent physical activity and active engagement with life; and in 1991/2: self-expressed health and confidence; and recent physical activity and engagement with life.

The model was then re-tested on the remaining random 50 per cent of the data. It also converged and with small modifications, the χ^2 was non-significant. This model was also a good fit to the data, although the structural relationships slightly differed from the first random sample. In particular, the function and risk factor in 1984/5 had more influence in the structure and on subsequent confidence in 1991/2 than in the first random model. In the measurement model, much the same indicator variables manifested strong path relationships with their factors, except that respira-

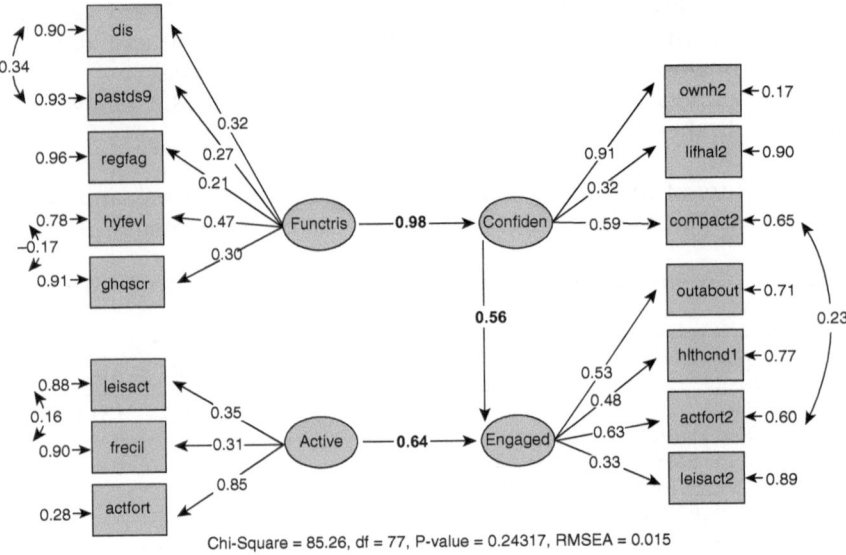

Chi-Square = 85.26, df = 77, P-value = 0.24317, RMSEA = 0.015

Figure 8.3 Other 50 per cent random sample

tory function was the strongest indicator of risk/function in 1984/5. This model is shown in Figure 8.3.

The Goodness of Fit Statistics are shown in Table 8.3 below, and explained in the appendix.

Table 8.3 Goodness of Fit Statistics for second 50 per cent of data

χ^2	RMSEA	CFI	SRMR	AIC
85.26	0.015	1.00	0.075	171.26
	90% Confidence Interval for RMSEA = (0.0 ; 0.030) P-Value for Test of Close Fit (RMSEA < 0.05) = 1.00			

Discussion

The findings of this analysis suggest that successful ageing is somewhat more complicated than suggested in the extant literature. Successful ageing is more than healthy ageing and includes an important subjective element. In these British data, two aspects of successful ageing are discernible, which can be understood as 1) confidence in one's own position and 2) level of engagement. True to the Rowe and Kahn model, past activities such as physical exercise, hobbies, leisure and social contact were important factors. Additionally, however, how one felt about one's own health, physical capabilities and the kind of life one had led was an important factor determining what one could subsequently do. Physical function and risk factors mediated the outcome indirectly, through building subjects' confidence in their ability. This also differed to the Rowe and Kahn proposal, where risk, function and active engagement directly influenced one outcome called 'success'. The model stood up to re-testing on random samples of the dataset, indicating reproducibility.

Implications for future policy

'Successful ageing' therefore can be expressed, and could be used to guide policy in future. It is mainly manifest as social engagement, physical activities and recent health experience, rather than objective measures of disease and disability. Thus, finding ways to support older people to continue to engage in social, cultural and physical activities would seem essential in future. The concept of adding life to years as well as years to life has had widespread acceptance as a reasonable aim, albeit somewhat lacking in detail. This is reflected in current English public health policy (Department of Health, 2004). However, social participation is uneven. For example, research on poor people aged over 85 years living in the east end of London has shown that, although over 80 per cent were healthy enough to engage in normal daily activities without restriction, only about 33 per cent regularly visited friends and relatives and only 34 per cent had other regular activities (Bowling, 1993). Higher levels of inactivity are found in minority ethnic groups (Lawton, 2006), women (Branch *et al.*, 1991), obese people (Nusselder and Peeters, 2005) and the less affluent (Harrison *et al.*, 2005).

These inequalities in participation are more worrying given that previous fitness and activity level influence present fitness and activity in this model. Research shows that although people may know about the health benefits of physical activity, those who do not exercise have low interest and doubt that the effort is worthwhile to them personally, have poor social support, and may perceive their environment not to be conducive to social and physical engagement (East, 1998; McNeill, 2006). These findings have particular implications for what people in mid-life should do to prepare for what is likely to be a long old age. The importance of active engagement with life, on terms that make the individual feel in control, is a golden thread in the model. Policy solutions might include supported 'health walks' or targeted programmes with professional support (Wormald, 2006), aimed at people in mid-life as well as in older age.

It is not clear whether the 'confidence' factor in the model is really signifying something more fundamental such as self-efficacy. This would be better ascertained through interviewing people. It is known that older people who feel confident in achieving hoped-for selves are higher performers in daily activities than those who have negative views of themselves in old age (Hoppmann *et al.*, 2007).

However, others can enable this process. The concept of the 'successfully ageing society' is used to describe a society that would be itself adapting in socially esteemed ways to the presence and needs of growing numbers of older people (Featherman *et al.*, 1993). There might be several aspects to this. Already there are changing attitudes to the economic role of older people (Bloom and Canning, 2000). Given that developed economies are dependent on the workforce, health status is having an increasing impact on economic output, and timely investment in the health and engagement of people before they age can make economic sense. Real income per capita grows faster in countries where life expectancy is five years longer than a country comparable in other respects (Bloom and Canning, 2000). This has a direct bearing on UK government policies aimed at eliminating age barriers in the formal labour market, flexible retirement practices, and the concurrent training of the older workforce for new roles. Changes to the state pension age will challenge the peculiarity of the sudden disappearance of people aged over 65 years from the workforce despite labour shortages and the potential desire of some people to continue at work. Given that the relationship between being active and being healthy is a recursive one, for their own health and quality of life they should be encouraged to continue in paid employment for as long as they are able.

In addition to being involved as grandparents in raising children, older people increasingly act as givers of care to the oldest old who will make up an increasing proportion of populations by 2030 (Robine, 2007). At the moment in Britain, however, their impact is weak and their image is predominantly negative, usually in pejorative language about their demand on public services. While older people can help their cause by using political or social routes to articulate what they expect in return for their contributions, it is the responsibility of opinion leaders to promote a positive image of ageing. The Plan of Action on Ageing that emerged from the United Nations 2002 World Assembly highlights the particular role of the media in creating these negative images, and stresses the untapped social capital locked in older people, advising that many would be ideal as mentors, mediators and advisers (UN, 2002).

One final point for consideration here relates to the housing of older people. Fifty years ago 27 per cent of dwellings in England and Wales were owner-occupied: today the proportion is 66 per cent (Appleton, 2002). Self-determination is important and ownership gives older people more control over their environment. However, remaining at home makes some vulnerable and lonely. Alternatives arrangements are increasingly available to meet the needs of older people who wish to stay independent, but who need support. These new residential options link nursing care with more integrated housing and planned environments, and may in effect promote successful ageing, as they enable social connections such as participation in voluntary work and physical activities. A retirement community started in York in 1998 and funded by the Joseph Rowntree Foundation represents one such promising alternative. The important difference between this model and an enclosed community is continuity with the surrounding area, aiming to create a sense of home through belonging rather than exclusion (Appleton, 2002). While appearing to offer ready-made social activities for people within a safe environment, other pre-adapted built environments such as gated communities may debar wider social integration, and thus inhibit successful ageing.

Weaknesses of the study

The analysis reported here indicates the critical aspects of successful ageing and contributes insights to guide future policymaking around ageing. On the other hand, SEM will not identify 'super-elders' or combinations of people within a group being modeled who are good insurance bets. There is no magic number to indicate when a perfect model has been achieved. The researcher must use her judgment about how plausible the model is epidemiologically and only then how strong the model statistics are – of which there are a number.

As in any model, however, those insights are only as good as the quality of the data and the reliability of the assumptions in the model. The data are of overall reasonable quality but the missing cases in the second round of the study, many of whom died and were older people, differed from those who survived. This will have the effect of extracting a number of people who were compromised in health and function.

More fundamentally, the model has pursued a particular hypothesis about ageing based to some degree on a preconceived model of success. The nature of the research also did not allow modification of the model with the input of the subjects themselves – or indeed any qualitative aspect.

Conclusions

The nature of ageing in western democracies and its positive and negative impacts on society is one of the major debates of the forthcoming decades. It is particularly interesting that a spate of strategies and policies have appeared from the constituent countries of the British mainland in the past five years, reflecting a pressing interest in how to plan for the future of their populations. This is good government, but these policies signal the commencement of a successfully ageing society, not the conclusion.

In terms of policy, the discussion about old age has so far centred on pensions and social care for the frail; it has now moved on to the workforce. It will increasingly focus on active retirement – initially concerning those who have done well enough in previous life to have spending power in old age. Eventually it may address uncomfortable areas such as expectations of society from fitter older people, inequalities in old age, and how to rationally address the end of life.

How the world's population addresses ageing has also caught the public attention rapidly in recent years. However, the popular conception of old age is largely determined by views which are out of date. There will be wealthier and increasingly assertive older people, in larger numbers, who look like winners in life. As business perceives their spending power, they will be courted. Later years may become a noisy place just like the rest of life. The media will come to promote attractive older men and women. The changing nature of the older population will eventually become more visible around us.

There has been insufficient attention to the views of older people themselves in this process, as well as to how these are likely to change in the future, as new cohorts enter old age whose experience in earlier life has been quite different to that of previous generations. Active contributions to the debate from middle-aged and older people are needed and websites such as the recently launched International Longevity Centre-UK allow for this via a tailored blog (ILC-UK, 2006).

'Successful' ageing is still a problematic phrase. It captures something indefinable, superficially attractive but inherently competitive. It signifies winner and losers. Yet we want to avoid the widening trend of inequalities in old age, as has occurred in Britain in other age groups. Active aging may be a better concept. Everyone can aspire to optimise their opportunities for wellbeing in old age. This captures the need for engagement that is apparently so important to a successfully aging society, underpinned by confidence and having goals. The positive components of adding life to years – productivity, participation and fulfillment – need encouragement. For the prevention of inequalities in old age, a purposeful tracking of different groups and action to avert different groups' disengagement, are important challenges for all societies from here on.

Appendix

A range of other measures contributed to the analysis of the model as robust, including the Adjusted Goodness of Fit, the parsimony of the model and the information provided within the structural equations themselves as to the proportion of the variance accounted for by the model. Below are explanations of these measures:

Goodness of fit (GOF) indices

A GOF index only indicates the overall fit of a model, and some parts of the model may fit better than others. A range of measures are presented in printouts. In addition to the classic measure which is the χ^2, there are a large number of GOF indices. There is an overlap between classifications, and some indices fall into one or more categories. There is no consensus on which indices should be used, but in general one index from each classification is chosen (Mulaik *et al.*, 1989). The following have been chosen for the current analysis because they are the preferred measures in modern practice.

Absolute fit indices (χ^2 and SRMR)

The χ^2 is a "badness of fit" measure, in that a finding of significance means the given model's covariance structure is significantly different from the observed covariance matrix. Thus the χ^2 should not be significant if there is a good model fit, while a significant χ^2 indicates lack of satisfactory model fit. The Satorra-Bentler χ^2 statistic was used to provide a test of the null hypothesis that the reproduced covariance matrix had the specified model structure, that is, that the model fit the data.

The standardised root mean square residuals (SRMR) index measures the agreement between the observed and predicted correlation matrix. The closer to 0 it is, the better the fit. Values less than 0.1 are considered adequate.

Incremental fit index (CFI)

These indices compare the relative improvement in a model compared to a base model. A value of the Comparative Fit Index (CFI) of between .90 and .95 is acceptable, and above .95 is good.

Parsimony index (RMSEA)

These indices incorporate a penalty function for poor model parsimony. The root mean square error of approximation (RMSEA) is a measure of absolute fit adjusted for parsimony. There is good model fit if RMSEA less than or equal to .05. There is adequate fit if RMSEA is less than or equal to .08. Hu and Bentler in 1999 suggested RMSEA *bl= .06 as the cut-off for a good model fit.

Information fit index (CAIC)

The Consistent Akaike Information Criteria (CAIC) is population based. This measure indicates a better fit when it is smaller.

Note

1 Full details of the Health and Lifestyle Surveys can be found via the UK data archive: http://www.data-archive.ac.uk/.

References

N. J. W. Appleton, *Planning for Older People in New Osbaldwick* (York: Joseph Rowntree Foundation, 2002).

P. B. Baltes and M. M. Baltes, 'Psychological Perspectives on Successful Aging: The Model of Selective Optimisation with Compensation', in P. B. Baltes and M. M. Baltes (eds), *Successful Aging: Perspectives from the Behavioural* Sciences (Cambridge: Cambridge University Press, 1993), pp. 1–34.

L. F. Berkman, T. E. Seeman, M. Albert, D. Blazer, R. Kahn and R. Mohs, 'High, Usual and Impaired Functioning in Community-Dwelling Older Men and Women: Findings from the Macarthur Foundation Research Network on Successful Aging', *Journal of Clinical Epidemiology*, 46 (1993) 1129–40.

B. Bissett, 'Healthy life expectancy in England at subnational level', *National Statistics*, 14 (2002) 21–9.

D. E. Bloom and D. Canning, 'The health and wealth of nations', *Science*, 287 (2000) 1207–9.

A. Bowling, M. Farquhar, E. Grundy and J. Formby, 'Changes in Life Satisfaction over a Two and a Half Year Period among Very Elderly People Living in London', *Social Science and Medicine*, 36 (1993) 641–55.

A. Bowling and S. Iliffe, 'Which model of successful ageing should be used? Baseline findings from a British longitudinal survey of ageing', *Age and Aging*, 35 (2006) 607–14.

L. G. Branch, J. M. Guralnik, D. J. Foley, F. J. Kohout, T. T. Wetle, A. Ostfeld and S. Katz, 'Active life expectancy for 10,000 Caucasian men and women in three communities', *Journal of Gerontology: Medical Sciences*, 46 (1991) M145–50.

B. D. Cox, M. Blaxter, A. L. J. Buckle, N. P. Fenner, J. F. Golding and M. Gore, *The Health and Lifestyle Survey* (London: The Health Promotion Trust, 1987).

B. D. Cox, F. A. Hupper and M. J. Whichelow, *The Health and Lifestyle Survey: Seven Years On.* (Aldershot: Dartmouth Publishing Company, 1993).

R. Craig and J. Mindell, *Health Survey for England 2005: The Health of Older People* (London: Office for National Statistics and The Information Centre, 2007).

Department of Health, *Better health in old age* (London: Department of Health, 2004).

L. East, 'The quality of social relationships as a public health issue: exploring the relationship between health and community in a disadvantaged neighbourhood', *Health & Social Care in the Community*, 6:3 (1998) 189–95.

D. L. Featherman, J. Smith and J. G. Peterson, 'Successful Aging in a post-retired society', in P. M. Baltes and M. M. Baltes (eds), *Successful Aging: Perspectives from the Behavioural Sciences* (Cambridge: Cambridge University Press, 1993), pp. 50–93.

J. F. Fries, 'Aging, Natural Death, and the Compression of Morbidity', *New England Journal of Medicine*, 303 (1980) 130–6.

R. A. Harrison, P. McEnduff and R. Edwards, 'Planning to win: Health and lifestyles associated with physical activity amongst 15,423 adults', *Public Health*, 120:3 (2005) 206–12.

C. Hoppmann and D. Gerstorf *et al.* 'Linking possible selves and behavior: do domain-specific hopes and fears translate into daily activities in very old age?' *Journal of Gerontology & Psychological Sciences and Social Sciences*, 62 (2007), 104–11.

L. Hu and P.M. Bentler, 'Cut-off criteria for fit indices in covariance structure analysis: Conventional criteria versus new alternatives', *Structural Equation Modelling*, 6 (1999) 1–55.

S. Jacobzine, E. Cambois and J. M. Robine, 'Is the Health of Older Persons in the OECD Countries Improving Fast Enough to Compensate for Population Ageing'? (Paris: Organisation for Economic Cooperation and Development, 2002).

K. G. Joreskog and D. Sorbom, 'LISREL 8: User's Reference Guide' (Chicago: Scientific Software International, 1996).

J. Lawton, N. Ahmad, L. Hanna, M. Douglas and N. Hallowell, '"I can't do any serious exercise": Barriers to physical activity amongst people of Pakistani and Indian origin with Type 2 diabetes', *Health Education Research*, 21:1 (2006) 43–53.

K. G. Manton, L. Corder and E. Stallard, 'Chronic Disability Trends in Elderly United States Populations: 1982–1994, Proceedings of the National Academy of Sciences of the USA', 94 (1997) 2590–8.

L. H. McNeill, K. W. Wyrwich, R. C. Brownson, E. M. Clark and M. W. Kreuter, 'Individual, social environmental, and physical environmental influences on physical activity among black and white adults: A structural equation analysis', *Annals of Behavioral Medicine*, 31:1 (2006) 36–44.

L. P. Montross, C. Depp, J. Daly, J. Reichstadt, S. Golshan, D. Moore, D. Sitzer, D. V. Jeste, 'Correlates of Self-Rated Successful Aging Among Community-Dwelling Older Adults', *American Journal of Geriatric Psychiatry*, 14 (2006), 43–51.

S. A. Mulaik, L. R. James, J. Van Alstin, N. Bennett, S. Lind and D. Stilwell, 'Evaluation of Goodness-of-Fit Indices for Structural Equation Models', *Psychological Bulletin*, 105 (1989) 430–45.

W. J. Nusselder and A. Peeters, 'Successful aging: measuring the years lived with functional loss', *Journal of Epidemiology and Community Health*, 60 (2005) 448–55.

M. G. Parker and M. Thorslund, 'Health trends in the elderly population: getting better and getting worse', *Gerontologist*, 47 (2007) 150–8.

Y. Reisinger and L. Turner, 'Structural equation modelling with Lisrel: application in tourism', *Tourism Management*, 20 (1999) 71–88.

J. M. Robine, J. P. Michel and F. R. Herrmann, 'Who Will Care for the Oldest People?', *British Medical Journal*, 334 (2007) 570–1.

N. Roos and B. Havens, 'Predictors of Successful Aging: A 12 Year Study of Manitoba Elderly', *American Journal of Public Health*, 81 (1991) 63–8.

J. W. Rowe and R. L. Kahn, 'Human Aging: Usual and Successful', *Science*, 237 (1987) 143–9.

A. Satorra and P. M. Bentler, 'Corrections for test statistics and standard errors in covariance structure analysis', in A. von Eve and C. C. Clogg (eds), Latent Variable Analysis: applications for developmental research (Thousand Oaks, CA: Sage, 1994), pp. 399–419.

K. W. Schaie, 'The Optimization of Cognitive Functioning in Old Age: Predictions Based on Cohort Sequential and Longitudinal Data', in P. B. Baltes and M. M. Baltes (eds), *Successful Aging: Perspectives from the Behavioural Sciences* (Cambridge: Cambridge University Press, 1993), pp. 94–117.

K. W. Schaie and S. M. Hofer, 'Longitudinal Studies in Aging Research', in J. E. Birren and K. W. Schaie (eds), *Handbook of the Psychology of Aging*, 5th edn (San Diego: Academic Press, 2001), pp. 53–77.

Stata Corporation, Stata Statistical Software (9.2) (College Station, TX: StataCorp, 2006).

W. J. Strawbridge, M. I. Wallhagen and R. D. Cohen, 'Successful Aging and Well-Being: Self-Rated Compared with Rowe and Kahn', *The Gerontologist*, 42 (2002) 727.

The International Longevity Centre (ILC-UK) http://blog.ilcuk.org.uk/.

United Nations, *Second World Assembly on Aging* (Madrid: United Nations, 2002).

University College London, The Institute for Fiscal Studies and The National Centre for Social Research, *Health, Wealth and Lifestyles of the Older Population in England: The 2002 English Longitudinal Study of Ageing* (London: The Institute for Fiscal Studies, 2003).

G. E. Vaillant and K. Mukamal, 'Successful Aging', *American Journal of Psychiatry*, 158 (1980) 839–47.

H. V. Vintners, 'Aging and the Human Nervous System', in J. E. Birren and K. W. Schaie (eds), *Handbook of the Psychology of Aging*, 5th edn (San Diego: Academic Press, 2001), pp. 135–60.

I. Visco, 'Economic Policy for Aging Societies', Kiel Week Conference, 18–19 June 2001: Aging Populations: Economic issues and policy challenges.

M. Von Faber, A. Bootsma-van der Wiel, E. van Exel, J. Gusekkloo, A. Lagaay, E. van Dongen, D. Knook, S. van der Geest and R. Westendorp, 'Successful aging in the oldest old', *Archives of Internal Medicine*, 161 (2001) 2694–700.

H. Wormald, H. Waters, M. Sleap and L. Ingle, 'Participants' Perceptions of a Lifestyle Approach to Promoting Physical Activity: Targeting Deprived Communities in Kingston-Upon-Hull', *BMC Public Health*, 6 (2006) 202.

9
Developing an Index of Capability for Older People: A New Form of Measure for Public Health Interventions?*

Joanna Coast, Terry Flynn, Ini Grewal, Jane Lewis, Lucy Natarajan, Kerry Sproston and Tim Peters

Introduction

Economic evaluation requires monetary measures or a single outcome for use across all interventions to assist decisions about service provision. Monetary values can be estimated through willingness to pay methods but there are difficulties, with few analyses successfully using these methods to value all outcomes (Drummond *et al.*, 2005). Instead, economic evaluation most often uses a single outcome. The quality-adjusted life-year (QALY), as recommended by the National Institute for Health and Clinical Excellence (NICE) in the UK (NICE, 2004), has become the dominant measure within economic evaluation. QALYs may be formed from a number of different measures, including the EQ-5D (Brooks, 1996), the SF-36 (Brazier *et al.*, 2002) and the Health Utility Index (Horsman *et al.*, 2003), but all focus entirely on health as the outcome of interest. The majority of analyses in the UK are currently conducted using EQ-5D, a measure with five dimensions (mobility, self-care, usual activities, pain/discomfort and anxiety/depression) each with three levels (Brooks, 1996).

There are a number of weaknesses of such an approach for the measurement of outcomes in public health interventions. The first is that QALYs measure health and not quality of life; they are proxies for quality of life (Hyde *et al.*, 2003). This matters when health is not the primary attribute of quality of life, but rather is an influence on an individual's ability to achieve quality of life, by reducing their independence, for example. This is discussed in greater detail in Grewal *et al.* (2006).

The second weakness of the QALY stems from the first, which is that complex and public health interventions, which may impact on quality of life rather than health *per se* (Kelly *et al.*, 2005), are not well served by these measures. This is in large part because their benefits may cross outside of

---

*This chapter contains preliminary analysis of valuation data; the full analysis of these data has been published elsewhere in Coast *et al.*, 2008.

the health sector. For example, an intervention to reduce unwanted pregnancies may lead to improved educational opportunities and thus impact on an individual's quality of life through routes other than health (Swann *et al.*, 2003). Interventions to reduce falls in older people may impact on quality of life through older people's ability to participate in their community not just through their health. Similarly, an intervention to reduce alcohol consumption may impact on quality of life through changes in criminal behaviour, not just health (Waller *et al.*, 2002). Use of QALYs to assess the outcome of such interventions is likely to underestimate the impact of such interventions and thus, potentially, disadvantage them unfairly in decisions about funding given current funding arrangements.

In the UK, resource allocation decisions for providing care for older people are confounded by difficulties in providing services through two distinct branches of government with different administrations, financing and policies. For older people the distinction between 'health needs' and 'social service needs' is often unclear (Lewis, 2001). Current UK policy, however, with respect to the provision of health and social care for older people, suggests that greater integration is required between these two areas (Glendinning, 2003; Department of Health, 2001). Many interventions in these areas are concerned with the public health of older people: reducing falls; continence services; mental health services to improve and detect depression, dementia and loneliness; opportunities to increase physical activity that include marginalised groups. Older people also often have complex needs which may require a broader assessment of outcome than is traditionally associated with QALYs.

Economic evaluation for complex and public health interventions thus requires outcome measures that go beyond health whilst still being amenable for use within economic evaluation. A broader measure would improve the ability of decisionmakers to maximise the benefits of health care to the population and thus enhance overall quality of life. It would ultimately be useful across all health interventions.

This paper reports an attempt to develop a new index for use in economic evaluation, clearly focusing on quality of life (for older people) rather than health or other influences on quality of life. Work was conducted in three progressive stages. First, there was the development of conceptual quality of life attributes using in-depth qualitative work with older people (Grewal *et al.*, 2006). Second, these conceptual attributes were developed further with iterative qualitative work, again with older people, to check meaning and understanding (Coast *et al.*, 2006). Third, a discrete choice experiment[1] was designed, piloted and analysed, to provide values for the attributes of quality of life developed in the first two stages of the work. The final discussion section considers the potential use of this new measure in future economic evaluation, as well as highlighting aspects for future development to ensure its applicability to a wider group.

Stage 1   Development of conceptual attributes

Methods

The starting point of the research was to develop attributes of quality of life grounded in the experience of older people. In-depth interviews were used to obtain conceptual attributes for use in the new questionnaire. For the in-depth interviews, 40 informants aged 65 and over were purposively selected to include the range of personal characteristics (sex, age, health status, household composition, and most recent occupation). Interviews were informant-led and opened with broad questioning about what was important to the older person and what they valued in their lives. Responsive questioning then probed underlying attributes of quality of life. A topic guide was used to ensure systematic coverage of the issues across interviews. This included: background information; the informant's current activities; aspects of quality of life bringing pleasure or satisfaction; aspects of quality of life present and absent in the informant's life. The topic guide also ensured that factors emerging from the prior literature review (Brown *et al.*, 2004) were addressed during the interview.

Interviews were transcribed verbatim and analysed using Framework (Ritchie *et al.*, 2003). Framework uses a systematic, comprehensive and rigorous thematic approach to summarise and classify data. Here, the process of analysis involved two distinct stages: (i) the identification of factors that informants valued or enjoyed or thought were important in their lives; and (ii) the conceptual grouping of data to identify mutually exclusive attributes of quality of life. Analysis comprised researchers reading, reflecting upon, and rereading transcripts to distinguish attributes of quality of life from the influences upon it. Full details of methods are given elsewhere (Grewal *et al.*, 2006).

Findings

Interviews were conducted with 40 older people during July and August 2003. Although discussion initially concentrated upon factors influencing quality of life (activities, relationships, health, wealth, surroundings and religion/faith/spirituality) further probing and analysis suggested that five conceptual attributes were important to these older people. Full details of findings are presented elsewhere (Grewal *et al.*, 2006).

The five attributes of quality of life for these older people were:

Attachment (incorporating feelings of love, friendship, affection and companionship),

> ... family love is different because it's part of you, it's love that extends from the time that they're born, from the cradle to the grave, that love will always be there...(female, aged 85)

We're going on holiday next week with my daughter, her husband and two grandchildren, and – yeah, it's the company, I suppose, that's what – that's what they give us, they give us company (male, aged 70)

Role (incorporating the idea of having a purpose or 'doing something' that is valued by the individual and/or by others),

But when we're doing the big lunches... it's giving isn't it? Making people happy. And... they all enjoy the food I cook, which is nice. (female, aged 69)

Enjoyment (incorporating notions of pleasure and joy, and a sense of satisfaction),

But I used to get a great feeling of upliftment and walking up in the woods – they're just next to our house – and just being at one with everything. And I'd see something different every day. A beautiful butterfly or something that would lift your heart, really beautiful... (female, aged 70)

Security (incorporating ideas of feeling safe and secure, not having to worry and not feeling vulnerable)

I should knock on the door of one of... neighbours and then they take you down to GP clinic then... you can rely on them... I think it helps you 'cos you know you're secure, I think. (male, aged 69)

Control (involving being independent and able to make one's own decisions).

...I wouldn't want to have to rely on other people... no, if it got to the stage whereby I couldn't do anything for myself, again I would just rather that I went 'down the road like', you know (male, aged 70)

Importantly, this work also suggested that the quality of informants' lives was limited by loss in ability to pursue these attributes (Grewal *et al.*, 2006). In other words, it was not poor health itself which reduced quality of life, but rather the influence of that poor health upon each informant's ability to achieve the attributes outlined above.

This finding led the research team to link the findings (Grewal *et al.*, 2006) with the extensive literature on capabilities (Sen, 1992; Robeyns, 2003; Robeyns, 2005; Nussbaum, 2003) and to interpret the five conceptual attributes as a set of functionings, as it was the capability to achieve these functionings which appeared most important in determining the informants' quality of life. Rather than use a more conventional preference-based utility measure to describe the quality of life of older people, the research team developed an index to measure the capability of older people to achieve specific functionings.

The next stage of research was the development of an index of capability which required the transformation of the formal attributes into concepts that had meaning for older people.

Stage 2   Development of lay terminology and meaning

Methods

The conceptual terms arising from the initial qualitative work were defined by and had meaning to the researchers (Grewal *et al.*, 2006), but were not necessarily meaningful either to older people or to policymakers. The conceptual labels needed to be translated into lay language, ensuring that the language used evoked the same meaning for informants (that is, conjured up similar factors) as the conceptual labels developed in the first stage of the research. Any 'translation' process also had to maintain the mutually exclusive nature of the attributes.

A second stage of qualitative work, using iterative techniques to refine the language used, was conducted. Semi-structured interviews were conducted with 19 of the informants interviewed during the earlier work. Informants were approached and asked if they would be willing to take part in a further interview. Informants who gave consent were visited in their own homes. All interviews were tape recorded, again with consent, and transcribed verbatim.

The research team brainstormed for lay terminology that might represent the conceptual attributes. For example, the 'attachment' attribute was defined originally by the research team as 'incorporating feelings of love, friendship, affection and companionship, sources of which appear to include partners, family, friends, and pets'. A number of different ways of expressing this concept were initially proposed, including: love, friendship, companionship and having good relationships. These terms were explored with informants during interviews, as were similar terms for each attribute (Coast *et al.*, 2006). Changes were made to the interview schedule after each small group of interviews, such that topics for which saturation had been achieved (that is, the research team were satisfied that the terminology had been established with the meanings of the terms being clear to respondents) were no longer considered.

Analysis was iterative and ongoing throughout the research, with a small number of interviews being conducted and then analysed before the next few interviews. Analysis used the techniques of constant comparison (Glaser and Strauss, 1968; Strauss and Corbin, 1990) and the writing of accounts to elucidate the different areas (Coast *et al.*, 2006).

Findings

It is not possible here to list all the different terms that were tried for each of the attributes. As a brief exemplar, the attachment attribute tried four terms: companionship, relationships, love and friendship. Companionship and relationships were, however, found to be used as terminology mainly related to sexual relationships, which was not the conceptual notion of attachment derived from the initial interviews:

> ... the only companionship you get is with a person of the opposite sex... (female, aged 73)

Love and friendship were found to have different meanings to informants, both of which contributed to the meaning of the attachment attribute, and so both were included in the final description of the attribute.

> Love... is... your family more... Friendship is people outside... Having people in your life that you care about, who care about you. That's obviously very important. (male, aged 77)

Language used in the eventual measure was 'love and friendship' (attachment), 'doing things that make you feel valued' (role), 'enjoyment and pleasure' (enjoyment), 'thinking about the future without concern' (security) and 'being independent' (control). Attributes that were the most difficult to clarify were the 'security' attribute (where it was difficult to remove the notion of security in relation to crime) and control (where introducing the notion of making choices made people focus exclusively on decisionmaking and not other aspects of control).

Once these terms were agreed, a discrete choice experiment was designed, piloted and analysed, to provide values for the attributes of quality of life developed in the first two stages of the work.

Stage 3   Obtaining values for attributes

Methods

Experimental design

A discrete choice experiment incorporating a best-worst scaling study was used (Marley and Louviere, 2005; McIntosh and Louviere, 2002; Flynn *et al.*, 2007) to estimate values for the index of capability. In best-worst scaling, respondents are presented with a number of hypothetical scenarios. For each scenario, respondents are offered a set of attributes at different levels, and are asked to choose which attribute is the best and which the worst within that scenario. This is equivalent to asking respondents to pick that pair of attributes that maximises the difference in value between them.

Best-worst scaling was chosen because it allows estimation of the impact of entire attributes, not just the levels of those attributes, and because it appears to be a less cognitively demanding task than other forms of discrete choice experiment. Respondents were also asked to decide whether they would value the entire scenario as better or worse than their own current quality of life, and to answer a question about whether the scenario was a life worth living. An example is provided in Appendix 9.1.

Given the number of attributes (five) obtained during the qualitative work, including all possible scenarios of four levels for each within the questionnaire would have required respondents to consider 1024 scenarios. Clearly this was not feasible. It was, however possible to reduce the number of scenarios using appropriate design methodology. The minimum number of scenarios required to estimate values for all the attributes was 16. An orthogonal main effects plan (OMEP) design with 16 scenarios was obtained via the website http://www.research.att.com/~njas/oadir/oa.16.5.4.2.txt. An OMEP would allow the value people derive from each level of each attribute to be estimated independently of all the others. However, estimating the relatively large number of parameters of interest from such a relatively small design can lead to imprecision in the statistical estimates. It was therefore decided to randomly assign respondents to one of two groups, the first of which received the OMEP from the website (group A) and the second of which received a variation of this design (a different OMEP known as the foldover) (group B). Each group therefore received 16 different scenarios. Attributes and scenarios were ordered randomly within the questionnaire.

Sampling

Sampling was restricted to those aged 65 and over, using the sampling frame of respondents to the Health Survey for England (HSE), who were interviewed as part of HSE 2005 and agreed to be reinterviewed. The HSE is a general population sample, taken from the publicly available Postcode Address File and stratified by Local Authority and the percentage of non-manual workers in the postcode sector. Clusters of postcode sectors were randomly selected from within fieldwork areas, with all eligible people in the selected areas being included.

Sample size

Insufficient relevant information was available for the use of power calculations to determine the sample size for this survey. Instead simulations were used, demonstrating that for the design (five attributes each with four levels, and 16 scenarios completed per individual), 100 completed questionnaires would be sufficient to estimate the underlying values (for a wide range of likely variances such that an R-squared of at least 90 per cent would be achieved when regressing estimated values against the true values). These simulations, however, are based on individuals with similar preferences, and there was a desire here ultimately to explore any variations in preferences. A sample size of 300 completed questionnaires was therefore aimed for. Allowing for a response rate of 65 per cent, it was decided to approach 460 households requiring 92 postcode sectors to be sampled.

A total of 478 individuals were sampled. Of these, 319 produced fully productive interviews (in that respondents reached the end of the questionnaire) and a further six resulted in interviews that were abandoned part way through (response rate 68 per cent). Non-responders were categorised as those who refused (n=106, 22 per cent), those who were not available through illness or incapacitation, death or house move (n=37, 8 per cent) and those with whom the interviewer was unable to make contact (n=10, 2 per cent).

Data collection

Data were collected between October 2005 and January 2006. Data were collected by an interviewer attending the respondent's home. All interviewers attended a briefing prior to interviewing. A structured survey schedule was used[2] to administer the questionnaire. Cards were used to describe 16 different scenarios to each individual, one at a time. Each scenario card had on it a list of attributes, each with a level ranging from good to bad. Thus a card might describe a scenario where a person enjoyed little attachment but considerable independence, for example (see Appendix 9.1). For each scenario, the respondent was asked to select the best and worst attributes of that scenario. They were then asked two supplementary questions: whether they would prefer that particular hypothetical scenario to their own health state and, if not, whether they felt that the hypothetical scenario represented a life worth living. They were asked these two questions each time they considered a particular card scenario. Information from completed questionnaires was input initially into SPSS.

Data analysis

Best-worst data can be analysed in a number of different ways (Flynn *et al.*, 2007). For the early analysis of the data presented here, values were estimated using a best-worst model using only questionnaires completed by group A. Therefore responses from 168 people were included in the analysis. Best-worst ratio estimates were first calculated by dividing the frequency that an attribute level was picked as best, across all scenarios and people, by the frequency that it was picked as worst. These best-worst ratios were then square-rooted, following Marley and Louviere (2005), to obtain values on a ratio scale. Stata version 9SE was used for analysis (Stata Corporation, 2006).

Findings

Table 9.1 shows the impact of each attribute, defined as the average quality of life across the four levels. All the attributes found by the qualitative work

Table 9.1   Impact weights for quality of life
attributes as a whole from group A (n=168)

Attribute	Weight
Attachment	2.001
Security	1.146
Role	1.544
Enjoyment	1.361
Control	1.730

Table 9.2   Values obtained for the different levels of the different attributes
from group A (n=168)

Attribute	Value
Attachment	
I can have all of the love and friendship that I want	3.096
I can have a lot of the love and friendship that I want	2.877
I can have a little of the love and friendship that I want	1.557
I cannot have any of the love and friendship that I want	0.474
Security	
I can think about the future without any concern	1.905
I can think about the future with only a little concern	1.207
I can only think about the future with some concern	0.885
I can only think about the future with a lot of concern	0.587
Role	
I am able to do all of the things that make me feel valued	2.244
I am able to do many of the things that make me feel valued	1.986
I am able to do a few of the things that make me feel valued	1.491
I am unable to do any of the things that make me feel valued	0.456
Enjoyment	
I can have all of the enjoyment and pleasure that I want	1.813
I can have a lot of the enjoyment and pleasure that I want	1.826
I can have a little of the enjoyment and pleasure that I want	1.321
I cannot have any of the enjoyment and pleasure that I want	0.484
Control	
I am able to be completely independent	2.745
I am able to be independent in many things	2.357
I am able to be independent in a few things	1.455
I am unable to be at all independent	0.361

to be important (Grewal *et al.*, 2006), were also found to be important in this quantitative work; that is, all attributes were selected by a number of respondents. Table 9.2 reveals that the attribute with the greatest impact is attachment with a value of 2.001, whilst security has least impact (1.146), with increasing levels of impact through enjoyment, role and control. Attachment thus provides the greatest contribution of all five attributes to the value of quality of life.

Table 9.2 shows results in terms of the quality of life for each level of each attribute. These are shown diagrammatically in Figure 9.1 and are informative in terms of indicating the changes in quality of life that have most value to respondents. For example, there are large changes in value between 'none' and 'a little', and between 'a little' and 'a lot' in terms of love and friendship (attachment). The greatest jumps in value are not consistent across levels for the different attributes, with the greatest jump in value for security being between the third and fourth levels (next best to best level) but the greatest jumps for role being between the worst and next to worst level, and for attachment being between the second ('a little') and third ('a lot') levels. For some attributes, particularly enjoyment, there is little difference between the third ('a lot') and fourth ('all') levels, suggesting little difference in the additional values for this group of older people for changes at these levels.

Summing the quality of life scores for each attribute enables estimation of a total score for a given state. Therefore, the data can also be considered in terms of the value of moving from the worst quality of life state (11111), which has a value of 2.361 to the best state (44444) with its value of 11.802. This means that it is possible to estimate the relative impact on quality of life of changes following interventions and to determine which interventions provide the greatest change in quality of life.

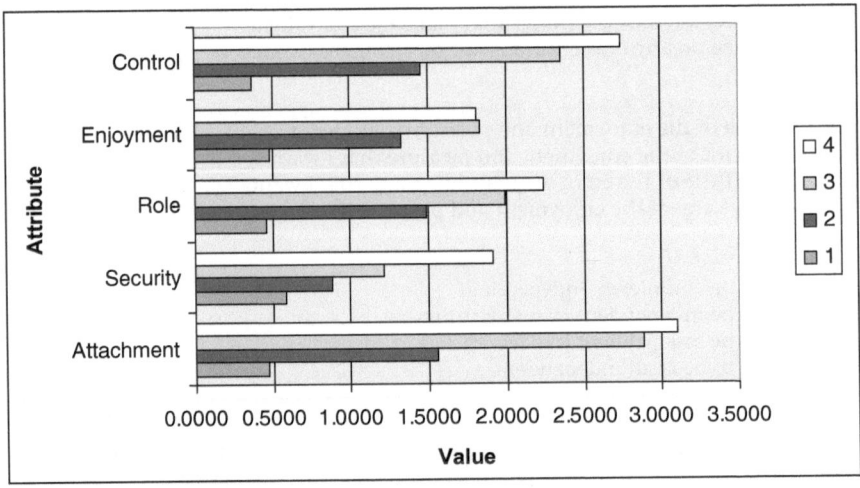

Figure 9.1 Values for the levels of the attributes shown graphically

Discussion

These data provide an important step towards a broader measure of quality of life for use in economic evaluation of public health interventions. They demonstrate the relevance of non-health attributes to quality of life amongst older people and suggest ways in which quality of life could be measured more comprehensively in future, and in ways that do not disadvantage public health interventions in economic evaluations. They also demonstrate the feasibility of measuring capabilities for such purposes. The measure includes attributes which are clearly influenced by health but will also be influenced by other aspects of policy relevant to public health, such as changes in crime, education and social care.

This measure has the potential to be used in economic evaluation of public health interventions, to provide an assessment of the impact of interventions on quality of life capabilities. This could be vital in avoiding underestimating the true impact of interventions. There are, however, a number of research questions that remain to be resolved before these data can be applied in practice to intervention studies and thus used to assist in making policy decisions, in the manner of the current QALY. Current analysis of the data is only preliminary. Additional analysis will be required to compare the impact of analysing under alternative models of human decisionmaking, and to utilise the entire dataset. The measure still needs to be used in groups of older people, to assess its validity, reliability, sensitivity to change and feasibility of use. This work is currently ongoing. Furthermore, this measure is currently only based on the quality of life of older people. This limits its use in the public health arena, where many interventions are based on the relatively young sectors of the population. Possibilities for expanding this work to the general UK population are currently being explored and have the potential to increase the application of the index in future.

Additional questions will include further discussion around anchoring. In a QALY measure, the index is anchored at zero, representing death and thus allowing the potential mortality resulting from an intervention to be combined with quality of life, but the capabilities literature does not advocate any such anchoring. This research is left with a number of options:

1. To not anchor at death. This would be in line with the capabilities literature but would make the measure much less useful for economic evaluation, even in areas such as public health.
2. To anchor according to responses from a (new) survey of older people which would elicit the value of having no capability – being in state 11111 – on a zero to one scale. This could be achieved by asking a single time trade-off question of the type used in the main EQ-5D valuation exercise. The disadvantage is that the cognitive difficulties and statistical limitations of the time trade-off may lead to considerable imprecision in the estimated value of the anchor.

3. To anchor by definition, in that it could be argued that no capability on any of the attributes is essentially equivalent to being dead.

Additional work, both in analysing the data, and at a conceptual level, is required here before any decision can be made with respect to anchoring these data.

The capabilities literature does not recommend that values are based on preferences elicited from a group of the population. One possible means of dealing with this would be to use these values from older people to provide evidence of a final value for the capability index, but to use discussion and debate with a wide variety of groups to further inform a final set of values for use in decisionmaking (Cookson, 2005). Such work may be important, given the finding here that, for a number of attributes, there was little difference in value found between the next to highest and highest levels of the attributes: it is interesting to speculate whether this might be related in part to expectations among this group, and whether, in a group of younger persons, these values would be different.

Conclusion

Policymakers increasingly aim to show that resources are being utilised where they provide the greatest benefit to society. To achieve this, they need broad outcome measures that are able to compare diverse interventions administered from any one of a range of government departments. Such outcome measures must take into account the health, social and other consequences of any proposed intervention and should take into account what is important to people. Evidence from this work suggests that capabilities are important to people, and the capabilities literature also provides a theoretical underpinning for the use of broader measures of outcome. Public health as a discipline is well placed to develop such measures: interventions in this field often impact outside the health of individuals and include interventions that can be thought of as lifestyle interventions. However, NICE's focus on health outcomes, which is apparent from its preference for QALYs to evaluate health interventions, is likely to disadvantage public health interventions. This is a real challenge for public health but it may provide the opportunity for the discipline to lead the way in terms of encouraging the use of broader outcome measures within health care evaluation. The capability index presented here potentially provides a way forward for the evaluation of public health interventions, which will help older people, a group in society who are in particular need of an integrated approach to public policy.

Acknowledgements

This work would not have been possible without the time given up by informants during the qualitative work and respondents to the surveys.

Thanks are also due to the survey interviewers. This work was supported by the MRC Health Services Research Collaboration.

Appendix 9.1 Example card scenario shown to participants

Quality of life

You can have a little of the love and friendship that you want
You can only think about the future with some concern
You are able to do many of the things that make you feel valued
You cannot have any of the enjoyment and pleasure that you want
You are able to be completely independent

Please look at this card and tell me which you think is the best thing, and which is the worst thing in this situation.

Is the situation on this card...

...as good as, or better than, your own quality of life.	1
or is it not as good as your own quality of life?	2

And, is the situation on this card a life worth living?

Yes	1
No	2

Notes

1 Discrete choice experiments are used to quantify choices.
2 The questionnaire was piloted with 30 respondents prior to the main survey.

References

J. Brazier, J Roberts and M. Deverill, 'The estimation of a preference-based measure of health from the SF-36', *Journal of Health Economics*, 21:2 (2002) 271–92.

R. Brooks, 'EuroQol: The current state of play', *Health Policy*, 37:1 (1996) 53–72.

J. Brown, A. Bowling and T. N. Flynn, *Models of quality of life: A taxonomy and systematic review of the literature* (Sheffield: University of Sheffield and European Forum on Population Ageing Research/Quality of Life, 2004).

J. Coast, T. N. Flynn, I. Grewal, L. Natarajan, J. Lewis, K. Sproston, 'Developing an index of capability for heath and social policy evaluation for older people: theoretical and methodological challenges', paper presented to Health Economists' Study Group, London, January 2006.

J. Coast, T. N. Flynn, L. Natarajan, K. Sproston, J. Lewis, J. J. Louviere and T. J. Peters, 'Valuing the ICECAP capability index for older people', *Social Science & Medicine*, 67 (2008) 878–82.

R. Cookson, 'QALYs and the capability approach', *Health Economics*, 14:8 (2005) 817–29.

Department of Health, *National Service Framework for Older People* (London: Department of Health, 2001).

M. F. Drummond, M. J. Sculpher, G. W. Torrance, B. J. O'Brien and G. L. Stoddart, *Methods for the economic evaluation of health care programmes* (Oxford: Oxford University Press, 2005).

T. N. Flynn, J. J. Louviere, T. J. Peters and J. Coast, 'Best-Worst Scaling – what it can do for health care and how to do it', *Journal of Health Economics*, 26:1 (2007) 171–89.

B. G. Glaser and A. L. Strauss, *The discovery of grounded theory: strategies for qualitative research* (London: Weidenfeld and Nicolson, 1968).

C. Glendinning, 'Breaking down barriers: integrating health and social care services for older people in England', *Health Policy*, 65:2 (2003) 139–51.

I. Grewal, J. Lewis, T. N. Flynn, J. Brown, J. Bond and J. Coast, 'Developing attributes for a generic quality of life measure for older people: preferences or capabilities?', *Social Science and Medicine*, 62:8 (2006) 1891–901.

J. Horsman, W. Furlong, D. Feeny and G. Torrance, 'The Health Utilities Index (HUI): concepts, measurement properties and applications', *Health and Quality of Life Outcomes*, 1 (2003) 54.

M. Hyde, R. D. Wiggins, P. Higgs and D. B. Blane, 'A measure of quality of life in early old age: the theory, development and properties of a needs satisfaction model (CASP-19)', *Aging and Mental Health*, 7:3 (2003) 186–94.

M. P. Kelly, D. McDaid, A. Ludbrook and J. Powell, 'Economic appraisal of public health interventions'. Briefing paper (London: Health Development Agency, 2005).

J. Lewis, 'Older people and the health-social care boundary in the UK: half a century of hidden policy conflict', *Social Policy & Administration*, 35:4 (2001) 343–59.

A. A. J. Marley and J. J. Louviere, 'Some probabilistic models of best, worst and best-worst choices', *Journal of Mathematical Psychology*, 49:6 (2005) 464–80.

E. McIntosh and J. J. Louviere, 'Separating weight and scale value: an exploration of best-attribute scaling in health economics', paper presented to Health Economists' Study Group Meeting, Brunel University, 2002.

National Institute for Clinical Excellence, *Guide to the methods of technology appraisal* (London: National Institute for Clinical Excellence, 2004).

M. C. Nussbaum, 'Capabilities as fundamental entitlements: Sen and social justice', *Feminist Economics*, 9:2–3 (2003) 33–59.

I. Philip, Department of Health and OPD(PIP), *Better health in old age* (London: Department of Health, 2004).

J. Ritchie, L. Spencer, and W. O'Connor, 'Carrying out qualitative analysis', in J. Ritchie and J. Lewis (eds), *Qualitative Research Practice: A Guide for Social Science Students and Researchers* (London: Sage, 2003), pp. 219–62.

I. Robeyns, 'Sen's capability approach and gender inequality: selecting relevant capabilities', *Feminist Economics*, 9:2–3 (2003) 61–92.

I. Robeyns, 'The capability approach: a theoretical survey', *Journal of Human Development*, 6:1 (2005) 93–114.

A. Sen, *Inequality reexamined* (New York: Russell Sage Foundation, 1992).

Stata Corporation, *Stata Statistical Software (9SE.0)* (College Station, TX: StataCorp, 2006.

A. Strauss and J. Corbin, *Basics of qualitative research: Grounded theory procedures and techniques* (London: Sage, 1990).

C. Swann, K. Bowe, G. McCormick and M. Kosmin, *Teenage pregnancy and parenthood: A review of reviews. Evidence briefing* (London: Health Development Agency, 2003).

S. Waller, B. Naidoo and B. Thom, *Prevention and reduction of alcohol misuse. Evidence briefing* (London: Health Development Agency, 2002).

10
Recruitment into Lifestyle Modification Programmes: A Cross-Atlantic Perspective

Sarita Bhalotra and Donald S. Shepard

Introduction: the need for lifestyle modification

Demographic and epidemiological trends

In 1962, Leonard W. Larson, MD, then president of the American Medical Association, called for a 'revolution in aging'. He charged physicians to reformulate medicine from 'defence to offence' by emphasising healthy behaviour in the individual throughout the life course (Larson, 2003). Dr. Larson recognised that these changes in medicine were especially important in the context of an ageing society. Since then, the US population has aged significantly, and technological advances have changed the length and nature of the aging process. Chronic, disabling illnesses dominate the landscape of health care needs, while the delivery system remains devoted to acute care. 'The role of (acute) medical care in preventing sickness and premature death is secondary to that of other influences; yet society's investment in health care is based on the premise that it is the major determinant' (McKeown, 1979).

The US Census Bureau estimates that in the year 2000 approximately 35 million people were elderly, defined as 65 or older. This group now makes up 13 per cent of the US population and is projected to increase to 20 per cent by 2030. Life expectancy has increased substantially, to 79.8 years for women and 74.4 years for men in 2001 (Arias, 2006). Moreover, current life expectancy is 18 years for those reaching 65 years of age and seven years for those reaching 85. As life expectancy has increased, those over 85, often referred to as the oldest old, have become the fastest growing segment of the elderly population, comprising two per cent of the population in 2000 and projected to increase to five per cent by 2050. In fact, the number of centenarians, or those 100 or older, is expected to grow from 19,000 in 2000 to 381,000 in 2030 (Federal Interagency Forum on Aging-Related Statistics, 2000).

Currently 125 million Americans, 45 per cent of the population, suffer from at least one chronic condition. Approximately 60 million people, or

48 per cent of the people with chronic conditions, have more than one chronic illness (Faulkner, 2003). By 2020, an estimated 157 million Americans will have a chronic condition, and 81 million of those people (25 per cent of the population) will suffer from at least two chronic conditions. Today people with chronic conditions account for 76 per cent of hospital admissions, 88 per cent of all prescriptions filled, and 72 per cent of all physician visits (Faulkner, 2003). The costs associated with treating the suffering and disability caused by chronic diseases account for 78 per cent of the nation's total medical care costs, including almost 80 per cent of Medicaid expenditures (Faulkner, 2003). In 1990, chronic care costs amounted to $435.5 billion in direct costs (payments for medical services) and $234.2 billion in indirect costs (lost wages and productivity). Treatment for chronic disease accounts for 96 cents of every health care dollar for persons aged 65 and older (Hoffman *et al.*, 1996).

As in the US, the UK also suffers from an increasing burden of chronic illness. In 2005, 16 per cent of the UK population was aged 65 and over and 1.2 million people were over 85 years of age. Further population ageing is projected as baby boomers retire and are replaced by fewer numbers born since 1960 (National Statistics UK, 2006). It is estimated that 80 per cent of all consultations with general practitioners (GPs) in the UK are for chronic illness and that over 17.5 million people live with chronic conditions; further, it is estimated that the incidence of chronic disease in the over 65s will double by the 2030s (Reid, 2004).

The health care system and its need to respond with lifestyle modification: the chronic care model of health care delivery

In both the US and the UK, the increasing prevalence of chronic diseases will require changes in how health services are delivered. The current medical care model focuses on treating acute problems and does not deal as well with chronic illness (Lee, 1998; Havranek *et al.*, 2003; Rothman *et al.*, 2003). Chronic illness care requires a transformation of health care, from an essentially reactive system responding to the already sick, to a proactive system focused on keeping people as healthy as possible and reducing the incidence of preventable chronic health problems (for example, those due to smoking, lack of exercise, or poor diet). As an example, the chronic care model developed by Dr. Edward Wagner through the Improving Chronic Illness Care Program and sponsored by the Robert Wood Johnson Foundation, emphasises high quality chronic disease management at the community, organisation, practice, and patient levels, with a focus on improving collaboration between the community and the health care system (Wagner *et al.*, 1999).

Effective chronic illness management requires an organised delivery system linked with complementary community resources and effective self-management supports and ideally leads to an informed patient and family who are better able to deal with chronic illness. While this model offers great potential to improve care for those with chronic illness, the system improvements and process changes needed require much planning and commitment.

It also requires greater involvement from the patient. Self-management support is a central feature of the chronic care model since the informed, active patient is central to productive patient-provider interactions (Glasgow *et al.*, 2002b). Traditionally, physicians and other health professionals are the experts, but the new chronic disease paradigm portrays people with chronic conditions as their own expert caregivers and health professionals as consultants supporting them in this role (Holman and Lorig, 2000). Emphasis on the importance of patient self-care and healthy lifestyles is increasing throughout the medical system (Salsberry, 1993; Rapley and Fruin, 1999; Stearns *et al.*, 2000; Draper and Sorell, 2002; Miche *et al.*, 2003; Bourbeau *et al.*, 2004).

Current models of disease management and lifestyle modification programmes

One response to the demand for increased self-management and personal responsibility is the development of integrated disease management and lifestyle modification programmes. Fernandez *et al.* (2001) define disease management programmes as 'structured packages of care for patients with a specified disease, often combining medical care with case management and health education services provided by nurses and other personnel'. Instead of treating individual health problems, disease management and chronic care models coordinate resources across the health care delivery system to manage the entire continuum of care (Svensk, 1996; Harvey and DePue, 1997). Well-designed disease management programmes incorporate disease-specific standards and protocols for high risk patients and optimise the use of resources such as personnel, information, and technology to affect efficient preventive and interventional care.

Existing disease management programmes tend to include the following common features: 1) identification of the patient and intervention that is matched with need; 2) use of evidence-based practice guidelines; 3) support for adherence to care plans; 4) support for physicians in monitoring their patients; 5) self-management services to enhance patient adherence; 6) routine reporting with communication between patient, physician and ancillary providers via team conferences, collaborative practice patterns; and 7) collection and analysis of process and outcome measures.

Disease management programmes have been more prevalent in the treatment of some diseases, such as diabetes and congestive heart failure, than of others. Criteria for the selection of targeted diseases include: high dollar cost and high volume conditions; high rate of preventable complications to avoid emergency room and hospital admissions; common low technology and non-surgical chronic outpatient conditions; high degree of variability in patterns of therapeutics; high rates of non-compliance with therapeutic regimens and amenability to education; existence of practice guidelines for the disease; consensus on good treatment, outcome measurements and quality improvement; and no constraints to intervention (Plocher, 1996). In a physician survey Fernandez *et al.* (2001) found that disease management programmes were most commonly available for diabetes (available to 40 per cent of physicians surveyed), asthma (available to 38 per cent), congestive heart failure (available to 22 per cent), and AIDS (available to 16 per cent). They also report that most programmes (88 per cent) were voluntary, meaning that physicians were not required to use them for all eligible patients.

In the UK, self-management is presently an increasingly important policy agenda. For example, the 'Expert Patients Programme' (EPP) was initiated in 2002 by Department of Health to provide skills to people living with long-term chronic conditions to manage their conditions, based on a US model (Department of Health, 2001). The experience of programmes in the US is therefore of direct interest to developing services that support public health in the future. In both countries recruitment to self-care programmes is an issue.

This chapter analyses the experience of the Medicare Lifestyle Modification Program Demonstration (LMPD) in the US, focusing in particular on the problems of recruitment, barriers to enrolment, and suggestions for ways forward.

CMS Medicare Lifestyle Modification Programme Demonstration

Description

The US Centers for Medicare & Medicaid Services (CMS) is the financing body that pays for the health care for US elders aged 65 and over, the disabled, and those with end-stage renal disease (ESRD). CMS regularly initiates demonstration projects aimed at examining opportunities to improve the Medicare programme. Recognising that chronic illness was increasingly responsible for escalating costs at the same time that the benefits did not include its management, the US Congress directed Medicare to conduct the Medicare Lifestyle Modification Programme Demonstration (LMPD).

LMPD tests two cardiac lifestyle modification programmes, which attempt to reduce risk factors for heart disease by assisting people to make changes in their diets and physical activity patterns and to learn better ways to control stress in their lives. CMS selected Brandeis University, Waltham, Massachusetts, USA, to evaluate the Demonstration project, which ran from November 1999 to February 2006. In the LMPD, Medicare beneficiaries with cardiac risk factors or coronary artery disease were invited to participate in one of two 12-month lifestyle programmes: the Dr. Dean Ornish Program for Reversing Heart Disease of the Preventive Medicine Research Institute, or the Cardiac Wellness Program of the Benson-Henry Institute for

Mind/Body Medicine. Each lifestyle programme could enrol up to 1800 Medicare beneficiaries who met eligibility criteria (bypass surgery, heart attack, stent, or stable angina) within the previous 12 months.

The Dr. Dean Ornish Program for Reversing Heart Disease has four main components: diet, exercise, stress management and group support. Twice or thrice a week, participants attend an intensive 12-week programme that teaches them to eat properly, exercise safely, identify and manage stress and feelings such as loneliness or isolation that may affect their health and well-being. Exercise programmes include low-impact aerobic exercise (e.g., walking, biking), as well as strength training. Three hours of exercise per week and one hour of stress management each day are required. Group support sessions are conducted by a licensed facilitator. Diet is vegetarian, limited to less than 10 per cent of calories from fat, with very little or no oil and no egg yolks. Participants are permitted to consume egg whites and fat free dairy products. It is rich in whole grains, whole-wheat pastas, soy products, beans, brown rice, and fruits and vegetables. Following the initial 12-week period, participants are assigned a programme schedule based on the extent of their risk for significant cardiac events and their degree of compliance with the intervention. Following completion of the 12-month programme, ongoing support is available as needed.

The Cardiac Wellness Program was developed by Dr. Herbert Benson and is based on moderate aerobic exercise, individual nutrition counselling (20–25 per cent fat, plant-based diet) and a comprehensive stress management programme. Participants in this programme are required to attend 13 weekly three-hour sessions, which include onsite supervised exercise, nutrition counselling and a comprehensive stress management programme. These sessions include interaction with a Cardiac Wellness team, consisting of clinical nurse specialists, dieticians, and exercise specialists. Ongoing support after completion of the programme includes optional maintenance sessions twice a month and a manual for home use.

The two programmes are similar in that participants alter their eating and exercise habits, engage in stress reduction activities, and participate in support groups. Since patient safety requires trained personnel and medical equipment to be in close proximity, the programmes tend to be hospital-based. While these two cardiac lifestyle programmes encourage many of the changes that are becoming increasingly necessary on a wide scale, there were some important limitations in implementing these programmes. To better understand the challenges faced in promoting lifestyle modification and new models of dealing with chronic diseases, it is useful to highlight and examine the major barriers faced by these trials.

Enrolment in the demonstration

The most serious problem faced in this Demonstration was the extremely low participation rate. In an attempt to determine the extent of the

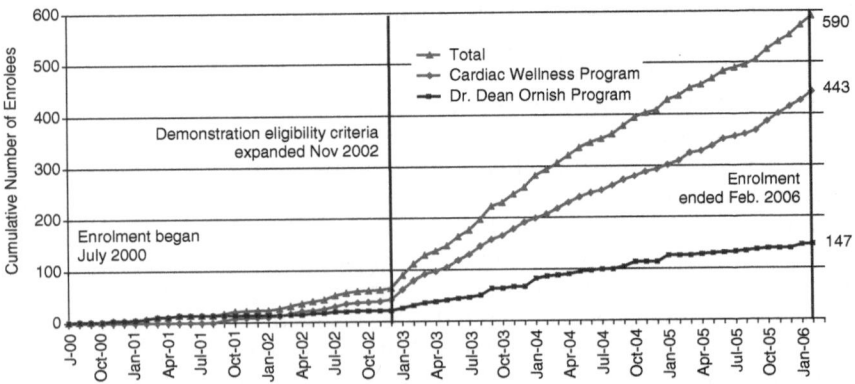

Figure 10.1   Cumulative enrolment in medicare lifestyle demonstration by program

problem, the Brandeis University evaluators first examined statistics from Delmarva Foundation for Medical Care, the quality monitoring contractor for the LMPD. Delmarva requires necessary information to be submitted in writing; it then carefully reviews each applicant's data to ensure that they satisfy the eligibility criteria and that they are not precluded from participating by any exclusion criteria.

Figure 10.1 shows the cumulative enrolment in the Demonstration by programme. Initially, CMS limited enrolment to patients with stable angina and current evidence of substantial coronary blockage, as documented by an angiogram or similar test. These criteria were established to limit the intervention to those patients who needed it most. As of November 2002, after more than two years of enrolment, only 62 patients had been approved and had entered the Demonstration.

In order to enlarge the eligible patient base, CMS expanded the criteria so that patients who had had a heart attack, had cardiac surgery, or received a cardiac stent also became eligible. Enrolment rates were higher over the remaining three years of intake, ending at 590 participants. The final number was only 16 per cent of the legislative ceiling (and projected enrolment) of 3600 participants for the two programmes combined.

The nurse recruitment initiative

In response to inadequate enrolment, the Dr. Dean Ornish Program for Reversing Heart Disease piloted nurse-recruiter positions at several participating West Virginia Hospitals. The programme hired and trained nurse case manager recruitment specialists to focus exclusively on participant recruitment. These nurse recruiters worked with health care providers in the community and in the participating hospitals to educate them on the programme in order to enhance the identification of potential enrolees.

They then met with eligible patients and their families to review the programme and describe how it could help them.

The Dr. Dean Ornish Program developed a resource packet and educational tools for the nurse recruiters, which included both audio-visual and print materials with specific information on the patient's medical condition and the ways in which the programme might benefit that condition. Nurse recruitment specialists carried out eligibility screening, and kept records of patient contact, including any reasons why eligible patients did not enrol. While the recruitment specialists spoke with about 2000 patients, very few patients ended up enrolling, and funding for the nurse recruiter initiative was eventually discontinued.

Enrolment rates in other lifestyle programmes

A review of the literature was undertaken to understand why enrolment had been so low. We were interested in the types of patients who were more likely to choose to participate in lifestyle modification programmes and the factors that made a difference in encouraging eligible patients to enrol.

Who enrols?

In general, studies that report on the demographic and health characteristics of participants in lifestyle modification programmes and of those who decline to participate tend to find that these groups are very similar (Glasgow *et al.*, 1991; Glasgow *et al.*, 2002a), with some suggestion that participation rates are particularly low for lower income, elderly, and less educated patients [National Health Intervention Study], as cited in (Toobert *et al.*, 2002).

Current data also suggests little difference between participants and non-participants in terms of their health status. For example, in their study of recruitment of women with type 2 diabetes into a lifestyle programme based on the Dr. Dean Ornish programmes, Toobert *et al.* (2002) found no statistically significant differences in age, body mass, age diagnosed with diabetes, type of diabetes medication, or percent of smokers between those eligible patients who chose to participate and those who did not, but did find that participants typically tended to have fewer years of taking medications and fewer years diagnosed with diabetes.

The most common reasons for refusal – time commitments, lack of interest in the proposed diet, and lack of interest overall – were not specifically linked to the health or demographic status of the patients (Toobert *et al.*, 2002). Hampson *et al.* (1995) found that diabetes patients' individual beliefs, particularly beliefs about the efficacy of treatments, influence the likelihood that they would adhere to certain diets and engage in physical activities. This conclusion suggests the need to specifically address such perceptions when recruiting potential participants to the programme.

There is a particular interest in encouraging elderly or sicker populations to join these programmes and some researchers have focused specifically on these groups (Glasgow *et al.*, 1991). This literature is particularly relevant for the LMPD trials. Mills *et al.* (1996) compared enrolees and non-enrolees in a physical activity programme that targeted older lower-income adults. The main differences between enrolees and non-enrolees were that enrolees were younger, more likely to be native English speakers, less likely to be completely sedentary, and more likely to be overweight. Similarly, Wagner *et al.* (1991) compared participants and non-participants in a senior health promotion programme. While the two groups were generally similar in health status indicators, participants were generally higher-income and better educated, were more involved in community activities, smoked less, and self-rated their health status as better than non-participants. Moreover, older people who are in good health and already have a history of exercise activity tend to be more likely to participate in exercise programmes (Boyette *et al.*, 2002). These findings suggest that, overall, programmes that target elderly populations are better at recruiting people of higher socioeconomic status who are more engaged in their communities and are in slightly better health.

Other researchers have addressed the issue of reaching out to underserved and harder-to-reach populations. It is not clear exactly why participation in these groups is lower, whether it is a result of system oversight, patient self-selection, or lower overall contact between these patients and the medical system. In particular, a number of studies note the importance of actively targeting African-American populations (Vollmer *et al.*, 1998; Warren-Findlow *et al.*, 2003; Parra-Medina *et al.*, 2004). Programme location, programme involvement with a community centre, and specifically targeted recruitment messages in particular, seem to be important in recruiting and retaining underserved groups (Warren-Findlow *et al.*, 2003; Parra-Medina *et al.*, 2004).

Importance of method of contact

One of the most important factors in determining who enrols in lifestyle programmes appears to be method of contact. There are two important pieces to this process – referral of patients by health care providers and recruitment of potential participants by programme staff. First, it appears that some patients are less likely to be referred by their physicians. For example, Toobert *et al.* (2000) found that women tended to be referred to cardiac rehabilitation programmes less frequently than men. Physician referral is an important step in recruitment referral, as trusted contacts increase the likelihood that a person will participate in these programmes.

How patients are recruited is also important in determining who will choose to participate in a lifestyle programme. Sarkin *et al.* (1998) found that participants who had been recruited using passive methods (where literature was sent to patients who were asked to respond if interested) tended to be more physically active and to have lower blood pressure. Active recruiting methods, where people were telephoned and asked to participate, resulted in a more representative sample and a higher overall recruitment rate. Manjer *et al.* (2002) compared participants in a cancer and diabetes lifestyle programme. They found that people who were successfully recruited through passive methods were generally older, more likely to be female, and had more financial resources. Passive method recruits in this study were also more likely to already be engaged in healthy lifestyle activities and had lower frequencies of disease, lower cancer incidence, and lower mortality rates than those recruited through active methods (Manjer *et al.*, 2002).

Barriers to programme success

As LMPD demonstrates, the biggest barrier to achieving short- or long-term health outcomes may be an inability to recruit and enrol enough patients into interventions such as lifestyle modification, chronic illness care, or disease management. While in theory lifestyle and behaviour programmes may be an effective way of dealing with chronic health problems, there are a number of practical barriers to successful implementation of these programmes which exist at the patient, provider, and organisational levels.

Patient barriers

A major group to be convinced of the importance and efficacy of lifestyle programmes is, of course, the patients who will potentially benefit from them. As our discussion of recruitment and enrolment indicate, patients have been slow to respond to these programmes, partly because of the responsibility and the serious changes that full participation in these programmes requires. In the LMPD trial, major barriers for patients included out-of-pocket costs, transportation and other logistical problems getting to the programme site, difficulty adapting to programme requirements they felt were too rigorous and time-consuming, too much paperwork, and a screening process that was too long. Three additional barriers impede the spread of self-management education from a patient's perspective. First there is a lack of trained personnel, which makes these programmes unavailable in many primary care settings. Second, people with chronic conditions are attuned to the medical model in which they depend on professionals, rather than a patient-physician partnership model. Finally, Medicare, Medicaid, and most private health insurance companies do not reimburse the costs of self-management education programmes.

Provider barriers: community physicians and other referral sources

To treat chronic illness successfully, disease management and lifestyle modification programmes rely on crucial referrals from community physicians.

While these programmes and lifestyle interventions have become increasingly popular in managed care organisations, they are still not widely supported by primary care physicians (Waters *et al.*, 2001). HMOs and other payers complain that doctors have remained reluctant to buy into disease management programmes even though numerous guidelines and protocols have been developed for their implementation (Leider, 2001).

Many of the concerns that physicians voiced in the LMPD were typical of the concerns that appear in the literature about these programmes. First, there was doubt regarding the clinical efficacy of these programmes and concerns that information about the programme was incomplete and outdated. Further, even if effective, they doubted that patients would really comply with programme guidelines. They did not want to refer patients they thought might fail, and were frustrated when patients they did refer faced long delays or were found to be ineligible. In addition, they reported that it was easier to prescribe drugs or use other medical or surgical interventions. They also had practical concerns about the bureaucratic implications of these programmes, for example, the potential loss of revenue and patients, and too much time taken away from patient care activities.

Physician compliance with treatment guidelines similar to those in the LMPD trials tends to be fairly poor for a number of reasons (Jamison *et al.*, 2002). Some physicians who participated in a disease management programme for patients' chronic pain resented the notion that they needed to be told how to change their practice and did not like the 'cookie cutter' aspects of these treatment methods, which did not allow for subjective decisionmaking (Jamison *et al.*, 2002). In addition, they felt that using the suggested treatment algorithms took too much time away from office visits and that the guidelines were too complicated to be practical (Jamison *et al.*, 2002). Even though most physicians have accepted the importance of physical activity and healthy diet in reducing risk for a number of morbidity and mortality measures (Lewis *et al.*, 1986; Green *et al.*, 1988), relatively few of them are willing to incorporate interventions which include these activities into their daily practice (Pinto *et al.*, 1998; Albright *et al.*, 2000).

Physicians tend to suggest diet and behaviour changes less often for some groups than for others, for example, offering such advice less frequently to blacks, males, rural and younger patients (Friedman *et al.*, 1994). Goldberg *et al.* (1993) surveyed physicians regarding their practice of counselling patients to quit smoking. Physicians reported that they were more likely to give smoking cessation advice to patients who were young, to those who had reversible conditions, to those they felt were receptive to interventions, and to those who had attempted to quit smoking in the past. Taira *et al.* (1997) found that physicians were more likely to discuss diet and exercise programmes with high-income patients needing such advice than with clinically similar low-income patients but more likely to discuss smoking with low-income patients.

Physician attitude is an especially important predictor of intervention. Specifically, physicians must believe not only in the efficacy of available treatment programmes for lifestyle factors, but they must also feel that they personally can successfully encourage people to pursue these programmes. After reviewing and analysing these trends, (Albright *et al.*, 2000) conclude that barriers to physician intervention include lack of the skills required for exercise counselling, lack of confidence in the effectiveness of physician advice, lack of institutional support and referral options, time pressures, and little or no reimbursement for preventive care. (They cite Rosen *et al.*, 1984; Wells *et al.*, 1984; Orleans *et al.*, 1985; Lewis *et al.*, 1986; Kottke *et al.*, 1987; Lewis *et al.*, 1991; Pinto *et al.*, 1998).

Clearly, it is not simply the case that physicians lack interest in encouraging healthy lifestyles. Larme and Pugh (1998) find that health care providers are generally frustrated by what they perceive is a lack of organisational support for treating complicated chronic diseases like diabetes. Lack of institutional support operates as a deterrent for engaging in lifestyle interventions. Physicians surveyed about preventive interventions reported that they felt this work was important, but worried about the time and resources it took away from curative work, and their own ability to cope with their workload (Bruce and Burnett, 1991).

Organisational and financial barriers

In the LMPD trial programme, some staff members shared their concerns and hesitations about participating in these Medicare trials. Some were not convinced of the clinical efficacy of these programmes, others wondered about their impact on established programmes and services. These reservations are major barriers, as they reduce the likelihood that staff members will be willing to make changes. The programmes were seen as being financial loss leaders, taking resources from other needs, and they were sometimes seen as too 'political'. Other barriers included the expense of mailings to patients, limited time available for targeted recruitment, and the extensive documentation required for programme tracking. A major focus of concerns from a provider organisation perspective is that reimbursement schemes do not appropriately compensate for what the programme is asked to do, especially in light of the questions about clinical efficacy.

LMPD required a co-payment from patients unless the organisation chose to waive it for all patients. The two most common methods of cost-sharing (co-payments and co-insurance) require patients to pay some of the costs of prescriptions and medical services out-of-pocket at the point of service. Economic theory suggests that these mechanisms will result in reductions in utilisation of health services; this impact of cost-sharing has been well documented in the health services literature [(Roemer *et al.*, 1975; Solanki and Schauffler, 1999; Joyce *et al.*, 2002), for competing outcomes see (Blais *et al.*,

2001; Pilote *et al.*, 2002)]. Co-payments do not need to be very high to have a deterrent effect (Simon *et al.*, 1996).

Researchers have also attempted to evaluate the nuances of how cost-sharing reduces costs in different populations and for different medical services. While it is preferable to reduce the use of non-essential services, there is concern that cost-sharing will lead to utilisation reductions in essential and preventive services. Liu and Romeis (2004) found a decrease in the utilisation of essential drugs. Other studies have also found reduced use of both essential and non-essential medications (Joyce *et al.*, 2002). Solanki and Schauffler (1999) found that the largest negative use effects of cost-sharing were on preventive counselling in indemnity plans and on mammograms in all health plans. Both major forms of cost-sharing (co-payments and co-insurance) were found to have direct negative effects on preventive counselling, pap smears, and mammography (in PPOs) (Solanki *et al.*, 2000).

The specific impacts of cost-sharing on poor and elderly populations have been cause for concern. It has been hypothesised that cost-sharing measures will be particularly burdensome for these groups and that they will be more likely than other groups to reduce their use of essential services (Trude, 2003). A number of studies support this theory, noting that cost-saving measures have reduced the use of both essential and non-essential medications among low-income and elderly groups (Tamblyn *et al.*, 2001; Joyce *et al.*, 2002). Further, reductions in the utilisation of essential services are more likely to be harmful for elderly patients (Tamblyn *et al.*, 2001). There is also concern that cost-sharing mechanisms will adversely affect sicker, chronically ill patients (Trude, 2003).

Ways forward

Incentives to patients to overcome financial barriers

Initially in the LMPD, sites were expected to collect co-payments from participants equal to 20 per cent of the total programme fee, consistent with general Medicare policy. For approved Medicare services, many beneficiaries purchase supplementary medical insurance to cover these co-payments. For the poor, the Medicaid programme generally covers co-payments. These options were not available in LMPD. The resulting co-payment proved to be a psychological barrier, if not an actual one in many cases. To increase participation, programme sites later waived the co-payment to participants and accepted the decrease as a financial loss.

The extensive literature regarding patient cost-sharing referenced earlier confirms the increased likelihood that patients will use fewer treatments, especially non-urgent treatments, if they are required to pay more for these services. Services with high co-payments would be utilised only by patients with extreme need, who would utilise more resources and staff time. By waiving co-payments, organisations may benefit by attracting a greater number and broader spectrum of patients.

Improving physician cooperation

Financial incentives for physicians can be aligned to encourage preventive work. Waters *et al.* (2001) found that financial incentives for case management programmes and for improving management information systems were positively linked to physician participation in and attitudes towards preventive care. A number of research groups have conducted intervention trials to find ways to improve physician cooperation and efficacy. Some propose fairly simple solutions. For example, Leider (2001) suggests that to encourage doctors to buy into disease management programmes, HMOs should share the cost savings with participating physicians.

Another straightforward suggestion based on the literature is to convince physicians to try these types of programmes. Those who have participated in behavioural intervention programmes tend to rate them fairly highly. A survey of physicians in California familiar with disease management programmes found that physicians considered disease management programmes effective in increasing the overall quality of patient care and the quality of care for the targeted disease without negatively affecting physician workload, income, or patient satisfaction (Fernandez *et al.*, 2001). In general, physicians have been receptive to incorporating short, healthy-lifestyle talks into office visits when specifically asked to do so (Albright *et al.*, 2000).

Institutional support and training are key ingredients. Physicians who had received training in lifestyle counselling were more likely than other physicians to bring these issues up in office visits (Thompson *et al.*, 1993). Sherman and Hershman (1993) found that a major predictor of physicians' counselling patients on lifestyle change was the physicians' belief in their ability to counsel patients effectively. Cohen *et al.* (1989) found that basic interventions such as labelling patients' charts and having nicotine gum available encourage physicians to counsel patients about quitting smoking. The finding that physicians believe they already provide high quality care and do not want to engage in system changes (Wagner *et al.*, 2000) suggests that most health care organisations need to implement system improvements to provide support for lifestyle modification programmes.

Organisational changes for health care institutions

To encourage financial investment in these programmes, their benefits must be marketed to health care organisations as well as to patients and physicians. For these prevention programmes to be implemented on a wider scale there must be some reorganisation of service delivery as well as of the financing system and larger medical care systems will have to agree that this is a beneficial and clinically sound method of delivering care.

Specific aspects of lifestyle programme organisation were also highlighted in the literature. Leonard *et al.* (2003) identify four key aspects of successful longitudinal programmes: 1) effective partnerships with community-based agencies, 2) selection and training of motivated programme staff, 3) participant-focused interventions, and 4) motivated professional research staff and organisations. They argue that successful recruitment depends on the programme's ability to establish interpersonal relationships with potential participants, including demonstrating respect for them and showing interest in their lives and experiences. The initial recruitment attempt is key in establishing these relationships (Leonard *et al.*, 2003).

Designing programmes around the needs of target populations

Addressing patient concerns will require ensuring that these programmes are specifically designed around the needs of targeted populations and that treatments are individualised. Self-management is a complex process for patients and should include addressing the emotional aspects of these programmes (Whittemore *et al.*, 2002). Older adults have different needs and require more support and socialisation to participate in lifestyle programmes, with interpersonal interaction being particularly important in these groups. Krichbaum *et al.* (2003) found that teaching patients to self-manage diabetes required interaction and not just lectures. To successfully retain elderly patients, programmes must be targeted to their needs (Miller and Iris, 2002). Timmerman (1999) found that the key success factors for patients making lifestyle changes were having specific goals, planning for barriers and challenges, and having the flexibility to make adjustments throughout the process. The ability to be in control of the process was a key ingredient.

One solution for overcoming barriers: social marketing

Some aspects of lifestyle programmes are even more difficult to implement than others. Researchers have noted in particular the difficulty in convincing patients to incorporate physical exercise or new eating plans into their daily routines (Gaede *et al.*, 2001). Education and specific instructions alone are not enough to influence these behaviours. For example, (Gordon *et al.*, 2002) found that educating patients and providing them with a specialist nurse led to only modest improvements in these areas.

To deal with one major participant enrolment barrier, lack of interest or belief that the programme is appropriate, programmes will need to be marketed more effectively to convince potential participants that the benefits outweigh the costs. Attempts at convincing individuals to alter their lifestyles for personal or societal good have proven difficult. Leonard *et al.* (2003) estimate that participation in intervention studies is generally around 20 per cent with retention rates ranging between 45 per cent and 65 per cent. Traditional methods of marketing do not seem to be successful in campaigns encouraging social change. Rangan *et al.* (1996) highlight specific challenges that must be faced by social change campaigns, two of which they see as especially applicable to lifestyle programmes. First, the target community may oppose the change that is being advocated. Second, adoption costs may actually exceed tangible benefits, especially if the costs are immediate and benefits are long term, for example with smoking cessation or diet programmes.

One response to these challenges has been the development and utilisation of social marketing techniques – the use of commercial marketing techniques to achieve a social good. See Chapter 4 this volume, Andreasen defines these techniques as 'the application of commercial marketing technologies to the analysis, planning, execution, and evaluation of programmes designed to influence the voluntary behaviour of target audiences in order to improve their personal welfare and that of their society' (as cited in Neiger *et al.*, 2003). The main difference between social marketing and most health education campaigns is that social marketing campaigns are persistently focused on consumers (Neiger *et al.*, 2003). While a number of studies refer to these techniques, critics note that only rarely is social marketing employed fully and appropriately. Specifically, health promotion interventions often lack an overarching marketing plan (Neiger *et al.*, 2003).

If a project is to be successful at convincing a target audience to behave in certain ways, then the first step is to tailor a message that highlights the particular benefits of joining and adhering to a programme. If a group is resistant to a message, researchers may need to disseminate scientific evidence. For instance, early smoking cessation programmes were once considered pushy, unnecessary interferences into people's personal lives. Current lifestyle programmes could be seen the same way, so there is first a need to reinforce information about the short- and long-term consequences of not changing behaviours (Rangan *et al.*, 1996). For example, one group found that in the short term, health promotions for mammographies that were targeted to an individual's need for information were more likely to persuade people to get a mammography (Williams-Piehota *et al.*, 2003). Changing people's attitudes requires, in part, affecting normative behaviour for the groups they belong to and strategies by one group (in this case, the proponents of lifestyle modification) to influence another group (in this case, those who would benefit) (Kotler *et al.*, 2002).

Messages that are targeted to a specific group or those which involve interaction with the target audience are more likely to be successful. Marcus *et al.* (1998) found that individuals had high recall of mass media messages but were not generally convinced by these campaigns to change their behaviour. Interventions that used telephone contacts in addition to print messages were able to change behaviour in the short term. The most effective interventions, however, were those that had more personal contacts and were tailored to the target audience (Marcus *et al.*, 1998). One campaign that aimed to reduce cardiovascular risk among Hispanic Americans found it necessary to break down the target population into six subgroups, each of which was thought to respond to distinct types of messages (Williams and Flora, 1995).

Education is a necessary, but not sufficient, component of successful social marketing campaigns. After initial contact, it seems that repeated interactions and reinforcements encourage specific behaviours and continued participation. According to Johnson *et al.* (2003), health campaigns that combined education with mailed reminders were more successful than either alone at encouraging elderly rural individuals to get pneumococcal immunizations. Lifestyle changes were more likely to occur when contacts from the programme included some form of personalised support. Patients who received counselling about cardiovascular risk prevention made improvements in several physiological risk factors (Simpson *et al.*, 2004). Similarly, patients who received monthly home visits from pharmacists or weekly calls and menus from nutritionists were also more successful at adhering to lifestyle programmes than comparison groups who received traditional care (Gleason *et al.*, 2002; Peterson *et al.*, 2004).

Rangan *et al.* (1996) take the analysis a step further and create a typology with categories of social change programmes. The Medicare LMPD programme falls into the category in their typology in which the costs of participation are high but the benefits are tangible and personal as well as society-wide. For this type of programme they suggest a specific type of marketing that balances communication efforts with a strong support system. Programmes of this kind require intensive community-level support for the target community. Successful social marketing campaigns must be 'mission driven, but market led' (Rangan *et al.*, 1996). In other words the focus must be on how to appeal to specific target groups, not only on the programme's agenda.

The UK has taken a lead in suggesting the use of social marketing techniques to accomplish changes in lifestyle, for example, as described in the public health white paper from the Department of Health, *Choosing Health* (2004). For more on social marketing, see Chapter 4, this volume.

Implications for the United Kingdom

As evaluators working in the US, the authors have reflected on the implications of this evaluation for the UK and other countries. While some elements of this demonstration are linked to the health care system in the US, many transcend this context. Factors that favour or impede enrolment operate at many levels, from the individual patient to the health care system. At one end of the spectrum, patient factors appear to be similar. Ischemic heart disease is a major cause of morbidity and mortality in the UK as it is in the US, representing seven per cent and nine per cent, respectively, of the countries' total disease burden in Disability Adjusted Life Years (DALYs) (World Health Organisation).

At the other end, system and institutional factors paint the largest contrasts. The US health care system is pluralistic. One important set of institutions is the group of sites offering the Medicare demonstration programme. They were mostly independent, non-profit hospitals. Each hospital depends on Medicare, private insurers, patient payments, and other payers for its financial viability. By contrast, hospitals in the UK depend almost entirely on the National Health Service for funding.

Referring physicians (often cardiologists, surgeons, or internists) represent another contrasting institution between the two countries. Physicians in the US receive compensation from a multiplicity of payment sources, while physicians in the UK generally have a single payment arrangement – salaried employment for hospital-based specialists or contracts for GPs.

The pluralism of the US health system may mean that hospital and physician factors have posed greater challenges for the LMPD than if a comparable demonstration had been conducted in the UK. In fact, the UK's single source of funding for hospitals and physicians and the unified database being assembled may provide powerful tools for implementing changes so that medical practice will more closely follow medical evidence. For example, in 2005, England's Department of Health announced the first results from the application of its Quality Outcomes Framework (QOF) for General Medical Services. On average, primary care practices achieved 91 per cent of the available QOF points and earned an average annual bonus of £74,299 (England Department of Health, 2005). Although GP practices can earn many QOF points for appropriate treatment of cardiac diseases, participation in lifestyle modification or cardiac rehabilitation are not parts of the current indicators. On the other hand, existing indicators already embody two important principles: the use of population-based indicators for important services, such as vaccinations, and an incentive for regular management visits for patients with chronic diseases, such as heart disease (Department of Health, 2005). Further, as the UK is more likely to implement such programmes in the community (as opposed to LMPD, which was largely hospital-based), associated costs should be less, and therefore pose less of a barrier.

This evaluation suggests that each side of the Atlantic can garner lessons from the other. England's QOF has parallels to Medicare's 'Pay for Performance' initiative in hospitals and physicians' practices. England's QOF experience suggests that measurement and incentives can be powerful tools for physicians' practices, while the US experience demonstrates the ability to monitor and improve hospital performance. A service such as lifestyle modification requires collaboration from both types of institutions.

When LMPD was planned, enrolment was not expected to be a problem, as there were a large number of eligible Medicare beneficiaries with ischemic heart disease. The barrier to participation was thought to be largely financial. However, the experience from 2000 through 2006 showed the challenges of enrolment and identified key success factors, such as champions of the programme within the institution providing the service; interest by referring physicians; data systems for tracking patients across institutions; and patient support systems for encouragement, relieving anxiety and, when needed, arranging transportation. Results from the outcomes evaluation of LMPD will soon be available, and can provide further information for improving the implementation of needed programmes such as LMPD. As researchers and evaluators, the authors hope that health care systems on both sides of the Atlantic can continue to put these measures in place and to reward stakeholders for their successes.

References

C. Albright, S. Cohen, L. Gibbons, S. Miller, B. Marcus, J. Sallis, K. Imai, J. Jernick and D. Simons-Morton, 'Incorporating physical activity advice into primary care: Physician-delivered advice within the activity counseling trial', *American Journal of Preventive Medicine*, 18:3 (2000) 225–34.

E. Arias, 'United States Life Tables 2003', *National Vital Statistics Reports*, 54:14 (2006).

L. Blais, J. Boucher, J. Couture, E. Rahme and J. LeLorier, 'Impact of a cost-sharing drug insurance plan on drug utilization among older people', *Journal of the American Geriatrics Society*, 49:4 (2001) 410–14.

J. Bourbeau, D. Nault and T. Dang-Tan, 'Self-management and behaviour modification in COPD', *Patient Education and Counseling*, 52:3 (2004) 271–7.

L. Boyette, W. Lloyd, J. Boyette, E. Watkins, L. Furbush, S. Dunbar and L. Brandon, 'Personal characteristics that influence exercise behavior of older adults', *Journal of Rehabilitation Research and Development*, 39:1 (2002) 95–103.

N. Bruce and S. Burnett, 'Prevention of lifestyle-related disease: General practitioners' views about their role, effectiveness and resources', *Family Practice*, 8:4 (1991) 373–7.

S. Cohen, G. Stookey, B. Katz, C. Drook and D. Smith, 'Encouraging Primary Care Physicians to Help Smokers Quit. A Randomized, Controlled Trial', *Annals of Internal Medicine* 110 (1989) 648–52.

Department of Health, *The Expert Patient: A New Approach to Chronic Disease Management for the 21st Century* (London: Department of Health, 2001).

Department of Health, *Choosing Health: Making Healthier Choices Easier* (London: HM Stationary Office, 2004).

Department of Health, 'NHS patients and staff reap rewards of GP incentive scheme as world's biggest health database goes live', press release reference number 2005/ 0306 (London, Department of Health, 2005).

H. Draper and T. Sorell, 'Patients' responsibilities in medical ethics', *Bioethics*, 16:4 (2002) 335–52.

L. Faulkner, *Issue Brief: Disease Management Programs: The New Tool for Cost Containment* (Washington DC National Governor's Association Center for Best Practices, Health Policy Studies Division, 2003).

Federal Interagency Forum on Aging-Related Statistics: *Older Americans 2000, Key Indicators of Well-Being* (Washington DC: Federal Interagency Forum on Aging-Related Statistics, US Government Printing Office, 2000).

A. Fernandez, K. Grumbach, K. Vranizan, D. Osmond and A. Bindman, 'Primary care physicians' experience with disease management programs', *Journal of General Internal Medicine*, 16:3 (2001) 163–7.

C. Friedman, R. Brownson, D. Peterson and J. Wilkerson, 'Physician Advice to Reduce Chronic Disease Risk Factors', *American Journal of Preventive Medicine*, 10 (1994) 367–71.

P. Gaede, M. Beck, P. Vedel and O. Pedersen, 'Limited impact of lifestyle education in patients with Type 2 diabetes mellitus and microalbuminuria: results from a randomized intervention study', *Diabetic Medicine*, 18:2 (2001) 104–8.

R. Glasgow, S. Bull, C. Gillette, L. Klesges and D. Dzewaltowski, 'Behavior change intervention research in healthcare settings: A review of recent reports with emphasis on external validity', *American Journal of Preventive Medicine*, 23:1 (2002a) 62–9.

R. Glasgow, M. Funnell, A. Bonomi, C. Davis, V. Beckham and E. Wagner, 'Self-management aspects of the improving chronic illness care breakthrough series: implementation with diabetes and heart failure teams', *Annals of Behavioral Medicine: A Publication of the Society of Behavioral Medicine*, 24 (2002b) 80–7.

R. Glasgow, D. Toobert and S. Hampson, 'Participation in outpatient diabetes education programs: how many patients take part and how representative are they?', *Diabetes Educator*, 17 (1991) 376–80.

J. Gleason, K. Bourdet, K. Koehn, S. Holay and E. Schaefer, 'Cardiovascular risk reduction and dietary compliance with a home-delivered diet and lifestyle modification program', *Journal of the American Dietetic Association*, 102:10 (2002) 1445–51.

R. Goldberg, I. Ockene, J. Ockene, P. Merriam and J. Kristeller, 'Physicians' attitudes and reported practices toward smoking intervention', *Journal of Cancer Education*, 8 (1993) 133–9.

M. Gordon, E. Thomson, R. Madhok and H. Capell, 'Can intervention modify adverse lifestyle variables in a rheumatoid population? Results of a pilot study', *Annals of the Rheumatic Diseases*, 61:1 (2002) 66–9.

L. Green, M. Eriksen and E. Schor, 'Preventive practices by physicians: behavioral determinants and potential interventions', *American Journal of Preventive Medicine*, 4 (1988) 101–7; discussion 108–10.

S. Hampson, R. Glasgow and L. Foster, 'Personal Models of Diabetes among Older Adults: Relationship to Self-Management and Other Variables', *Diabetes Education* 21:4 (1995) 330–7.

N. Harvey and D. DePue, 'Disease management: a continuum approach', *Healthcare Financial Management*, 51:6 (1997) 35–7.

E. Havranek, F. Masoudi, J. Rumsfeld and J. Steiner, 'A broader paradigm for understanding and treating heart failure', *Journal of Cardiac Failure*, 9:2 (2003) 147–52.

C. Hoffman, D. Rice and H. Sung, 'Persons with chronic conditions: Their prevalence and costs', *Journal of the American Medical Association*, 276:18 (1996) 1473–9.

H. Holman and K. Lorig, 'Patients as partners in managing chronic disease. Partnership is a prerequisite for effective and efficient health care', *BMJ (Clinical Research Ed.)*, 320:7234 (2000) 526–7.

R. Jamison, L. Gintner and J. Rogers, 'Fairchild DG disease management for chronic pain: barriers of program implementation with primary care physicians', *Pain Medicine*, 3:2 (2002) 92–101.

E. Johnson, T. Harwell, P. Donahue, M. Weisner, M. McInerney, G. Holzman and S. D. Helgerson, 'Promoting pneumococcal immunizations among rural Medicare beneficiaries using multiple strategies', *Journal of Rural Health* 19:4 (2003) 506–10.

G. Joyce, J. Escarce, D. Solomon and D. Goldman, *Cost Sharing Cuts Employers' Drug Spending – But Employees Don't Get the Savings* (Santa Monica, CA: RAND, 2002).

P. Kotler, P., N. Roberto and N. Lee, *Social Marketing: Improving the Quality of Life*, 2nd edn (Thousand Oaks, CA: SAGE, 2002).

T. Kottke, H. Blackburn, M. Brekke and L. Solberg, 'The Systematic Practice of Preventive Cardiology', *American Journal of Cardiology*, 59:6 (1987) 690–4.

K. Krichbaum, V. Aarestad and M. Buethe, 'Exploring the connection between self-efficacy and effective diabetes self-management', *Diabetes Educator*, 29 (2003) 653–62.

A. Larme and J. Pugh, 'Attitudes of Primary Care Providers toward Diabetes: Barriers to Guideline Implementation', *Diabetes Care* 21:9 (1998) 1391–6.

L. Larson, 'The revolution in aging is here', *Journal of the American Geriatrics Society*, 51:6 (2003) 874–6.

A. Lee, 'Seamless health care for chronic diseases in a dual health care system: managed care and the role of family physicians', *Journal of Management in Medicine*, 45:6 (1998) 398–405.

H. Leider, 'HMOs need to share gains of Dm programs. Physicians are more likely to buy in if they see better outcomes – and Financial Rewards that go with them', *Managed Care*, 10:7 (2001) 33–4.

N. Leonard, P. Lester, M. Rotheram-Borus, K. Mattes, M. Gwadz, and B. Ferns, 'Successful recruitment and retention of participants in longitudinal behavioral research', *AIDS Education and Prevention*, 15:3 (2003) 269–81.

C. Lewis, C. Clancy, B. Leake and J. Schwartz, 'The counseling practices of internists', *Annals of Internal Medicine*, 114:11 (1991) 54–8.

C. Lewis, K. Wells and J. Ware, 'A model for predicting the counseling practices of physicians', *Journal of General Internal Medicine*, 1:1 (1986) 14–19.

S. Liu and J. Romeis, 'Changes in drug utilization following the outpatient prescription drug cost-sharing program-evidence from Taiwan's elderly', *Health Policy*, 68:3 (2004) 227–87.

J. Manjer, S. Elmstahl, L. Janzon and G. Berglund, 'Invitation to a population-based cohort study: differences between subjects recruited using various strategies', *Scandinavian Journal of Public Health*, 30:2 (2002) 103–12.

B. Marcus, N. Owen, L. Forsyth, N. Cavill and F. Fridinger, 'Physical activity interventions using mass media, print media, and information technology', *American Journal of Preventive Medicine*, 15:4 (1998) 362–78.

T. McKeown, *The Role of Medicine: Dream, Mirage, or Nemesis?* (Princeton, NJ: Princeton University Press, 1979).

E. Miche, G. Herrmann, U. Wirtz, H. Laki, M. Barth and A. Radzewitz, 'Effects of education, self-care instruction and physical exercise on patients with chronic heart failure', *Zeitschrift Für Kardiologie*, 92 (2003) 985–93.

A. Miller and M. Iris, 'Health promotion attitudes and strategies in older adults', *Health Education & Behavior*, 29:2 (2002) 249–67.

K. Mills, A. Stewart, A. King, K. Roitz, P. Sepsis, P. Ritter and W. Bortz II, 'Factors associated with enrollment of older adults into a physical activity promotion program', *Journal of Aging and Health*, 8:1 (1996) 96–113.

National Statistics UK (2006) 'Population: Aging', *National Statistics Website*. http://www.statistics.gov.uk/cci/nugget.asp?ID=949

B. Neiger, R. Thackeray, M. Barnes and J. McKenzie, 'Positioning social marketing as a planning process for health education', *American Journal of Health Studies*, 18:2–3 (2003) 75–81.

C. Orleans, L. George, J. Houpt and K. Brodie, 'Health promotion in primary care: a survey of US family practitioners', *Preventive Medicine*, 14:5 (1985) 636–47.

D. Parra-Medina, A. D'Antonio, S. Smith, S. Levin, G. Kirkner and E. Mayer-Davis, 'Successful recruitment and retention strategies for a randomized weight management trial for people with diabetes living in rural, medically underserved counties of South Carolina: the power study', *Journal of the American Dietetic Association*, 104:1 (2004) 70–5.

G. Peterson, K. Fitzmaurice, M. Naunton, J. Vial, K. Stewart and H. Krum, 'Impact of pharmacist-conducted home visits on the outcomes of lipid-lowering drug therapy', *Journal of Clinical Pharmacy and Therapeutics*, 29:1 (2004) 23–30.

L. Pilote, C. Beck, H. Richard and M. Eisenberg, 'The effects of cost-sharing on essential drug prescriptions, utilization of medical care and outcomes after acute myocardial infarction in elderly patients', *Canadian Medical Association Journal*, 167:3 (2002) 246–52.

B. Pinto, M. Goldstein, J. DePue and F. Milan, 'Acceptability and feasibility of physician-based activity counseling: The Pal Project', *American Journal of Preventive Medicine*, 15:2 (1998) 95–102.

D. Plocher, 'Disease Management', in P. Kongstvedt (ed.), *The Managed Health Care Handbook* (Gaithersburg, MD: Aspen Publishers, Inc., 1996).

V. Rangan, S. Karim and S. Sandberg, 'Do Better at Doing Good', *Harvard Business Review*, May–June (1996).

P. Rapley and D. Fruin, 'Self-efficacy in chronic illness: the juxtaposition of general and regimen-specific efficacy', *International Journal of Nursing Practice*, 5:4 (1999) 209–15.

J. Reid, 'Managing new realities – integrating the care landscape', Speech given 11 March 2004.

M. Roemer, C. Hopkins, L. Carr and F. Gartside, 'Copayments for ambulatory care: penny-wise and pound-foolish', *Medical Care*, 13 (1975) 457–66.

M. Rosen, D. Logsdon and M. Demak, 'Prevention and health promotion in primary care: baseline results on physicians from the Insure Project on lifecycle preventive health services', *Preventive Medicine*, 13:5 (1984) 535–48.

R. Rothman, R. Malone, B. Bryant, C. Horlen and M. Pignone, 'Pharmacist-led, primary care-based disease management improves hemoglobin A1c in high-risk patients with diabetes', *American Journal Of Medical Quality*, 18:2 (2003) 51–8.

P. Salsberry, 'Assuming responsibility for one's health – an analysis of a key assumption in Nursing's Agenda for Health Care Reform', *Nursing Outlook*, 41:5 (1993) 212–16.

J. Sarkin, S. Marshall, K. Larson, K. Calfas and J. Sallis, 'A Comparison of methods of recruitment to a health promotion program for university seniors', *Preventive Medicine*, 27:4 (1998) 562–71.

S. Sherman and W. Hershman, 'Exercise Counseling: How Do General Internists Do?', *Journal of General Internal Medicine* 8:5 (1993) 243–8.

G. Simon, L. Grothaus, M. Durham, M. VonKorff and C. Pabiniak, 'Impact of visit copayments on outpatient mental health utilization by members of a health maintenance organization', *American Journal of Psychiatry*, 153:3 (1996) 331–8.

D. Simpson, B. Dixon and P. Bolli, 'Effectiveness of multidisciplinary patient counselling in reducing cardiovascular disease risk factors through nonpharmacological intervention: results from the Healthy Heart Program', *Canadian Journal of Cardiology*, 20:2 (2004) 177–86.

G. Solanki and H. Schauffler, 'Cost-sharing and the utilization of clinical preventive services', *American Journal of Preventive Medicine*, 17:2 (1999) 127–33.

G. Solanki, H. Schauffler and L. Miller, 'The direct and indirect effects of cost-sharing on the use of preventive services', *Health Services Research*, 34:6 (2000) 1331–50.

S. Stearns, S. Bernard, S. Fasick, R. Schwartz, T. R. Konrad, M. G. Ory and G. H. DeFriese, 'The economic implications of self-care: the effect of lifestyle, functional adaptations, and medical self-care among a national sample of medicare beneficiaries', *American Journal of Public Health*, 90:10 (2000) 1608–12.

U. Svensk, 'Disease management at the system level – an effective way to improve health care', *International Journal of Health Care Quality Assurance*, 9:7 (1996) 4–8.

D. Taira, D. Safran, T. Seto, W. Rogers and A. Tarlov, 'The relationship between patient income and physician discussion of health risk behaviors', *Journal of the American Medical Association*, 278:17 (1997) 1412–17.

R. Tamblyn, R. Laprise, J. Hanley, M. Abrahamowicz, S. Scott, N. Mayo, J. Hurley, R. Grad, E. Latimer, R. Perreault, P. McLeod, A. Huang, P. Larochelle, L. Mallet, 'Adverse events associated with prescription drug cost-sharing among poor and elderly persons', *Journal of the American Medical Association*, 285:4 (2001) 421–9.

S. Thompson, L. Schwankovsky and J. Pitts, 'Counselling patients to make lifestyle changes: the role of physician self-efficacy, training and beliefs about causes', *Family Practice*, 10:1 (1993) 70–5.

G. Timmerman, 'Using self-care strategies to make lifestyle changes', *Journal of Holistic Nursing*, 17:2 (1999) 169–83.

D. Toobert, R. Glasgow an J. Radcliffe, 'Physiologic and related behavioral outcomes from the Women's Lifestyle Heart Trial', *Annals of Behavioral Medicine* 22:1 (2000) 1–9.

D. Toobert, L. Strycker, R. Glasgow and J. Bagdade, 'If you build it, will they come? Reach and adoption associated with a comprehensive lifestyle management program for women with type 2 diabetes', *Patient Education and Counseling*, 48:2 (2002) 99–105.

S. Trude, *Patient cost sharing: how much is too much?* (Washington, DC: Center for Studying Health System Change, 2003).

W. Vollmer, L. Svetkey, L. Appel, E. Obarzanek, P. Reams, B. Kennedy, K. Aicher, J. Charleston, P. R. Conlin, M. Evans, D. Harsha, S. Hertert, 'Recruitment and retention of minority participants in the dash controlled feeding trial. Dash Collaborative Research Group. Dietary approaches to stop hypertension', *Ethnicity & Disease*, 8:2 (1998) 198–208.

E. Wagner, C. Davis, J. Schaefer, M. Von Korff and B. Austin, 'A survey of leading chronic disease management programs: are they consistent with the literature?', *Managed Care Quarterly*, 7:3 (1999) 56–66.

E. Wagner, L. Grothaus, J. Hecht and A. LaCroix, 'Factors Associated with Participation in a Senior Health Promotion Program', *Gerontologist*, 31:5 (1991) 598–602.

E. Wagner, T. Wickizer, A. Cheadle, B. Psaty, T. Koepsell, P. Diehr, S. Curry, M. Von Korff, C. Anderman, W. Beery, D. Pearson and E. Perrin, 'The Kaiser Family Foundation Community Health Promotion Grants Program: findings from an outcome evaluation', *Health Services Research*, 35:3 (2000) 561–89.

J. Warren-Findlow, T. Prohaska and D. Freedman, 'Challenges and opportunities in recruiting and retaining underrepresented populations into health promotion research', *Gerontologist*, 43 (2003) 37–46.

T. Waters, P. Budetti, K. Reynolds, R. Gillies, H. Zuckerman, J. Alexander, L. Burns and S. Shortell, 'Factors associated with physician involvement in care management', *Medical Care*, 39:7 (2001) 179–91.

K. Wells, C. Lewis, B. Leake and J. Ware Jr., 'Do physicians preach what they practice? A study of physicians' health habits and counseling practices', *Journal of the American Medical Association*, 252:20 (1984) 2846–8.

R. Whittemore, S. Chase, C. Mandle and C. Roy, 'Lifestyle change in Type 2 Diabetes – a process model', *Nursing Research*, 51:1 (2002) 18–25.

P. Williams-Piehota, T. Schneider, J. Pizarro, L. Mowad and P. Salovey, 'Matching health messages to information-processing styles: need for cognition and mammography utilization', *Health Communication*, 15:4 (2003) 375–92.

J. Williams and J. Flora, 'Health behavior segmentation and campaign planning to reduce cardiovascular disease risk among Hispanics', *Health Education and Behavior*, 22:1 (1995) 36–48.

World Health Organization: Countries, United Kingdom. *World Health Organization.* http://www.who.int/countries/gbr/en/

Part III

Evaluation and Measurement for Public Health

11
Evaluating the Societal Costs of Potentially Preventable Illnesses: Developing A Common Approach

Graham Lister, Richard Fordham, Miranda Mugford,
Abiodun Olukoga, Edward Wilson and Dominic McVey

1 Introduction

This paper is based on a review produced for the National Consumer Council to support their report on social marketing for health, *It's our health* (National Social Marketing Centre, 2006). The aims were to explore ways of assessing the cost to society of risky behaviour and preventable illnesses based on the best available evidence,[1] and to demonstrate the value of adopting a consistent approach across different types of preventable behaviours. The analysis presented here focuses on alcohol misuse, tobacco, obesity, preventable Coronary Vascular Disease (CVD) and preventable mental illness. Estimates of the health impact for each behaviour or condition are made, and the costs associated with it calculated. Unresolved issues are identified, and work for future development is suggested.

A rapid overview of existing work was conducted, and adjusted to apply to England at 2005 prices. In order to avoid gaps and inconsistencies a pragmatic layered framework for analysis was used, as recommended in the Michael Kelly policy guidelines published by the Health Development Agency in 2005. Where no other data were available estimates were made by the research team. Less than one week of research time could be allocated to each field. The answers produced need to be refined and improved in the future, but it was found that in most cases an initial estimate of costs could be derived for public and private sector health and social care, other related welfare services, individuals and households, employers and intangible societal values.

The most useful entry point for analysing the cost of preventable illness was by examining preventable behaviours and the illnesses attributable to them. Attempts to assess the total cost of an illness were less successful if there was no clear link to prevention actions. While this analysis produced a useful snapshot of current costs, it was noted that in several fields trends in behaviours were leading to an increase in the potential for long-term illness. Thus a further analysis of long-term costs was recommended.

The review suggested that total societal costs are considerably greater than indicated by most previous studies, which have often been limited to NHS costs. The broader societal costs bear most heavily on the individuals with the illness and their families and may also include significant costs to employers, other welfare services and wider society. Most studies have ignored these costs as either too difficult to measure or irrelevant to narrow cost impact studies. Yet because an effective social marketing campaign should mobilise all sectors of society, cost benefit analysis must demonstrate these wider social costs to engage all those who need to take action. This is the aim, for example, of the Healthy Living Programme (Department of Health, 2005).

It is hoped that the pragmatic, layered framework proposed here can be developed to establish consensus amongst policymakers and advisers on the best way of reflecting costs to society of preventable illness. Such a framework may provide a consistent methodology for measuring and monitoring the impact of social marketing and other measures to prevent behaviour leading to ill health in the future.

Table 11.1   Framework for analysis of societal health impacts and costs

Health Impacts as indicated by Health Attribution Fractions (HAF)	Health life expectancy (HALE)	Disability/ Quality adjusted life years (DALYS/QALYs)	Years lived with disability Yrs of life lost (YLDs)	Premature deaths, economically active (EYLL)
Costs to Individuals and households	Related expenditure on products and services + taxes/charges	Copayments to NHS + private sector + self medication	Informal care Household cost of crime/ violence	Income loss: early death and reduced employment + benefits
Costs to NHS and public care services	Prevention and Social marketing	NHS Treatment services	Care services	Indirect health and care costs
Costs and income to other public services	Income from taxes and charges	Criminal Justice System and Social services	Education and other services	Benefit payments
Costs to employers	Health and safety + Occupational health	Efficiency/ Productivity	Absenteeism	Accidents at work
Wider social impacts/ intangible human costs	Intangible values	Social capital participation	Fear of crime and violence	Other

2 Framework for analysis of societal health impacts and costs

The framework for the analysis of societal health impacts and costs used to guide this review provides a simple map of the types of health impacts and costs and where they fall. These are summarised in Table 11.1.

The framework encompasses different types of societal health impacts and costs. The first row shows total health impacts as measured by the disease outcomes attributed to the behaviour or condition – Health Attribution Fractions (HAFs), the impact on healthy life expectancy – Health Adjusted Life Expectancy (HALE), the outcome in terms of Disability Adjusted Life Years (DALYs) or Quality Adjusted Life Years (QALYs), Years Lived with Disability (YLD) and premature deaths, measured as Years of Life Lost (YLL) and years of economically active life lost (EYLL).

The rows in Table 11.1 show cost impacts at various levels in society: the second row shows costs to individuals and households, the third row shows impacts on the NHS and other public care services, the fourth row shows costs to other public services such as the criminal justice system, the fifth row shows costs to employers, and the sixth row shows wider cost and value impacts on society. In principle this framework can be applied to identify the cost and value impacts of any type of preventable illness and behaviour, though in practice data may be incomplete.

The framework encompasses several different types of cost, including direct household or institutional expenditures, projections of future income losses, tax income and benefits payment, which are transfer payments within the economy. The final row includes the intangible costs of death and disability as values foregone based on how much people say they would be willing to pay to avoid risk of the outcome. Expenditure, future income loss and values foregone are all equally valid societal costs, but care should be taken in summarising the total impact on the economy to avoid potential double counting.

The review was intended to provide a demonstration of the principles of societal costing of preventable illness and behaviours and a broad estimate of the level of these costs, rather than detailed estimates of specific costs. The review followed the general economic principles outlined in the Treasury Green Book (HM Treasury, 2003), which stresses that it is important to avoid being spuriously accurate when concluding from, and presenting the results of data generated by an appraisal. It is important to acknowledge that there remain inconsistencies arising from the different sources used and there is scope to improve the estimates in subsequent phases of review.

The framework shown in Table 11.1 raises many questions; it is not claimed that it is the only way of analysing societal costs but it is hoped it will prompt discussion and consensus for future studies.

3 Data sources

Health impacts

Health impact estimates were based on the Murray and Lopez study and subsequent updates available from the World Health Organisation (WHO) web sites (Murray and Lopez, 1996). These data provide estimates of the attribution fraction of disease outcomes from different causes based on data from low mortality countries in Europe. These data were applied to UK incidence data to derive estimates of Disability Adjusted Life Years (DALYs), Years Lived with Disability (YLD) and Years of Life Lost (YLL). Where DALYs were not available QALY data were used. In some cases figures were derived from the definition: DALYS = YLL + YLD. While these data are adjusted for UK disease incidence, they are still general estimates of attribution fractions which need to be updated for UK experience. Attribution fractions for CVD caused by obesity, smoking and heart disease account for about 55 per cent of morbidity so the team assumed that 12 per cent of CVD cannot be linked to a cause and 33 per cent may be linked to other prevention measures such as control of cholesterol and lipid levels, this assumption needs further examination but accords with current thinking. Years of economically active life lost before the age of 65 were estimated by the team by consideration of the average age of death and YLL. Premature deaths were usually available from sources specific to each cause, however, it was not always clear that these matched the attribution fractions.

Cost data

Cost data was derived from a range of recent studies and other information sources for each topic; a total of over 110 sources are referenced in the detailed papers. The analysis of the costs of alcohol misuse took as its starting point the Cabinet Office Alcohol Harm Reduction Strategy (Prime Minister's Strategy Unit, 2004). The review of smoking considered a range of sources including the Health Development Agency review *Smoking and Public Health* (Naidoo, Warm, Quigley and Taylor, 2004). The review of obesity also drew on *Tackling Obesity in England* (Comptroller & Auditor General, 2001). The review of the cost of CVD took as a starting point, 'The economic burden of coronary heart disease in the UK' (Liu, Maniadakis, Gray, and Rayner, 2002). The review of lung cancer examined a range of sources including *Tackling cancer in England: saving more lives* (National Audit Office, 2004). The review of the cost of HIV/AIDS also drew a range of resources including *Focus on Prevention: HIV and other Sexually Transmitted Infections in the United Kingdom in 2003* (UK Collaborative Group for HIV and STI Surveillance, 2004). The resources used to examine the societal cost of mental illness included *Costs of mental illness in England* (Patel and Knapp, 1998).

All data were updated for 2005 based on retail price inflation, increases in NHS spend, trends in the behaviour and trends in nominal GDP growth as appropriate. UK, England and Wales figures were applied to England on the basis of population, even though in some cases there were slight differences in behaviour between home countries.

Costs to individuals and households

Costs to households of related expenditures were estimated on the basis of market data. This included spending on: over-the-counter medicines, supplements and vitamins, subscribing to gym membership, calorie reduced or diet products allocated to obesity and CVD according to QALYs. Such expenditures were related to specific behavioural and disease outcomes wherever possible, including, for example expenditure on alcohol over the level of guidelines for alcohol consumption and all expenditure on tobacco. Only costs associated with excessive alcohol consumption were taken into account since many studies suggest that moderate alcohol consumption is beneficial to health. However, these assumptions need further examination. For example, consumption of fat reduced or diet products do not necessarily relate to fear of obesity or CVD; they may simply represent preferences for these products and similarly some people enjoy gym membership and exercise without thinking of their health. At this stage these costs have been used as a proxy for the costs that arise from fear of obesity and CVD.

Private expenditure on health treatments and co-payments were estimated as 16 per cent of NHS expenditure in line with Treasury estimates (HM Treasury, 2005). Private expenditure on long-term care was estimated as 33 per cent of total long-term care expenditure of £8.5 billion (Lister and Robinson, 2006) attributed to causes in proportion to YLDs. Informal care time inputs were derived from the 2002 Carers UK Report. However, the Carers UK report valued informal carer time at the same cost as formal care, equivalent to £9.95 per hour in 2005. This was adjusted because many carers are beyond employment age and therefore a cost reflecting a mix of leisure time and employment costs of £5.50 per hour was used. This was attributed to preventable illnesses on the basis of the years lived with disability (YLDs) arising from each cause. Income loss from early death was estimated on the basis of years of work lost from under-employment or early death valued at £25,250 per year, the average wage level for 2005.

Costs to NHS treatment and care services

Estimates of NHS treatment expenditure were obtained from various studies including those listed above. Prevention and social marketing expenditure was not available by programme, while estimates of the total cost in this field vary between £0.8 billion and £4 billion depending upon whether Primary Care costs are included. An estimate of £1.1 billion was derived from Treasury estimates for 2004/5 but no allocation to programmes could be found. Social marketing expenditure was estimated as £70 million. Public sector long term care costs were estimated as 66 per cent of the total allocated according to YLDs.

Other public sector costs and income

Costs to other public services were not always available. In particular, education and social services related costs were missing. Criminal justice system cost estimates were available for alcohol misuse (Prime Minister's Strategy Unit, 2004). Social services costs were not generally available, however, it was unrealistic to ignore this factor in relation to alcohol misuse so an allocation was made of the total social service costs on the basis of the average proportion of attributable health and criminal justice system costs.

Incapacity and sickness benefits were attributed to causes in proportion to YLDS and taxes and charges for alcohol and tobacco were derived from Treasury estimates. However in the case of alcohol only the proportion of taxes and charges relating to consumption in excess of guidelines was taken into account. It is important to note that these payments are transfers costs from one group in society to another without any consumption of real resources (except perhaps bureaucratic costs). Thus by including them as costs at one level and offsetting income at another their impact on different layers is taken into account but they cancel each other out in the overall analysis of the total impact on the economy.

Costs to employers

Estimates of the total cost to employers of absenteeism were derived from the CBI/AXA annual survey quoted by the Faculty of Medicine review (2006). Estimates of the costs of fires and crimes related to health causes were derived from the Prime Minister's Strategy Unit 2004 paper. A total cost to employers of £10 billion was identified as a result of absenteeism related to preventable illness. There were also costs of £1.1 billion relating to crime and accidents at work. Attributing total absence costs to these preventable illnesses is an over-estimate since preventable illness makes up only 70 per cent of total illness but as the review failed to find data relating to employers' expenditure on occupational health or health and safety nor were data found relating to the loss of productivity when people with preventable illnesses were at work, this was accepted as a reflection of total costs. It is recognised that this is a gap in the current review.

Wider social impacts and intangible human costs

Wider costs to society were estimated on the basis of £31,750 per DALY or QALY. This figure is an update of the estimate of £30,000 used in the Salisbury Centre study of the cost of mental illness (2003). Applying these costs gives the following figures:

- Alcohol misuse – DALYs £10.8 billion + crime £5.3 billion
- Smoking – DALYs £16.8 billion
- Obesity – DALYs £7.4 billion
- Other CVD – DALYs £8.8 billion
- Mental illness – QALYs £34.4 billion

This gives a total intangible human cost for the preventable illnesses and deaths arising from the causes considered here of £83.5 billion. Note that for CVD the total has been adjusted to exclude deaths arising from alcohol, smoking and obesity.

4 Societal health impacts and cost estimate results

Breakdowns of the health and cost impacts for each behaviour/disease are shown in Appendices 11.1–11.5. Table 11.2 summarises these health and cost impacts. Note that figures for 'Other Preventable CVD' are one third of those shown in Appendix 11.3 since these apply to causes other than alcohol abuse, smoking and obesity.

While it should be stressed that further work is necessary to confirm and complete such cost estimates, it already provides some useful insights into the scale of societal health impacts and costs involved and their relative magnitude. It shows for example that the economic impact of mental health to society is the largest amongst the behaviours and illness included in the review. The greatest impact is on social impacts/intangible human values but even in this case the economic costs to the other levels of society are greater. The greatest impact of alcohol misuse, the second largest cost to society, is borne by individuals and households with substantial costs to employers and wider society.

While the analysis of total societal costs and values is of interest for broad policy and priority setting, the layered nature of the framework also makes it possible to assess cost impacts at different levels, for example, to examine total NHS treatment and care costs, or to focus on employer costs.

Table 11.2   Comparison of societal health and cost impacts

Behaviour/Illness	Alcohol misuse	Smoking	Obesity	Other CVD	Mental Illness	Total
Health Impacts						
Premature deaths	18,500	130,000	10,000	17,700	3,100	179,300
Years of life lost	365,000	307,000	70,050	203,600	11,490	957,140
DALY	460,000	528,000	233,000	276,000	709,000	2,206,000
Costs to Individuals and households	£21.6b	£18b	£4.1b	£4.2b	£5.4b	£53.3b
Costs to NHS and public care services	£3.2b	£2.7b	£1.2b	£0.6b	£9.1b	£16.8b
Costs to other public services and (income)	£5.0b (£2.9b)	£1.1b (£9.1b)	£0.1b	£0.1b	£10.2b	£16.5b (£12b)
Costs to employers	£2.6b	£2.0b	£1.5b	£0.7b	£4.2b	£11b
Social impacts/ intangible human values	£16.1b	£16.8b	£7.4b	£8.8b	£34.4b	£83.5b
Total Cost	£45.6b	£31.5b	£14.3b	£14.4b	£63.3b	£169.1b

When considering specific health promotion activities the most relevant perspective may be that of marginal cost and benefit analysis. Thus to determine the value of an intervention, which may only affect say one per cent of behaviour in a specific area, it would be necessary to scale down the national cost and value figures to examine the effect of a small change. It is not only possible but preferable to use the framework in this way since one of the key uncertainties in relation to, for example, mental illness, is how much of the total illness is in fact preventable. For this reason the average costs that can be generated by the framework are likely to be more realistic than the total cost.

5 Conclusions and implications for the future

This chapter describes a pragmatic approach to evaluating the societal cost of potentially preventable illnesses using a layered framework for analysis as called for in the policy guidelines proposed by Michael Kelly in 2005. The fact that it was possible to complete most of this analysis in a rapid review, allowing less than one week per topic demonstrates the feasibility of such an approach.

This review and analysis provides a number of lessons for taking the agenda forward and developing practical solutions. It is not claimed that this is the only possible framework or that the method of analysis used here is superior to every other approach. It is simply intended to show the great value of establishing a consistent approach to such analyses. Any method that provides a consistent and realistic assessment of the value of health promotion and illness prevention would be preferable to the current incoherence.

The review revealed that while there are many studies of specific aspects of health prevention almost none of them adopted a comprehensive societal cost approach and most used diverse assumptions and methods of analysis. The review also found gaps in information, including measures of the current expenditure on health prevention by programme, measures of the costs incurred by employers and analysis of cost impacts on services other than the NHS.

An important next step is to establish consensus on the framework and the conventions used to estimate societal costs as a basis for economic evaluation of public health interventions. It will be of particular importance to resolve contentious issues including: the development of a realistic null hypothesis or counterfactual, problems of double counting, how to evaluate intangible human costs and how to address long-term impacts on health and society, including intergenerational impacts.

A clear statement of the societal cost of preventable illness will be a helpful starting point for future analysis of the costs and benefits of prevention and positive health programmes. This would address the concern raised by Wanless in his 2004 report about the lack of cost benefit analyses of public health interventions.

It could also be used in social marketing to raise awareness and stimulate action. For example, it is clear that cost impacts on individuals and households are far higher than costs to the NHS, and that in many cases employer costs are also high. This sort of analysis could be used in social marketing to raise awareness of impact and show how families and employers could reduce their costs by taking action to improve health.

It is also clear that a focus on investment in public health to reduce NHS costs is ill founded. In many cases reducing death or disability from one cause may in fact lead to the need for more care for survivors. The reason for investing in public health is not to save NHS money, but to improve health and well-being, and it is important to develop cost benefit appraisal techniques which can justify such decisions alongside any other element of social investment. Whilst there are many difficulties in assessing the complex interrelationship between prevention measures, behaviour, outcomes and costs, there are great prizes at stake for society. Work in Australia (Ableson, 2003) shows that public health programmes can produce very high levels of return to societal costs and generate significant cost savings for the public sector. An analysis along these lines would not only be helpful in assessing potential costs and benefits, it would also establish a clear basis for monitoring and evaluating disease prevention and health promotion activities including social marketing for health. A WHO report, Comparative Quantification of Health Risk (Ezzati, Lopez, Rodgers and Murray, 2006), drawing together the work of over 100 researchers applying a common analytical framework, provides an excellent starting point.

Appendices

Appendix 11.1   Alcohol misuse summary England at 2005 prices average values

Health impacts	Healthy Life Expectancy Reduced by up to 20 years	Disability Adjusted Life Years DALYS 7.4% of total 460,000	Years lived with disability YLDs 15.6% of total	Premature deaths 18,500 Years of life lost YLL 365,000 total 155,000 to 65
Costs to Individuals and households	Related expenditure £12.2b	Private +NHS co pay +OTC + long-term care £0.85b	Informal care £4.1b	Income loss: early death and reduced employment £6b less £1.6b benefits
Costs to NHS and public care services	Prevention + Social marketing unknown	Treatment services £2.3b	Care services £0.9b	Indirect health service costs
Costs and income to other public services	Income from taxes and charges (£2.9b)	Criminal Justice System £1.8b	Education and social services £1.6b	Incapacity benefits + Income support £1.6b

Appendix 11.1 Alcohol misuse summary England at 2005 prices average values – *continued*

Costs to employers	Health and safety + Occupational health	Efficiency/ Productivity	Absenteeism £1.5b	Accidents at work + crime £1.1b
Wider social impacts/ intangible human costs	Intangible values £10.8b	Social capital participation	Crime and violence £5.3b	Other

Appendix 11.2 Smoking summary England at 2005 prices average values

Health impacts	Smoking reduces life expectancy by 2–8 years	Wellness or health risk impact Up to 8.5% of all DALYs = 528,000	Disablement Up to 307,000 YLL 221,000 YLD	Premature deaths 130,000 deaths
Costs to Individuals and households	Related exp. (expenditure on tobacco products) £14.04b	Private costs of treatment £0.6b	Informal care £2.4b	Loss of income £1.9b less £0.97b benefits
Costs to NHS and public care services	Prevention/ Social marketing £0.13b	Treatment and care £1.7b	Social care £0.53b	Indirect Treatment costs passive smokers £0.36b
Costs and income to other public services	Income from taxes on tobacco £9.1b	Fires etc. £0.15b	Incapacity benefits & Income support £0.97b	
Costs to employers	Health and safety/positive health at work	Absenteeism £2.0b	Productivity No data available but considered in overall estimate	
Wider social impacts/ intangible human costs	Intangible social costs 528000 DALYs at £31,750 £16.8b	Social Capital	Crime and violence Smuggling	Other Litter

Appendix 11.3   Obesity summary England 2005 prices average values

Health impacts Risk factor for many chronic diseases. 36% hypertension, 47% type 2 diabetes, 18% Myocardial Infarction (MIs) 1%–29% colorectal, ovarian, prostate and endometrial cancers.	Disease incidence / prevalence 31.9m overweight or obese, 12.4m obese, 1m morbidly obese. 5.9m hypertensives, 150,000 angina cases 14,000 MIs	DALYs Estimate 233,045 DALYs attributable to consequences of obesity. = 3.75% of DALYs	Years lived with disability YLD= 163,000	Premature deaths 6% premature deaths attribut able to obesity 10,007 YLLs 70,050
Costs to Individuals and households	Related expenditure Reduced fat & low calorie food £6.7b attributable to fear of obesity say 33% Total: £2.2b	Private treatment and care related to obesity: treatment £0.23b Long-term care £0.03b Total £0.26b	Informal care £0.6b	Loss of income £1b
Costs to NHS and public care services	Prevention/social marketing Unknown		Health and care costs Primary and secondary care, plus prescribing for obesity = £0.05b Primary and secondary care, plus prescribing for comorbidities = £1.09b Long-term care = £0.06b Total cost: £1.2b	
Costs and income to other public services	Education related costs £0.13b	Disability benefits unknown	Social care costs unknown	Income support unknown
Costs to employers	Health and safety/positive health at work unknown	Absenteeism Estimated £1.5b from certified sickness in 2005		Productivity No data available but in estimate
Wider social impacts/ intangible human values	Intangible values £7.4b	Social capital/ social stigma unknown	Crime and violence Not applicable	DALYs to others

Appendix 11.4   CVD summary England at 2005 prices average values

Health impacts	Wellness or health risk impact IHD is the leading cause of death in England. At age 40, the lifetime risk is 50% for men and 33% for women.	Disease incidence/ prevalence Approximately 77,000 MIs, 91,000 new cases of angina and 56,050 new cases of heart failure.	DALYs Approximately 829,000 DALYs attributable to cardiovascular disease.	Premature deaths 35% of premature deaths in men & 27% in women Total 53,038 YLL 610,650
Costs to Individuals and households But note 2/3rds attributed to obesity alcohol and smoking 1/3rd = £4.2b	Related expenditure e.g. OTC medicines, diet food £13.01b	Costs of treatment Estimated £0.43b private care	Informal care estimated 343,000 carers for CHD patients in England, providing care worth £1.3b	Loss of income 129,800 working years lost in 2005, costing £0.7b Less benefits £1b
Costs to NHS and public care services × 1/3 = £0.6b	Prevention/social marketing Expenditure in England in 2005 estimated at £0.01b		Health care costs Primary, secondary & tertiary activity, drugs estimated to cost £1.66b	
Costs and income to other public services × 1/3 = £0.1b	Education related costs unknown	Disability benefits unknown	Social care costs Community health and social services expenditure of £0.29	Income support unknown
Costs to employers × 1/3 = £0.7b	Health and safety/positive health at work unknown	Absenteeism 56,400,000 certified lost working days, costing £2.21b		Productivity No data but considered in estimate
Wider social impacts/ intangible human costs × 1/3 = £8.8 b	Intangible values £26.4b	Social capital/ participation	Crime and violence	Other

Appendix 11.5   Mental health summary England at 2005 prices average values

Health impacts	Wellness or health risk impact Disabling consequences and stigma	Disease incidence/ prevalence 9 million adults 8.25m have moderate mental health problems and 770,000 severe.	QALYs/ DALYs QALYs = 1.085m DALYs = 708,574.	Premature deaths Estimated 3,087 Years of Life Lost due to mental illness 11,490
Costs to Individuals and households	Related expenditure Not Known	Costs of treatment Private costs 16% of NHS = £1.4b	Informal care £4.13b	Loss of income 400,000 person-years of lost employment. Valued at £10.1b less £10.2b benefits
Costs to NHS and public care services	Prevention / social marketing No direct prevention of mental health cost is available.			Health care costs £9.1b
Costs and income to other public services	Education related costs Significant but no data	Disability benefits and income support £10.2b		Social care costs Significant but not estimated
Costs to employers	Health and safety/positive health at work Not available	Absenteeism SCMH (2003) estimate the cost due to mental health at £4.2b for England in 2005 prices (incl. loss of income by the self-employed).		Productivity No data but considered in estimate
Wider social impacts/ intangible human costs	Intangible costs QALYs lost = 1.085m valued at £31,750 per QALY the total is £34.4b	Social capital/ participation Participation in paid and unpaid work has been included in the other estimates and should not be double-counted.	Crime and violence Unknown	Other Spouses and relatives of those who suffer from a mental illness are also more likely to suffer with mental health problems.

Note

1   The detailed report is available online at http://www.nsms.org.uk/images/CoreFiles/
NSMC-R10-EconomicAnalysis.pdf

References

National Social Marketing Centre, *It's Our Health: Realising the potential of effective social marketing* (London: National Consumer Council, 2006).

G. Lister, R. Fordham, M. Mugford, A. Olukoga, E. Wilson and D. McVey, *'The Societal Costs of Potentially Preventable Illnesses: A Rapid Review'*, NSMC Report 10 (London: National Social Marketing Centre, 2006). Available 10 October 2007: http://www.nsms.org.uk/images/corefiles/NSMC-R10 societal costs.pdf.

Department of Health, *Healthy Living Programme* (London: Department of Health, 2005). Available 7 September 2006: http://www.dh.gov.uk/PolicyAndGuidance/HealthAndSocialCareTopics/HealthyLiving/fs/en.

M. P. Kelly, D. Mcdaid, A. Ludbrook, A. and J. Powell, *Economic Appraisal of Public Health Interventions* (London: Health Development Agency, 2005). Available 7 September 2006: http://www.nice.org.uk/page.aspx?o=513210.

HM Treasury, *Green Book, Appraisal and evaluation in central government* (London: HM Treasury, 2003). Available 7 September 2006: http://www.hm-treasury.gov.uk/ economic_data_and_tools/greenbook/data_greenbook_index.cfm.

C. Murray and A. Lopez, (eds) *The Global Burden of Disease: A comprehensive assessment of mortality and disability from diseases, injuries and risk factors in 1990 and projected to 2020* (Cambridge, MA: Harvard University Press on behalf of the World Health Organization and the World Bank, 1996).

Prime Minister's Strategy Unit, *Alcohol Harm reduction Strategy for England* (London: Cabinet Office, 2004). Available 7 September 2007: http://image.guardian.co.uk/sys-files/Society/documents/2004/03/15/alcoholstrategy.pdf.

Prime Minister's Strategy Unit, *Alcohol misuse: How much does it cost* (London: Cabinet Office, 2003) Available: 7 September 2006: http://sia.dfc.unifi.it/costi%20uk. pdf. See also Annexes at http://www.cabinetoffice.gov.uk/upload/assets/www.cabinetoffice.gov.uk/strategy/econ_annexes.pdf.

B. Naidoo, D. Warm, R. Quigley and L. Taylor, *Smoking and public health: a review of reviews of interventions to increase smoking cessation, reduce smoking initiation and prevent further uptake of smoking* (London: Health Development Agency, 2004).

Comptroller and Auditor General, *Tackling Obesity in England* (London: HM Stationary Office, 2001).

J. L. Liu, N. Maniadakis, A. Gray and M. Rayner, The economic burden of coronary heart disease in the UK, *Heart*, 88: 6 (2002) 597–603.

National Audit Office, *Tackling cancer in England: saving more lives* (London: National Audit Office, 2004).

The UK Collaborative Group for HIV And STI Surveillance, *Focus on Prevention – HIV and other Sexually Transmitted Infections in the United Kingdom in 2003* (London: Health Protection Agency Centre for Infections, 2004).

A. Patel and M. Knapp, 'Costs of mental illness in England', *London Mental Health Research Review* PSRU London Issue 5, 4–10 June 1998.

HM Treasury, *Treasury Expenditure Estimates 2004–2005* (London: HM Treasury, 2005). Available 7 September 2006: http://www.hm-treasury.gov.uk/media/801/75/sr2004_ch8.pdf

G. Lister and R. Robinson, 'What will health cost?', in Z. Morris, L. Chang, S. Dawson and P. Garside (eds), *Health Policy Futures* (Oxford: Radcliffe Publishing, 2006), pp. 155–77.

Carers UK, *Without Us: Calculating the value of carers' support* (London: Carers UK, 2002). Available 7 September 2006: http://www.carersuk.org/Policyandpractice/ PolicyResources/Research#1095432875

Occupational Health Group of the Faculty of Public Health and Faculty of Occupational Medicine, *Creating a healthy workplace* (London: Faculty of Public Health, 2006).

Sainsbury Centre for Mental Health, *Policy Paper 3: The economic and social cost of mental illness* (London: Sainsbury Centre, 2003).

Transport and Road Research Laboratory, *Highways Economics Note No. 1: 2005 Valuation of the Benefits of Prevention of Road Accidents and Casualties* (London: Department for Transport, 2007). Available 10 October 2007: http://www.dft.gov.uk/ pgr/road-safety/ea/pdfeconnote105.

D. Wanless, *Securing Good Health for the Whole Population* (London: HM Treasury, 2004).

E. Wilson and R. Fordham, *A model to estimate the health impacts and cost of obesity in Norfolk over the next 10 years* (Norwich: Health Economics Support, 2006). Available 7 September 2006: http://www.med.uea.ac.uk/research/research_econ/hesp/docs/ Obesity.pdf.

P. Abelson, *Returns on Investment in Public Health* (Canberra: Department of Health and Ageing, Government of Australia, 2003).

M. Ezzati, A. Lopez, A. Rodgers and C. Murray, *Comparative Quantification of Health Risks: Global and Regional Burden of Disease Attributable to Selected Major Risk Factors* (Geneva: World Health Organisation, 2006). Available 7 September 2006: http://www.who.int/publications/cra/chapters/volume1/0000i-xxiv.pdf

12
What Use Has Been Made of Economic Evaluation in Public Health? A Systematic Review of the Literature*

David Mcdaid and Justin Needle

Introduction

The last 15 years have seen a dramatic increase in both the volume and quality of economic evaluations of health care interventions (Elixhauser *et al.*, 1998; Sassi *et al.*, 2002). The demand for evidence on the cost-effectiveness of such interventions has grown, with many countries now having formal or semiformal mechanisms, such as the National Institute for Health and Clinical Excellence (NICE) in England and Wales or the Scottish Medicines Consortium, to feed such information into the policy-making process in the UK.

The overwhelming majority of such evaluations have examined (often expensive and new) health care interventions, most notably pharmaceuticals, medical technologies and surgical procedures. In comparison, budgets for pubic health are modest and there appear to have been few incentives to undertake economic evaluations of public health and health promoting interventions (Godfrey, 2001; Hale, 2000; Holland, 2004; Kelly *et al.*, 2005). Alongside this has run a several decade old debate amongst health economists, public health practitioners, health promotion campaigners and others over how to properly assess the economic case for prevention and promotion interventions (Fuchs, 1983).

Effective public health and health promoting interventions are an essential element of health policy. Much morbidity and mortality may be avoidable, but are best tackled outside health care systems (Nolte and McKee, 2003). Potentially, public health interventions can help generate substantial health and wider societal benefits by reducing the likelihood of becoming ill as well as promoting positive wellbeing, rather than just the absence of disease.

*This study was commissioned by the Welsh Assembly Government Health Promotion Division as part of their Wanless Health Economics Research Programme. The views expressed in this chapter are those of the authors alone and not the Welsh Assembly Government.

There are potential gains to be made by reducing or delaying the need for the consumption of future health care resources, and from limiting the wider costs to society resulting from absenteeism and health-related early retirement from the paid labour force. There are also productivity gains to be made by improving/maintaining the health of those who do not engage in paid work but nonetheless contribute to the economy through voluntary work, domestic activities and the consumption of leisure services. There may also be non-health related benefits such as increased community cohesiveness (Hills *et al.*, 2007).

While these potential benefits may be substantial, any decision to invest in public health interventions needs to consider the human and infrastructure costs associated with their delivery. For instance, is it really more cost-effective overall to prevent health problems through population-wide preventive measures rather than simply treating that smaller group of individuals who actually develop problems? Thus the imperative for identifying both effective and (more recently) cost-effective ways of promoting good health through public health and health promotion activities has become a major health policy question in many countries, including England.

The economic case for public health was examined as part of a review commissioned by the Treasury on the potential impact of better population health in the final Wanless report (2004). It concluded that the evidence base on the economic case for public health interventions remained limited, and that robust evidence on cost-effectiveness was only found in a small number of areas.

There are a number or explanations of why public health interventions are not well covered in economic analyses. The first relates to the complexity inherent in running public health interventions, compared with, say, randomised controlled trials (RCTs) for health care pharmaceuticals: the impact of variables that do not lie within the remit, or budgets, of health policy; the problem of discounting (Ganiats, 1997; Sheldon, 1992) and long-term outcomes – particularly in a political context which demands immediate rewards and focuses attention on health care; and the associated issues of evaluations focusing on process variables and proxy outcomes, e.g. numbers in smoking cessation projects, instead of numbers of ex-smokers. Adding to the complexity is that many interventions are not seen as being within the province of health care systems and require investment from other budget holders such as those in transport, education or the environment.

The complexity in practice has led some public health professionals to criticise traditional approaches to economic evaluation for adopting a 'reductionist' perspective that does not capture all the benefits of maintaining good health and averting illness. For instance, benefits from community interventions such as regeneration schemes may also serve to strengthen community cohesion and thus build social capital. These benefits are not picked up by measures such as the Quality Adjusted Life Year (QALY); thus they argue that when it comes to public health, economic evaluation is simply not feasible (Burrows *et al.*, 1995).

The real practical challenge may not lie in scepticism over methodologies of evaluation, but rather in the very limited levels of resources available for evaluating public health and health promoting interventions. Public funding remains modest and, as there is little opportunity to generate a profit from investment, this research is largely reliant on funding from charitable institutions and private foundations.

Another explanation is that the apparent lack of economic evaluation might simply be an artefact of the challenge of identifying such studies in the literature. Economic evaluations of public health interventions might be published in one of many journals covering a wide range of disciplines (Jackson and Waters, 2004). This may make studies difficult to identify, particularly by those more accustomed to trawling through the medical literature alone (Petticrew and Roberts, 2005). Non-medical-literature databases may be cumbersome to search and may not provide access to abstracts of papers (Powell *et al.*, 2004).

This chapter reports the results of a review of the economic literature which aimed to see if this perception of a dearth of evidence was in fact borne out in the literature, using a range of databases in order to capture any non-medical literature which included economic evaluations. The results of the search are presented to illustrate the extent of current literature which can feed into developing the evidence base in future. Specific areas of public health, settings of the intervention and the methods of economic evaluation used are all considered, and areas of patchiness in the evaluation literature highlighted. Some areas for future development and policy implications of the findings are considered.

Methods

A literature review protocol was developed, in line with guidance published by the NHS Centre for Reviews and Dissemination (2001). Full details are available elsewhere (McDaid and Needle, 2006).

A broad range of medical and non-medical databases were searched including Medline, CINAHL, Psychinfo, Econlit, the International Bibliography of the Social Sciences, the Public Administration and Information Service, Geobase, and ERIC (an education related resource). There were no language restrictions and we covered the 40 years from 1966 to 2005. A hand search of 35 key journals was also conducted and references of relevant papers checked.

Inclusion criteria for public health and health promoting interventions covered those that alter individual behaviours/lifestyles; control and prevent infectious diseases; tackle the broader determinants of health; and provide secondary prevention, in particular screening for disease.

We identified studies using conventional economic analyses of public health and health promoting interventions: cost minimisation analysis (CMA), cost-effectiveness analysis (CEA), cost-utility analysis (CUA) and cost benefit analysis (CBA). We also included cost-consequences analysis (CCA) which is less common in economic evaluations.[1]

Kelly *et al.* (2005) have argued that in thinking about public health there could be a greater role for econometric modelling studies and innovative approaches combining qualitative methods alongside economic evaluation – something that has been coined as 'holistic' or 'ecological' economic evaluation (Hawe *et al.*, 2004; Jan *et al.*, 2004). For example, economic analysis of the impact of changes in taxation on the demand for cigarettes or alcohol would lie outside the conventional definition of an economic evaluation, as they tend to rely heavily on econometric analysis, but clearly these are highly relevant to research and policymaking. Similarly, the effectiveness of legislation and regulatory instruments in improving public health may not easily be assessed using conventional methods and again may rely on econometric analysis. Thus although these studies rarely assess implementation costs we have sought to include them where identified.

Abstracts of papers for review were checked independently and then compared by the two authors. We also included findings from two published reviews of economic evaluations for health promotion interventions, one undertaken at the University of Calgary (Rush *et al.*, 2004) and the other in Switzerland (Winterthurer Institut fur Gesundheitssokonomie, 2004).

Results

Is there a lack of relevant publications?

Over 7000 references were identified. After initial screening 2109 publications were further examined and almost 1700 studies met the inclusion criteria and were included in our final analysis.

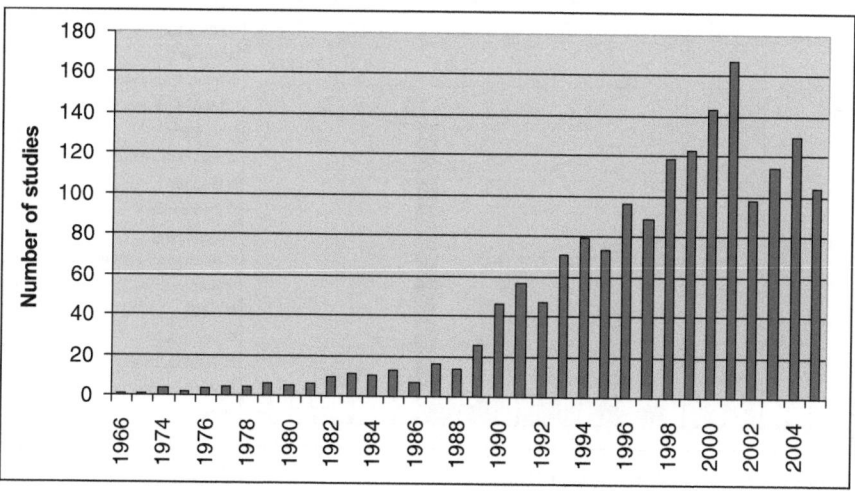

Figure 12.1 Total number of included studies

There has been a sustained increase in the number of economic evaluations over time. Figure 12.1 illustrates this growth. Only 12 per cent of papers date back to before 1990, although studies dating back to the 1960s were identified. While the number of studies appears to peak in 2001, this is an artefact of the inclusion of papers identified by the Calgary review (the period for this review ran from 1990 to 2001). There may also be a publication lag effect for 2004 and 2005 papers.

Unsurprisingly, but consistent with economic evaluation more generally, the majority of studies (49 per cent) are produced in the United States. The UK accounts for 13 per cent, followed by Canada (five per cent) and Australia and the Netherlands (both 4 per cent).

Which areas of public health and health promotion have made use of economic evaluation?

Figure 12.2 illustrates the different areas of public health and health promotion where economic evaluation has been used. Evaluations at the medical end of the public health spectrum dominate, with more than 60 per cent of all studies having some focus on the prevention of communicable diseases such as influenza as well as early detection and preventive measures against cancer. More than 35 per cent of all studies evaluated screening and early diagnostic tools, particularly for breast and colon cancer. HIV/AIDS-related

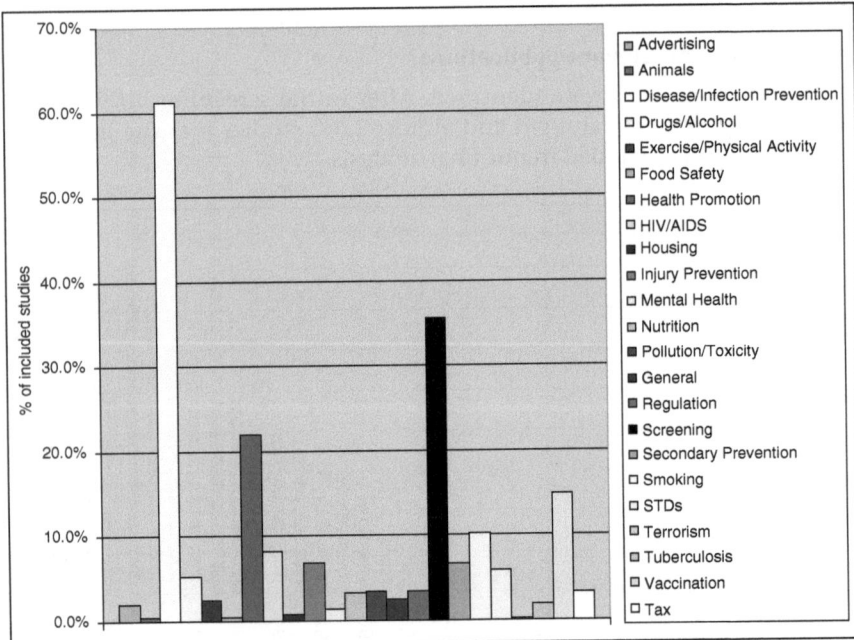

Figure 12.2   Areas for intervention

prevention strategies, interventions to reduce the risk of maternal transmission to infants and vaccination programmes were also common.

Other areas of public health are more complex and in them economic evaluations are less frequent. Nonetheless, we were able to identify more than 550 examples of broad health promoting interventions, including the merits of exercise, smoking prevention, nutrition change and drug/alcohol consumption. The majority of these general lifestyle interventions were aimed at changing individual behaviours rather than targeted at a population level.

We also found a substantial number of studies focusing on injury and accident prevention, including the use of bicycle helmets and seatbelts in cars and adaptations in the home to reduce the risk and/or consequence of accidents such as falls or fires.

Some areas remained weak. Consistent with the findings of previous studies we found few studies that looked at the value of tackling the wider socio-economic determinants of health, such as poverty and unemployment, from a health-economic perspective. There also appeared to be little on the economic case for mental health promotion outside the workplace, although a small number of suicide prevention interventions, including some targeted at ethnic minorities and university students, were identified (de Castro *et al.*, 2004; Zaloshnja *et al.*, 2003). A major systematic review undertaken by the US Preventive Services Task Force failed, however, to find any evidence on the economic case of screening for suicide risk (Gaynes *et al.*, 2004).

Where did the interventions take place?

In terms of studies where settings were specified, 22 per cent were located in the workplace. This is one specialist area where not only is there an extensive literature on effectiveness but many studies looking at the resource consequences of poor employee health. In the US, Employee Assistance Programmes intended to help prevent both stress and physical health problems have been the subject of much evaluation. Other schemes evaluated include physical exercise programmes, the provision of lifestyle advice and workplace screening programmes. Excluding screening, with very few exceptions, where evaluated these studies appear to be cost-effective (Pelletier, 2005a; Pelletier, 2001; Pelletier, 1991).

The overwhelming majority of workplace studies are from the US, where employers usually provide health care benefits for their employees and their families. The economic case has been based strongly around reducing the direct health care costs to employers of poor employee health. In other settings where the state, social health insurance or even the individual are the primary sources of health care funding, the burdens on employers may be considerably less and benefits more fragmented, thus the incentives to commission such evaluations and take subsequent action more limited (Dewa *et al.*, 2007). Nevertheless, it is perhaps surprising that so few workplace health promotion evaluations have been conducted outside the US. Long-term absenteeism and premature retirement from the labour force, largely due to stress and musculoskeletal problems, have contributed to the substantial rise in disability related social welfare payments seen in many European countries in the last decade (McDaid *et al.*, 2005).

Almost 8 per cent of studies were set in schools or in colleges of higher education. Many of these school-based studies were concerned with evaluating screening interventions (Chatterji *et al.*, 2004; Konig and Barry, 2004; Lowin *et al.*, 2000; Wang *et al.*, 2002), although economic evaluations of interventions targeted at changing behavioural risk factors such as smoking (Elder *et al.*, 1993) and unsafe sex (Berrios *et al.*, 2004) can also be identified. There have been a handful of economic evaluations of school-based interventions intended to impact on the chances of adult obesity. For example, one RCT conducted in Boston in ten middle schools examined the impact of an inter-disciplinary curriculum intended to decrease TV and fatty food consumption as well as increase the intake of fruit, vegetables and moderate exercise. In the short term, changes in body mass index were recorded; modelling was then used to predict the transition to obesity from age 14 to 40. The programme only appeared to be effective in girls (perhaps emphasising the need for more contextual research) and overall the programme was estimated to cost just over $4000 per QALY saved (Wang *et al.*, 2003). This compares with the NICE threshold of £20K to £30K.

What methods of economic evaluation were used?

Figure 12.3 provides a breakdown of the types of evaluation methodology used. More than three quarters of all studies were simple CEA or CCAs. CUA,

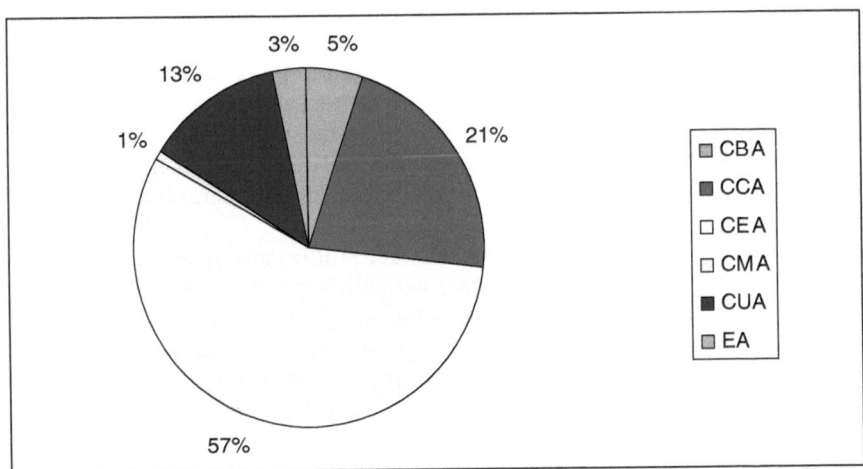

Figure 12.3 Economic evaluation methodologies used

which uses the QALY as a common outcome measure, accounted for just 13 per cent of all studies found. CBAs accounted for five per cent of all studies identified. The technique did appear to have been most often applied to areas of injury prevention and pollution prevention. This is not surprising given that there is a strong history of CBA in both environmental economics and in transport economics (many of the interventions are transport safety measures).

A small, but not insignificant, number of studies (three per cent) used econometric techniques. Studies identified typically looked at tobacco and alcohol, although nutritional interventions (where the impact of price controls and subsidies on the consumption of healthy foods or the avoidance of fatty foods) were the focus of some studies. A number of studies also assessed the impact of regulatory measures. For instance, one used three-year data from the US nationwide Fatal Accident Reporting System to assess the impact of mandatory retesting of vision as part of driver relicensing. The study concluded that sight tests were effective in reducing road traffic fatalities and might avert more than $31 million in costs (Shipp, 1998).

It was not unusual for different approaches to be used in different areas of public health. For example, screening and vaccinations studies tended to use cost-effectiveness or cost-consequence analyses using decision analytical models to estimate long-term consequences to different sectors of the population (Mandelbatt *et al.*, 2003; Roberts, 2006). A common factor in both screening and vaccination interventions which differentiates them from many other public health interventions is the relative ease of measuring short-term outcomes in terms of true positive cases detected or successful immunisations conducted, while initial costs incurred are also easily identifiable. The principle challenge is modelling lifetime benefits.

Discussion

This review clearly demonstrates that the whole gamut of economic evaluation techniques have been used as part of the assessment of a wide range of public health interventions. Yet our findings are conservative – we are acutely aware of the potentially significant amount of literature that we might have identified had we gone even further with our search protocol.

Our findings support those of earlier reviews, and thus add to their validity. The Calgary review concluded that more than 400 economic evaluations of health promoting interventions alone had been published between 1990 and 2001. They found little in the areas of population health advocacy or in tackling the biological and behavioural determinants of health (Rush *et al.*, 2004). They also observed that studies tended to be concentrated in a few areas, most notably workplace health promotion and smoking cessation. Our review confirms this trend, although our analysis indicates an emerging interest in studies across a wider number of public health areas in the last few years. The Swiss review, meanwhile, similarly found a majority of health promoting interventions to be from the US, and only 13 per cent to be from the UK (Winterthurer Institut fur Gesundheitssokonomie, 2004).

Despite the increased availability of literature, however, there remain concerns about research quality. In reviewing US-based studies of the cost-effectiveness of workplace interventions, one expert commented that there has been a marked decline in both quality and quantity of economic evaluations over time (Pelletier, 2005b). Whilst, overall, our analysis would suggest that the economic case for investment in preventive measures is becoming more robust and has been undertaken in more settings, it is also patchy.

The review also highlighted areas of policy where there are gaps, for example around mental health. One review of workplace mental health promoting interventions could only find six studies that were evaluated using rigorous methods, not one of which presented information on cost-effectiveness (Michie and Williams, 2003).

Some methods of economic evaluation are more common than others. Our review found relatively few examples of econometric analysis, although this may reflect our search strategy which did not specifically include econometric search terms, rather than an indication of the scale of work produced using these techniques.

There is continued debate on the appropriateness of the methods used in economic evaluation for health promotion and public health interventions (Godfrey, 2001; Kelly *et al.*, 2005; Richardson, 1998; Shiell and Hawe, 1996). Of particular interest, as it is recommended by NICE, has been the questioning of the QALY as a suitable outcome measure for public health interventions. Hunter is one of many in the public health community to question whether 'it is feasible to collapse the multifaceted phenomena of life and its quality into a single valid scale' (1997). Yet at the same time, it is also interesting that the QALY is becoming of interest to those working outside the traditional boundaries of health care. It has been put forward as an alternative to CBA in environmental economics, for example, for issues such as the regulation of air pollution (Hubbell, 2002).

CBA theoretically overcomes the limitations of the QALY as it can capture all potential outcomes of interest and may present an appropriate way forward, despite the practical and conceptual problems associated with contingent valuation methods (Cookson, 2003). Whether estimates of individual willingness to pay adequately reflect the societal benefits in those health areas that may be influenced by stigma and discrimination, as in the case of mental illness, is one example of the problems encountered in this approach. Furthermore, we can only speculate as to whether the positive exclusion by NICE (and several other Health Technology Assessment agencies) of CBA from formal technology assessment procedures may have discouraged greater use of the approach – and thus hampered opportunities to overcome some of its limitations.

Discrete choice methods may represent one alternative to the willingness to pay approach. This approach allows individuals to choose between a range of realistic scenarios, taking account of process factors, and may be used to elicit values for both health and non-health outcomes (Lancsar and Donaldson, 2005; Ryan *et al.*, 2001). A key challenge, however, is determining which attributes to include in scenarios. Approaches might draw on the expert opinion of professional stakeholders or the general public. Other techniques, such as enhanced synthesis of qualitative literature, perhaps making use of meta-ethnographic techniques (Noblitt and Hare, 1988) or Q-methodology, which combines elements of quantitative analysis with qualitative techniques to explore subjectivity and beliefs (Baker *et al.*, 2006), might also be used to inform analysis; such applications, however, remain rare within health economics.

CCAs do not strictly meet the definition of economic evaluation laid down in many standard texts; they do however represent a significant proportion of studies undertaken. In the absence of confidence in methods of CBA and the acknowledged limitations of QALYs, CCA may provide a pragmatic solution for decisionmakers. It is not insignificant that NICE now allows CCA to form part of the process of assessing public health interventions, albeit only alongside the use of CUA (Kelly, 2005).

Future analysis by NICE and other bodies might place more emphasis on instruments such as taxes, subsidies and regulations. The potential role of taxation in reducing binge drinking is currently the subject of some prominence both in England and elsewhere in Europe (Anderson and Baumberg, 2006; BBC News Online, 2006). As noted, most analysis of these economic incentives does not take the form of economic evaluation but rather econometric analysis. This is potentially extremely valuable to policymakers, but the costs associated with introducing and enforcing such measures have received much less attention.

We have indicated the critical importance of context in understanding what influences individual behaviours and the uptake of interventions. Again, future methodological development might consider how to enhance and increase the use of holistic approaches to economic evaluation that make use of qualitative methods to obtain contextual information on the implementation of interventions (Jan, 1998; Jan *et al.*, 2004). Approaches such as 'Theory of Change' may merit further consideration. This involves the identification of why and how intervention planners believe that change in behaviour or practice will occur, and subsequently how this will link to changes in short, mid and long-term outcomes (Connell and Kubisch, 1998). As yet such approaches have only rarely been used by health economists alongside economic evaluation; equally it is true to say that proponents of these types of 'realistic evaluation' rarely incorporate an economic dimension into their analyses.

Finally, regardless of study method used, more might be done to improve transparency in reporting study findings. There are numerous standards and recommendations available on how to report outcome studies (both qualitative and quantitative) and economic evaluations. It is not just a question of transparent reporting – policymakers require rapid, accessible and independent interpretation of studies to help inform the decisionmaking progress. Methods put forward by the US Center for Disease Control and Task Force on Community Preventive Services which include guidance on how to identify as well as rapidly judge the quality of effectiveness and economic studies may well be worth adopting (Briss *et al.*, 2000; Briss *et al.*, 2004).

Guides such as that developed specifically for economic evaluation of health promoting interventions (Hale *et al.*, 2005) can also play an important role in aiding this process. They can also help in disseminating the message that, when commissioning an effectiveness evaluation, it would be helpful to incorporate economic evaluation, or at least put the measurement tools in place to record resource use for some future evaluation. Although not ideal, one way of reducing the knowledge gap would be through adding an economic dimension retrospectively in those areas of public health where evidence on effectiveness is available.

Future policy implications

Our focus in this review has not been to assess methodological quality in great detail, but to get a better overall sense of the breadth of the literature and the use of economic evaluation techniques. We believe that the view that few economic evaluations have been conducted in the field of public health cannot be sustained. The rapid expansion of the evidence base in recent years and the growing interest of policymakers is recognition of the importance of the economic case for public health, including health promotion.

Our review raises a number of challenges for future public health policymaking, which may require a distinctively different role for economic evaluation compared to its use in health care policy. Perhaps the most fundamental challenge is the need to undertake or commission evaluations of interventions that are delivered outside the health sector, such as in school or the workplace. Evaluation of these interventions requires coordination across government departments and cooperation with non-governmental stakeholders. It also raises questions about incentive structures and the current role of bodies such as NICE whose guidance is only binding, at present, within the health care system.

Consider, for instance, a hypothetical early intervention in school for children with behavioural problems that is shown to be highly cost-effective, not only in terms of long-term health outcomes, but also in other areas such as educational performance. NICE might conclude that such an intervention should be made available in all schools – yet the responsibility for the funding and delivery of such interventions may lay with local authority education departments. From the perspective of the education sector, the intervention may appear very expensive and, because most of the benefits are accrued in adulthood, not to benefit the local authority education department. Incentives may be required, such as additional funding from central government, or perhaps in the longer term, a transfer of funding from those sectors that will benefit most to those where the intervention is delivered. This also would be consistent with the increased focus on assessing the health impacts of all policies now in vogue (see Stahl *et al.*, 2006).

Another key policy challenge is linked to outcome measurement. What if a hypothetical intervention in fact does not generate significant additional health gains at all, but nevertheless does demonstrate substantial non-health related outcomes such as improved community cohesion, educational attainment, or workplace performance? In this case any economic evaluation which focuses solely on health outcomes will probably conclude that the intervention is not cost-effective. In England the change in NICE guidance to allow the use of cost-consequences analysis alongside the measurement of QALY outcomes will certainly help highlight the potential importance of non-health outcomes.

Yet even if these non-health related outcomes are measured, what influence could or should they have over the decision to allow access to an intervention with only modest health benefits? Well conducted CBA would theoretically overcome this problem, but there are practical challenges in generating meaningful values and it is still not permitted by NICE. In the absence of CBA, how can different benefits be prioritised? Cooperation may be required across sectors, such that results of evaluation are shared with other relevant sectors and decisions can be made on whether or not a public health investment represents good value for money. If provided within the health sector, a transfer of resources may be required from those sectors which have most to gain.

Increased cooperation with the private sector, including the use of incentives such as tax breaks, may also be required. Few economic evaluations of workplace health promotions are found outside the United States, yet effective interventions can not only enhance health in the workplace, but also reduce premature retirement and long-term absence from the labour force, both of which not only have implications for the future use of health care resources, but also the level of disability and sickness welfare payments.

The nature of many public health interventions, which often may be delivered in community wide settings and do not lend themselves easily to experimental controlled trials, also requires a high degree of collaboration between the public health and health economics communities. The dominance of US-based research identified in our review raises major questions about the generalisability of many study findings, and an understanding of the extent to which local adaptations may need to be made requires a multidisciplinary response. Policymakers might help to enhance such cooperation by explicitly calling for multidisciplinary research teams when commissioning research.

Potentially, the economic benefits of investing in many public health areas are very high, but it is important that well designed evaluations are undertaken prior to large-scale investment. Adding an economic dimension retrospectively to those areas of public health where evidence on effectiveness is strong may be one pragmatic and relatively rapid way of helping to inform decisionmaking. Modelling can also play a critical role in helping to provide information on the potential long-term impacts of public health interventions. Even simple threshold analysis, which looks at the potential level of effectiveness that an intervention would need to demonstrate in order to make an intervention cost-effective, might be assessed. Given the potential cost saving nature of many interventions, the level of improvement in effectiveness required may well be very modest, as may well be the case for suicide prevention strategies (Platt *et al.*, 2006).

Funding remains an overarching issue of concern. Evaluation and investment in public health interventions by the private sector is limited, as typically, unlike with health care interventions, there is little opportunity for a market return on investment. Instead the onus must remain on governments and charitable foundations (and perhaps employers) to fund the majority of such evaluations and to aid in their interpretation and dissemination. Despite the growing body of evidence, major gaps, especially in non-US evaluation, persist. Without additional funding for evaluation and to make better use of or adapt existing evidence, proponents of public health will continue to fight an uneven struggle against those arguing for more investment in the health care system.

Note

1 For a full discussion of these methodologies see, for instance, Drummond *et al.*, 1997 and Hale *et al.*, 2005.

References

S. Allin, E. Mossialos, M. McKee and W. Holland, *Making Decisions on Public Health: A Review of Eight Countries* (Copenhagen: World Health Organization, 2004).

P. Anderson and B. Baumberg, *Alcohol in Europe* (London: Institute of Alcohol Studies, 2006).

R. Baker, C. Thompson and R. Mannion, 'Q methodology in health economics', *Journal of Health Services Research and Policy*, 11:1 (2006) 38–45.

BBC News Online, Hewitt asks for alcohol tax rise (London: BBC, 2006).

X. Berrios, P. Bedregal and B. Guzman, 'Costo-efectividad de la promocion de la salud en Chile: Experiencia del programa "Mirame"! [Cost-effectiveness of health promotion in Chile: Experience with the "Mirame!" programme]', *Revista Medica Chile*, 132:3 (2004) 361–70.

P. A. Briss, R. C. Brownson, J. E. Fielding and S. Zaza, 'Developing and using the guide to community preventive services: lessons learned about evidence-based public health', *Annual Review of Public Health*, 25 (2004) 281–302.

P. A. Briss, S. Zaza, M. Pappaioanou, J. Fielding, L. Wright-De Aguero, B. I. Truman, D. P. Hopkins, P. D. Mullen, R. S. Thompson, S. H. Woolf, V. G. Carande-Kulis, L. Anderson, A. R. Hinman, D. V. McQueen, S. M. Teutsch and J. R. Harris, 'Developing an evidence-based guide to community preventive services – methods: The task force on community preventive services', *American Journal of Preventive Medicine*, 18:S1 (2000) 35–43.

R. Burrows, R. Bunton, S. Muncer and K. Gillen, 'The efficacy of health promotion, health economics and late modernism', *Health Education Research*, 10:2 (1995) 241–9.

Centre for Reviews and Dissemination, *Undertaking Systematic Reviews of Research on Effectiveness: CRD Report No 4'* (York: NHS Centre for Reviews and Dissemination, 2001).

P. Chatterji, C. M. Caffray, M. Crowe, L. Freeman and P. Jensen, 'Cost assessment of a school-based mental health screening and treatment program in New York City', *Mental Health Services Research*, 6:3 (2004) 155–66.

D. Chisholm, J. Rehm, M. Van Ommeren and M. Monteiro, 'Reducing the global burden of hazardous alcohol use: a comparative cost-effectiveness analysis', *Journal of Studies on Alcohol*, 65 (2004) 782–93.

J. Connell and A. Kubisch, 'Applying a theory of change approach to the evaluation of comprehensive community initiatives: progress, prospects and problems', in K. Fulbright-Anderson, A. Kubisch and J. Connell (eds), *New approaches to evaluating community initiatives, Volume 2: theory, measurement, and analysis* (Washington DC: The Aspen Institute, 1998), accessed 21 January 2008 at http://www.aspeninstitute.org/site/c.huLWJeMRKpH/b.613709/k.B547/Applying_a_Theory_of_Change_Approach_to_the_Evaluation_of_Comprehensive_Community_Initiatives_Progress_Prospects_and_Problems.htm

R. Cookson, 'Willingness to pay methods in health care: a sceptical view', *Health Economics*, 12:11 (2003) 891–4.

S. de Castro, F. Newman, G. Mills and N. Sari, 'Economic evaluation of suicide prevention programs for young adults in Florida', *Business Review Cambridge*, 3:1 (2004) 14–20.

Department of Health, *Our Health, Our Care, Our Say: A New Direction for Community Services* (Norwich: HM Stationary Office, 2006).

C. S. Dewa, D. McDaid and S. L. Ettner, 'An international perspective on worker mental health problems: who bears the burden and how are costs addressed?', *Canadian Journal of Psychiatry*, 52 (2007), 346–56.

M. Drummond, B. O'Brien, G. Stoddart and G. Torrance, *Methods for the Economic Evaluation of Health Care Programmes* (Oxford: Oxford Medical Publications, 1997).

J. P. Elder, M. Wildey, C. de Moor, J. F. Sallis, Jr, L. Eckhardt, C. Edwards, A. Erickson, A. Golbeck, M. Hovell and D. Johnston 'The long-term prevention of tobacco use among junior high school students: classroom and telephone interventions', *American Journal of Public Health*, 83:9 (1993) 1239–44.

A. Elixhauser, M. Halpern, J. Schmier, B. R. Luce, 'Health care CBA and CEA from 1991 to 1996: an updated bibliography', *Medical Care*, 36:5, S1 (1998) MS1–MS9.

D. B. Evans, T. T. Edejer, T. Adam and S. S. Lim, 'Methods to assess the costs and health effects of interventions for improving health in developing countries', *British Medical Journal*, 331:7525 (2005) 1137–40.

R. Fordham, 'Towards investment in public health: the emergence of a burden of economic proof', this volume.

V. Fuchs, 'Setting priorities in health education and promotion', *Health Affairs*, 2:4 (1983) 56–69.

T. G. Ganiats, 'Prevention, policy, and paradox: what is the value of future health?', *American Journal of Preventive Medicine*, 13:1 (1997) 12–17.

B. Gaynes, S. West, C. Ford, P. Frame, J. Klein and K. N. Lohr, *Screening for Suicide Risk: A Systematic Evidence Review for the U.S. Preventive Services Task Force* (Rockville, Maryland: Agency for Healthcare Research and Quality, 2004).

C. Godfrey, 'Economic evaluation of health promotion', *WHO Reg Publ Eur Ser*, 92 (2001) 149–70.

J. Hale, 'What contribution can health economics make to health promotion?', *Health Promotion International*, 15:4 (2000) 341–8.

J. Hale, D. Cohen, A. Ludbrook, C. Phillips, M. Duffy and N. Parry-Langdon, *Moving from Evaluation into Economic Evaluation: A Health Economics Manual for Programmes to Improve Health and Well-being* (Cardiff: National Assembly for Wales, 2005).

P. Hawe, A. Shiell, T. Riley and L. Gold, 'Methods for exploring implementation variation and local context within a cluster randomised community intervention trial', *Journal of Epidemiology and Community Health*, 58 (2004) 788–93.

D. Hills, E. Elliot, U. Kowarzik, F. Sullivan, E. Stern, S. Platt, L. Boydell, J. Popay, G. Williams, M. Petticrew, E. McGregor, S. Russell, E. Wilkinson, J. Rugkasa, M. Gibson and D. McDaid, *The evaluation of the Big Lottery Fund Healthy Living Centres Programme* (London: Big Lottery Fund, 2007).

W. Holland, 'Health technology assessment and public health: a commentary', *International Journal of Technology Assessment in Health Care*, 20:1 (2004) 77–80.

B. J. Hubbell, *Implementing QALYs in the Analysis of Air Pollution Regulations* (Washington DC: US Environment Protection Agency, 2002).

D. J. Hunter, *Desperately Seeking Solutions: Rationing Health Care* (London: Longman, 1997).

N. Jackson and E. Waters, 'The challenges of systematically reviewing public health interventions', *Journal of Public Health Medicine*, 26:3 (2004) 303–7.

S. Jan, 'A holistic approach to the economic evaluation of health programs using institutionalist methodology', *Social Science & Medicine*, 47:10 (1998) 1565–72.

S. Jan, S. Conaty, R. Hecker, M. Bartlett, S. Delaney and T. Capon, 'A holistic economic evaluation of an Aboriginal community-controlled midwifery programme in Western Sydney', *Journal of Health Services Research and Policy*, 9:1 (2004) 14–21.

M. P. Kelly, 'Public health guidance and the role of new NICE', *Public Health*, 119 (2005) 960–8.

M. P. Kelly, D. McDaid, A. Ludbrook and J. Powell, *Economic Appraisal of Public Health Interventions* (London: National Institute for Health and Clinical Excellence, 2005).

H. H. Konig and J. C. Barry, 'Cost-utility analysis of orthoptic screening in kindergarten: a Markov model based on data from Germany', *Pediatrics*, 113:2 (2004) e95–108.

E. Lancsar and C. Donaldson, 'Discrete choice experiments in health economics', *European Journal of Health Economics*, 6:4 (2005) 314–16.

A. Lowin, J. Slater, J. Hall and G. Alperstein, 'Cost-effectiveness analysis of school based Mantoux screening for TB infection', *Australian and New Zealand Journal of Public Health*, 24:3 (2000) 247–53.

J. Mandelblatt, S. Saha, S. Teutsch, T. Hoerger, A. Siu, D. Atkins, J. Klein and M. Helfand, 'The cost-effectiveness of screening mammography beyond age 65 years: a systematic review for the U.S. Preventive Services Task Force', *Annals of Internal Medicine*, 139:10 (2003) 835–42.

D. McDaid, C. Curran and M. Knapp, 'Promoting mental well-being in the workplace: a European policy perspective', *International Review of Psychiatry*, 17:5 (2005) 365–73.

D. McDaid and J. Needle, *Economic Evaluation and Public Health: Mapping the Literature* (Cardiff: Health Promotion Division, Welsh Assembly Government, 2006).

S. Michie and S. Williams, 'Reducing work related psychological ill health and sickness absence: a systematic literature review', *Occupational and Environmental Medicine*, 60 (2003) 3–9.

G. W. Noblitt and D. R. Hare, *Meta-ethnography: Synthesizing Qualitative Studies* (Newbury Park, CA: Sage, 1988).

E. Nolte and M. McKee, 'Measuring the health of nations: analysis of mortality amenable to health care', *British Medical Journal*, 327:7424 (2003) 1129.

K. R. Pelletier, 'A review and analysis of the health and cost-effective outcome studies of comprehensive health promotion and disease prevention programs', *American Journal of Health Promotion*, 5:4 (1991) 311–15.

K. R. Pelletier, 'A review and analysis of the clinical- and cost-effectiveness studies of comprehensive health promotion and disease management programs at the worksite: 1998–2000 update', *American Journal of Health Promotion*, 16:2 (2001) 107–16.

K. R. Pelletier, 'International collaboration in health promotion and disease management: implications of US health promotion efforts on Japan's health care system', *American Journal of Health Promotion*, 19:3 (2005a) 216–29.

K. R. Pelletier, 'A review and analysis of the clinical and cost-effectiveness studies of comprehensive health promotion and disease management programs at the worksite: Update VI 2000–2004', *Journal of Occupational and Environmental Medicine*, 47:10 (2005b) 1051–7.

M. Petticrew and H. Roberts, *Systematic Reviews in the Social Sciences: A Practical Guide* (Oxford: Blackwell Publishing, 2005).

S. Platt, E. Halliday, M. Maxwell, A. McCollam, J. McLean, A. Woodhouse, A. Blamey, M. Mackenzie and D. McDaid, *Evaluation of the First Phase of Choose Life. Final Report* (Edinburgh: Scottish Executive, 2006).

J. Powell, J. Glanville and L. Mather, *Indexing of Databases Relevant to Public Health* (London: National Institute for Health and Clinical Excellence, 2004).

J. Richardson, 'Economic evaluation of health promotion: friend or foe?', *Australian and New Zealand Journal of Public Health*, 22:2 (1998) 247–53.

J. Roberts (ed.), *The Economics of Infectious Diseases* (Oxford: Oxford University Press, 2006).

B. Rush, A. Shiell and P. Hawe, 'A census of economic evaluations in health promotion', *Health Education Research*, 19:6 (2004) 707–19.

M. Ryan, A. Bate, C. J. Eastmond and A. Ludbrook, 'Use of discrete choice experiments to elicit preferences', *Quality and Safety in Health Care*, 10:S1 (2001) i55–i60.

L. Rychetnik, M. Frommer, P. Hawe and A. Shiell, 'Criteria for evaluating evidence on public health interventions', *Journal of Epidemiology and Community Health*, 56:2 (2002) 119–27.

F. Sassi, L. Archard and D. McDaid, 'Searching literature databases for health care economic evaluations: how systematic can we afford to be?', *Medical Care*, 40:5 (2002) 387–94.

T. A. Sheldon, 'Discounting in health care decision-making: time for a change?', *Journal of Public Health Medicine*, 14:3 (1992) 250–6.

A. Shiell and P. Hawe, 'Health promotion community development and the tyranny of individualism', *Health Economics*, 5:3 (1996) 241–7.

M. D. Shipp, 'Potential human and economic cost-savings attributable to vision testing policies for driver license renewal, 1989–1991', *Optometry and Vision Science*, 75:2 (1998) 103–18.

T. Stahl, M. Wismar, E. Ollila, E. Lahtinen and K. Leppo (eds), *Health in All Policies: Prospects and Potentials* (Helsinki: Ministry of Social Affairs and Health, 2006).

L. Y. Wang, G. R. Burstein and D. A. Cohen, 'An economic evaluation of a school-based sexually transmitted disease screening program', *Sexually Transmitted Diseases*, 29:1 (2002) 737–45.

L. Y. Wang, Q. Yang, R. Lowry and H. Wechsler, 'Economic analysis of a school-based obesity prevention program', *Obesity Research*, 11:11 (2003) 1313–24.

D. Wanless, *Securing Good Health for the Whole Population* (Norwich: HM Stationary Office, 2004).

Winterthurer Institut fur Gesundheitssokonomie, *Ökonomische Beurteilung von Gesundheitsförderung und Prävention* (Winterthurer: Winterthurer Institut, 2004).

E. Zaloshnja, T. R. Miller, M. S. Galbraith, B. A. Lawrence, L. M. DeBruyn, N. Bill, K. R. Hicks, M. Keiffer and R. Perkins, 'Reducing injuries among Native Americans: five cost-outcome analyses', *Accident Analysis and Prevention*, 35:5 (2003) 631–9.

13
Towards Investment in Public Health: The Emergence of a Burden of Economic Proof

Richard J. Fordham

Introduction

The Wanless Report (2002) called for evidence-based policy in public health and warned that without an economic evaluation evidence base, investment in public health would be hard to justify. In fact, depending on the definition of public health used there have been a considerable number of economic evaluations of these interventions to date, albeit in different countries and across a wide variety of programmes and using varying economic evaluation techniques. Although no simple evaluation framework exists, the consistent message is that many public health programmes can be cost-effective and affordable at currently accepted international thresholds.

Wider interpretation of economic evaluation parameters is required to accommodate the special features of population versus individual programmes in particular. Study designs and methodologies used in this field are not as consistent as pharmacological interventions where a single end-point is often all that may be required. Historically, much evaluation of public health concentrates on 'process' or intermediate outcomes more than final outcomes. Indeed, it may be argued that it is not possible to use this framework at all without taking into consideration other types of cost (such as costs to the community at large, or individual and even anonymous third- parties). The National Institute for Health and Clinical Excellence 'Reference Case' analytical method, to which submissions for drug funding are submitted, currently includes the UK NHS and Personal and Social Services perspectives. But NICE now recognises (in principal at least) these wider impacts and has broadened the scope of costs and benefits that evaluations be allowed to be included in the future. Possible public sector agencies to have their perspectives accounted for could include education, law enforcement, and the criminal justice system.

The main economic issue here is the presence of 'externalities' (indirect costs and/or benefits to others outside of the immediate economic 'transaction'), something which occurs less often with one-to-one treatments applied to individual patients. An example of an 'externality' is the impact of a vaccination and immunisation programme on the whole population – the so-called 'herd immunity' effect. Additionally, benefits and costs may 'spill over' onto particular groups such as the old or the vulnerable. Evaluations, however, may overlook these wider benefits. For example, conventional economic evaluation of pneumococcal vaccine for infants may not include the subsidiary benefits to adults (parents and, in particular, older grandparents) in reduced mortality and hospital admissions. Of course, externalities can be negative as well as positive. Pollution is a classic environmental 'negative externality', in that it is a cost which falls on third parties who have often had no part in either the consumption or the production of the harmful goods and services.

Despite the limitations of existing studies there is nevertheless a significant body of research that can offer many useful insights into the cost-effectiveness of public health interventions. Many of these studies adopt a useful, if somewhat compressed, form of economic analysis known as 'cost-utility' analysis (CUA). This incorporates the 'quality-adjusted life-year' (QALY) as the main measure of health outcome. The product of years of extra survival and improved quality of life, the QALY enables programmes of different types to be readily compared (Williams, 1985). The incremental cost of producing an extra QALY is then compared in an incremental cost-effectiveness ratio. These ratios may be combined in 'league tables' in rank order or they may be looked at in terms of cost-effectiveness thresholds. As well as allowing external judgements by decisionmakers to be made about the acceptability of how much extra value is produced for a given cost (the so-called 'threshold of acceptability'), they also make it easier for public health interventions to be compared with wider medical interventions such as drugs and devices.

But this is still only potentially possible and we are still a long way from making such choices 'at the margins' of treatment and prevention given the present dominant distribution of resources in favour of treatment services. However, the notion that disinvestments in inefficient acute care areas and a subsequent reinvestment in public health could be sanctioned using these studies is unlikely until much better methods of economic evaluation are used and there is much more robust evidence in both acute and preventive medicine. Even in acute medicine presently few interventions are presently subject to this level of economic evaluation.

A precondition for this kind of debate would be to agree to a standard economic methodology for appraising public health interventions among researchers, perhaps one that reconsidered the cost-effectiveness threshold. If the presently accepted threshold of £30,000 per QALY was lowered, it would be much easier for less expensive and more cost-effective public health programmes to compete with acute interventions. At present the higher threshold allows more expensive, usually acute treatments, to be funded despite many public health programmes falling well below this maximum threshold. The result is a much higher 'opportunity cost' than may be efficient in terms of the more cost-effective prevention programmes foregone.

Obviously, a mix of both treatment and prevention is required in any health care system. But how much confidence can be placed in reinvestment in public health when the evidence is uncertain and based on different assumptions? Also there is often natural variability in outcomes of public health interventions. Wide confidence limits are much more common (and indeed more widely acceptable) in such programmes because of greater variability between intended subjects and hence interpersonal outcomes. It is commonly held in public health that if one is to change certain behaviours, such as 'binge drinking' for instance, then reducing the mean consumption rate for all the population, not just heavy 'at risk' consumers, is necessary. The rationale is that drinking is on a continuum and that reducing the average number of daily units consumed will be prevent moderate drinkers moving into the heavy drinking category. However, this may take a much greater effort (and hence cost) and it will not have the targeted effect of say, a prescription drug. It may stand to reason therefore that a drug for 'binge drinking' – if one were to be invented and available in every nightclub – may find greater favour on economic grounds than a population-wide education programme.

Background

Public health is a wide-ranging discipline delivering interventions that take place both on a one-to-one basis (for example, vaccinations) as well as population-wide (for example, smoking cessation). But its core functions mean different things to different public health professionals, so it is not surprising that it sometimes has widely varying objectives which are hard to capture in a single evaluation framework. Many practitioners believe that their role is to engage the community, or help hard-to-reach disadvantaged groups. Hence, for many, equity plays a key role in the delivery of public health, not only because it is desirable but because it is seen as central to ensuring the health of a whole public. Whilst redistribution of resources from one group to another may be a key policy goal for public health, there will be occasional, inevitable conflicts between that goal and that of achieving conventional economic efficiency where, for example, the cost per QALY of an intervention can be much higher than existing thresholds. Unless equity promoting programmes are explicitly addressed in the same metrics as other health interventions, the 'trade-offs' will be unknown and hence the 'price' to be paid for achieving greater equity will not be transparent.

Public health is also concerned with risk-taking behaviours and involves changing perceptions and attitudes, particularly those associated with harmful consumption patterns. Some programmes may require a series of incremental step changes to achieve a goal and often result in much more complex intervention strategies than found in clinical trials. Capturing the longer-term effects on quality of life or disease reduction in which they ultimately result is challenging epidemiologically, economically and politically. For example, trying to justify better parenting programmes on the grounds of future educational attainment at 18 years of age depends on the level of long-term follow-up that is achieved. However, there are countless other intervening, but independent, factors that may arise during this long period. For this reason, such studies tend to chose shorter-term process outcomes, but these may be less useful to economists.

In addition, costing frameworks for public health interventions are still in their infancy and there is still a lack of consensus about which costs to include in public health investment analysis. As this is, by definition, usually concerned with whole populations, the scope of these costs should be broader than private investments in, for example, the population's demand for fitted kitchens! Although no consensus has yet been reached on which costs to include when evaluating public health measures, this also occurs in acute medicine, where only a small proportion of what is still done has actually received any formal evaluation. Hence researchers have been free to determine the scope of costs when designing studies. It seems then perhaps a little unfair that public health must prove itself in a way that much of acute medicine has never actually been required to do.

Public health is also hampered by timing and uncertainty. Anything occurring in the future in economic analysis is subject to the customary practice of 'discounting' (that is, having present values adjusted below their expected value to take account of society's 'positive time preference' for benefits now and costs later). Additionally, the benefits of public health programmes are usually further away in time. Secondly, investments in public health are sometimes inherently risky, in that they do not always result in the expected (or any) future returns. This is not to deny the uncertainty of future benefits present in acute medicine; however, in acute medicine control over the selection of appropriate patients is easier is to undertake.

Recent progress in economic evaluation in public health

A major change in public health evaluation in recent years has been the use of various economic evaluation techniques. Such attempts have often been based on incomparable economic evaluations, rendering their implications in the wider context of policy choices difficult to compare. Few guidelines exist to assist in choice of technique.

The three standard types of analyses that exist are cost-effectiveness, cost-benefit and cost-utility analysis. A fourth one, cost-consequence analysis, has recently been added. It may be more applicable to public health because it does not lose the complexity of capturing multidimensional outcomes often found in public health. However, each of these methods imposes restrictions on analysts and there is not a best solution. While measuring costs might be expected to be easier – everyone can measure cost, or so they think – resource measurement can be subject to wide interpretation. Costs might include those to individuals, their families, the workplace, the community and society as a whole.

Each of these four types of analysis is reviewed below with regard to public health.

Cost-effectiveness

Perhaps the most 'user-friendly' design is cost-effectiveness (CEA), where the end-point of the studies is acceptable in what economists call 'natural' units, that is, units based on actual clinical or specific outcomes measurements. The greatest difficulty here is that these studies tend to be programme or condition specific. A particular programme will have specific goals which can be translated into various local outcomes. Where these have been established before an economic evaluation is undertaken, the evaluator has no choice but to use them (e.g. the number of children immunised or the number of units mmHg reduced). Whilst clearly convenient for clinicians, this makes comparison across different public health programmes nearly impossible. Furthermore, the chosen end-point could be appropriate for some local purposes but less appropriate for wider goals. Is the number of patients screened, for example, more relevant than the number of cases prevented? The answer can depend on the perspective taken. If the goal is simply equity, then achieving coverage of a population in terms of screening uptake may be more important than actual clinical outcomes. But if the goal is efficiency (obtaining the best outcomes for the resources provided), then the number of disease episodes, life years or, better still, avoided quality-adjusted life years lost, is the most relevant measure to use.

Until recently the cost-effectiveness literature in public health has not been well surveyed. Such literature normally requires the presence of both effectiveness and cost data. One problem has been the lack of cost data associated with undertaking evaluations of effectiveness. It is always preferable for there to be contemporaneous collection of resource use or cost information alongside effectiveness data, but in many studies this only takes place retrospectively. For example, only average costs of the interventions and associated costs will be known retrospectively, but during the study it is possible to collect resource use on individual patients. Variation in use of a NHS smoking cessation programme, for example, could be high, depending on a patient's willingness to engage with the programme and follow the advice given. If the patient does not attend, then usage could be much lower than for another patient who attends all sessions. However, resource use would be difficult to measure without recourse to retrospective examination of individual patient records. Additionally, levels of uptake and engagement with programmes such as health promotion will determine outcomes, so it is important to know how much cessation rates were related to exposure to an intervention.

When similar programmes with identical objectives are under consideration, CEA can be useful in identifying the most technically efficient option. Whilst this improves 'technical efficiency', the option which fulfils the goal at least cost does little to change the balance of resources between different programmes – known to economists as improving 'allocative efficiency' (selecting the right mix of programmes).

Cost-utility

Cost-utility analysis (CUA) is a specific form of cost-effectiveness which uses the quality-adjusted life-year (QALY) as the measure of outcome. It is also NICE's methodology of choice. The QALY is a composite outcome measure derived from the total gain in the number of years of survival but also valuing these years in terms of overall quality of life. Some commentators have queried the relevance of QALYs to public health practice, mainly because they fail to take account of externalities. Based on the economic notion of 'utility' or satisfaction to the individual consumer, a QALY is a construct that does not capture change that affects other parties. Since these wider social goals are often a crucial part of public health, important consequences of many programmes (e.g. peace of mind for parents of immunised children) are not captured. It is perhaps not surprising therefore that CUA has been put to limited use by the public health profession.

A fundamental limitation of the QALY is its inability to take into account the size of the public health problem in a defined population. Williams' utilitarian principle that a 'QALY is a QALY is a QALY' (Weinstein, 1988) not only gives equal weight to a recipient of a QALY, but also does not distinguish between individual and group level decisions. For instance a gain of ten QALYs for one individual is considered the same as a gain of one QALY for ten individuals. This has limitations for use in public health where the population and not the individual is frequently the focus of an intervention. For this reason, commissioners have only taken QALYs into partial account and use other criteria in making choices about their use of scarce resources.

Recognising the limitations of a single utility measure, analysts have suggested alternative methodologies. A 'multi-criteria utility function' is one such attempt to ensure that a combination of several objectives are maximised. The main benefit of this approach is that it may include effectiveness, equity, convenience, cost and other policy goals in a single benefit score. Since not all these goals will be afforded the same importance, individual criteria can be weighted to reflect the relative importance of each (Wilson, Rees and Fordham, 2006). Other methods have included population cost-impact analysis. Here decisionmakers are asked to assess the population impact of different interventions and the cost in terms of population utility by a simple ranking process (Heller *et al.*, 2006). In one such local experiment, community and health care representatives scored and ranked a list of new treatments according to a set of criteria they had helped to define in an exploratory workshop. Notably, the new technologies recommended and mandated by NICE were at the bottom of their list.

The cost-utility of public health interventions has been more comprehensively pursued in the United States, where such evidence has been used by health insurers and providers to determine which preventive measures should be carried out. In 2004, the National Commission on Prevention Priorities in the US reviewed effectiveness and cost literature to determine which public health strategies should be recommended as cost-effective (Maciosek *et al.*, 2006). This study also incorporated the burden of disease on the population from a 'clinically preventable condition'. The measure of effectiveness chosen was the QALY. The potential number of QALYs saved was calculated per a population of four million (the size of current US birth cohorts). Each intervention was ranked according to its potential QALY improvement and also the (discounted) cost per QALY of achieving it. Once these pieces of information had been assembled, an arbitrary score between one and five was assigned to both measures by a panel of experts, producing a maximum possible score for any public health programme of ten. Finally, being rational consumers, decisionmakers were assumed to adopt the highest scoring programmes first and to continue to work down the list of these services until the allocated budget was spent. Interestingly, questions about public health as a 'private' or a 'public' good also arose. As its name suggests, public health should be a 'public good' (that is, owned, or at least accessible to, everyone, and hence 'non-rivalrous') – a situation where one person's consumption of a good does not reduce that of another's. Clean air is an example of such non-excludability. But in a predominately private market like the US, information is often turned into a private transaction between physician and 'patient'.

What were the most cost-effective measures adopted? They mainly consisted of immunisation and screening programmes, including the childhood immunisation schedule, elderly pneumococcal vaccination, and screening for hypertension, colorectal cancer, impaired vision, and cervical and cholesterol screening. Interestingly, not all diseases and conditions screened were equally cost-effective. This was particularly so where lifestyle changes were necessary to bring about successful outcomes. These included programmes with benefit scores of less than five which addressed obesity, depression, hearing, injury prevention, high risk cholesterol, diabetes and diet. The authors attributed poor outcome scores mainly to poor adherence or programme participation.

How useful would this exercise be if adopted in the UK? Its main advantage was that it was comprehensive and also based on a single methodology. The approach that the NCPP took is possibly more relevant to interventions that can be recommended during a physician consultation than at a population or community level. There were also some technical weaknesses in its execution, although they are not insurmountable. For example, the ranking of cost-effectiveness belied an underlying complexity in the results of some of the studies used, with wide variance in baseline effectiveness results. The scope of the costs was also restricted to health care and personal costs and savings to the wider economy were excluded. This might be an acceptable definition of costs from a health provider perspective, but the cost of some preventable diseases such as obesity, stress/depression, cardiovascular events and cancer fall heavily on the workplace and elsewhere in society. More importantly, the exercise was not incremental in its analytical approach; it did not look at the extra gains and costs of adopting a new technology. Instead, it took an average approach to cost-effectiveness calculations and so made the assumption that none of the current target population had ever had the intervention – and all subjects were *de novo* recipients. This is clearly a naïve assumption. Hence each programme was valued for the entire population as opposed to the percentage of the population who might still need to receive it. From a public health viewpoint, it is more relevant to assess the costs and benefits to the population who at current levels of provision are not receiving any of the programmes, as these may be quite different than average cost-effectiveness, given that the difficult-to-access parts of the population are often more expensive to treat.

In other studies the cost per QALY has been found to compare very favourably with treatment. In a recent review of 226 cost-utility studies, 85 per cent had a cost per QALY well below the present NICE threshold for pharmacological interventions of around £25,000 (Fordham and Pritchard, 2006). Six major groupings of interventions were identified (infectious diseases, HIV/AIDS, coronary heart disease, diabetes, cancer and smoking). Smoking control programmes were the most cost-effective of any public health intervention. In almost all cases, public health measures represented much better value-for-money than equivalent pharmacological agents. Only two of the 34 programmes in the infectious disease prevention grouping had a mean cost per QALY of more than £25,000 per QALY.

It is sometimes useful to have multiple studies of the same technology; in some areas cost-utility results were confirmed in up to nine different studies of the same type of intervention (for example, pneumococcal vaccination). However, in many single studies the variance in the cost per QALY range was very high, making some of the promising results less certain. There is also variation in these results depending on the target population. However, some types of intervention were consistently less cost-effective than others irrespective of their target audience. For example, drug therapies for cholesterol reduction were consistently less cost-effective than lifestyle and dietary modifications used overall for the same purpose.

Cost-benefit

Economists are very specific about the definition of a cost-benefit (CBA) study as a measure of both benefits and costs of a programme in monetary terms. Hence, to be included in a cost-benefit study, all relevant costs and benefits must be capable of being expressed financially. They are more common in some areas of public health than others and widespread in health promotion and drug and alcohol prevention studies. Drummond (2005) has called cost-benefit 'a formula in search of data'. The technique is powerful if it can capture the full range of costs and benefits, although as he points out, it is frequently impractical to do so. For example, in cost-benefit appraisal it is important to obtain total willingness-to-pay estimates. This is rarely done in many areas of health care, let alone public health. We rarely ask people to state how much they would be willing to pay for a service or to avoid a disease (or indeed be compensated for having it). Yet there is no reason to presuppose that such contingent valuation experiments could not be set up in public health. To this end, many CBAs simply exclude non-monetary benefits and costs where they are difficult to collect or measure. Hence the definition of what is included in a CBA is highly variable and analysts may have completely different interpretations of their scope. These are interpreted differently as various social impacts, depending on the viewpoint of the analyst. For example, including or excluding absenteeism costs in the workplace due to an infectious disease like flu can significantly change the decision to invest in immunisation programmes. NICE explicitly excludes such productivity losses (because of bias effects of wage differentials), whereas it would be seen as essential from a company's perspective to include them if considering whether to invest in such services.

Workplace health promotion is perhaps one area where the cost-benefit approach has been developing most rapidly (Pelletier, 2001). Although not common in the UK, some workplaces are beginning to recognise the value of addressing health issues at work. Whilst firms are keen to maintain a healthy workforce, they also want to know the level of 'return on investment' they might expect from Workplace Health Programmes (WHPs). This 'pay-back' ethic has encouraged the development of cost-benefit in this field.

Since firms and organisations in the US are responsible for their employees' health care costs and wage compensation for sickness, they have an incentive to invest in public health programmes. Though many of the published studies are company or sector specific (and may therefore have limited generalisability), there is a mounting number of studies demonstrating a very positive return to such investments. A regular review of these studies has shown that they consistently report benefit-cost ratios (BCRs) of around 4:1 (although the ranges around this estimate can be wide), typically within one year after the intervention (Pelletier, 2001). The reported benefits are usually expressed in terms of the averted costs of absenteeism and health care which are variously included in the reported studies. Several commentators have called for more consistent economic methodologies, including greater use of randomised controlled trials in evaluations (Aldana, 2001). What appears to be most cost-beneficial to date are company supported programmes that keep healthy, but 'high-risk', individuals healthy. The level of participation in WHPs is also a key factor, with those with high levels of participation having better outcomes (Pelletier, 2001).

Other prevention areas where the cost-benefit method is well established are drug and alcohol interventions. Again, most of these still originate in the US. This field is perhaps even more dependent on correctly capturing intangible costs and externalities. Studies to date variously report the impact of programmes. For example, the 'Perry Preschool Project' – a school-based drug education programme – reported benefits to (parental) work productivity and reduced health care, crime, legal and other social costs (Karoly *et al.*, 1998). Within the drug prevention field, however, the range of BCR estimates is not as consistently good as for workplace health, ranging from 2:1 to 400:1, not because of the impact of the programme but more unusually because of the scope of costs/savings included (Fordham *et al.*, 2007).

Conclusion

Wanless (2002) called for a greater burden of economic proof for public health to match that generated in acute care where technical efficiency arguments have, for over a decade, ensured the domination of expenditure on treatment, especially pharmacological management of patients. Some have argued that this has ensured the growth of acute care budgets and programmes, as technology has been adopted additively, without at the same time losing other unproven treatments (Gafni and Birch, 2003).

It has been demonstrated that there is already a body of good evidence available for public health specialists to access and interpret in their local contexts. *Prima facie* evidence suggests that many of these public health interventions appear to be below cost-effectiveness thresholds adopted for acute care. But the literature at present consists of many possible types of economic evaluation, definitions of costs and benefits and also weaknesses of approach in capturing public as opposed to private benefits. This still makes interpretation difficult.

Hence although the burden of proof is still inconclusive, major inroads have been made, with a growing body of literature on the cost-effectiveness of public health interventions now available within the context of the UK's health system. More work needs to be done on providing guidance to researchers planning to undertake economic evaluations. NICE has made a good start (see Chapter 14, this Volume), but its agenda is limited to the referrals made to it by the government and its own capacity to undertake such demanding and complex work. Only when methodological practices are standardised for public health in ways that address the concerns raised in this paper will it become easier to accept the conclusions of economic evaluations of public health. Hopefully then the balance between acute care and public health will change to reflect the relative efficiency of the public health approach to keeping people healthy.

References

S. G. Aldana, 'Financial impact of health promotion programs: a comprehensive review of the literature', *American Journal of Health Promotion*, 15:5 (2001) 296–320.

M. F. Drummond, M. J. Sculpher, G. W. Torrance, B. J. O'Brien and G. L. Stoddart, *Methods for the Economic Evaluation of Health Care Programmes*, 3rd edition (Oxford: Oxford University Press, 2005).

R. J. Fordham and C. Pritchard, 'What have QALYs ever done for public health: The dilemma of shifting priorities towards the well', paper presented at 'The Future of Health: Burdens, Challenges and Opportunities', July 12–13, 2006 (University of Cambridge).

R. J. Fordham, L. Jones, H. Sumnall, J. McVeigh and M. Bellis, *The Economics of Preventing Drug Misuse: An Introduction to the Issue* (Liverpool: National Collaborating Centre for Drug Prevention, Centre for Public Health and John Moores University, 2007).

A. Gafni and S. Birch, 'NICE methodological guidelines and decision making in the National Health Service in England and Wales', *Pharmacoeconomics*, 21:3 (2003), 149–57.

R. Heller, I. Gemmel, E. Wilson, R. J. Fordham and R. D. Smith, 'Using economic analyses for local priority setting: the population cost-impact approach', *Applied Health Economics and Health Policy*, 5:1 (2006), 45–54.

L. A. Karoly, P. W. Greenwood and S. S. Everingham, J. Hoube, M. R. Kilburn, C. P. Rydell, M. Sanders and J. Chiesa, *Investing in our Children* (Santa Monica: RAND, 1998).

M. V. Maciosek, A. B. Coffield, N. M. Edwards, T. J. Flottemesch, M. J. Goodman and L. I. Solberg, 'Priorities among effective clinical preventive services: results of a systematic review and analysis', *American Journal of Preventive Medicine*, 31:1 (2006) 52–61.

K. R. A. Pelletier, 'Review and analysis of the clinical and cost-effectiveness studies of comprehensive health promotion and disease management programs at the worksite: 1998–2000 update', *Journal of Health Promotion*, 16 (2001) 107–16.

D. Wanless, *Securing Our Future Health: Taking a Long-Term View. Final Report* (London: HM Treasury, 2002).

J. Weinstein, 'A QALY is a QALY is a QALY – Or is it?', *Journal of Health Economics*, 7:3 (1988) 289–90.

A. Williams, 'The economics of coronary artery bypass grafting', *British Medical Journal*, 291 (1985) 326–9.

E. Wilson, J. Rees and R. J. Fordham, 'Developing a prioritisation framework in an English Primary Care Trust', *Cost Effectiveness and Resource Allocation*, 4:3 (2006).

14

The Challenges of Developing Cost-Effective Public Health Guidance: A NICE Perspective

Kalipso Chalkidou, Anthony J. Culyer, Bhash Naidoo and Peter Littlejohns

Introduction

In his first report on the financial viability of the NHS, Derek Wanless held that 'health promotion and disease prevention play an important role in moderating the need for care' (2002, page 117), and went on to conclude:

> 'Thanks to the health outcome benefits associated with investment in public health, the UK would find itself much better placed to deal with the (financial) pressures under the "fully engaged"[1] scenario, [characterised by] a step change in the way public health is viewed, resourced and delivered nationally' (page 118).

In his follow-up report, focusing on the fully engaged scenario, he made explicit the need for economic evaluation for all health policies: 'The total costs of an intervention to the government and society must be kept to a minimum and be less than the expected benefits over the life of the policy: interventions should be prioritised to select those which represent best value' (Wanless, 2004, page 183). He pointed out the conceptual similarity of the economic evaluation of public health interventions to that of other health care interventions and concludes that 'where [evidence] exists it does suggest that the former can be more cost-effective than the latter, even along the same disease pathway' (Wanless, 2004, page 134). Finally, in terms of the economic evaluation of public health interventions, Wanless observed that NICE, then the National Institute for Clinical Excellence and now the National Institute for Health and Clinical Excellence, already had a model, albeit one needing some modification from its current format: 'A consistent framework – such as the methodology developed by NICE – should be used to evaluate the cost-effectiveness of interventions and initiatives across health care and public health' (Wanless, 2004, page 136).

In April 2005, NICE's remit was expanded to include the development of cost-effective, evidence-based public health guidance. NICE took over the functions of the Health Development Agency (HDA) and a new Centre for Public Health Excellence (CPHE) was formed within NICE (Littlejohns and Kelly, 2005). This provided an opportunity for NICE to adopt an integrated approach to improving the health of the population through the production of guidance ranging from disease and accident prevention, through health promotion, to treatment. However, it has also posed new challenges, particularly in testing the suitability of the existing NICE principles of economic evaluation for developing public health guidance.

This chapter describes the continuing process of development that started with the establishment of the CPHE within NICE in 2005. It reflects on the experiences and lessons learned so far and the challenges faced by NICE in developing public health guidance based on scientific evidence of clinical and cost effectiveness. There remain more questions than answers; NICE's thinking in the field is evolving and it is keen to engage with stakeholders in deciding the best ways forward. Thus, the final part of the chapter sets out a number of issues in need of resolution in future.

NICE

NICE provides guidance on the promotion of good health and prevention of disease in England. Evaluating the effectiveness and cost-effectiveness of public health interventions is a relatively recent function for NICE, and is therefore still being developed. Our focus in this chapter is on developing the process of economic evaluation of public health interventions.

The NICE Reference Case

NICE's establishment in 1999 was an explicit acknowledgment by the government of the need to account for costs when making decisions in the health care sector. The 'effective use of available resources in the health service' was a key objective embedded in NICE's statutory instruments from the very beginning. In accordance with its core principles of transparency, inclusiveness and methodological robustness, NICE adopted an explicit framework for undertaking the economic evaluation of the medical technologies and care pathways. This is the NICE Reference Case. It specifies the methods of evaluation considered to be most appropriate to meeting NHS objectives (NICE, 2004). Its key features are set out in Table 14.1.

The Reference Case was developed in collaboration with leading health economists and in consultation with NICE's stakeholders (Claxton *et al.*, 2005). It aims to fulfil a triple objective:

1). Ensure the fitness-for-purpose of the final NICE product. The key objective of the Reference Case is to ensure that the needs of the decision-maker (NICE), in the context of a health care system operating with finite resources (NHS), are met by the economic analyses submitted to NICE. In that

Table 14.1 The NICE reference case applicable to clinical guidelines and technology appraisals

Comparator	Alternatives routinely used in the NHS
Perspective on costs	NHS/personal and social services (PSS)
Perspective on outcomes	All health effects on individuals
Type of economic evaluation	Cost-effectiveness analysis
Synthesis of evidence on outcomes	Based on systematic review
Measure of health benefits	QALYs
Description of health states	Standardised-validated generic instrument
Preference elicitation	Choice-based (e.g. TTO, SG)
Source of preference data	Representation sample of the public
Discount rate	3.5% pa on costs and health effects
Equity position	A QALY is a QALY is a QALY ...

sense, the Reference Case is in fact a prescriptive, but hopefully not overly restrictive, framework.

2).   Encourage consistency in guidance development methods and comparability of the final products. This involves different NICE products, such as clinical guidelines and technology appraisals, as well as non-NICE guidance.

3).   Ensure that all NICE stakeholders, including patients, industry and the academic community working with NICE, are clear about the key principles underpinning NICE economic analysis.

The Reference Case may also improve the quality standards of economic evaluation across the board.

The Reference Case has now been adopted by all three NICE guidance production centres (Clinical Practice, Health Technologies, and Public Health guidance), in the latter case with some major deviations which are discussed below.

The NICE preferred economic evaluation

One of the key parameters defined in the NICE Reference Case has to do with the type of economic evaluation. Broadly speaking, there are various ways of undertaking economic evaluation in health care. Each involves examining the benefits of a medical or public health intervention in conjunction with its costs. NICE's preferred method is cost-utility analysis (CUA), which extends from cost-effectiveness analysis (CEA).

In CEA, a common measurement unit is used to quantify the outcomes (for example, life years saved, mg/dl reduction in cholesterol levels). An incremental cost-effectiveness ratio (ICER) is calculated which shows the additional cost per unit gain in effectiveness with the new intervention rather than the comparator. Interventions with lower ICERs represent better value for money (Drummond *et al.*, 2005).

In CUA, the measure of health outcome is a generic measure reflecting quality of life and survival. An advantage of this technique is that it allows direct and explicit comparability between interventions having different types of outcomes. The most common index of health outcome is the Quality Adjusted Life Year (or QALY), measured with the EQ5D[2] by NICE. One QALY is one year of life in full health; it can also mean two years of life in 'half health' (health is expressed in a scale from 0, representing death to 1, representing full life). It is assumed that QALYs arising for different individuals can be added up. For example, supposing that it was agreed that a QALY had the same social significance to whomever received it and having more or fewer of them did not affect this value, then two QALYs for one person might be considered to be of equal social significance as one QALY each for two people. Alternatively, different QALYs could receive different weights and then be added up. The results of CUA are, like those in CEAs, usually presented as ICERs, showing the expected cost per additional QALY gained by the use of one intervention rather than another. This figure is often compared with a benchmark cost-effectiveness threshold, representing an estimate of the maximum ability (or willingness) of a health care system to pay for an additional QALY or, alternatively, the cost of an additional QALY in a situation in which the health gain has been maximised for the size of the available NHS resources (Culyer *et al.*, 2007).

The broad use of CUA and the QALY ensures consistency of methods and can allow baseline comparisons across different health care interventions and programmes. However, the QALY has a number of limitations, being a measure of health changes and not of non-health related outcomes such as those relating to education or transport. While the QALY raises equity and distributional issues very explicitly, to date there has been no consensus as to how best to resolve these.

These economic evaluation methods are by no means mutually exclusive; they can be complementary depending on the clinical and public health setting for each piece of guidance. Furthermore, the NICE Reference Case is not dogmatically prescriptive; it encourages the use of alternative methods as long as their application can be justified.

Developing methods for guidance for public health

Soon after the HDA joined NICE, and in accordance with the NICE core principles of inclusiveness and transparency, NICE sought to review current thinking about the economic evaluation of public health interventions and began to engage actively with key external stakeholders.

The starting point was open recognition that the proper way in which economic evaluation should be used in developing public health guidance was a matter for debate. NICE considered it essential that a variety of methodological approaches be reviewed and compared with the existing

Reference Case for evaluating health care technologies, with contentious issues and practical challenges being openly confronted and possible means of addressing them identified as soon as possible in the guidance development process.

To help inform the debate and set out the basic principles that would underpin NICE's future economic analysis of public health interventions, a workshop was held in May 2005. The focus was on how NICE could frame, measure, and compare the cost-effectiveness of public health interventions and programmes. The main aims of the workshop were to: describe the problems of carrying out health economic evaluation in public health, explore possible economic approaches to address these problems, seek input from a wide range of potential CPHE stakeholders, describe the implementation challenges of this exercise and ways of tackling them, and to identify key R&D questions necessary to advancing CPHE's methods.

Table 14.2 The general principles currently adopted for NICE evaluation

Economic analysis should form an integral part of the public health guidance development process undertaken by the Centre for Public Health Excellence (CPHE). The methodological basis for the economic evaluation should be the same for both public health interventions and programmes.

Cost-utility (CUA) should be adopted for undertaking economic evaluation in public health, with the QALY as the preferred outcome measure.

The QALY is a well-established measure that should form part of economic evaluation in public health, both to serve as a baseline comparator across other health interventions and to assist with the prioritisation process at the local level.

Cost-consequence analysis (CCA) should also be employed to allow consideration by the Committees of non-health related or hard to quantify outcomes that cannot be captured by the QALY, including distributional (equity) considerations.

A public sector perspective should be adopted in all economic evaluation analysis in public health as defined by NICE's statutory instruments.

NICE Public Health Committees need to be multidisciplinary. In addition, experts should be invited to participate in Committees' deliberations on an *ad hoc* basis as required by the nature of the guidance being developed.

NICE Committees should be given clear guidance as to how to account for factors additional to cost per QALY in their decisionmaking. Papers such as Social Value Judgements (NICE, 2005b, currently under revision) would help formalise this part of the decisionmaking process.

The topic referral process needs to ensure that the objective of the guidance was clearly stated in the remit in order to guide the scoping process.

Health economists and policymakers from the UK and abroad, government representatives and public health practitioners, NICE committee members and CPHE researchers and analysts engaged in the debate and helped build a picture of where NICE stood at the time and what the key issues were. The debate was continued internally and a set of core principles (detailed in Table 14.2) were agreed upon which helped inform the CPHE Methods Manual (NICE, 2006a), published in early 2006. The CPHE Methods Manual draws on the principles that emerged from the workshop and a broad public consultation. The 'incorporating health economics' section details the proposed approach to undertaking economic analysis to underpin NICE's public health recommendations. There are two major departures from the NICE Reference Case, which are summarised in Table 14.1.

The first relates to the perspective of the economic analysis. Upon the arrival of the HDA, NICE's statutory instruments were amended to include 'functions in connection with the promotion of excellence in public health provision and promotion and in that connection the effective use of resources available in the health service and other available public funds' (NICE, 2005a, italics added). As a result, CPHE considers the public sector in addition to the NHS and personal and social services perspectives (PSS) when developing its guidance. All other programmes across NICE continue to consider NHS/PSS cost consequences only.

The second way in which CPHE deviates from the NICE clinical Reference Case is in accepting the use of cost-consequence analysis (CCA) to supplement cost-utility analysis, where appropriate. In cost-consequence analysis (CCA), consequences are measured in terms of multiple outcome indicators and listed so that decisionmakers form their own opinions about the relative importance of the various outcomes relative to their cost – elements of which are not necessarily in monetary form. Options are contrasted explicitly in a balance sheet enumerating all the relevant costs and consequences. Both quantitative and qualitative information may be made available in the balance sheet. Information about implications for equity, different subgroups, and other relevant parameters may be presented as well as information about the health and non-health outcomes affecting non-patients (for example, informal carers). One clear benefit of this approach is that it is easily understood. However, the decision rules are not explicit. Instead, the decisionmakers use their discretion in qualitatively 'weighing up' the different elements according to implicit criteria. This may lead to arbitrariness, lack of consistency in analytical treatment from study to study, and lack of effective accountability.

Given the complexity and multidimensionality of public health interventions and programmes, CCA provides an appealing tool for performing economic evaluation. The explicitness and transparency of the approach makes it 'user-friendly' for the decisionmaker at both the NICE and local levels. However, when applied on its own, CCA has two major weaknesses from NICE's perspective. In the absence of a quantifiable measure such as the cost per QALY, CCA lacks an outcome measure that can be used to compare interventions. Secondly, CCA's lack of clarity over the classification of negative and positive costs and consequences was perceived to lead to possible inconsistencies with other economic evaluations and to compromise transparency. As a result, CCA is recommended as a means of supplementing CUA only when it can help communicate decisions to the stakeholders and the public, or when it is likely to modify advice based solely on cost per QALY data.

The principles described in the Methods Manual (NICE, 2004) drove the development of the first pieces of NICE public health guidance. At the same time, the challenges and experiences in developing the guidance identified areas of methodological controversy and uncertainty.

Producing public health guidance: the challenges

In 2006, NICE published two items of public health guidance, on smoking cessation and on physical activity, as well as a comprehensive guidance on managing obesity, in collaboration with the NICE Clinical Guidelines team. Work is currently under way on a number of key public health priority areas such as obesity and sexually transmitted diseases (see Table 14.3 for details of future work).

In developing its public health guidance, CPHE adhered to the basic framework of the NICE Reference Case while ensuring that the methodology remained fit for purpose in the public health context. While holding the principle of a consistent framework as put forward by Wanless, we consider below the most challenging dimensions of the NICE Reference Case as applied to the production of public health guidance. Theoretical questions are supplemented by practical examples drawn from the NICE experience to date, and unresolved questions associated with the particular nature of economic evaluations of public health are identified for future discussion.

Measuring benefit

To measure benefit is a challenging task at the best of times, whether for public health or clinical interventions. It is even more challenging when the outcome of interest is poorly defined as, for example, in the topic referred to by CPHE as 'an assessment of community engagement and community development approaches including the collaborative methodology and community champions' (title of guidance expected to be issued 2008; see Table 14.3 for a complete list of public topics reviewed or scheduled for review by NICE). Even when outcomes are clearly defined, it may still sometimes be difficult or inappropriate to use QALYs as an outcome measure. For example, a QALY is not obviously the best (and certainly not the only) outcome measure when a major benefit from preventing teenage pregnancies

Table 14.3   NICE's public health guidance; published and in development as of April 2007. For more information visit: http://www.nice.org.uk/guidance/type

Public Health Guidance Topic	Guidance Type	Status
Four commonly used methods to increase physical activity: brief interventions in primary care, exercise referral schemes, pedometers and community-based exercise programmes for walking and cycling	intervention	published: March 2006
Brief interventions and referral for smoking cessation in primary care and other settings	intervention	published: March 2006
Obesity: the prevention, identification, assessment and management of overweight and obesity in adults and children	joint clinical and public health guidance	published: December 2006
Guidance for use in primary and secondary schools on sensible alcohol consumption	intervention	expected: November 2007
Guidance for primary care and for residential care institutions on the promotion of good mental health in older people	intervention	expected: March 2008
Guidance on promoting the mental wellbeing of children in primary schools	intervention	expected: February 2008
Guidance for the NHS and other sectors on what works in driving down population mortality rates in disadvantaged areas where risk of early death is higher than average	intervention	expected: April 2008
Guidance on the prevention of the uptake of smoking in children and young people	intervention	expected: June 2008
Guidance for workplaces on the promotion of good mental health in employees	intervention	expected: August 2008
Intervention guidance on workplace health promotion with reference to physical activity	intervention	expected: May 2008
Intervention guidance on workplace health promotion with reference to smoking	intervention	Published: April 2007
Preventing STI and reducing under-18 conceptions especially in vulnerable and at-risk groups	intervention	published: February 2007
An assessment of community-based interventions to reduce substance misuse among the most vulnerable and disadvantaged young people	intervention	published: March 2007

Table 14.3   NICE's public health guidance; published and in development as of April 2007. For more information visit: http://www.nice.org.uk/guidance/type

Public Health Guidance Topic	Guidance Type	Status
Guidance for midwives, health visitors, pharmacists and other primary care services to improve the nutrition of pregnant and breastfeeding mothers and children in low-income households	programme	expected: February 2008
The most appropriate means of generic and specific interventions to support attitude and behaviour change at population and community levels	programme	expected: October 2007
An assessment of community engagement and community development approaches including the collaborative methodology and community champions	programme	expected: February 2008
Guidance on school, college and community-based personal, social and health education	programme	expected: July 2009
Guidance for primary care and employers on the management of long-term sickness and incapacity	programme	expected: December 2008
Guidance on the promotion and creation of physical environments that support increased levels of physical activity	programme	expected: January 2008
Smoking cessation services, including the use of pharmacotherapies, in primary care, pharmacies, local authorities and workplaces, with particular reference to manual working groups, pregnant smokers and hard to reach communities	programme	expected: November 2007
Guidance on physical activity, play and sport for pre-school and school age children	programme	expected: December 2008

is uninterrupted education. In other cases, the data may just not be available; for instance, there is a paucity of QALY data associated with sexually transmitted diseases in the majority of extant studies.

It is clear from these examples that there can be a tension between the need to ensure consistency of measurement and the need to ensure that whatever measures are used are valid and acceptable constructs for the evaluation at hand. In public health, relevant QALY data are scarce and the benefit of interest often has one (or more) non-health dimensions, such as a reduction in crime, better access to education or a safer transport system.

This raises the question of whether a new form of the QALY ought to replace the Reference Case's recommendation of the EQ5D, or if more than one outcome measure ought to be used (which then raises issues concerning the appropriate weights to be attached to each outcome).

Public versus individual: special features of population-based interventions

The consequences of public health interventions may include significant effects that are not normally considered in the evaluation of other health interventions in terms of public versus individual benefit. An example relates to the 'publicness' of many public health interventions, as when smoking cessation interventions reduce the non-smoking public's exposure to second-hand smoke, or when there are benefits for children of interventions that enhance mothers' health (intergenerational benefits), or there are benefits to untreated people from treating those having sexually transmitted disease. 'Publicness' in this sense refers to a situation in which individuals cannot be excluded from experiencing the effects (good or bad) of a procedure: the service effectively denies individuals the opportunity to choose. Individuals cannot, for example, decide to stop breathing filtered air in their workplace, nor can someone drink non-fluoridated tap water when the whole supply has been fluoridated. If the intervention is provided for one it is provided for all. How can these externalities (whether positive or negative) be suitably captured?

In an environment where 'choice' is pursued as a key policy priority, ought cost-effectiveness analysis to take account of such effects and, if so, how? How ought the positive and negative effects of 'publicness' in provision be accounted for? Can it be argued, where the intervention is not selectively distributed, that the cost-effectiveness range acceptable by NICE's Advisory Bodies should be higher and the 'harms' of the regulation taken into account?

Equity versus efficiency and other distributional concerns

Equity has not yet been successfully addressed within existing frameworks of economic evaluation. At present, NICE's Advisory Bodies are presented with all relevant information, including an economic model where applicable, and asked to apply their own judgements within a transparent and deliberative framework, before reaching a decision. The Reference Case specifies that

...an additional QALY has the same weight regardless of other characteristics of the individual receiving the health benefit. This position reflects the absence of consensus regarding whether these or other characteristics of individuals should result in differential weights being attached to QALYs gained (NICE, 2004, page 29).

NICE has adopted a positive approach to resolving the distributional concerns in economic evaluation. NICE's Social Value Judgements paper (2005b)

attempts to ensure that the values and trade-offs applied by Advisory Bodies when making decisions reflect the views of the broader public as identified through the deliberations of the Citizens' Council.

The challenge posed by equity is often more pressing in the context of public health interventions, considering that a frequent objective of public health is to tackle health inequalities. Indeed, programme guidance on smoking cessation and under-18 conceptions explicitly identifies hard to reach, disadvantaged groups as target populations of the guidance, even though they may be relatively high cost groups to treat. To address this challenge in the context of public health, CPHE recommends CCA as a supplement to cost effectiveness analysis where distributional or equity concerns are central to the development of guidance. In this way transparency and the provision of comprehensive and relevant information, including effects that cannot be captured by the QALY, are explicitly embodied both in NICE's decisionmaking process and in the public rationale for NICE advice.

Does the provisional assumption that 'a QALY is a QALY is a QALY' (a phrase widely used by health economists) need to be reconsidered in the context of public health (or, indeed, clinical) guidance? If so, can distributional concerns be addressed solely through the economic evaluation framework? Social welfare functions, willingness-to-pay and cost-value analysis have all been put forward as potential models for doing so. Or is a transparent deliberative process, at the level of the Advisory Bodies, a more pragmatic, case-sensitive and publicly credible way forward?

The perspective of the analysis

NICE's perspective was broadened, for public health guidance only, to include the full public sector perspective. However, as the delineation is not always clear between NHS-specific and broader public interventions across public health and clinical guidelines (even in the case of technology appraisals), this prescription could lead to inconsistency, not only in the frequency with which the Reference Case was deemed unsuitable but at a more fundamental level: why exclude some of the public sector consequences in some appraisals but not others? And why make the scope of analysis subject to a sometimes arbitrary and artificial definition of 'public health'? For example, the NICE guideline on tuberculosis (NICE, 2006b) addresses a 'public health' issue, but the cost perspective there has to be that of the NHS/PSS.

A challenge stemming from the broader perspective adopted for public health guidance has to do with failing to account for the opportunity cost to the individual associated with behavioural change. For instance, attending a gym to increase physical activity or going shopping for healthier food entails a personal cost that does not figure in the public sector accounts. These types of activities can have strong behavioural effects with consequences for health inequalities, and can delay demand for health care services, which raises the question of the manner in which such personal costs ought to be accounted for, and how.

Lengthy time-horizons

Many of the payoffs from preventive interventions accrue far in the future, while the evidence is often based on short follow-up periods. This poses a number of problems. Firstly, the methodological basis needs to be developed further, with active input from econometricians and epidemiologists, to enable the extrapolation of data over longer time horizons.

The time horizon chosen also affects the way relevant costs and savings are identified and accounted for in both modelling and budget impact calculations. This is crucial for preventive interventions, where any benefits of short-term investment tend to be long term. For example, immediate benefits resulting from successful diagnosis of lung cancer using PET scanning may be of more relevance to NHS commissioners compared to the long-term benefits of preventing lung cancer through smoking cessation interventions. But what is the appropriate time horizon in modelling and costing calculations?

Quality of research evidence

The evidence base in public health is weaker in terms of internal validity compared to clinical medicine. This could be explained in part by the relatively small investment in public health research – 2.5 per cent of the total investment in health research (UK Clinical Research Collaboration, 2006) – and the particular characteristics of public health interventions that make controlled trials either impossible or excessively costly.

Weak evidence affects the overall guidance development process and poses new methodological challenges. Particularly problematic areas include the often inappropriate comparators used and the consequential need to undertake indirect comparisons. The frequent lack of control for confounding factors compared to clinical research is another common problem. Estimates of effect have to be derived from observational studies. In a well-designed study this can enhance external validity but does not attain the same level of internal validity of the randomised control trial (RCT). In addition, there are significant evidence gaps around equity and a paucity of good evidence on the long-term effectiveness of most public health interventions. The lack of easily available and consistent costing data poses another significant challenge when assessing the cost-effectiveness of an intervention.

Another big methodological challenge has to do with means of synthesising public health evidence. In the absence of rigorous meta-analyses of randomised trials, new methodological tools for pooling different data types need to be developed and validated. In the meantime, interpreting the limited evidence base is often difficult and even misleading.

A methodological research agenda needs to be developed in response to the needs of and in collaboration with the decisionmakers for scientifically robust evidence-based public health guidance to be produced.

Is the acceptable cost-effectiveness range right?

The interventions recommended in the recently published NICE public health guidance on smoking cessation and physical activity were shown to be extremely cost-effective (NICE 2006c, 2006d). The incremental cost-effectiveness ratios (ICERs) were well below the NICE threshold range of £20–30k and were remarkably insensitive to varying key parameters such as the intervention unit cost, compliance rates or effect size. This was the case in even the most pessimistic scenarios. For example, in the age group with the least cost-effective outcomes, it was estimated that for brief advice to give up smoking (usually delivered in five minutes) the ICER would not reach the NICE threshold range until the time spent exceeded one hour. Similarly, in the case of brief interventions to encourage physical activity, the ICER was always below the NICE threshold range, even for drop-off rates as high as 97 per cent. Indeed, even if only 3 per cent of participants maintained their new exercise levels following the intervention, all brief interventions considered still had an ICER of less than £7000. It seems that the public health interventions for which there is an evidence base demonstrating effectiveness are highly cost-effective relative to the NICE range of acceptable ICERs.

If this proves more generally to be the case, the £20–30k threshold across NICE guidance may be too high. The threshold range may therefore require revision. If this implied that fewer pharmacological and other medical procedures might pass the cost-effectiveness test, the implications for innovation and the other wider impacts on the economy would need careful assessment. The possibility of multiple thresholds arises, as well as a more explicit consideration of these wider consequences in the determination of the so-called threshold.

Implementing public health interventions

Implementing public health guidance in the context of the health care system is often challenging because of the lack of a sponsor or a strong lobbying group, unlike the usual case for new medical technologies. However, when public health recommendations apply to organisations outside health care, such as workplaces or schools, this task becomes even harder for a number of reasons. First, NICE has no designated authority outside the NHS. Second, there is a lack of an underpinning cross-government framework to ensure that public health guidance is promoted through appropriate channels in different government sectors. Thirdly, public sector non-health organisations often operate differently from the rather centralised NHS; for example, local authorities and schools have a significant degree of autonomy compared to their equivalents in health care. This calls for an adaptation of the public health regulations within these structures. Lastly, NICE's influence on private sector organisations such as workplaces is particularly weak, not least because differences in organisational culture and communication can create barriers to successful implementation. New modes of delivering guidance and incentivising uptake need to be developed for the NICE public health message to reach these audiences (Tompa *et al.*, 2008).

Conclusions and implications for the future

NICE has embarked on the challenging journey of developing cost-effective public health guidance, within the broad framework set out by the Wanless reports (Wanless, 2002; 2004). It has adopted a pragmatic approach of developing high quality, fit for purpose guidance using the best available evidence and utilising, where appropriate, the existing methodological guidance. At the same time, NICE remains committed to improving the evidence base and the methodological tools available for this task.

Comment, discussion and innovation in academic and policy circles will, we hope, advance these developments. Furthermore, NICE will aim to engage with a wide range of stakeholders during the update of its Guide to Methods for Developing Public Health Guidance, planned for 2007. Some of the key questions raised below will be addressed during this update, through both public consultation and direct iterations with experts in the field. Finally, we are hoping that key methodological questions such as these will be addressed through relevant methods research funded by NHS R&D, as recommended in the recently published Cooksey Review (2006).[3]

The complex nature of public health evaluation raises a number of issues around the measurement of costs and benefits. The principal issues posed by trying to apply economic evaluation in public health in the future can be summarised as follows:

1). Appropriate outcome measures should be developed which, where appropriate, supplement or replace the QALY as a health-related quality of life measure. Better outcome measures might include ways of measuring and valuing both positive and negative externalities. They would include the costs and benefits of unconventional goods and services, such as the characteristics of services – their 'responsiveness' for example – or preserving or enlarging the range of individuals' choices. More appropriate outcome measures might also reflect a weighting system of other methods with which to compare multiple outcomes and their costs as part of an evaluation.

2). Ways should also be developed of synthesising and summarising research literatures that tend to employ widely varying techniques, few of which equate to the particular type of rigour expected from a randomised controlled trial.

3). The unsettled matter of weighting costs and benefits appropriately should be resolved in a way that is perceived by the public as fair and equitable whilst acknowledging that 'the public' is not a homogenous group. This suggests a need to find a process for addressing some of the questions that rely on value judgements, perhaps through social surveys, controlled experiments, or by the use of instruments such as the Citizens' Council.

4). The role and significance of equity in setting public health priorities should be resolved and made more explicit.

5). Many public health technologies can best be applied in non-health care environments, such as workplaces or schools. Because health as such is not the prime objective of these organisations and their managers and professionals have different motives and incentives, issues surrounding the dissemination and implementation of public health technologies need to be addressed.

Notes

1 According to Wanless, in the 'fully engaged' scenario levels of public engagement in relation to their health are high: life expectancy increases go beyond current forecasts, health status improves dramatically and people are confident in the health system and demand high quality care. The health service is responsive with high rates of technology uptake, particularly in relation to disease prevention and use of resources is more efficient.

2 EQ5D stands for EuroQol – 5 Dimensions, and is a simple measure of an individual's health and wellbeing, designed by the EuroQol Group. More information can be found at http://www.euroqol.org/.

References

K. Claxton, M. Sculpher, C. McCabe, A. Briggs, R. Akehurst, M. Buxton, J. Brazier and T. O'Hagan, 'Probabilistic Sensitivity Analysis for NICE Technology Assessment: Not an Optional Extra', *Health Economics*, 14:4 (2005) 339–47.

D. Cooksey, *A Review of Health Research Funding* (London: HM Treasury, 2006).

A. J. Culyer, C. McCabe, A. H. Briggs, K. Claxton, M. Buxton, R. L. Akehurst, M. Sculpher and J. Brazier, 'Searching for a Threshold, Not Setting One: The Role of the National Institute of Health and Clinical Excellence', *Journal of Health Service Research and Policy*, 12:1 (2007) 56–8.

M. F. Drummond, M. J. Sculpher, G. W. Torrance, B. J. O'Brien, and G. L. Stoddart, *Methods for the Economic Evaluation of Health Care Programmes*, 3rd edn (Oxford: Oxford University Press, 2005).

P. Littlejohns and M. Kelly, 'The Changing Face of NICE: The Same but Different', *Lancet*, 366: 9488 (2005) 791–4.

National Institute for Health and Clinical Excellence, *Guide to the Methods of Technology Appraisal* (London: HM Stationary Office, 2004).

National Institute for Health and Clinical Excellence, *The National Institute for Clinical Excellence (Establishment and Constitution) Amendment Order* (London: HM Stationary Office, 2005a).

National Institute for Health and Clinical Excellence, *Social Value Judgements: Principles for the development of NICE guidance* (final report) (London: HM Stationary Office, 2005b).

National Institute for Health and Clinical Excellence, *Methods for the Development of NICE Public Health Guidance* (London: HM Stationary Office, 2006a).

National Institute for Health and Clinical Excellence, *Clinical diagnosis and management of tuberculosis, and measures for its prevention and control* (London: HM Stationary Office, 2006b).

National Institute for Health and Clinical Excellence, *Brief interventions and referral for smoking cessation in primary care and other settings* (London: HM Stationary Office, 2006c).

National Institute for Health and Clinical Excellence, *Four commonly used methods to increase physical activity: Brief interventions in primary care, exercise referral schemes, pedometers and community-based exercise programmes for walking and cycling* (London: HM Stationary Office, 2006d).

National Institute for Health and Clinical Excellence, *An assessment of community engagement and community Development approaches including the collaborative methodology and community champions* (London: HM Stationary Office, forthcoming).

E. Tompa, A. J. Culyer and R. Dolinschi (eds), *Economic Evaluation of Interventions for Occupational Health and Safety: Developing Good Practice* (Oxford: Oxford University Press, 2008).

UK Clinical Research Collaboration, *UK Health Research Analysis* (London: UK Clinical Research Collaboration, 2006).

D. Wanless, *Securing Our Future: Taking a Long-Term View* (London: HM Treasury, 2002).

D. Wanless, *Securing Good Health for the Whole Population* (London: HM Treasury, 2004).

Conclusion: Accepting Burdens, Meeting Challenges and Creating Opportunities

Sandra Dawson

Public health in the UK encompasses a trio of policies and practices gathered under the rubric of health promotion, health protection and health improvement. They each, separately and in concert, are designed to secure improvements in the indices of public health, which, through statistics on mortality, morbidity and quality of life, reveal whether people in a given population are living longer, healthier and higher quality lives than their forbears, and whether, for any given population, variation in the statistics for subgroups show greater or less variation over time.

Health promotion concerns all manner of interventions which promote or sell particular behaviours as a route to improve health status of individuals and thereby populations. Health promotion efforts are directed at health and other 'expert' professionals as well as directly to lay members of the public. Examples of health promotion efforts include the 5-a-day programme to encourage the eating of fresh fruit (Department of Health, 2003) and smoking cessation programmes (http://gosmokefree.nhs.uk).

Health protection concerns all manner of interventions that aim to prevent a deterioration of health status, such as sanitary water systems, immunisation, or early screening for treatable diseases. The distinction between health promotion and protection is imprecise, and one of emphasis. In the main, 'protection' is stimulated by major public infrastructural investments, from which the layperson can be the almost by-standing beneficiary, whereas 'promotion' normally requires active engagement from those who will benefit.

Health improvement largely focuses on improving the impact and effectiveness of interventions by health professionals, who in turn operate largely but not exclusively within what are considered to be the health care services. Any number of examples can be drawn from underneath the umbrella of 'evidence-based medicine', such as the prescription of statins to manage cardiovascular disease (NICE, 2006). An example of health improvement directed directly at the public rather than at health care professionals is the *cleanyourhands* campaign, which urges patients to ask their caregivers to wash their hands through posters in hospitals (Department of Health, 2004). It is in health improvement that the commissioning of health services is most directly involved in public health, since the contract can specify expected procedures and clinical audit; and data on performance is now readily available (patients can compare hospitals at www.nhs.uk/scorecard). Health improvement is a vital part of public health, but not the focus of this book, which is instead concerned with the agenda for promotion and protection.

Our emphasis on those aspects of public health that impact upon both behaviour and those systems that reach beyond the health care system is deliberate. There is overlap, of course, between the health care and health systems (beyond improving health), most notably in personnel. Many health care employees – doctors, nurses and therapists – are agents in health prevention and promotion, focusing on behaviours and actions experienced far beyond the boundaries of the health care system which employs them. Public health interacts in complex ways with a broad landscape of social and political institutions at local community as well as at regional and national levels. It is a poor respecter of professional, geographic, institutional and organisational boundaries. Critical complexities and interactions were discussed in many of the chapters in this Volume and were the focus for Atkinson who provided us in Chapter 2 with the book's first visualisation built around individual characteristics, borrowing a figure from Dahlgren and Whitehead. Figure C.1 provides another illustration that situates individual health within the social and environmental context, but also depicts relationships with the policy context and public health outcomes.

Indicators of public health, shown in the diamond, are aggregate measurements of data about individual morbidity, mortality and quality of life. These in turn can only be understood as a product of the three octagonal boxes describing individual factors of biological profile, social profile and the intention and execution of behaviours that impact health. Likewise, these individual factors are affected by the physical and social environment in which those individuals are embedded, illustrated in the figure by the two cross-shaped boxes. All is set in the policy context created by the impact of different sources and quanta of funds, sectional interests and political will and mandate.

The impact of environmental factors on individual actions and experiences is most clearly demonstrated in the early heydays of public health, when advances were made through cleaner air and water, and vaccinations. An understanding of the social context of behaviour took longer to reach the policy arena, but now is clear for all to see and is a strong theme of this book, with ample evidence of the impact of variations in depth and direction of community cohesion, family structure, social class, education, lifestyles and peer influence on the very habits of eating, drinking, sexual activity, substance misuse, exercise, compliance with prescribed medication, and immunisation programmes which are directly translated into indices of public health.

A further example of the relationship between social experience and health, if one is needed, is found in the subject of violence, which is increasingly seen as a health matter. The World Health Organisation (WHO) launched its global campaign of Violence Prevention in 2002[1] amid growing evidence revealing the negative health consequences of childhood experiences of verbal and physical violence, including substance misuse, mental illness and suicide, and unsafe sexual behaviour. There are negative consequences for children who are the victims of violence in educational outcomes, social engagement and cohesion. Violence disproportionally is experienced by the poor in any society and so exaggerates health and social inequalities.

The embedded nature of individual health in given characteristics of individual profiles and social, physical and political context mean that those charged with securing improvements in public health are presented with a daunting prospect. Where should they place their attention and how and when will they know the efficiency and effect of their interventions?

The chapters in this book throw light upon answers to these testing questions. In Part I on policy frameworks we were reminded that the scene is set by politics; that the billowing clouds of the policy context in Figure C.1

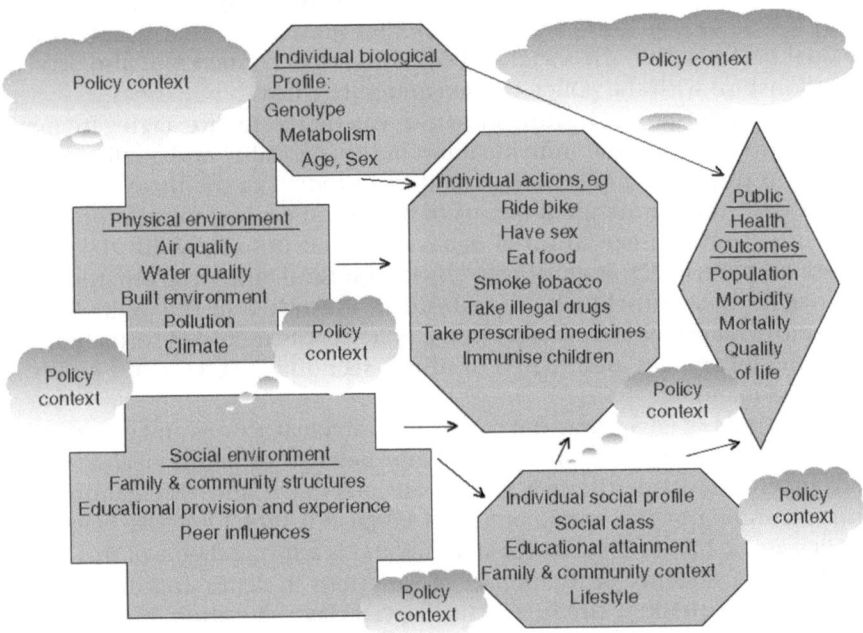

Figure C.1 Understanding health in context

are indeed all encompassing and move to some extent with the political wind, sometimes, to stretch the metaphor, promising refreshing rain combined with bright sunshine and at other times, threatening serious and unpredictable storms. Greer's account of the experience of devolution in the UK shows that a government of the same party will be differently motivated to action when placed in the more communitarian political alliances of Wales and Scotland than in market dominated, individualistic England. Amery and Gillam remind us of the inevitability of the links between primary care provision and public health outcomes, even when we focus on health protection and promotion rather than health improvement. Atkinson stresses that the natural centrifugal forces in Whitehall need to be tempered by an urgent and sustained need for interdepartmental and intersectoral collaboration in situations where we know that health status is at least as heavily influenced by expenditure and policy in education and the social and physical environment as it is by health care. French moves entirely to the social, and proselytises for widespread, yet targeted, employment of the tools of social marketing.

Part II gave examples and guidance on how public health outcomes could actually be influenced for improvement. Corbett places emphasis on evidence from psychology on influence processes on individual behaviour and motivation. She advocates a mix of mass communications, improvement schemes and skills development in contexts sensitive to the need for community development at a local level. Morris and Dawson continue to train the spotlight on the interaction of individual behaviour and social context with a focus on perceptions of risk associated with aspects of sexual behaviour. Three chapters then follow focusing on public health implications of the 21st Century western demographic time bomb of an ageing population. Karlsson and colleagues discuss the positive associations of cohabitation in old age. Doyle and colleagues show that successful ageing, which places less call on health care and is characterised by prolonged, active independent life, is strongly linked to aspects of social environment. Coast develops a measurement system to give emphasis to older people's quality of life and wellbeing rather than more narrow biomedical status. Pointing out that while a great deal of research goes into which interventions and programmes might work best for those at risk of heart attack, the real trouble is in getting individuals to participate in those programmes, Bhalotra and Shepard engage in a postmortem of two programmes from the US that failed to attract or retain many participants.

Part III addresses the question of evaluation. Three chapters acknowledge the complexity illustrated in Figure C.1, by including the societal costs of not taking action (Lister *et al.*), the need for evaluation to reach across agencies and budgets, for example into costs and benefits of programmes in schools and workplaces (McDaid *et al.*) and an appreciation of the impact of incurring social costs and influencing social outcomes in the creation of public health status (Fordham). In the final chapter in this part, Chalkidou and colleagues detail the challenges of developing cost-effective public health guidance from within the National Institute for Health and Clinical Excellence (NICE). They discuss the challenges of meeting imperatives for consistency, comparability, robustness and fairness of evaluation and usability of resulting guidance, and illustrate how they are picking their way on the basis of pragmatism and principle.

The aim in the collection is to reveal the importance of the linkages illustrated in Figure C.1 in the creation of positive and negative public health outcomes. Individual behaviour must be understood in a complex context, one in which targeted actions produce outcomes that appropriate evaluation will adjudicate for effect. It is hoped that this figure will prove fertile ground for developing further programmatic interventions and approaches to evaluation.

In conclusion we turn to the title of the collection, and summarise the revealed burdens, challenges and opportunities for the future of public health. Classification into these three groups is, of course, a matter of judgement; a 'burden' could be seen as a 'challenge' which needs to be overcome or an 'opportunity' to make a substantial change. We give our pragmatic definitions of each as a basis for concluding this discussion.

Burdens

Our approach is to describe burdens as those things that for the next decade, if not century, represent political, economic, social and environmental trends which even the most optimistic public health policymaker or practitioner must acknowledge are beyond their direct impact. Thus they may react and seek to manage around them, to mitigate their effects in the margins, and indeed to lobby for action with others in different domains of power and influence. In this sense, burdens embody risks and major threats to public health, they need to be managed at community, national and international levels, both in crisis and in emergent steady state. Alone they cannot be placed at the heart of active policy, yet they will all impact on the public health outcomes in the diamond-shaped box in Figure C.1. We highlight four burdens.

- Climate change with attendant floods, food shortages, and drought.
- Environmental degradation of air and water.
- Terrorism with release of biological agents or other damaging materials in 'dirty bombs' and other distribution channels.
- Demographic changes reflecting migration flows, with impacts on local social structures and trends of increasing economic affluence being associated with people living longer, with rising expectations of quality of life.

Challenges

Challenges are taken to be developments or events that may create obstacles on the road to improving public health, but which within a holistic view of the determinants of public health as in Figure C.1 can be seen as realistic and legitimate targets for public health policy and interventions. We highlight five.

• Persistent, if not increasing, inequalities in health status, which are arguably the most significant challenge for the future of public health in the UK. It is serious, almost tragic, that one of the unintended consequences of public health interventions is that their positive effects, mediated through a level of engagement with the programmes themselves, often mean that inequalities are exaggerated. The articulate, relatively wealthier, better educated, higher income earners respond more positively to pleas to eat healthier, take more exercise and renounce tobacco and other addictive substances and so get healthier, whilst those with poorer economic prospects, low educational attainment or living in dysfunctional communities continue to exhibit relatively poor health, even though they too have apparently had the benefit of the programmes, and may indeed have had a disproportionate amount spent on them as the target groups. While from 1994 to 2002 the infant mortality rate fell 16 per cent in the UK, for babies of fathers in routine and semi-routine occupations it fell by only five per cent (ONS, 2004). Nine per cent of people in professional occupations report a neurotic disorder, compared with 20 per cent of those in unskilled occupations. Men and women living in the most deprived fifth of local areas in England and Wales are twice as likely to commit suicide as those living in the least deprived fifth (Baker *et al.*, 2006).
• The intensity and speed of the spread of communicable disease, not least through the medium of mass global travel, creates a major challenge, as one's memories of the SARS outbreak illustrate (BBC, 2004). Malaria occurs in over 100 countries and more than 40 per cent of the people in the world are at risk. Trends in the spread of communicable diseases are complicated by the emergence of antibiotic-resistant strains, often the ironic result of therapeutic interventions and other times associated with the incidence of HIV/AIDS and other conditions that attack the immune system. The WHO in 2006 expressed concern over the emergence of virulent drug-resistant strains of tuberculosis (TB) and called for measures to be implemented to prevent the global spread of multidrug resistant XDR-TB strains (WHO, 2006). In February 2008, the BBC reported a WHO release that drug resistant tuberculosis had hit the highest levels ever recorded and that, whilst the incidence was concentrated in places with poor economic outlooks like Azerbaijan's capital, Baku, in parts of east

London rates of TB were higher then in some developing nations (BBC, 2008). AIDS/HIV is still a major cause for concern in the UK and there is realistic apprehension about a flu pandemic (Department of Health, 2005).

- Challenging patterns of non-communicable (often chronic) diseases, notably diabetes, heart and lung disease and various forms of mental illness. By 2010 2.5 million people in England will be living with diabetes (Department of Health, 2007b). Ninety per cent of these people will be living with Type 2 Diabetes, of which 58 per cent are attributable to excess body fat (Department of Health, 2007a). It is predicted that by 2050 60 per cent of men, 50 per cent of women, and 25 per cent of children will be obese if nothing is done to curb today's trends (Foresight, 2007). While the proportion of the population suffering from anxiety, depression or both appears to have remained largely stable in recent decades, in the seven years leading up to 2000 the number in treatment doubled (ONS, 2006). Despite this increase, it is estimated that only a quarter of sufferers receive treatment, evidence of both unmet need and growing demand for care (Mental Health Policy Group, 2006). The number of sufferers will grow as the population becomes older and more ethnically diverse (McCrone *et al.* 2008). There is also an increasing prevalence of dementia (associated with the demographic changes in our age structure). As we get older, our chances of suffering from some form of dementia increase steeply. A Kings Fund review recently projected that the 0.58 million dementia sufferers in England will grow to 0.94 million by 2026, a 61 per cent increase (McCrone *et al.*, 2008).
- Trends in community cohesion. Fragmented communities of isolated inhabitants cannot provide the vital social support on which most public health interventions depend. Cohesion alone is not necessarily an ally of public health, however, as a highly cohesive community in which it is socially acceptable and expected to take illegal drugs and binge on alcohol is as much an enemy of public health as is a fragmented one where experience of alienation and dispossession is strong. Crossley (2004) suggests that gay men continue to have sex without condoms as a form of rebellion, and describes this as an important value in gay culture. Morris and Dawson, in Chapter 6, cite several researchers who describe individuals who choose to engage in risky sexual behaviour rather than risk their relationship, and for whom that choice may even act as an affirmation of their affection and trust. These summary points provide a glimpse of the scope of the challenge to understand the public health implications of paths of identity formation, and the experienced balance between an individualistic or communitarian approach to health.
- The last challenge selected for emphasis in this book is the definition and realisation of the skills and experience needed in the public health workforce, including their readiness to engage with citizens in terms of personal and social inclinations and responsibilities. This workforce must include

specialists trained in medicine, epidemiology, crisis management, community development, social marketing, genetic counselling, education and indeed complex policymaking. The landscape of public health is complex and broad interventions essential, thus specialists must not only be excellent in their fields but also have a passion and determination to work collaboratively across professional boundaries in interdisciplinary teams.

Opportunities

The challenges are awesome, but so too are the opportunities. They, just like the challenges, derive from the broad, complex and interconnected landscape of public health as illustrated in Figure C.1. Provided that one is not beguiled by the (very important) use of the word health into thinking that to improve public health one can focus on health care; and providing that one acknowledges that the mainsprings of human behaviour that most public health interventions target are a complex interaction of the physical, social, economic and political environment with the individual, who in turn is both a biological system and a social being, then the opportunities for focused and well evaluated interventions are many and varied. Thus whilst, as Amery and Gillam show us, primary health care is a vital source of advice, guidance and action in, for example, tackling obesity, substance dependence and unsafe sexual behaviour, public health must be set in a context of a joined up intersectoral approach at a community level.

- Thus the first opportunity is to champion an intersectoral policymaking framework that fundamentally acknowledges the potential for programme delivery through intersectoral systems and structures.
- Secondly, there is an urgent opportunity to invest in a sustainable surveillance and knowledge system for quantifying and then prioritising risk, unhealthy behaviours, interventions and public preferences. This needs to be coupled with robust evaluation frameworks with clear targets to tackle inequalities as well as mean performance and to develop systems for data collection and analysis which will enable us to track trends in a confident and robust fashion, and to establish priorities, as a product of degree of risk and amenability to mitigation or eradication.
- This book has laid great stress on the creation of individual health and wellbeing in a social context, and this perspective provides our third opportunity: to see public health as a matter of everyday behaviour. The 19th century was a time for public health as a force to clean up the misdeeds of others, often industrialists, who were polluting our planet and creating ill-health. This book comes at a time when we are once again preoccupied by the burden of environmental pollution, but it is now seen as

much as a product of our consumption as well as of the means of production, and so solutions lie in part at least with altering our everyday behaviour. Similarly, unhealthy lifestyles and dysfunctional communities are our own creation. Thus the opportunity is to understand our own responsibilities in creating the indices of public health, and to emphasise the way our own behaviour reflects and creates the social, political and economic contexts that have such a profound impact on public health.

- Discussion in this book shows that a determination to educate or influence individuals in isolation from their social context has very limited impact – at least with the present state of knowledge. However, casting our eyes to the future, we may be looking to developments in the field of genetics, which will facilitate target screening and preventive interventions and so the pendulum may again swing back to the individual biological system. Where the policy focus should be, where there is greatest leverage for public, charitable and individual investment will change over time, as our understanding of the dynamic complexities described in this book interacts with scientific advances in understanding biological systems and human expectation.

Securing public health is always work-in-progress. It is never work-completed. The sources of mortality and morbidity change; people's definition of what is healthy and health change. One always has to examine the complex interactions between what is, at one time, given, and what may be changed. Where we see change as possible then we have to determine direction and speed of travel, taking care to plan the route and take all necessary interacting parts alongside. Today, public health policy requires a breadth of vision illustrated in Figure C.1; a relentless realism in its chosen targets and a sustained commitment to evaluate on as wide a canvas as is necessary in order to capture the positive lessons. Our canvas has been one in which we foreground the social context as we seek to mitigate the burdens and meet the challenges of improving public health.

Note

1 http://www.who.int/violence_injury_prevention/violence/global_campaign/en/index.html

References

A. Baker, A. Brock, G. Fegan, C. Griffiths, G. Jackson, D. Marshall, 'Suicide trends and geographical variations in the United Kingdom, 1991–2004', *Health Statistics Quarterly*, 31 (2006), 6–22.

BBC, *Timeline: SARS Virus*, http://news.bbc.co.uk/1/hi/world/asia-pacific/2973415.stm, 7 July 2004, accessed 14 July 2008.

BBC, *Drug resistant TB 'at new high'*, http://news.bbc.co.uk/2/hi/health/7265464.stm, 26 February 2008, accessed 18 June 2008.

M. L. Crossley, 'Making Sense of "Barebacking": Gay Men's Narratives, Unsafe Sex and the "Resistance Habitus"', *British Journal of Social Psychology*, 43 (2004), 225–44.

Department of Health, *5 a Day: Just Eat More (Fruit and Veg)* (London: Department of Health, 2003).

Department of Health, *Towards Cleaner Hospitals and Lower Rates of Infection: a Summary of Action* (London: Department of Health, 2004).

Department of Health, *Explaining Pandemic Flu: a guide from the CMO* (London: Department of Health, 2005).

Department of Health A, *The Way Ahead: The Local Challenge. Improving diabetes services: the National Service Framework four years on* (London: Department of Health, 2007).

Department of Health B, *Health risks and costs of obesity*, http://www.dh.gov.uk/en/ Publichealth/Healthimprovement/Obesity/DH_4133949, 3 September 2007, accessed 18 June 2008.

Foresight, *Tackling Obesities: Future Choices* (London: Government Office for Science, 2007).

P. McCrone, S. Dhanasiri, A. Patel, M. Knapp and S. Lawton-Smith, *Paying the Price: The Cost of Mental Health Care in England to 2026* (London: King's Fund, 2008).

Mental Health Policy Group, *The Depression Report: A New Deal For Depression and Anxiety Disorders* (London: Centre for Economic Performance, 2006).

National Institute for Health and Clinical and Excellence, *Statins for the prevention of cardiovascular disease: technology appraisal 94* (London: NICE, 2006).

Office for National Statistics, *Focus on Social Inequalities* (London: Office for National Statistics, 2004).

Office for National Statistics, *Mental Health: 1 in 6 Adults Have Neurotic Disorder*, http://www.statistics.gov.uk/cci/nugget.asp?id=1333, 17 January 2006, accessed 14 June 2008.

World Health Organisation, *Emergence of XDR-TB: WHO concern over extensive drug resistant TB strains that are virtually untreatable*, http://www.who.int/mediacentre/ news/notes/2006/np23/en/index.html, 5 September 2006, accessed 18 June 2008.

Index